KU-470-391

Our Daily Journey with God

WRITERS:
Poh Fang Chia, Winn Collier, Tom Felten, Regina Franklin, Tim Gustafson, Jeff Olson, Roxanne Robbins, Jennifer Benson Schuldt, K.T. Sim, Sheridan Voysey, Marvin Williams, Mike Wittmer

ACKNOWLEDGMENTS:
Unless otherwise indicated, all Scripture quotations are taken from the Holy Bible, New Living Translation, copyright 1996, 2004. Used by permission of Tyndale House Publishers, Inc., Wheaton, Illinois 60189. All rights reserved.

MANAGING EDITOR:
Tom Felten

ASSOCIATE EDITOR:
Cindy Kasper

STAFF EDITORS:
Clair Hess, Alyson Kieda

EDITORIAL REVIEWERS:
Bill Crowder, Kevin Gregory, K.T. Sim

ART DIRECTOR:
Alex Soh

GRAPHIC DESIGNER:
Joshua Tan

COVER PHOTO:
Angkor Wat, Cambodia ©Alex Soh

INTERIOR PHOTOGRAPHY:
Alex Soh, stock.xchng

© 2011 RBC Ministries Headquarters
Grand Rapids, MI 49555-0001, USA

All Rights Reserved
Printed by KHL Printing Co Pte Ltd,
57 Loyang Drive, Singapore 508968

We're glad you've come along for a journey into a deeper relationship with Jesus Christ!

This annual edition of *Our Daily Journey* gives you an inspiring look into God's Word each day of the year. On the following page, you'll find some helpful tips on how to get the most out of using this devotional. Take time to read through this brief list.

Then sit down and spend a few minutes reading today's devotional article. You'll find our writers speak to real-life issues—relationship struggles, raising kids, serving and lifting others up, pursuing holiness while living in an unholy world—all written from a biblical perspective.

We welcome your questions and comments, so please don't hesitate to contact us at comments@ourdailyjourney.org

Welcome to *ODJ*! May God bless you on this journey with Him,

—The *Our Daily Journey* Staff

using ODJ

How to get the most out of using this *ODJ* devotional:

1. **Select a time and place.** Choose a specific time and place to get into *ODJ* each day.

2. **Read the Bible verses.** Begin your time with God by reading the Bible passage printed beneath the **read>** section. The Word of God is the most important part of your daily *ODJ* diet.

3. **Note the key verse.** It points to a key theme and provides a good launching point for reading the article.

4. **Read the article thoughtfully.** As you read, seek to learn more about God, your relationship with Him, and how He wants you to live.

5. **Take time for more>.** This feature contains additional Scripture for you to consider and meditate on.

6. **Consider what is next>.** The questions in this feature will help you bring the message of the devotional home to your heart. Strive to answer each question with complete honesty and transparency before God.

7. **Take time to pray.** After working through the article and its features, talk with God about what you've just learnt and experienced. Share your response with Him.

8. **Share it with others!** Look for opportunities to share what you've learnt in *ODJ* with others. Help them get into God's Word by using *ODJ* each day!

when to forget

read>
Isaiah 43:14-21
But forget all that—it is nothing compared with what I am going to do (v.18).

more>
- 2 Corinthians 5:17
- Jeremiah 14:7
- Jeremiah 31:22

next>
How are you cynical toward God's promises or locked in your view of how God should care for you? What "new thing" do you think God may be wanting to do in or for you?

After our first son was born, my wife Miska and I entered a rough stretch in our marriage. We had been extremely close, but now another little person interrupted all that. We loved Wyatt very much, but our relational dynamic had changed forever. Selfishly, I kept insisting that our marriage get back to the way it was before the upheaval. One day, amid a fight, Miska said, "Winn, you are going to have to stop insisting our marriage be what it was. It will be good again, but it will be different."

Isaiah wrote to the people of Judah prior to their Babylonian exile. He reminded them of how God miraculously rescued them generations earlier during their Egyptian exile. He recounted how God was the one who "opened a way through the waters" and made a "dry path through the sea" (Isaiah 43:16). The Exodus story, Moses going toe-to-toe with Pharaoh, plagues raining down, and the people crossing the Red Sea on dry ground had been their defining marker of God's power and goodwill toward them.

So, in the face of their prophesied future exile, some of God's people may have assumed that God intended to send another prophet and another battery of stunning plagues, another miraculous trek across a sea to deliver them. They may have expected God to act in a certain way. Maybe others, when they heard Isaiah's words, felt cynical. *We've heard these stories before, for hundreds of years. But nothing is going to change.*

Either way, the people had to let go of what they were holding so tightly (either their cynical doubts or their ideas of how God would act). They had to forget what they thought they knew so they could receive the new thing God wanted to do. As novelist L. P. Hartley said, "The past is a foreign country. They do things differently there." —Winn Collier

abandoned by me

read>
Luke 23:44-49
By this time it was noon, and darkness fell across the whole land until three o'clock (v.44).

Things had started well enough. Crowds had flocked to Him—astounded by His miracles (Mark 1:27), amazed at His power and His teaching (Luke 4:36). Soon, however, public sentiment changed.

The religious leaders were first to question His credentials, offended by the company He kept (Mark 2:16) and the "blasphemous" claims He made (14:64), and stating that the power by which He healed was from "Satan" (3:22). His neighborhood "scoffed" at Him (6:3). His synagogue tried to kill Him (Luke 4:29), and even His family felt embarrassed by His actions and antics (Mark 3:21). By the end of His days He'd been betrayed by a disciple (Luke 22:4), disowned by a friend (v.60), deserted by His followers (Mark 14:50), cursed by a criminal (Luke 23:39), and faced the abandonment of His Father (Mark 15:34).

Now we find Him in darkness—cold and alone, naked and exposed, abandoned by all on a cross of shame. The crowd's hollow praise has fallen silent, His followers' loyalty pledges have proven false. Those He'd fed, befriended, healed, and forgiven are nowhere to be seen. All that remains is the muffled sniggers from His betrayers, the whimpers of His grief-stricken mother, and the murmurs of soldiers.

A "political disturber" quashed. A "blasphemous healer" silenced. A darkened sky. A tear from heaven. The sins of the world resting on the shoulders of a man.

Would I have mourned for Jesus, or scoffed? Would I have stayed "uninvolved" or, like the centurion, lamented His wrongful death? (Luke 23:47).

The one thing I know is that I would have abandoned Jesus too. And that makes His death for my sins so much more amazing. —Sheridan Voysey

more>
Yet it was our weaknesses He carried; it was our sorrows that weighed Him down. . . . He was beaten so we could be whole. He was whipped so we could be healed (Isaiah 53:4-5).

next>
Picture yourself at Jesus' crucifixion. Where are you in the crowd, and what are you saying? What is Jesus saying to you?

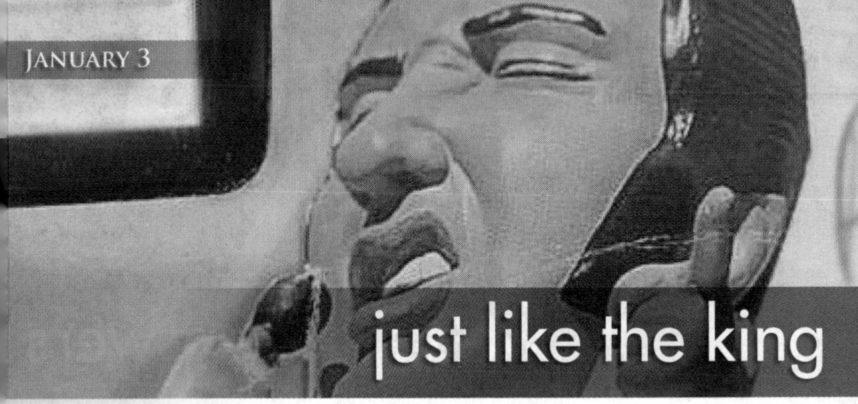

just like the king

read>
Ephesians 5:1-21
Imitate God, therefore, in everything you do (v.1).

more>
Put on your new nature, created to be like God—truly righteous and holy (Ephesians 4:24).

next>
If people were examining your "walk," would they call you an imitator of God? Why is it impossible for us to imitate God without the power of the Holy Spirit?

I hoped our dinner guest wouldn't notice that I was staring at him. I knew it was impolite, but I was trying to decide if he looked like Elvis Presley. Let me explain. My husband had invited a friend over to eat with us who was an "Elvis tribute artist." He told us stories of swaggering to the stage with his guitar at backyard birthday parties, weddings, and even in college dorms.

Imitating "The King of rock and roll" was just a hobby for our friend, but as Christians we're called to "imitate God . . . in everything [we] do" (Ephesians 5:1). Fortunately, Paul left us with some specifics on how to live just like "The King of heaven." We're supposed to be God-followers who:

Walk in love—because "God is love" (1 John 4:8). We need to love our fellow Christians and put their needs above our own, just as Jesus did for us (Eph. 5:2).

Walk in light—because "God is light, and there is no darkness in Him" (1 John 1:5). This means not getting tangled in sinful patterns of living. Rather, our lives should be characterized by what is "good and right and true" (Ephesians 5:9).

Walk in wisdom—because "God is so wise" (Job 9:4). We're supposed to be careful about the life choices we make and be filled with God's Holy Spirit (Ephesians 5:15,18).

As Christians, we need to remember that other people are studying us, looking for any likeness to God that they can see. And God wants us to live so that our lives will encourage people to get to know Him. This is why He says: "Be holy because I am holy" (Leviticus 11:45). —Jennifer Benson Schuldt

we've got answers

read>
Job 11:1-20
True wisdom and power are found in God; counsel and understanding are His (12:13).

more>
Read Job 12 to see some of Job's honest and angry responses to his friends. What was Job's ultimate conclusion? (see ch.42).

next>
How have you been comforted by someone when you were hurting? Do you feel that you have the answers to everyone's questions? How might this be misinterpreted by others?

While in college, I volunteered at a center that provided emergency housing assistance. One winter day, a distraught woman called to complain about her negligent landlord. She couldn't stay in her rental home because of severe maintenance problems. In a panic, she asked what she could do to care for her children in the cold weather. I gave the standard answer, which was to move into a hotel until the problem was resolved. Under our state's consumer protection laws, she could bill the landlord. But she angrily hung up on me, believing I had failed to take her seriously.

I may have known the textbook response to that woman's question, but I didn't grasp her real need. She needed someone to comprehend her fear and desperation. She needed to feel she was not alone in her dilemma. I had done nothing to address her *heartfelt cry*.

In the Bible, Job stands as a paragon of patience. He too had a heartfelt cry. He had lost everything in a cosmic game no human being could comprehend (see Job 1–2). And he had friends with thoughtless textbook answers.

"Can you solve the mysteries of God?" asked his friend Zophar, drunk on his own self-righteousness (11:7). "If only you would prepare your heart and lift up your hands to Him in prayer!" (v.13). Naturally, that only elicited a bitter retort from Job. "You people really know everything, don't you? And when you die, wisdom will die with you!" (12:1).

We malign Job's friends for their failure to see the big picture. But I'm no different. I'm quick with answers to questions I've never faced.

"You've got questions, we've got answers," says an advertising campaign. For life's big questions, people *do* want and need answers. Most of all, they want to know someone truly cares. —Tim Gustafson

lampstand

read>
Revelation 2:1-7
Look how far you have fallen! Turn back to me and do the works you did at first. If you don't repent, I will come and remove your lampstand from its place among the churches (v.5).

more>
This is what the Lord says: "I remember how eager you were to please Me as a young bride long ago, how you loved Me and followed Me even through the barren wilderness" (Jeremiah 2:2).

next>
How strong is your love for Jesus? What steps can you take to remember, return, and repent?

One evening, while waiting for a friend at a church, I chatted with a security guard. He said, "This church just installed a new state-of-the-art sound system, and they spent a hefty sum on it." Then he added, "But it's a pity, the church doesn't have many activities."

While the number of activities does not necessarily reflect the health of a church, I couldn't help but wonder if this church's lampstand had been removed (Rev. 2:5).

In the book of Revelation, Jesus states that "the seven lampstands are the seven churches" (1:20). As lampstands, the churches are light-bearers. They're not the light themselves, but they hold or bear the light. The illumination comes from Jesus—"the light of the world" (John 9:5). So it's the mission of the church to point lost people to Him.

In Revelation 2, we see the reason a church can lose its impact upon a community and also the solution to that problem. The negative issue for the church of Ephesus wasn't a lack of industry, service, toil, and effort (2:2-3). In fact, their activity, theology, conduct, and perseverance were all looking good. Their *hearts* were the problem. They had forsaken their first love (v.4). In fact, their relationship with Jesus had become routine, no longer vibrant and alive. The solution given was: "Look how far you have fallen! *Turn back . . . repent*" (v.5). Our heart for Jesus must be restored before we can light up our world.

An atheist once said to an evangelical Christian in the British Isles: "If I believed what you say you believe, I would cross Britain upon my knees on broken glass to tell men about it." When we walk closer with Jesus and really experience His light, we can't help but let the whole world see Him!

—Poh Fang Chia

long commute

read>
1 Corinthians 7:1-7
The husband should fulfill his wife's sexual needs, and the wife should fulfill her husband's needs (v.3).

more>
Note that Paul also lifts up singleness as a God-glorifying way to live (1 Cor. 7:7). Check out verses 32 to 35 for the unique ways the single person can glorify God.

next>
If you're married, what is keeping you and your spouse from a healthy intimate relationship? How does God want you to change?

Michael Hanley traded an 8-minute commute to work for an 8-*hour* one. When his autoworker job in Wisconsin was phased out, he stayed with the company and took the only position available—in Kansas. His weekly round-trip commute is now more than 1,600 kilometers (1,000 miles). He's gone from his family each workweek, seeing them only on the weekends. But he chose to stay with the company because of the good wages, a retirement package he's working toward, and medical benefits. Being apart from his wife, however, has been brutal.

The apostle Paul recognized how important it is for husbands and wives to spend time together. He knew that distance can make the heart wander—not necessarily cause it to *grow fonder*. And so he told the married believers in Corinth, "Do not deprive each other of sexual relations" (1 Corinthians 7:5). He supported this instruction with two points about sex: (1) Husbands and wives should fulfill each other's needs for intimacy (v.3); (2) When the two wed, their bodies were no longer their own—but were to be shared by their spouse (v.4). It's essential, however, that we live out these truths in gentle and tender ways (Ephesians 5:28-29; 1 Peter 3:7). Sex in marriage is meant to be selfless, not selfish.

Husbands and wives have the God-given gift of sex as something to be enjoyed (Proverbs 5:18-19). But sometimes we drift apart emotionally . . . and physically. It might not be a long commute that keeps us apart, but things like the lack of loving communication, being unhealthily busy, and not being affectionate throughout the day.

God desires for us to "remain faithful" to our spouses (Hebrews 13:4). To do so requires that we keep the stuff of life from coming between us and them. If we don't, the results can be brutal. —Tom Felten

dismembered

read>
Galatians 5:13-26
If you are always biting and devouring one another, watch out! Beware of destroying one another (v.15).

more>
- John 13:34-35
- 1 Corinthians 1:10
- 2 Corinthians 12:20

next>
How have you allowed a personal hurt to shape your view of the church or others within the church? Why is Jesus so insistent that we understand that the true measure of our discipleship is our love for one another?

Because my husband and I live in the "Bible Belt" (historically, the South and parts of the Midwest of the US), we can drive for miles around town with at least one church always in view. While the variations of buildings and denominations can be seen as a demonstration of the diversity within the body of Christ, sadly we can also mark far too many of them as divisions from another body. Having experienced a major split in our own church almost 4 years ago, I'm still trying to process the complexity of the situation and the resulting hurt and disillusionment.

Scripture clearly indicates that there are times and seasons when God works within the factions of man. In the Old Testament, God specifically told Rehoboam and his people not to pursue the tribes that were leaving to follow Jeroboam, for their departure was "[the Lord's] doing" (1 Kings 12:24). Later in the New Testament, irreconcilable differences brought Paul and Barnabas to the point of separation (Acts 15:39).

However, in a world where human trafficking, slavery, and destitution still exist and believers around the world suffer death for the gospel, I often wonder what God thinks of our church disagreements. When we enjoy prosperity, we can forget that church is not really about us. While there are justifiable reasons to rebuild and tear down (Eccl. 3:3), we must realize the high level of accountability in such decisions. Ultimately, the justification should not be our comfort, but God's Word.

Ephesians 6:12 reminds us that our battle is not against flesh and blood, but against the sinister and divisive powers of the enemy. When our feelings are hurt and our frustration level runs high, it's a difficult truth to remember. May we live watchful of the hour, so that we might be a pure bride ready for the Bridegroom's return and not a bride dismembered by factions. —Regina Franklin

all things are possible

read>
Luke 18:18-30
He replied, "What is impossible for people is possible with God" (v.27).

more>
Now all glory to God, who is able, through His mighty power at work within us, to accomplish infinitely more than we might ask or think (Ephesians 3:20).

next>
What is God asking you to lay down that seems impossible to surrender? How does Jesus' example inspire you?

The movie *The Blind Side* tells the true story of Michael Oher, a homeless, quiet teen from a broken home. He flourished into an All-American college football player and first-round National Football League draft pick with the help of a compassionate woman and her family.

The movie included two quick shots of what appears to be an arch entering the private Christian school that Oher attended. Inscribed over the arch were the following words, "With men this is possible, but with God all things are possible." The phrase over the arch is clearly based on Jesus' words in Matthew 19:26, but it's not entirely accurate. Here's what Jesus actually said: "Humanly speaking, it *is* impossible. But with God everything is possible."

It's anybody's guess as to why the words were changed, but I would like to believe it was a deliberate attempt to acknowledge that while man is able to do some great things, only God can do the impossible.

There are certain things that look absolutely impossible that only God can accomplish. That was Jesus' point (Luke 18:27). Remember, He was referring to the rich young ruler who was unwilling to sell his possessions and give up his identity as a man of great wealth in order to follow Him (v.22). On the surface it seemed like an impossible sacrifice, like a camel walking through the eye of a needle (v.25). But with God all things are possible.

All of us are in the same situation as the rich young ruler was. While our issues may be different, we all have things we cling to that, with God's help, we can lay down in order to follow Jesus and become all He intends for us to be. It can be costly to follow Jesus, but it's so worth the cost! (vv.29-30).

—Jeff Olson

higher logic

read>
Matthew 18:21-35
The king called in the man . . . and said, "You evil servant! I forgave you that tremendous debt because you pleaded with me. Shouldn't you have mercy on your fellow servant?" (vv.32-33).

more>
Get rid of all bitterness, rage, anger, harsh words, and slander . . . . Instead, be kind to each other, tenderhearted, forgiving one another, just as God through Christ has forgiven you (Ephesians 4:31-32).

next>
When you forgive someone, what consequences must you release and what ones must remain?

While Khalid Sheikh Mohammed awaited trial for plotting the 9/11 terrorist attacks, some US citizens were nervous that he might be acquitted by an inept jury. Others hoped that *that* would be precisely what happened. If they had turned Khalid out into the angry streets, it wouldn't have taken long for New Yorkers to exact their revenge. I certainly understand the reason why, but it overlooks the bigger picture.

If you've ever been to the top of the Empire State Building, you know that—from God's perspective—the people of New York City look like ants. If God is to us as we are to ants, imagine a colony of carpenter ants systematically chewing up the foundation of your house. You could call the exterminator, but for reasons that aren't entirely clear you decide to stop their destruction by becoming an ant yourself.

The ant leaders are threatened by your arrival, and not knowing what else to do, they incite a mob that mocks and then kills you. What they don't realize is that you will come back from the dead—for you are more than just an ant—and that your death and resurrection will grant forgiveness and everlasting life to any ant who repents of his destructive ways and follows you (1 John 1:9).

Now imagine that one of those ants that believes in you is bullied by another ant. The aggressive ant commits unspeakable acts that heap incalculable misery upon the redeemed ant. It would be normal for the victimized ant to strike back and get revenge. But what if she remembers the higher logic of the human who became an ant?

We are that ant, and every time we are sinned against we get to choose: Will we live by the laws of the anthill or forgive as God has forgiven us? (Matthew 18:35).

—Mike Wittmer

company you keep

read>
1 John 3:16-19
We think of your faithful work, your loving deeds (1 Thessalonians 1:3).

more>
We wanted to give you an example to follow (2 Thessalonians 3:9).

next>
Schedule a meeting with someone who is actively serving others. What steps should you take to serve others in a similar way?

One of the highlights of living in East Africa is meeting men and women from around the world who come through the region to participate in short or long-term missions. Today, for example, while sitting in a Kampala, Uganda, coffee shop, I met a young married couple from Charleston, South Carolina. Amanda and Michael recently moved to Uganda to help their church build a medical center in one of the country's most impoverished areas.

I enjoyed learning about the couple's work and how the Lord had led them to leave home and serve in Africa. Our conversation reminded me that whether in our own neighborhood or abroad, it's inspiring to hear about and spend time with people who have experienced God's love and are in turn sharing it with others.

Such individuals strive to live out the essence of 1 John 3 by enthusiastically . . .

- Giving up their lives and comforts in behalf of their brothers and sisters around the world (v.16).
- Demonstrating God's love by sharing their money and resources with the poor—showing compassion to brothers and sisters in need (v.17).
- Demonstrating love through their actions rather than merely professing love to others (v.18).
- Letting their behavior convey God's truth (v.19).

In his bestselling book *Today Matters,* John C. Maxwell writes, "It's a fact that you become more like the people you spend time with. If you desire to increase your faith, spend time with others who exercise theirs. Learn from them. Find out how they think." And, I might add, how they act.

As God nudges you to engage in service to others, be intentional about building friendships with people who are already doing so and who can lead you by their example. —Roxanne Robbins

a healthy lifestyle

read>
Proverbs 4:20–5:2
So be careful how you live. Don't live like fools, but like those who are wise (Ephesians 5:15).

more>
Give me an eagerness for Your laws rather than a love for money! Turn my eyes from worthless things, and give me life through Your Word (Psalm 119:36-37).

next>
What lifestyle choices should you make for a healthier spiritual life? How does Jesus' example help you live a healthy life?

Recently, I attended a presentation on heart attack prevention. The speaker reminded us to make healthy lifestyle choices that help reduce the risks of having a heart attack. We were told that not smoking, eating the right foods, maintaining a proper weight, reducing and managing stress, and participating in physical activities can contribute to a healthy heart.

In Proverbs we find some instruction can make us spiritually healthy (4:23):

• *Keep your mouth right* (Proverbs 4:24). Our Lord says, "Whatever is in your heart determines what you say" (Matthew 12:34-37). Our words should be godly (2 Timothy 2:16), wholesome and encouraging (Ephesians 4:29), gracious and attractive (Colossians 4:6). This means speaking the truth in love (Ephesians 4:15).

• *Keep your eyes right* (Proverbs 4:25). The eyes are the most influential parts of the body. What the eyes see, the heart wants (Genesis 3:6; Matthew 5:28). Keeping our eyes on Jesus (Hebrews 12:1-2) will overcome our "craving for everything we see" (1 John 2:16).

• *Keep your ears right* (Proverbs 4:20-22, 5:1-2). Listen carefully to God's Word. Let God's Word penetrate deep into your heart (v.21), and you will live (Proverbs 4:4). For God's words are "life to those who find them and health to a man's whole body" (v.22 NIV; John 6:68).

• *Keep your feet right* (Proverbs 4:26-27). Be careful where you walk (Proverbs 4:11-15), with whom you walk (Proverbs 2:20), and how you walk (Jeremiah 6:16). Walk as Jesus did (1 Peter 2:21; 1 John 2:6), led by His Spirit (Galatians 5:16,25), in light (1 John 1:7), in love, in obedience (2 John 1:6), and in truth (3 John 1:3-4).

Choose to avoid the risks that lead to spiritual sickness. Use your mouth, eyes, ears, and feet to pursue a healthy lifestyle in Jesus today. —K.T. Sim

into temptation

read>
Luke 4:1-13
[Jesus] was tempted by the devil for forty days (v.2).

more>
- Psalm 23:3
- 1 Corinthians 10:13
- James 5:11

next>
Read each temptation in Luke 4. What would be your equivalent temptation of turning stone to bread, worshiping the devil, and testing God by leaping off the temple? How would you handle each temptation?

One of the most distressing portions of Scripture is the part of Luke's gospel that tells us Jesus "was led by the Spirit in the wilderness" to be tempted by the devil (4:1). The Spirit took Jesus *into* the dark wilderness? We think of God as the One who keeps danger at bay, not One who invites us to face difficulties.

But God never promises to steer us clear of temptation or intense difficulty. Far better, the Spirit promises to go with us into the mouth of the dragon. God went through the tumultuous waters of the Red Sea with Israel (Isaiah 43), and God was present with the young Hebrew men in the fiery furnace (Daniel 3). God was present with Jesus, and God will be with us.

In the wilderness, Satan's temptation was a multistep ploy to get Jesus to go on His own, separating Himself from the very One who was with Him there. Satan tempted Jesus to:

- turn stone to bread (providing for Himself rather than trusting God, (Luke 4:3).
- worship Satan and gain all Satan's domain (grabbing His own kingdom rather than remaining under God's rule, v.5).
- hurl Himself off the temple's pinnacle (taking life into His own hands rather than simply trusting God's goodness, v.9).

With each temptation, however, Jesus answered Satan with Scripture—rebuking Satan's words with God's words. Jesus knew the truth, and He knew God was with Him even in that vile place.

I have a friend who's angry at God for not averting suffering and pain at a particular moment in his life. I believe Jesus *was* with my friend, however, even in his pain. If he would trust God's kind presence, he would discover something far better than release from his painful circumstances. —Winn Collier

four hearts

read>
Mark 4:1-20
Still other seeds fell on fertile soil, and they sprouted, grew, and produced a crop that was thirty, sixty, and even a hundred times as much as had been planted! (v.8).

more>
Read Isaiah 53:1. It seems that God's prophets have always had a hard time being heard. Read Revelation 3:20 to hear Jesus' response to an open heart.

next>
Which heart type would you use to describe yourself—hard, shallow, distracted, or attentive? How can you open your heart to Jesus today?

Theologian C. H. Dodd described Jesus' parables as stories that tease us into thought. They provoke us—shock us even—into deep soul-searching.

The first parable in Mark 4 is a good example. Jesus compared His preaching mission to a farmer sowing seed that fell on different types of soil. Jesus' missional success depended not on His message (the "seed"), but on how receptive hearts were to receive it (the "soil"). He categorized His audience into four heart types:

- *The hard heart,* where the seed can't penetrate (Mark 4:4,15). I once asked an author if he would ever consider Jesus' claim to be the Messiah. His reply was that there was nothing that would sway him from his religion. In this case, Jesus' message couldn't even get a hearing.
- *The shallow heart,* where initial faith is abandoned because of hardship (vv.5-6,16-17). I knew a girl who needed to decide whether Jesus or her boyfriend would be her priority. She returned to her boyfriend, to the demise of her faith. Her faith wasn't yet deep enough to face the costs of discipleship.
- *The distracted heart,* where the worries, riches, and pleasures of life compete for our attention (vv.7,18-19). At one time, this was me. When I came to faith, my life changed but my old lifestyle of nightclubs and music vied for allegiance. I gave in and my faith began to wither.
- *The attentive heart,* where the message is received and pursued for life (vv.8,20). This heart produces a miraculous harvest of fruit!

Jesus invited His audience to wrestle with this parable and wring out its meaning (v.9). Failure to do so would prove there was little interest in Him and His forgiveness (v.12). Jesus' invitation extends to us today. How open is our heart to His voice and message? How open is our heart to *Him*? —Sheridan Voysey

bubble trouble

read>
2 Timothy 3:10-17
All Scripture is inspired by God and is useful to teach us what is true and to make us realize what is wrong in our lives (v.16).

more>
Read Psalm 119:97-104 to see the benefits of reading God's Word. Read Deuteronomy 8:11-14 to learn why it's important to read and remember God's Word.

next>
What's the connection between reading the Bible and a God-honoring lifestyle? Why is it so difficult to read the Bible regularly? How can you read God's Word more consistently?

The new eco-friendly dish detergent was super-concentrated, so I squirted much less than usual into the dishwasher. I cranked the knob and walked away. Minutes later, I heard a gurgling noise. Suds were bubbling out of the dishwasher and cascading onto the floor. After sopping up the mess, I read the label on the container: "Not for use with automatic dishwashers. Hand-wash only." *Ugh . . .*

Sadly, my approach to life is often the same as my approach to washing the dishes—I jump right in without reading the directions. But God's Word contains the instructions we need (Leviticus 18:5).

Paul pointed out that the Bible "teaches us to do what is right" (2 Timothy 3:16). In another letter, he outlined some of the basics: "Live peacefully with each other. . . . Encourage those who are timid. Take tender care of those who are weak. Be patient with everyone. . . . Always be joyful. Never stop praying. Be thankful in all circumstances" (1 Thessalonians 5:13-16).

The Bible also makes us "realize what is wrong in our lives" (2 Timothy 3:16). Since "the Word of God is alive and powerful" (Hebrews 4:12), it speaks to us when we're drooling over the neighbor's new car . . . *you must not covet.* It whispers, *you must not steal,* when we could easily exaggerate business expenses. God's Word shows us our sin (Romans 7:7).

When I become blind to my sin and when I "forget" how God wants me to live, His Word reminds me. The more I read the Bible, the more Scripture soaks into my soul, where it can cleanse my conduct. This is how as Christians we become "[equipped] . . . to do every good work" (2 Timothy 3:17).

—Jennifer Benson Schuldt

oscar for fathers

read>
Romans 8:12-17
Father to the fatherless, defender of widows—this is God, whose dwelling is holy (Psalm 68:5).

James Cameron, of *Avatar* and *Titanic* fame, has reportedly said, "Anybody can be a father or a husband. There are only five people in the world who can do what I do, and I'm going for that."

It isn't only Hollywood directors who succumb to the siren song of success. Clergymen also put ministry ahead of family. And even King David committed flagrant errors regarding marriage. He violated the Lord's explicit command not to take many wives (Deuteronomy 17:17). It's difficult to fulfill the unity intended in marriage or to spend quality time with your kids if you're rationing time between multiple women (2 Samuel 3:2-5, 5:13, 11:27). David may have been a man "after [God's] own heart" (Acts 13:22), but as a husband and father, he compels us to seek a better role model.

In my own life, I was blessed with a great adoptive father who loved and provided for me and my brother. But for many, "Dad" is absent, or disengaged, or emotionally or physically abusive. Where are we to turn when our fathers abandon, fail, or wound us?

For those who turn in faith to Jesus, we have this remarkable comfort: "Father to the fatherless," sings the psalmist, "this is God, whose dwelling is holy. God places the lonely in families" (Psalm 68:5-6). And the apostle Paul elaborated, "You received God's Spirit when He adopted you as His own children. Now we call Him, '*Abba*, Father'" (Romans 8:15). *Abba* is the Aramaic term for God the Father that conveys intimate trust and familiarity.

Despite what Mr. Cameron says, it's an unfathomable privilege to be a father—to enjoy the trust, mentorship, and intimacy intended for such a relationship. And God is our perfect example. He's the one Father who will never let us down.

—Tim Gustafson

more>
What does Genesis 1:24-28 tell us about God's plan for a man and a woman?

next>
Who are the role models in your life? Who sees you as a role model? In what ways can you be a better example to others?

david and the dwarf

read>
1 Samuel 17:1-37,45-47
I have done this to both lions and bears, and I'll do it to this pagan Philistine too, for he has defied the armies of the living God! (v.36).

more>
Read John 14:1 and find the comfort Jesus brought to His disciples when they were facing the "giants" of fear and uncertainty.

next>
What are the "giants" that may hinder you from living out your Christian faith? How does remembering who God is strengthen your courage today?

The towering enemy strides into the Valley of Elah. He stands more than 9 feet tall, with shining armor made of several hundred small bronze plates that glimmer in the sunlight. His spear is several inches thick, with a 15-pound spearhead (1 Samuel 17:7). It's wrapped with cords so it can be thrown farther and more accurately through the air. Goliath looks—and feels—invincible.

By contrast, Saul and his army have no iron weapons. They have no tall champion—except Saul. But he too is cowering at the rear of the lines in fear. No one will fight the giant.

Then a ruddy shepherd boy walks up. He's the youngest in his family and he lacks any form of military experience. Yet, *he* offers to fight the bigger-than-life enemy.

Goliath looks and acts like a giant. But in contrast to the living God, David knows the monstrous man is a dwarf. He has the right view of God and the right view of his situation. The Israelites see Goliath as unconquerable (v.25), but David sees him as a pagan Philistine who is defying the armies of the living God (v.26). So David walks toward Goliath in shepherd's clothes, armed with only his shepherd's staff and sling. His confidence isn't in *what* he has but in *who* is with him. He says, "You come to me with sword, spear, and javelin, but I come to you in the name of the Lord of Heaven's Armies—the God of the armies of Israel, whom you have defied" (v.45).

We can have that same confidence in God and His power. We can be courageous in living boldly for Jesus in a non-Christian world. With His help, we can face any foes—for they're all dwarfed by our great God! —Poh Fang Chia

illumination

read>
1 Corinthians 2:6-16
For His Spirit searches out everything and shows us God's deep secrets (v.10).

more>
In 2 Timothy 3:16-17, Paul reveals that the Scriptures came about by God's inspiration. How does this differ from the illumination of God's Word?

next>
How have you viewed Scripture through the wrong lens? How does the Holy Spirit open your eyes to the truths found in the Bible?

It's glossy and features the pics of people like Bono, Angelina Jolie, the Dalai Lama, and Che Guevara. If you glanced at the cover you might mistake it for a fashion magazine. What is it? A New Testament called *The Bible Illuminated.* The publishers, however, admit that they don't "support a specific faith." Many of the images of celebrities and well-known people are positioned next to specific verses to make political or social statements. The photos don't "illuminate" the text. Instead, they mislead and confuse the reader.

I'm grateful for the *illumination* that the Holy Spirit brings, so that we can truly understand God's Word (1 Corinthians 2:10). He "shows us God's deep secrets" as we read and study it. Like a lens that allows us to see what once was blurry and undefined, God's Spirit helps us grasp the truths in Scripture that nonbelievers can't possibly understand. To them it's foolishness (1:18).

As the Holy Spirit illumines God's Word for us, we move from false and distorted views to the clarity of what the Bible's authors are actually communicating (2 Peter 1:21). Then, after the Holy Spirit has opened our eyes to what the Word is saying, we can pray that He will also help us take it to heart and obey it.

Now, when a particular passage of the Bible is highly confusing or hard to understand, it's good to do two things: (1) Seek out helpful insights from godly commentators and theologians who have studied the Scriptures and experienced the Spirit's illuminating ways; (2) pray for the Spirit to shed His light on the verses in question. For "we have received God's Spirit (not the world's spirit), so we can know the wonderful things God has freely given us" (1 Corinthians 2:12).

Now *that's* illumination! —Tom Felten

waiting for rain

read>
Joel 2:18-32
Rejoice, you people of Jerusalem! Rejoice in the Lord your God! For the rain He sends demonstrates His faithfulness. Once more the autumn rains will come, as well as the rains of spring (v.23).

more>
Read Psalm 52:8-9 to see where we should be planted and what the attitude of our heart should be in all seasons—especially in those where rain is scarce.

next>
What circumstances in your life have caused you to give up hope for change? How have your circumstances shaded what you believe God wants to do in you?

Competing against the *thwap-thwap* sound of the windshield wipers, the rain beat a rhythmic pattern against the car. Driving out of town for a retreat with our youth leaders, I was thankful for the chance to spend time with them.

The rain outside, however, fell in contrast to the desert condition inside my heart. His presence real, I felt that Jesus was near, but I wrestled with feelings of significant disappointment in ministry. Soil that had seemed to promise such beauty now seemed hardened by relentless heat and wind. Nettles of discouragement readily flourished in the dry, wounded places of my heart.

Jeremiah 17:7-8 says, "Blessed are those who trust in the Lord and have made the Lord their hope and confidence. They are like trees planted along a riverbank, with roots that reach deep into the water. Such trees are not bothered by the heat or worried by long months of drought. Their leaves stay green, and they never stop producing fruit." In the moment of adversity, however, we sometimes believe that something has gone dreadfully awry. Wanting God to rescue us, we cry out in our pain. We wonder at His timing, at His seeming silence. All the while, in that place of confusion and uncertainty, our spirit presses through the hardened clay of surface living, pushes aside the gravel of self-focus, and—in a refusal to give up—finds living water at the point of desperation (John 7:38).

He is real, and so are His promises.

Jesus—who came and lived among us—"grew up in the Lord's presence like a tender green shoot, like a root in dry ground" (Isaiah 53:2). In the certainty of His grace and the steadfastness of His hand, He can be trusted. The refreshing, restoring rains will come again. —Regina Franklin

investment advice

read>
Luke 9:23-25
If you try to hang on to your life, you will lose it. But if you give up your life for My sake, you will save it (v.24).

more>
For My people have done two evil things: They have abandoned Me—the fountain of living water. And they have dug for themselves cracked cisterns that can hold no water at all! (Jeremiah 2:13).

next>
As we surrender all we have and are to Jesus, what happens? How do we then view the stuff of this world?

A stock market consultant recently suggested, "People should always sell when they have a better place to put their money." While true, the challenge is recognizing when one place is better than another, which, of course, no one can identify with any level of certainty.

I typically respond to this sort of financial advice with a resounding *"Duh! No kidding?"* It's like telling investors to buy low and sell high. *Please tell us something we don't already know.*

Jesus once gave a crowd of people some fresh "advice." He said, "If you try to hang on to your life, you will lose it. But if you give up your life for My sake, you will save it" (Luke 9:24). I doubt there were few, if any, in the crowd who said. "Well, duh." Instead, most stood there scratching their heads, thinking, *Huh?*

Although Jesus drove home this thought on more than one occasion (Matthew 16:25; Luke 17:33), it's not exactly the kind of advice people hear every day. And while it caused them to stop and think, those who truly heard Him understood He *wasn't* talking about holding on to our *physical* life. The word Jesus used for "life" is the word *psyche*, which is the Greek word for the soul. He was referring to our *inner* life and clinging solely to our own efforts and plans to secure it. In essence, Jesus was saying that without Him, joy and meaning will slip through our fingers.

Self-reliance is a poor investment to hold on to because it never works out the way we think it should. And it prevents us from discovering the life our souls crave in a friendship with Jesus and living for His purposes (John 15:15).

What might you be hanging on to that you need to "sell" in order to find your life in Him? —Jeff Olson

sin and self-worth

read>
2 Samuel 16:5-14
God showed His great love for us by sending Christ to die for us while we were still sinners (Romans 5:8).

more>
Compare Philippians 3:3-6 and 1 Timothy 1:15-17 to learn how Paul balanced a positive self-image with an equal appreciation of his own sin.

next>
Which is the best version of the hymn "At the Cross?" The original line that Jesus died "for such a worm as I" or the revised "for sinners such as I"?

A youth pastor avoids telling his teenagers that they're sinners because he doesn't want to leave the impression that they "suck" (that they're *bad* or *worthless*). A popular author denies that infants are born with a sin nature because that would mean that "babies suck." And a friend who confessed to an especially offensive sin said, "I guess this means I suck."

Despite their juvenile descriptions of sin, notice that each person confuses sin with self-worth. They assume that sin means they no longer matter, when in fact their sin matters only if *they* do. Sin is rebellion, and rebellion is a problem only when the rebel carries some weight. If we really were worthless, our sin wouldn't count for much.

When King David was fleeing Jerusalem, he met Shimei, an enraged loner from Saul's dethroned family who hurled stones and insults at the king's entourage (2 Samuel 16:9). David's men wanted to crush Shimei, but David told them to leave him alone, in part because he was not a threat (v.10). Far different was David's response to Absalom's army. He knew that those men could destroy him and his kingdom, and so David threw all of his weapons at them in the fight of his life (18:1-2).

God isn't threatened by our rebellion, but the cross informs us that He takes us and our sin seriously. If we had no value, would God have given His life to save us? The cost of our salvation reminds us that we and our sin matter to God. If we minimize our sin, we also minimize ourselves and the salvation which rescues us.

The surest way to tell someone they're worthless is to ignore their sin. Treat them like a Shimei whose rebellion is of no account. If you want them to know they matter, you're going to have to talk about sin. —Mike Wittmer

the oprah effect

read>
2 Kings 5
Is this the time to receive money and clothing, olive groves and vineyards, sheep and cattle, and male and female servants? (v.26).

more>
- Genesis 14:22-23
- Acts 20:33
- 1 Thessalonians 2:9

next>
List some instances where you might miss God's blessings by accepting material gifts. When is it appropriate to give and receive material gifts?

While managing media and public relations for a handful of leading Washington, DC-based nonprofits, I found that nearly every organization I worked for craved recognition on *The Oprah Winfrey Show*. Their aspiration came as no surprise. Oprah Winfrey, after all, is "The queen of talk, a cultural and financial icon and her impact on business (and charities) is worth billions," according to CNBC host Carl Quintanilla. "Oprah Winfrey is the most influential woman in America—maybe in the world."

Experts have coined the term "The Oprah Effect" to describe her unparalleled ability to boost companies' bottom lines and to take organizations from no name to brand name. Some of us would love to benefit from the Oprah Effect, or most any other "rainmaker." We can readily imagine what we would do with the potential added resources. Many of us would likely give more to the poor, expand our influence, and live more comfortably.

Scripture states, however, that there are times when we must refrain from pursuing or receiving material gifts. In the case of the prophet Elisha, for example, it would have been wrong for him to request or accept gifts for the healing of Naaman's leprosy (2 Kings 5:15-16).

Elisha knew that if he accepted Naaman's "thank you" gift, the army commander would credit man, not God, for his healing. So even when Naaman persisted, Elisha stood firm, saying, "As surely as the Lord lives . . . I will not accept any gifts" (v.16).

I know a sports chaplain who refuses to accept gifts from the professional athletes he works with because he doesn't want them to question his motives. He simply wants to teach them the Word of God.

Today, consider when you should refuse a gift in order to point someone to God.

—Roxanne Robbins

get low

read>
2 Chronicles 26:1-23
But after Uzziah became powerful, his pride led to his downfall. He was unfaithful to the Lord his God (v.16 NIV).

more>
- James 4:6
- Proverbs 6:17;16:18

next>
How is pride a contention for the supremacy of God? How has it manifested itself in your life lately? Humility attracts the gaze and grace of God. What is your personal plan for seeking humility?

Evangelist D. L. Moody once said, "When a man thinks he has a good deal of strength, and is self-confident, you may look for his downfall. It may be years before it comes to light, but it is already commenced." This was definitely true of King Uzziah.

Everything seemed to be going so well in the monarch's life. He lived in covenant obedience to the Lord and he sought God's guidance during most of his reign. As long as he asked God for guidance and help, God gave him great success. His success was evidenced by his many accomplishments (2 Chronicles 26:2,7-15). In fact, Uzziah's life could be considered a human success story—until he became blinded by his power and success, which caused him to be filled with pride.

Uzziah's pride was evidenced in several ways: He challenged God's holiness by trespassing into the temple and presuming upon a position he would never be able to have (v.16); he viewed God's power as nice but not absolutely necessary for his leadership and life (vv.5,16); when confronted with his pride, he refused godly correction and counsel; he refused to repent, and he ignored—instead of feared—the consequences of his sin (vv.18-19). Uzziah's pride motivated him to glorify himself and contend for God's supremacy. What a tragic ending to a promising life.

The story of Uzziah teaches us several important lessons on how to break the pride cycle and start the humility cycle in our lives: View God's help as absolutely necessary, remember the Source of all our blessings, thank God regularly for those blessings, and accept godly and worthwhile counsel. May we choose, as William Penn says, a "low and level dwelling!" For God opposes the proud, but gives grace to the humble (James 4:6).

—Marvin Williams

let it (all) go

read>
Genesis 22:1-14
[Abraham] tied his son, Isaac, and laid him on the altar on top of the wood (v.9).

more>
Read Luke 18:18-29. What did Jesus ask the young man to give up? What was the significance of this specific challenge to this particular man?

next>
What do you find most difficult to surrender to God? What does that thing represent, and why do you cling to it so tightly?

Karl Rabeder is an Austrian millionaire, but not for much longer. He's giving away his entire fortune, more than 3 million pounds. His 3,455-square-foot villa overlooking the Alps, his six gliders, his expensive Audi A8, his country estate—all have been or will be sold. As Rabeder told *The Daily Telegraph*, "My idea is to have nothing left. Absolutely nothing." The money will fund his microcredit charity that will serve underdeveloped countries. Rabeder said he kept hearing these words: "Stop what you are doing—all this luxury and consumerism—and start your real life." So that's what he's doing.

Abraham faced a moment where he had to decide if he would let go of all he held dear. In one of the Old Testament's more disturbing stories, God asked Abraham to take his beloved son Isaac to Moriah and "sacrifice him as a burnt offering on one of the mountains" (Genesis 22:2). Bewildered, Abraham must have wondered why God would make such a horrific request. Isaac was not only his *son* but also the fulfillment of God's promise—the promise to finally bring the joy of a child to Abraham and Sarah and the promise to build a great nation on the earth from Abraham's descendants (18:18-19).

And yet, God asked Abraham to give up his faith in these promises. To surrender—not his own life—but the life of the boy he loved. How will we respond when God asks us to give up everything, even the things He's given us?

Abraham bound Isaac and laid him on the altar. He raised his knife, prepared to obey God. Mercifully, the angel of the Lord bellowed, "Don't lay a hand on the boy! . . . for now I know that you truly fear God. You have not withheld from me even your son, your only son" (22:12).

God wanted Abraham to be willing to release absolutely everything to Him. Will *we*? —Winn Collier

follow Jesus . . . on twitter

read>
Mark 1:16-20
Jesus called out to them, "Come, follow Me, and I will show you how to fish for people!" (v.17).

more>
"Follow Me and be My disciple," Jesus said to him. So Levi got up and followed Him (Mark 2:13-14).

next>
What have you understood "following Jesus" to mean in the past? Have you ever slipped into "push button" following—believing in Jesus, but not necessarily surrendering your life to Him?

Jesus has His own Twitter account. Well, actually, hundreds of them. Search for "Jesus Christ" on the social networking site, and you'll find a plethora of twitterers all tweeting in His name—some well-meaning and many blasphemous. The most popular "Jesus" on Twitter has tens of thousands of followers!

Hmmm. Would the *real* Jesus use Twitter? I wonder.

"Follow me," Jesus said to those first disciples (Mark 1:17). Unlike the rabbis of His day, Jesus wasn't looking simply for students—people who would sit at His feet and ponder the law. And although it was His core message to others (vv.14-15), Jesus didn't even call Simon, Andrew, James, and John to "repent." He called them to *follow.* This was a greater call than mere belief.

"I will show you how to fish for people!" Jesus added (v.17). He had a vision for them, a calling that would change their identity—no longer "fishermen" but "fishers-of-men." This was a call to change.

"And they left their nets at once and followed Him" (v.18). Jesus' call claimed priority even over the disciples' livelihood. This call would reorder their economic lives.

While crowds flocked to Jesus to receive healing (3:7-10), such people were not His disciples. Demons fell prostrate at His feet, but they certainly weren't His followers (v.11). To follow Jesus meant giving up everything to do the will of God (3:35; Luke 14:33).

Would the real Jesus use Twitter? I don't know. I *do* know that following the real Jesus means surrendering our dreams, jobs, identities, and finances to Him and choosing His plans for us (Matthew 22:37-39).

That's not something you can do by simply pushing a button.

—Sheridan Voysey

criminally cute

read>
Romans 5:12-21
Just as sin ruled over all people and brought them to death, now God's wonderful grace rules instead (v.21).

more>
According to John 3:16-18, what is the reason God sent His Son Jesus into the world? What does it say is not the reason?

next>
Do you see God as eager to forgive or quick to judge? What does the Bible say about His character?

Giddy with delight, my young son Elias slipped out of the room that served as a temporary nursery to newborn kittens. His mother had warned him not to touch them, so she asked, "Did you touch the kitties, Elias?" "No!" he said earnestly.

Mom wasn't fooled, so she probed a bit further. "Were they soft?"

"Yes," he volunteered, "and the black one mewed."

In a toddler, such duplicity is cute. But Elias' disobedience underscores our human condition. No one had to teach the 4-year-old fabricator to fib. He lied because such self-centered behavior is as natural to us as breathing. "I was born a sinner," wrote the songwriter David in his classic confession. "Yes, from the moment my mother conceived me" (Psalm 51:5). The New Testament adds this: "When Adam sinned, sin entered the world. Adam's sin brought death, so death spread to everyone" (Romans 5:12). That depressing news applies equally to kings, 4-year-olds, and you and me.

Scripture passages that point out our hell-bent tendencies could leave us feeling hopelessly guilt-ridden. But, by God's grace, there's hope! "God's law was given so that all people could see how sinful they were," wrote Paul. "But as people sinned more and more, God's wonderful grace became more abundant" (Romans 5:20).

We sometimes have a vague view of God behaving as a divine policeman, waiting for us to blow it so He can cuff us and curtail our freedom. But the one who accuses us is not God. Rather, it's our archenemy the devil (see Revelation 12:7-10). Our heavenly Father is all about grace, forgiveness, and restoration. We have only to come to Him in faith and repentance.

The happy conclusion is this: "There is no condemnation for those who belong to Christ Jesus" (Romans 8:1). —Tim Gustafson

alone

read>
John 16:16-32
You will be scattered, each one going his own way, leaving Me alone. Yet I am not alone because the Father is with Me (v.32).

more>
Read Isaiah 41:10 to discover God's assurance. Read 1 Kings 19:8-15 to see how God dealt with Elijah when he felt he was the only prophet left in Israel.

next>
Who or what do you normally turn to when you feel lonely? How could you learn to recognize God's abiding presence?

I saw this quote on a friend's Facebook page: "It's not that I feel alone because I have no friends. I have lots of friends. I know that I have people who can hold me and reassure me and talk to me and care for me and think of me. But they can't be inside my head with me all the time—for all time."

Loneliness is a reality that all human beings experience at one time or another. Albert Einstein once said, "It is strange to be known so universally and yet be so lonely." Jesus understands our loneliness. During His earthly ministry He saw it in the eyes of lepers, heard it in the voices of the blind, and felt it in the touch of the pressing masses. But above all, He experienced it when His close friends deserted Him.

As He foretold the disciples' desertion, however, He also confessed His unshaken confidence in His Father's abiding presence. He said, "But the time is coming—indeed it's here now—when you will be scattered, each one going his own way, leaving Me alone. Yet I am not alone because the Father is with Me" (John 16:32).

Jesus knew the ultimate cure for loneliness, and He shared it with us. He told us that isolation doesn't need to lead to loneliness—for *we have the abiding presence of the Father with us*. God is eternal and omniscient and omnipresent. Only He could be with us all the time, for all time.

After Jesus said His words of comfort to the disciples (v.22), He took up the cross and the curse of loneliness for us. He made it possible for you and me to have a restored relationship with God and to be a member of His family—*all the time, for all time.* —Poh Fang Chia

power failure

read>
1 Samuel 13:5-14
Your kingdom must end, for the Lord has sought out a man after His own heart. The Lord has already appointed him to be the leader of His people, because you have not kept the Lord's command (v.14).

more>
If once wasn't enough, later Saul disobeyed another divine command (ch.15). Read verse 22 to learn what Samuel told the fallen king about what God truly values.

next>
What fear or concern is causing you to consider a decision that will defy God's commands? Why is it vital that you choose to obey God instead?

An impromptu high-wire act by a 26-year-old man caused a portion of Dongguan, a city in China, to experience a blackout. The man had lost his job and chose to drown his sorrows by drinking heavily. After his binge, the drunken one climbed a high voltage cable tower and began walking and hanging on the power cables. When firemen couldn't coax him down, they ordered the electricity to be shut off so he wouldn't electrocute himself. Four hours later, the guy finally fell . . . landing softly on a safety cushion where he was "greeted" by police.

King Saul once had a power *surge* (1 Samuel 10:6), but he lost it all due to a rash decision. In the span of just four chapters, we find the prophet Samuel anointing Saul as Israel's king (13:1) and then informing him that God had rejected him as ruler of His people (v.14). Why the abrupt change? Samuel made it plain to Saul: "Because you have not kept the Lord's command."

The command was clear. Samuel told Saul to camp out at Gilgal for a week until he arrived there to "sacrifice burnt offerings and peace offerings" (10:8). But the king got uptight when the mighty Philistine army with "as many warriors as the grains of sand on the seashore" (13:5) caused his army to begin "trembling with fear" (v.7).

With his army defecting and growing smaller by the hour, Saul (literally) chose to play with fire and did the burnt offering himself (v.9). That's when Samuel caught him red-*hot*-handed and gave him the bad news—his days on the throne were numbered.

Have you been tempted to make a rash decision—one that doesn't honor God? Fear can cause us to short-circuit our faith and future. Let's choose to obey God instead. He's got all the power we need. —Tom Felten

a time to learn

read>
2 Peter 1:3-11
Work hard to prove that you really are among those God has called and chosen. Do these things, and you will never fall away (v.10).

more>
Work hard to show the results of your salvation, obeying God with deep reverence and fear (Philippians 2:12).

next>
What's a lesson you've learned in the midst of working through a challenge? What would happen to you if God removed every challenge from your life?

A video on YouTube captured a mother squirrel trying to teach her baby how to scale a cement wall. Over and over the mother squirrel patiently showed how it was done, but the wall was simply too big for the younger rodent to conquer.

Eventually, a few college students intervened. They first placed a backpack up against the wall, hoping it would function as a step for the younger squirrel. But it wasn't tall enough. Next, they made a higher step by placing a couple of sandbags on top of one another. Finally the little squirrel climbed on top of the sandbags and scaled the daunting wall— having learned a valuable survival lesson.

This little drama from the animal kingdom reminds me of how God often deals with us. One of the reasons He doesn't instantly resolve our struggles or take us out of seemingly insurmountable challenges is because they provide valuable learning experiences. For instance, after He brought Pharaoh to his knees through a series of crippling plagues (Exodus 12:31-32), God didn't pack the Israelites' bags and march them out of Egypt. They had to do it themselves, learning the valuable lesson that faith and effort often go hand in hand.

Too often the Christian walk is seen as believers sitting back and letting God do everything for us. That's rarely the case. While God is always God, and we can do nothing apart from Him (John 15:5), He's not going to do all the work. Sometimes He will provide a "backpack" or a "sandbag," but He knows there are lessons for us to learn through effort that will make us better in the long run.

—Jeff Olson

embrace the cross

read>
Galatians 2:17–3:7
My old self has been crucified with Christ. It is no longer I who live, but Christ lives in me (2:20).

more>
If any of you wants to be My follower, you must turn from your selfish ways, take up your cross, and follow Me (Matthew 16:24).

next>
Extreme measures indicate that the situation is not only desperate but also important. What does the cross say about your value to God?

If desperate situations call for extreme measures, then extreme measures are a sign that we are in a desperate situation. If a police car flashed its lights behind me, my wife might say in her disapproving voice, "What did you do?" If my car were surrounded by police and a TV news helicopter hovered overhead, my wife's tone would likely become more accusatory, "*What* did you *do*?" If a jet fighter joined the chase, dropping bombs in the direction of our car, my wife might scream like the lead female actor in an action movie, "*What did you do?!*"

Consider what God did to save us. He didn't hand us a brochure, as if our problem were merely ignorance. He didn't hold an intervention, as if our problem were merely stubbornness. He answered our need with the cross, which can only mean that we have messed up big-time. If the cross is necessary to save us, then *What did we do?*

The cross is a dagger through the happy talk of "You're okay, I'm okay" and if we just try harder, we can change the world. The cross informs us that things have gone horribly wrong, and they won't be right unless somebody dies.

That somebody is *Jesus*. He paid our penalty, absorbing the Father's wrath so that we might live (Galatians 2:20). That somebody is *us*. Jesus died instead of us, but not without us. Karl Barth explains: "That Jesus Christ died for us does not mean, therefore, that we do not have to die, but that we have died in and with Him, that as the people we were we have been done away and destroyed, that we are no longer there and have no more future."

Salvation is free, but it's not cheap. It cost Jesus His life; and if you accept His gift, it will cost yours. —Mike Wittmer

prison break

read>
Isaiah 42:1-9
You will free the captives from prison (v.7).

more>
Read 2 Corinthians 5:11-21. How is Mosab Hassan Yousef living out verse 4? How are you doing that?

next>
Pray for your brothers and sisters around the world who are facing extreme persecution, even to the point of death, for following and proclaiming Jesus Christ. How will you proclaim the good news today?

"I absolutely know that in anybody's eyes I was a traitor," Mosab Hassan Yousef told the *Wall Street Journal* before the release of his book *Son of Hamas.* "To my family, to my nation, to my God. I crossed all the red lines in my society. I didn't leave one that I didn't cross."

By "traitor," Mosab—the son of Sheikh Hassan Yousef, a founder and leader of the terrorist group Hamas—refers to his radical conversion from an extreme faith to Christianity. It also reflects his departure from Hamas after more than a decade of serving the terrorist group alongside his father.

Though the terrorists he once served now threaten his life, Mosab considers himself a free man, a man depicted in Romans 6:19 who was previously a slave "to impurity and lawlessness, which led ever deeper into sin," but is now a slave "to righteous living so that [he] will become holy."

"I converted to Christianity because I was convinced by Jesus Christ as a character, as a personality. I loved Him, His wisdom, His love, His unconditional love," Mosab says. "I found that I was really drawn to the grace, love, and humility that Jesus talked about."

Mosab relishes following and proclaiming the God who sent His Son Jesus to "bring good news to the poor . . . comfort the brokenhearted . . . proclaim that captives will be released and prisoners will be freed . . . [bring forth] the Lord's favor . . . give a crown of beauty for ashes, a joyous blessing instead of mourning, festive praise instead of despair" (Isaiah 61:1-3).

A new man, Mosab now says, "My goal is not to defeat my enemy. It is to win over my enemy." —Roxanne Robbins

God's friend

read>
Genesis 18:16-19
The Lord is a friend to those who fear Him (Psalm 25:14).

If I were to tell you that the president of your country is my friend, it's likely you wouldn't believe me. You might even be tempted to call me a liar. But if your president were to go on national TV and say publicly that I'm his friend, then all doubts would fade away, right? The facts would back up my claim.

Now, what if I told you that God is my friend? Let's check the facts, starting with the reality that God once called Abraham "My friend" (Isaiah 41:8; see also 2 Chronicles 20:7; James 2:23). God said of Abraham, *"I have singled him out"* (Genesis 18:19). Other Bible translations render this as *"I have chosen him"* (NIV) or *"I have known him"* (NKJV). These words speak of divine election, of covenantal love, and of grace. Bible commentator H. C. Leupold translated the phrase this way: "For I acknowledge Him to be My intimate friend."

A friend is someone with whom we aren't afraid to share our true struggles and intimate secrets. Friends listen as we share our pain. When we have a problem, to whom do we turn? Our closest friend. Amazingly, when God had a burden, He shared it with His friend Abraham (v.17).

You and I enjoy the same covenantal relationship with God as the one Abraham experienced. We've been chosen by God to be in His family (Ephesians 1:4-7). And we're chosen by Jesus to be His friend. For He said, "You are My friends if you do what I command. . . . Now you are My friends, since I have told you everything the Father told Me. You didn't choose Me. I chose you" (John 15:14-16).

Your very best friend is Jesus. Even if others let you down, He will be "with you always" (Matthew 28:20). —K.T. Sim

more>
According to John 15:12-17, what did Jesus do for you, His friend?

next>
How would you describe your friendship with Jesus? How have you been showing Him that He's your best friend?

good fruit

The secret of good fruit is in the branch and root. Good parenting is the fruit of good character that is rooted and growing in God Himself. The Bible calls this character the fruit of the Spirit. That is to say that it comes from the Holy Spirit of God rather than from our own natural ability or energy. Listen to what the apostle Paul wrote, and think about how it assures good parenting: "But the Holy Spirit produces this kind of fruit in our lives: love, joy, peace, patience, kindness, goodness, faithfulness, gentleness, and self-control. There is no law against these things! Those who belong to Christ Jesus have nailed the passions and desires of their sinful nature to His cross and crucified them there. Since we are living by the Spirit, let us follow the Spirit's leading in every part of our lives" (Galatians 5:22-25).

The reason Paul's words are so important for parents is that they not only reflect the qualities that assure good parenting, but they also point to resources of the Spirit that we don't have to find in ourselves or in our own experience. If Paul is right, then our own sense of inadequacy and our own history in dysfunctional relationships can actually be put to work for us. Those can be the needs that drive us to find in the Spirit of our heavenly Father the parenting qualities that are not natural to us.

Listen to what Paul wrote to Christians who had been trying to live in their own strength: "How foolish can you be? After starting your Christian lives in the Spirit, why are you now trying to become perfect by your own human effort? Have you experienced so much for nothing? Surely it was not in vain, was it? I ask you again, does God give you the Holy Spirit and work miracles among you because you obey the law? Of course not! It is because you believe the message you heard about Christ" (3:3-5).

The spiritual resources of character Paul was talking about are not the result of

trying to live by the ideals of God. They come when we believe and trust what God says He is willing and able to do in us. We need to remind one another continually that the secret to good parenting is like fruit that is rooted in the branches and roots of the Spirit of Christ. When we are in agreement with Christ and His Word (John 15:1-14), then we will be growing in our experience of the fruit of the Spirit:

- supernatural love vs. sheer effort and fatigue
- good sense of humor (joy) vs. pessimism
- calm spirit vs. anxiety
- patient attitude vs. quick anger
- kindness vs. meanness
- good motives and intentions vs. selfishness
- promise-keeping vs. breaking your word
- gentleness vs. harshness
- self-control vs. addictive behavior

good instruction

In the Old Testament, God taught His people to build rock piles so that their children would one day ask why the stones were there. When the children asked, the parents were to be ready to tell the story of how the Lord of Israel had wonderfully met their needs in that place. The secret was in being ready for teachable moments.

"In the future your children will ask, 'What do these stones mean?' Then you can tell them, (Joshua 4:21-22). The parent-teachers of Israel were not to be boring. They were to do things that would encourage their children to ask, "Dad, Mom, why do we do this? Why do we always have an empty placesetting at our table?" (See also Deut. 6:6-9,20-25.)

The father who wrote the Proverbs for his son realized the power of a word spoken at just the right moment (Proverbs 15:23,25:11). He came from a tradition

that used creative ways to open the hearts of children to life-changing perspectives. The Jews used education by rock piles, by riddles, by object lessons, by drama, by word pictures, and by seeing children, overall, as being willing and active participants in their own learning. Such child-ready object lessons are different from the kind of family devotions that are forced, ritualistic, and academic. These seldom have the desired spiritual effect. Unless our words come at teachable moments, they are not likely to draw our children's hearts toward God.

All that forced devotions do is help a parent feel less guilty about something he feels he should do. Planning for and taking advantage of teachable moments is far better. Discussions about life while enjoying an afternoon in a fishing boat, a walk along a wooded field, a drive through the countryside, a spontaneous discussion during mealtime, or a tender Bible story and prayer at bedtime are usually far better received (Deuteronomy 6:6-9) and much more effective. The challenge is that you can't teach children this way without a lot of involvement and creative time spent with them. Now, I'm not saying that we should not have mealtime devotions with our children. If it is working well and doing what you hoped it would do, then continue. But if all you are doing is trying to force your children to learn something, chances are they may be learning to resent not only Bible reading and prayer, but also you and your Lord. —Mart De Haan

Adapted from the Discovery Series booklet *How Can A Parent Find Peace Of Mind?*
© 2011 RBC Ministries.

disturbing the peace

read>
John 14:23-30
I am leaving you with a gift—peace of mind and heart (v.27).

more>
Read Ephesians 2:14-18 to learn about how Jesus "Himself has brought peace to us." Read Revelation 21:3-4 to gain a picture of the peace that believers will experience in heaven.

next>
How have you tried to create peace for yourself? Why do we sometimes reject Jesus' gift of peace?

Sometimes I catch a glimpse of him as he drives by—reclined in his seat, one arm slung out of his rolled-down window. He's the guy with the car stereo that blasts seismic sound waves through our neighborhood. His sub-woofers pulse with a booming rhythm so loud that I can hardly feel my own heartbeat. In case you think I'm simply dull and cranky, let me assure you that I love music. And sometimes, I like it *really* loud. It's the jolt of the unexpected musical monster that sets me on edge; it steals my peace.

Jesus knew this world would furnish all sorts of unsettling situations. That's why He said, "I am leaving you with a gift—peace" (John 14:27). Amazingly, peace is a gift. We don't have to work for it; we just have to welcome it. As Christians, we're supposed to "let the peace that comes from Christ rule in [our] hearts" (Colossians 3:15).

Jesus' gift of peace doesn't mean that He'll resolve every issue in our lives. Our spouse may continue to overdraw from the checking account. Our kids may not lose interest in that dreaded rock band. The boss may never ease up. But somehow, Jesus said we could have "peace of mind and heart" (John 14:27). Jesus provides *inner* peace when outer peace isn't possible.

For most of us, peaceful life circumstances are impossible to obtain. And no amount of striving will create the calm we crave. Perfecting our relationships, simplifying our schedules, and organizing our homes won't lead us to long-term serenity. Jesus said, "The peace I give you is a gift the world cannot give" (v.27). We can't manufacture what only Christ can provide.

If something is disturbing your peace today, trust in Jesus' promise: "You may have peace in Me. . . . I have overcome the world" (John 16:33).

—Jennifer Benson Schuldt

dirty jobs

read>
Colossians 3:22–4:1
Work willingly at whatever you do, as though you were working for the Lord rather than for people (v.23).

more>
Read 1 Timothy 6:1-2 and Titus 2:9-10 to see more characteristics of a Christ-honoring employee.

next>
How would you rank your attitude toward your job, fellow employees, and your employer? If you did your work for Jesus every day, what difference would it make in the output and quality of your labor?

Spencer Johnson, author of *Who Moved My Cheese?* stated in an article: "I believe research may one day show that the only long-lasting motivation will come from employees who bring it to work in the form of God, spirituality, or something else that causes them to rise to a higher purpose." Long before Dr. Johnson came to that conclusion, the apostle Paul said that slaves (employees) and masters (employers) should be motivated by a higher purpose in their jobs—their relationship with Jesus.

In Colossians 3:22–4:1, Paul discussed three important aspects of work—*mandate, manner,* and *motivation*. Employees have the mandate to obey their bosses out of reverence for Christ (3:22). The manner in which they obey flows from a sincere heart and with a right attitude. Paul wrote, "Work willingly at whatever you do, as though you were working for the Lord rather than for people" (v.23). Employees can overcome the lack of motivation in their work and accept new responsibilities without a negative reaction by focusing on their true motivation: working for Jesus (v.24).

Paul also addressed the actions of employers. They should treat their employees with fairness and justice as they honor their Master in heaven (4:1; Philemon 16).

As followers of Jesus who work in the marketplace, we're called to rise to a higher purpose in our jobs. If we're employees, unless we know a task is sinful, we should do the job we were hired to do—every task, every workday. Even if our jobs are dirty or seem to lack meaning, we should perform them with excellence and the right attitude. If we're employers, we should create fair and just environments out of our reverence and love for Jesus.

In both roles, we're missionaries on assignment—representing the Master.

—Marvin Williams

no guide

read>
Jeremiah 2:1-13
My people have done two evil things: They have abandoned Me—the fountain of living water. And they have dug for themselves cracked cisterns that can hold no water at all! (v.13).

more>
Read Jeremiah 31:9 for a picture of a thirsty people returning to God. Read John 4:10-14 for a fresh vision of Jesus as living water.

next>
When have you thirsted for God? How are you seeking Him today?

Each week around the world, 10 million Girl Guides (or Girl Scouts) learn how to cook, knit, survive in the wilderness, and generally become good citizens. A girl becomes a Guide by making the Guide Promise—a pledge of duty to God, country, and the Guide Law.

In recent years, there's been discussion over the wording of the Promise, as a Canadian case illustrates. A Canadian Guide once pledged to "do my duty to God, the Queen, and my country." In 1994, this was changed to "be true to myself, my God/faith, and Canada," and in 2010 it was revised to "be true to myself, my beliefs, and Canada." The changes reflect an understandable desire to be inclusive in a pluralistic society. But one can't escape the obvious: a promise to self has replaced a promise to *God*. I often wonder how God feels about such headlines.

"What did your ancestors find wrong with Me?" God once said through the prophet Jeremiah (Jeremiah 2:5). In her youth, Israel had been devoted to God—eager to keep her bridal promise; valiantly following Him through the wilderness (vv.2-3). Then the love cooled. Israel no longer cared for God, nor did her priests, scribes, and prophets (vv.6-8). In fact, she replaced Him with human-engineered replicas (vv.11-12). Her promise to God was transferred to an idol.

"They have abandoned me—the fountain of living water," God cried out in poetic fashion. "And they have dug for themselves cracked cisterns that can hold no water at all!" (v.13). Here's the tragic irony: *Self-made replacements for the Source of life can only leave us dry and empty.*

The change in the Canadian Guides' Promise is symptomatic of a broader trend. When spiritual thirst overwhelms us, may we pledge ourselves again to the God of our youth. —Sheridan Voysey

read>
1 Peter 3:8-18
Turn away from evil and do good. Search for peace, and work to maintain it (v.11).

more>
Read John 14:26-27 to find out the role of the Holy Spirit in bringing real peace to your heart.

next>
In what area of your life are you attempting to keep peace or make peace? Thinking of a conflict you are currently facing, what can you do to "live in peace"? Do you trust God to work out the conflict or are you relying on your own efforts?

Checking the texting inbox on my phone, I understood my friend's frustration when I read her message: "I am sick of unresolved conflict!! I can't take it anymore!" Ironically, our Bible study the night before had been on peace. As I thought about her situation—and some of my own—I was reminded how easily conflict can arise and how difficult resolution can be.

In a world full of conflict, God's Word stands in stark contrast with its reminders that "God blesses those who work for peace" (Matthew 5:9), and "those who are peacemakers will plant seeds of peace and reap a harvest of righteousness" (James 3:18). Peter told his audience to be humble and loving, choosing to end conflicts by paying people "back with a blessing" (1 Peter 3:8-9). Peace*keeping* and peace*making* are similar in many ways, and yet different. The primary emphasis in keeping peace is to maintain it by enforcement or supervision (v.11; Hebrews 12:14).

Making peace, however, means getting to the root of the issue. Colossians 1:20 teaches that for us to be reconciled to God, our sin can be removed only through the work of the cross (1 Peter 3:18). Peace comes with a price. To make peace also means we have to be content to lose control. Isaiah 26:3 reminds us, "You will keep in perfect peace all who trust in You, all whose thoughts are fixed on You." We can't always make our circumstances or relationships peaceful, but we can find personal peace by:

- Recognizing that our peace is not measured by others' choices, but by our own (Romans 12:18).
- Growing in our relationship with the God of all peace (2 Peter 1:2).

Peace will not be found in what we can maneuver to bring us comfort, but in what we surrender to God. —Regina Franklin

something good

read>
Psalm 37:1-9
Trust in the Lord and do good. Then you will live safely in the land and prosper (v.3).

more>
Read Psalm 37 and note: God's *timing* and God's *action*.

next>
How would you describe your anticipation that God is up to something good in your world? Where can you see God's good activity?

In Johannesburg, South Africa, large crowds lined up to purchase tickets to the 2010 World Cup—the first Cup ever to be held on the African continent. One man (the 565th person in line) passed away as he waited to purchase tickets. A FIFA official told reporters that there was a "massive demand for tickets." Energy and excitement had struck the continent, as ecstatic fans eagerly awaited soccer's greatest tournament.

Scripture tells us that God's people are *waiting*. Waiting for God to make wrong right, to heal what is wounded, and to awaken to life that which is dead. And the Scripture tells us that this waiting isn't in vain. Our hopes aren't based in a fairytale. Our deepest hopes *will* be fulfilled. Something good *is* coming.

The psalmist tells us that the world we know pits the wicked (those who refuse God) against the righteous (those who find their hope in God). It often seems to us as though the wicked do well, while the righteous suffer. The psalmist, however, insists that the story's end will be much different. The wicked will "fade away," but those who trust (find hope in) the Lord will receive their "heart's desires" (Psalm 37:2,4).

The difficulty for us is to trust that God's promise is true. When those with power exploit the weak, when the political machine chews up the helpless, and when those bent on arrogance and selfishness and unscrupulous profit always seem to win, it requires deep faith to remain confident in God's ultimate triumph. It requires immense courage to resist the lie that we must join the ranks of the wicked in order to find fulfillment. Yet God tells us to "wait patiently for Him to act" (v.7).

God *will* act. Something good *is* coming. —Winn Collier

what we worship

read>
Psalm 115:1-8
Those who make idols are just like them, as are all who trust in them (v.8).

more>
Read Exodus 32:1-9 and Isaiah 48:4-5 to learn how God views those who worship idols instead of Him.

next>
What prevents you from hearing God's voice? What steps can you take to worship Him with all you are and possess?

We resemble what we revere. When we worship money, we view ourselves and others in terms of our cash value. We see people as creditors, debtors, and customers, rather than as human beings made in the image of God. When we worship sex, we treat ourselves and others as dehumanized objects of sexual pleasure—good for nothing other than the next orgasm. And when we worship power, we turn every relationship into a contest between competitors, managers, and pawns.

The tragedy of becoming what we worship is that our false gods "have mouths but cannot speak, and eyes but cannot see. They have ears but cannot hear, and noses but cannot smell" (Psalm 115:5-6). When God says that we become like idols, He means that we become mute, blind, and deaf to what matters most.

That's why God told Isaiah that idolatrous Israel would "not see with their eyes, nor hear with their ears, nor understand with their hearts and turn to [Him] for healing" (Isaiah 6:10). They had been serving idols for so long that they had become deaf to the very voice of God.

Nothing dulls our awareness of God as efficiently as the media. Movies and television shows ignore God in their pursuit of money, sex, and power. Have you ever heard an onscreen character say, "Let's pray about this" or "I wonder what God's Word says about our problem"?

We regain our ear for the music of God when we destroy our idols and practice living in His presence. Karl Barth explained that we become "like a latecomer slipping shamefacedly into creation's choir . . . which has never ceased its praise, but merely suffered and sighed . . . that in inconceivable folly and ingratitude its living center man does not hear its voice, its response, its echoing of the divine glory." Better late than never. —Mike Wittmer

feel

read>
Proverbs 3:1-8
We don't know what God wants us to pray for. But the Holy Spirit prays for us with groanings that cannot be expressed in words (Romans 8:26).

more>
Read Romans 8:1-17 to learn about the Holy Spirit's role in guiding our lives and decisions. In Matthew 16:1-4, what do you think is the "sign of Jonah"? (v.4).

next>
How do you seek God's guidance? Are your prayers sometimes attempts to manipulate Him? How well are you obeying God's Word?

My friend has a habit of asking God for signs. In doing so, His prayers tend to seek confirmation of his feelings, as in "God, if You want me to do 'X,' then please do 'Y,' and I'll know it's OK."

Not surprisingly, this has created a dilemma. For my friend feels that he should get back with his ex-girlfriend, based on the way he prays. His ex, on the other hand, feels strongly that God has told them *not* to get back together. Ah, *feelings*.

Jesus told the religious leaders of His day: "Only an evil, adulterous generation would demand a miraculous sign" (Matthew 16:4). But He wasn't making a blanket statement to prevent anyone from seeking God's guidance. Rather, Jesus was accusing them of ignoring the clear prophecies that told them He was the Messiah.

Proverbs gives us an abundance of direct signs as to how to live our lives. Solomon, who wrote most verses in the book, gave these instructions to his son: "Never let loyalty and kindness leave you" (3:3). "Trust in the Lord with all your heart; do not depend on your own understanding" (v.5). To drive his point home, Solomon concluded: "Don't be impressed with your own wisdom. Instead, fear the Lord and turn away from evil" (v.7).

God wants us to seek His guidance in prayer (James 1:5). He has given us the instruction of the Holy Spirit (John 14:26) and His Word, the Bible (1 Thessalonians 2:13). He gives us mentors and wise leaders. He's also given us the ultimate example seen in Jesus (Philippians 2:4-5).

It's wise to ask God for clear direction. But our prayers should never be formulaic attempts to manipulate God. Real Christianity is not a system; it's a relationship with Jesus Himself. —Tim Gustafson

training daze

read>
1 Kings 17:7-16
Then the Lord said to Elijah, "Go and live in the village of Zarephath, near the city of Sidon. I have instructed a widow there to feed you" (vv.8-9).

more>
Read John 15:2 to discover why, according to Jesus, God prunes us.

next>
What is your usual response when faced with difficulties? What new perspective should you work on?

After graduation from college, I worked for an organization that did not pay well. It was tough. Sometimes I couldn't even afford my next meal. During that time, my mother became sick. I felt awful not being able to help pay for her hospital expenses. It was one trial after another, and each new trial was harder than the previous one.

In 1 Kings 17, we find God training Elijah. By the waters of Kerith, God used ravens to bring Elijah his daily meals. But as the drought persisted, the babbling brook became a silent stream, and then it slowed to a mere trickle.

We read: "But after a while the brook dried up . . . *then* the Lord said to Elijah" (vv.7-8). Often we would rather have God show us the next step before our resources are totally depleted. Waiting can be nerve-racking. It can be frustrating. But this is all part of the training process. We need to learn that we're dependent on God, and Him alone. We need to learn that when our comfort zone is compromised, God is still in control.

Elijah was told by God, "Go and live in the village of Zarephath, near the city of Sidon. I have instructed a widow there to feed you" (v.9). Zarephath was enemy territory. Why would anyone offer Elijah shelter, especially a *widow*? They were often the poorest of the poor! Everything God told Elijah to do defied man's wisdom; it demanded trust. God was training His servant to walk by faith, not by sight (2 Corinthians 5:7).

He learned the lesson reflected in these lyrics: "Now I can see testing comes from above, God strengthens His children and purges in love. My Father knows best, and I trust in His care; through purging, more fruit I will bear." Are you ready for God's training? —Poh Fang Chia

a gift for Jesus

read>
Mark 14:3-9
Wherever the Good News is preached throughout the world, this woman's deed will be remembered and discussed (v.9).

more>
Read Romans 12:1, to learn the appropriate gift for you to give to Jesus for all He's done for you.

next>
This coming week, what's one good or beautiful thing you can do for Jesus? What keeps you from giving Him your all?

Consider this situation: Someone you deeply love is dying. Doctors tell you that this could be his last week of life. You want to do something memorable and meaningful for him. What would it be?

At a dinner held to honor Jesus (John 12:2), Mary anointed Him with expensive perfume made from essence of *nard* (or *spikenard*)—a special plant that grew only in the Himalayas of India. Mary's perfume cost the equivalent of a whole year's salary for a laborer in ancient Israel (Mark 14:5). In the Song of Solomon (1:12 and 4:13), *nard* symbolizes the sweet aroma worn by a bride, drawing her husband to her. Some Bible teachers believe that the perfume Mary was using to annoint Jesus was her personal dowry—a treasure she had been keeping for her own wedding. It was her most precious possession.

Mary's generous gift to Jesus invoked strong negative responses. Some dinner guests rebuked her harshly (vv.4-5). But Jesus commended her. For Mary had done a "beautiful" thing (v.6 NIV). She had placed the perfume on Jesus to prepare Him for His death (v.8). Leading up to this time, He had often said that He would be betrayed, killed, buried, and that He would rise again. His disciples didn't believe Him, for they didn't want it to happen (Mark 8:31-33, 9:31-32). But Mary had been listening to Jesus (Luke 10:39-42). Believing His words, she lovingly ministered to Him in His last week before He went to the cross.

The expensive perfume was Mary's funeral gift to Jesus. She gave her very best to honor Him. Today, we're part of Jesus' fulfilled prophecy—we're remembering what Mary did at that dinner (Mark 14:9).

If you were in Mary's place, what would you have done for Jesus? What "perfume" would you have given to honor Him? —K.T. Sim

flying fish

read>
Exodus 16:1-18
Each family had just what it needed (v.18).

more>
Numbers 11:31-35 presents an account of falling quail. Why did God discipline His people? How can you avoid following their sinful behavior?

next>
Why does God desire that you be content with His provision? How is He developing your faith by giving you what you need—not what you want?

The residents of Lajamanu, a remote Australian town, received a fishy gift in February 2010. Hundreds of small spangled perch dropped from the sky! Meteorologists believe the fish were sucked up into the clouds by a storm. "It could have scooped the fish up to 40,000 to 50,000 feet in the air. Once they get up into the system they [were] pretty much frozen. After some period they [were] released," said a weather expert. Surprisingly, Lajamanu has been bombarded by flying (frozen) fish twice before—in 1974 and 2004.

A month after being miraculously delivered from Egypt, the Israelites were looking for a nice, fresh fish dinner—or *something* fresh to eat (Exodus 16:1-3). The wilderness didn't allow for much, shall we say, delicious cuisine. God knew what His people needed, and He told Moses that He would "rain down food from heaven" (v.4). And that's just what He did!

God provided His complaining people with bread in the morning and meat in the evening (v.12). But, instead of fish, God gave them "vast numbers of quail [that] flew in and covered the camp" (v.13). So the Israelites had some tasty fowl to consume. In fact, "Each family had just what it needed" (v.18).

Why would God give His people simply what they needed and no more? He was teaching them to trust in Him alone and not in their own means. He was teaching them about real faith. Jesus reflected the same faith-building way of life in the Lord's Prayer, telling His disciples to pray, "Give us today the food we need" (Matthew 6:11).

Are you content with what God has provided for you today? If not, it's time to take a fresh look at your faith. God wants us to depend on Him for our daily provision—not the frozen fish in the freezer. —Tom Felten

not today!

read>
John 10:1-10
The thief's purpose is to steal and kill and destroy. My purpose is to give them a rich and satisfying life (v.10).

more>
Read Ephesians 6:10-18 to gain insight into how to resist the devil.

next>
How has Satan been trying to steal life from you? What has Jesus—your Good Shepherd—provided to help you withstand Satan's schemes?

A few years ago, an attempted bank robbery was thwarted when an armed and courageous customer stopped a man who claimed to have a bomb strapped to his chest. *Here's what happened.* Shortly after the bank opened, a man approached a teller and threatened to detonate a bomb if she didn't hand over the money. Another teller, who saw what was going down, alerted long-time customer Nabil Fawzi, who happened to be legally packing a handgun.

Calmly, Fawzi pulled out his concealed pistol, pointed it at the robber and firmly announced, "You are not robbing this bank today!" He then ordered the thief to sit in a chair and held him at gunpoint until police arrived.

Most of us won't witness a robbery at our local bank, but Jesus warned that we all are in danger of being *robbed*. When He described Himself as the "Good Shepherd" (John 10:11), Jesus reminded His followers that there is an unseen thief who is out "to steal and kill and destroy" the life He came to restore (John 10:10).

The "thief" Jesus referred to is Satan—the once mightiest of angels who fell when he became arrogant and turned against his Maker (Isaiah 14:12-14). Though God defeated Satan's attempt to overthrow heaven, Satan and his fallen angels are still active today.

Jesus wants to give us life, and Satan wants to steal it away. The evil one is bent on keeping us from the life with God that he once had but can never get back. It's imperative that we know this, so that we can be alert and resist him (1 Peter 5:8-9).

Satan is an accomplished thief, but we're far from helpless. Like Nabil Fawzi, we are armed (but with God's truth) and can firmly tell him, "Not today!"

—Jeff Olson

when faith is weak

read>
Psalm 136:23-26
He remembered us in our weakness (v.23).

more>
In Luke 12:28, Jesus decries the lack of faith by those who claim to believe in Him. What reason does He give for the importance of a strong faith in God?

next>
Talk with a Christian friend or two about the origin of their faith and what keeps it strong, even when circumstances threaten to make it weak. How have you grown in your faith this year?

To say my Christian faith is unflappable would be untrue. It's to the *contrary*. For even though I write devotions, engage in work on behalf of the poor in East Africa, and long for my confidence in Jesus Christ to be strong—often, too often, my faith is pathetically, embarrassingly weak. In the midst of personal hardships, I find it more natural to question God's goodness than to trust in His sovereignty and bask in His love.

I'm not confessing anything new to God. His Word states that, whether or not I admit it, God knows how weak I am—how weak we all are (Psalm 136:23). He knows we are "only dust" (103:14). Our Creator understands that it's easier to trust in what is "seen" than what is "unseen" (Hebrews 11), and that while our spirits may be willing, our bodies are weak (Matthew 26:41).

That's why, in His great mercy, God sent His Holy Spirit to dwell in our hearts, to give us the grace and strength we need to muster up faith in Jesus even in the darkest of trials (Romans 8:26). The Lord wants you and me to be made right with God through our faith and trust in *Him*. He also allows us to experience these faith-building things:

- Salvation (Luke 7:50)
- Healing (Mark 3:4; James 5:15)
- Righteousness (Romans 1:7; Galatians 3:24; Philippians 3:9)
- Growth with our brothers and sisters in the faith (Ephesians 4:16)
- Protection from the enemy (Psalm 136:24; Ephesians 6:16)

The apostle Paul wrote, "So faith comes from hearing, that is, hearing the Good News about Christ" (Romans 10:17). Let's strengthen our faith by relying on the Holy Spirit, God's Word, other believers, and His "faithful love" that endures forever (Psalm 136:25-26). —Roxanne Robbins

off-limits

read>
Hosea 14:1-9
The Lord says . . . "I will heal you of your faithlessness; My love will know no bounds" (v.4).

more>
Read 1 John 1:8-10 to grasp why confession is so critical when returning to God. Read Psalm 32:1-5 to understand what it feels like to be right with Him.

next>
Why is it so tempting to wander away from God? How does He respond when we return to Him after being in a spiritually off-limits area?

James Pell and three of his buddies wandered into treacherous territory while snowboarding in the French Alps. Reflecting on the incident, Pell said, "We came to a cliff ledge and quickly realized [we would not] be able to ride out of the area. But by [that] time . . . we were stuck."

If you've ever wandered off spiritually, you understand how easy it is to get into a situation that seems hopeless. The buzz of being in an off-limits area quickly grows quiet.

When the Israelites made the disastrous decision to worship Baal and some handcrafted silver idols (Hosea 13:1-2), God sent them a message through the prophet Hosea. He outlined what to do to get back to a place of spiritual safety.

First, Hosea instructed them to "Return to the Lord. Say to Him, 'Forgive all our sins'" (14:2). We too need to repent if we want to renew our relationship with Jesus after a time of wandering away.

Once we humbly admit our sin and continue no more in it, it's time to praise God for His mercy (v.3). The Bible assures us that "people who . . . confess [their sins] and turn from them, they will receive mercy" (Proverbs 28:13). While we may suffer some earthly consequences for backsliding, God makes it possible for our relationship with Him to be restored.

Finally, we have to trust in our Father's forgiveness. God said, "I will heal you of your faithlessness; My love will know no bounds, for My anger will be gone forever" (Hosea 14:4). Although guilt may try to stalk us, God's forgiveness sets us free from past sin.

If you're in an off-limits area, remember Hosea's words to the Israelites, "The paths of the Lord are true and right, and righteous people live by walking in them" (v.9). —Jennifer Benson Schuldt

letting go

read>
Matthew 10:32-42
If you love your father or mother more than you love Me, you are not worthy of being Mine; or if you love your son or daughter more than Me, you are not worthy of being Mine (v.37).

more>
Read Philippians 3:7-8 to see Paul's comparison between knowing Jesus Christ and knowing anything else.

next>
How can you tell if you're putting another person, hobby, or thing in the place reserved for God alone? How might you properly enjoy those things as God's gift to you?

Li Yue fell hard for Hou You Jing. They were from the same province, shared a love for badminton and western movies, and—as if by fate—met while working second shift at a microchip processor company in Shenzhen. Li Yue couldn't stand to be apart from Hou You Jing, and she didn't notice that her constant calls and weekend plans were beginning to smother him. He slowly pulled away—finally telling her that he was ending their relationship. Li Yue was devastated. In desperation, she pleaded, "But I love you!"

But was it *truly* love? Jonathan Edwards explained that we truly love another person only if we love them first *in* God. Any love that doesn't begin with God is actually a form of selfishness. We love ourselves rather than others, our family rather than another family, or our city or country rather than another town or nation. Our circle of love may widen to include everyone on planet Earth, yet we'll still prefer the people on our planet to the possible inhabitants of others. Edwards explained that "true virtue consists in love to Being [his term for God] in general" and only afterward "to any one particular being."

This is partially Jesus' point when He commands us to love Him more than our closest family and friends (Matthew 10:37). He isn't merely warning against idolatry, but He's also telling us how to *fully* enjoy our close relationships. When we love others more than God, we inevitably ask more from them than what they can deliver. Our neediness will eventually suffocate them and our relationship.

Jesus said that whatever we cling to we will lose, but "if you give up your life for Me, you will find it" (v.39). As the saying goes, "If you love someone, set them free"—in God. —Mike Wittmer

little platoons

read>
Colossians 4:7-18
These are the only Jewish believers among my co-workers; they are working with me here for the kingdom of God. And what a comfort they have been! (v.11).

more>
Read Romans 16 to view another list of Paul's friends and how they made a great impact on his life and ministry.

next>
Who are the members of your little platoon? How have they comforted, served, accepted, prayed for, and worked hard for you lately? What kind of platoon member are you?

In his book, *Waking the Dead,* John Eldredge writes: "When he left Rivendell, Frodo didn't head out with 1,000 elves. He had eight companions. Jesus didn't march around backed by hundreds of followers either. He had 12 men. . . . Though we are part of a great company, we are meant to live in little platoons. The little companies we form must be small enough for each of the members to know one another as friends and allies." In the closing section of Colossians, Paul listed and described his little platoon of friends and allies.

In describing his platoon, Paul used relational language. He said Tychicus was a "dear brother, a faithful minister," and a "fellow servant" in the Lord (4:7 NIV). It was probably Paul's theology of equality that allowed him to build a significant relationship with the slave Onesimus (v.9; Philemon 1:10). The apostle called him "a faithful and beloved brother." Another platoon member was Mark (Col. 4:10). This was the same Mark who abandoned Paul in the middle of a mission. When he went AWOL, it caused so much tension between Paul and Barnabas that they ended up separating (Acts 15:36-39). The fact that Mark was now ministering with (and to) Paul (2 Timothy 4:11) reveals that the two had renewed their relationship through forgiveness and reconciliation.

In addition to Tychicus, Onesimus, and Mark, Paul also listed Aristarchus, Jesus (who is called Justus), Luke, and Demas (Colossians 4:10-14). Lastly, Paul wrote that Epaphras also cared for him and the Colossians by praying "earnestly" for them (vv.12-13). The men made up a small platoon, but it had a big relational impact on the apostle Paul.

As believers in Jesus, we're called to live in little platoons as well. These groups of growing Christians will thrive as we accept, forgive, serve, comfort, pray for, and work hard for one another. —Marvin Williams

silence of God

read>
Psalm 13
O Lord, how long will You forget me? Forever? How long will You look the other way? (v.1).

more>
Read Psalm 5:1-3. What posture does David suggest we take in the midst of God's silence? How might Luke 18:6-8 provide encouragement as we wait?

next>
Recall a period of God's silence in your life. How did you grow through it? How can you help others who are experiencing the silence of God? How will you be God's comfort as they wait?

She sits alone in her room—dark circles under her eyes, tears running down her cheeks. Since her teenage years, God has been her fulfillment, but her heart still has gaps—empty places, hollow spaces, unmet longings. And she has prayed, oh how she has prayed for God to give her the desires of her heart. Or to take them away. One or the other. But neither has happened. Ten long years of waiting. "How long will you forget me?" she whispers. "Forever?"

We may celebrate the *goodness* of God during times of answered prayer and unexpected blessing, but sooner or later, we all face the *silence* of God. Israel did (1 Sam. 3:1). Job did (Job 23:1-9). Asaph did—crying to God all night without answer (Ps. 77:1-9). "Why do you hide when I am in trouble?" David prayed (10:1). "Do not turn a deaf ear to me," he demanded (28:1). "How long must I struggle with . . . sorrow in my heart every day?" he cried. "Turn and answer me" (13:2-3). Even Jesus experienced the deathly silence of the Father (Matt. 27:46).

What is God doing during His silence? Preparing the answer to our request? Maybe. Testing the depth of our devotion? Perhaps. Developing our character? Undoubtedly. Christian martyrs of old were sawn in two out of devotion to Jesus. Why shouldn't *we* endure a little pain as we mature? Sometimes, however, *we* may never know why God is keeping quiet.

Thankfully, God *does* break His silence. He spoke to Israel (1 Samuel 3:4-14) and Job (Job 38); the morning finally dawned for Asaph (Psalm 77:11-20) and David (28:6-9); the silence of Good Friday was followed by the shout of Easter (Matt. 28).

But, until she hears from God, that girl—representing so many others—sits in her room *alone*. Or is she? —Sheridan Voysey

principled

read>
Luke 13:10-21
This dear woman, a daughter of Abraham, has been held in bondage by Satan for eighteen years. Isn't it right that she be released, even on the Sabbath? (v.16).

more>
Read Micah 6:8 to discover how we should live out both God's mercy and His justice.

next>
Are there places in your life where you have become more focused on a principle than a person? In what specific areas have you experienced God's mercy? How have you been transformed by His grace?

Teaching in a Christian preparatory school, I am accustomed to including an "honor code" on each quiz and test that my students take. Because they live in a world of moral relativism, some students are accustomed to signing on the line even when they've cheated. Recently I had to turn a student in for cheating, and as I watched the administration seek to respond with grace and justice, I saw in action what Jesus tried to impart to those around Him. People and principles go hand-in-hand.

Comfortable in their list of rules, the Pharisees couldn't understand why Jesus would heal a woman on the Sabbath (Luke 13:12-14). Due to their own self-righteousness, they missed the point—and the grace of God. The rule was to put aside work in order to save the Sabbath for God's glory alone. Jesus' point? What better way to glorify God than by allowing Him to do the work of healing. They saw the law; Jesus saw the *person*.

In our dealings with others, we need to hold fast to the truth of God's Word and its principles. To become passive in our response to sin is to build our houses on shifting sand (Matthew 7:26). Jesus came to show us that the law for the sake of the law brings only death (Romans 4:15), but implementing the law to demonstrate our need for Jesus brings life (3:19-24).

God's justice and His mercy are not opposing forces. The purpose of mercy is to make way for grace, and extending grace doesn't mean setting aside principles. Grace understands that the true purpose behind any standard is found in what Jesus lifted up as the most important of all—God-centered love (Mark 12:30-31). —Regina Franklin

swallowing up death

read>
Isaiah 25:1-8
[God] will swallow up death forever! (v.8).

more>
How does 1 Corinthians 15:55-57 describe Jesus' victory?

next>
Where have you experienced death as an enemy? What does it mean for you to acknowledge Jesus as victor over death?

I met Stephen and Roxanne at a hotel. They needed help as they entered one of the most difficult days any parent could envision. Matt, a graduate student at the University of Virginia and member of our church community, died in a freakish bike collision. This should never happen. A father should never bury a son. A mother should never have to dig through her dead boy's lonely apartment. There is so much to celebrate in Matt's good life (his deep heart, for instance—his last hours were spent serving in a homeless shelter). There is much to curse, however, about his passing. Death is a menacing villain.

The prophet Isaiah wrote to his people in anticipation of their Babylonian captivity. Isaiah spoke with language that cast God as the powerful, conquering God—strong enough and bold enough to take on every enemy the besieged people faced. God was the One who would "turn mighty cities into heaps of ruin" and who would "silence the roar" of violent armies afflicting them (25:2,5).

The ultimate enemy our conquering God would crush, however, would be death itself. Death is our wretched foe—our enemy and, thankfully, God's enemy. In Jesus, God has defeated death, showing that He is Lord over all—even over death (1 Corinthians 15:54).

Melito of Sardis, a church father from the third century, powerfully captured this truth as he wrote:

When the Lord had clothed Himself with humanity, and had suffered for the sake of the sufferer, and had been bound for the sake of the imprisoned, and had been judged for the sake of the condemned, and buried for the sake of the one who was buried, He rose up from the dead, and cried with a loud voice: Who is he who contends with Me? —Winn Collier

judah and tamar

read>
Genesis 38:6-30
Judah was the father of Perez and Zerah (whose mother was Tamar) (Matthew 1:3).

more>
Read 2 Timothy 2:20-21 and note what God desires of the person who will be used "for every good work."

next>
What kind of qualifications do you think God looks for in His servants? Where in the Bible do you find people with these qualifications?

I know a guy who doesn't leave a very good first impression . . . or last one, for that matter. He's conniving and selfish, a man of double standards. He makes promises that he has no intention of keeping, and he's led a promiscuous lifestyle. Not exactly *Mr. Right,* huh?

Judah, Joseph's brother, was such a guy. In Genesis 38, we read that his eldest son married Tamar, but then God put him to death (1 Chr. 2:3). They had no children. In those days it was customary that the next oldest brother take the wife of his brother and raise a family for his deceased brother. This was called a levirate marriage. So the responsibility fell on Onan, the second son. Because of Onan's wickedness, however, God put him to death too (Genesis 38:10).

Judah had just one son left. He had no intention of having his only surviving son marry Tamar. So he lied in order to put her out of sight and out of mind. Tamar trusted him and followed his request—thinking Judah was looking out for her best interests. But after a long wait, she decided to take action. Apparently Judah had established himself as the kind of man who would use the services of a prostitute. So she disguised herself as one, and Judah, not knowing she was his daughter-in-law, slept with her.

It's a bizarre story, but that's not the end of it. For from this one-night stand, twins Perez and Zerah were born (vv.27-30). Surprisingly, God used Judah and Tamar in the lineage of Christ (Matt. 1:3).

While I'm not excusing or encouraging evil acts, it's evident that God can work even in our sin to bring glory to His name. So who are we to say, "I'm not qualified to serve God. There's no way He can possibly use me"? If God can use Judah and Tamar, He can use us to bring Him glory. —Poh Fang Chia

get real

read>
Psalm 84
Before daybreak the next morning, Jesus got up and went out to an isolated place to pray (Mark 1:35).

more>
Read Acts 2:42 to discover how believers in the early New Testament church lived out community.

next>
What do you do for relaxation? How do your times of solitude cause you to ponder God's character and help you to enjoy the company of others?

Slate magazine's William Saletan indicts our culture stating: "Every time you answer your cell phone in traffic, squander your workday on YouTube, text a colleague during dinner, or turn on the TV to escape your kids, you're leaving this world. You're neglecting the people around you, sometimes at the risk of killing them."

Wow! And he didn't even mention the addictive nature of online games. Or Internet porn and how it depersonalizes and destroys the sacredness of sex.

We might be tempted to debate Saletan. But rather than getting defensive, it may be wise to take a look at our own priorities. It's likely we'll all find something out of whack. I can reach out to the people God places in my path—those who need an encouraging word or who may be hurting and need my listening ear. But instead, I put on the headphones and vanish into iPod world or lose myself in a laptop DVD. I shun human community for the loneliness of something less.

Solitude has its place. Jesus had a habit of slipping away to be alone. But when He did, He found community with His heavenly Father. And then He returned to His ministry to others (Mark 1:35-38).

In the Psalms, we read how the poet yearned for community with God. "I long, yes, I faint with longing to enter the courts of the Lord," he wrote (84:2). And he craved the community with others that grows out of unity with the Father. "What joy for those who can live in Your house, always singing Your praises" (v.4).

Perhaps it's time to exchange our headphones for some bona fide interaction with God and His children. By doing so, we'll lose the loneliness of the virtual world and find the joy of genuine community. —Tim Gustafson

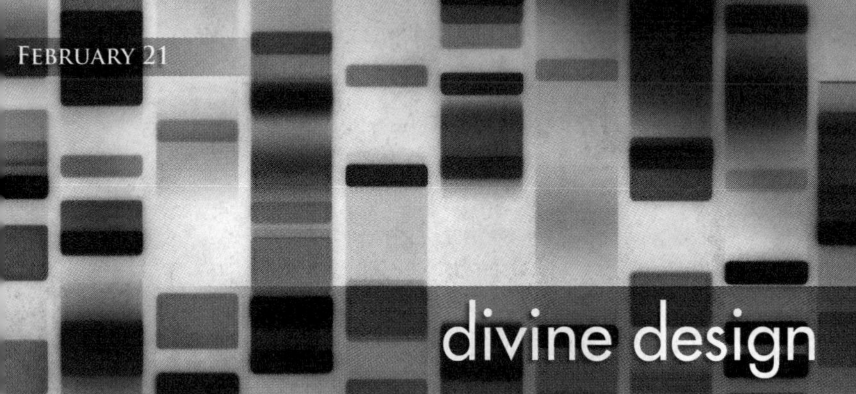

divine design

read>
Colossians 1:15-20
He made the things we can see and the things we can't see (v.16).

more>
Read Genesis 1:3 and John 1:3-4. What two kinds of light has Jesus brought us by His divine design?

next>
What comes to mind when you hear the words intelligent design? How has science encouraged you in your faith in Jesus?

Intelligent design. It's hard to go a day without encountering that phrase, and here's why. The more scientists study matter like molecular DNA—the building block of life—the more it points to a Creator. As Dr. Stephen Meyer, author of *Signature in the Cell,* writes, "The best, most causally adequate explanation for the origin of the specified, digitally encoded information in DNA is that it . . . had an intelligent source." Intelligent design = *divine* design.

It's not surprising that the more scientists study what can't be seen by the human eye, the more they see the fingerprints of God (Colossians 1:15). Paul stated, in what likely were lyrics of an early church hymn, the reality of Christ being behind DNA and every other part of creation. He wrote, "Through [Jesus] God created everything in the heavenly realms and on earth" (v.16).

Those words were significant for the believers in the church at Colosse, for they were dealing with false teachers who taught that angelic mediators were doing what only Jesus can do. But they also help us address the attacks by secular scientists against the Christian faith today. For, Paul says, "He made the things we can see and the things we can't see" (v.16).

Woven into every strand of DNA is the divine work of Jesus, the One who "holds all creation together" (v.17). He is our confidence, our hope, and the source of every created thing. And as we look at His amazing creation, we—like the Colossians—are able to stand for the truth found in His Word. Attacks on what we believe are to be expected, but they pale in the light of Jesus' reality (2:8).

Be encouraged! The more we sharpen the lens on even the tiniest parts of God's creation, the better we see His divine design. —Tom Felten

wild gourds

read>
2 Kings 4:38-41
The ear tests the words it hears just as the mouth distinguishes between foods (Job 34:3).

more>
What did the Bereans and the Thessalonians do to test the teachings they were hearing? (Acts 17:11; 1 Th. 5:21).

next>
Where do you go to get your spiritual food? Have you been feeding on the Word of God—reading and studying it daily? How have you been searching the Scriptures to see if what you've been taught is true?

As you probably know, not all mushrooms are safe to eat. In fact, only 3,000 of the 14,000 known mushroom species are edible. Poisonous mushrooms are also known as toadstools (thought to have originated from the German word *todes* which means death). That's why I rely on the experts, for I can't tell a good mushroom from a bad toadstool.

Due to a famine, Elisha once sent his servant to look for some food to eat (not necessarily mushrooms!). The young man came back with herbs and wild gourds, and shredded them to make a pot of hot stew.

The famine referenced in 2 Kings 4 came about because the people had rejected God's Word (Leviticus 26:3-4; 1 Kings 18:18). This resulted in both a natural famine and one of not hearing the word of the Lord (Amos 8:11).

I see a spiritual analogy here. For the world we live in is like that pot of stew—full of all kinds of ideas, beliefs, convictions, philosophies, and teachings. They're tossed in together, mixed, adapted, assimilated, and served to Christians as wholesome biblical truth.

God's people should be hungry for His Word. But there is no shortage of "wild gourds" out there. You or someone in your church family may read a book or go to a conference that presents what sounds like sound teaching from God's Word, but it's actually nothing but "wild gourds." Soon it's served in "a pot of stew" to the rest of the congregation. That's why it's so important that we grow in our knowledge of what God's Word actually says, and what it doesn't say (Hebrews 5:14; Ephesians 4:11-14).

Got some "wild gourds" that you've taken in? Test them by the scrutiny and authority of God's Word (Job 12:11; Mark 4:24). If you don't, their poison will pass from you to others. —K.T. Sim

point to Jesus

read>
John 6:60-69
Simon Peter replied, "Lord, to whom would we go? You have the words that give eternal life" (v.68).

more>
To find out what God's presence can mean in the midst of trying times, check out Psalm 16:11.

next>
What have you been doing to try to find peace in your life? Why can true peace and hope be found only in Jesus?

Two days after my daughter purchased her first used car, it wouldn't start. After fiddling with the battery, I tried hooking it back up. That was a big mistake. Little did I know that reattaching the battery cables would set off the most loud and obnoxious sounding car alarm I've ever heard (We didn't even know it was installed on the car.)

Not a good way to score points with the neighbors at 10 p.m.

After frantically trying everything I could think of to make it stop, I disconnected the battery. *Whew! Silence.*

Still, I was at a complete loss as to why it happened. So I asked the man who sold us the car if he knew how to shut off the alarm. He didn't, but He pointed me to the Internet. There I found a solution to hook up the battery and start the car without waking up the neighborhood.

The experience reminds me of how often I feel "at a loss" as a counselor. There are many times I'm deeply aware that I don't have all the answers for the pain and commotion in a client's life. But I know that I can point to the One who does.

Peter was a man who understood this. During a time when many of Jesus' disciples were turning away and deserting Him, Jesus asked His 12 closest followers, "Are you also going to leave?" (John 6:67). Peter, apparently speaking for the rest of the group, said, "Lord, to whom would we go? You have the words that give eternal life" (v.68).

Jesus is the One to point to, especially when it seems that there is nowhere else to go. He alone can bring us real peace and hope as we experience the loud commotions of this world. —Jeff Olson

lost

read>
Proverbs 2:1-11
Then you will understand what is right, just, and fair, and you will find the right way to go (v.9).

more>
According to Luke 15, what does God do when you're lost?

next>
When have you been lost in your relationship with God? How can you experience eternal salvation and find your way home? Why is repentance so important in our relationship with Jesus?

"We just witnessed a stunning, daring bit of TV storytelling that set the show on a new, series-ending path—one that will track the characters through parallel, alternate universes," wrote *USA Today's* Robert Bianco following the 2-hour premiere of the last season of *Lost.*

"We are now following two versions of their lives. "That's no easy task to pull off," Bianco insisted. "Few shows would even try. It worked because the script and actors so clearly delineated the difference between the two groups: one transformed by the island, one left as they were when we first met them."

It is indeed rare for television to delve so deeply into character study, to attempt to unravel the complexities of man's lost soul. While brilliant scriptwriting can help expose dark hearts, only God-inspired Scripture can provide a genuine map home and a formula for true and lasting change—salvation "through" Jesus Christ (John 14:6).

To find your way, "Don't copy the behavior and customs of this world," the apostle Paul teaches, "but let God transform you into a new person by changing the way you think. Then you will learn to know God's will for you, which is good and pleasing and perfect" (Romans 12:2).

As the Lord told the Israelites, when we come "weeping and seeking the Lord" our God in repentance, striving to find the way back home, then we will bind ourselves to the Lord "with an eternal covenant that will never be forgotten" (Jeremiah 50:4-5).

Are you lost? Then "stop at the crossroads and look around. Ask for the old, godly way, and walk in it. Travel its path, and you will find rest for your souls" (Jeremiah 6:16). —Roxanne Robbins

respecting God

read>
1 Chronicles 11:10-19
So the Three broke through the Philistine lines, drew some water from the well . . . and brought it back to David. But David . . . poured it out as an offering to the Lord (v.18).

more>
Read 2 Corinthians 8:1-9 to see how God showed respect to us, and how we might show respect to God and to each other.

next>
What has God done to show that He respects you? Think of some people who would benefit from your respect. How might you go above and beyond the norm to sacrifice for them?

In his book *Faith at the Edge,* philosopher Robert Wennberg describes attending a small church with his students as they traveled through Europe. The students were not greeted warmly by the church members, did not know enough of the language to follow the songs or the sermon, and generally considered their Sunday morning to be a complete waste of time. Wennberg assured them that it wasn't, for the effort they made to worship with fellow believers was an act of respect toward God.

Wennberg quoted Pascal: "Respect means; put yourself out. . . . It amounts to saying: I should certainly put myself out if you needed it, because I do so when you do not; besides, respect serves to distinguish the great. If respect meant sitting in an armchair we should be showing everyone respect and then there would be no way of marking distinction, but we make the distinction quite clear by putting ourselves out."

We respect others when we put ourselves out for them. It may be something small, such as standing to our feet when they enter the room, saluting or tipping our hat, or kneeling in front of their wheelchair. It might be huge, as when David's elite warriors crept behind enemy lines to bring him water from Bethlehem, or when David—overcome by the magnitude of their devotion—poured out the water as a drink offering to the Lord (1 Chronicles 11:17-19).

We respect God when we put ourselves out for Him. We all experience dry spells when the Bible seems irrelevant, our prayers don't seem to matter, and we'd rather sleep in than go to church. These down times are opportunities to express our allegiance and devotion to God. If we continue to put ourselves out, even when we don't feel any benefit, we pay God the highest respect.

—Mike Wittmer

wilderness experiences

read>
Mark 1:9-15
The Spirit then compelled Jesus to go into the wilderness, where He was tempted by Satan for forty days. He was out among the wild animals, and angels took care of Him (vv.12-13).

more>
Read Matthew 4:1-11 to see how Jesus combatted the attacks of the devil. Read Mark 1:16-39 to see what Jesus accomplished after His wilderness experience.

next>
Are you in a wilderness moment right now? What do you need to do today in order to take another step of faith with Jesus?

God sometimes works in strange ways. Jesus is baptized, and the next thing He experiences is *temptation*. Led into the wilderness by the Holy Spirit, He's tempted by Satan—His adversary. Such is the nature of our own wilderness experiences.

The wilderness stirred many emotions for the Jews of Jesus' day, evoking memories of their 40-year journey out of Egypt. To them, the wilderness was a place of vulnerability—a rough terrain in an unknown land, with uncertain provisions (Exodus 15:22-24; 16:2-3). It was a place of testing where the promises of God were all they had (Deuteronomy 8:1-5). For Jesus, His wilderness experience included both "wild animals" and Satan himself (Mark 1:12-13). In the wilderness, He was vulnerable to both physical and spiritual dangers.

The wilderness was not just a place of vulnerability for the Jews. It was also a place of transition that lay between their slavery and liberation (Exodus 3:17). Jesus' wilderness experience marked a transition for Him too. The private years were over; His public life had begun. John the Baptist's mission was done. Now it was Jesus' turn (Mark 1:14-15).

Have you ever had a wilderness experience—a time of vulnerability and testing far away from all that is familiar and certain? Perhaps it involved a risky step of faith, a period of doubt, or even disobedience. The terrain was rocky; you were cold and afraid. During that time, did you realize that the wilderness was where God trained Israel as His child? Spoke to His prophets? Prepared His people, and His Son, for a significant work?

The wilderness can be a scary place—full of dangers. But if you stay close to the God of Israel, close to Jesus, it may prove to be your transition into an unprecedented period of fruitfulness. —Sheridan Voysey

restrained

read>
1 Samuel 3:1-14
I have warned him that judgment is coming upon his family forever, because his sons are blaspheming God and he hasn't disciplined them (v.13).

more>
Read 2 Timothy 1:7 to see the connection between fear and a lack of self-control.

next>
In what area of your life is God challenging you to learn restraint? How should you be more consistent in your expectations of others, including (if applicable) your children?

Since my nephew's birthday is 11 days before mine, we often celebrate together. One year we decided to do something different, so the extended family—grandparents included—went to eat pizza and play laser tag. At one point, I inadvertently fired my laser gun at one of my own team members, thinking he was a spy. Somehow missing the point that I was an adult and he was a pre-teen, the young kid called out sarcastically, "I'm on your team, genius!" I had to crucify the desire to send him to time-out.

As parents, one of the greatest gifts we can give our children is self-control. Growing up in a society of instant gratification, they face significant challenges in learning the power of restraint. The problem, though, is not a new one. Eli, the priest of Israel during the time of Samuel's childhood, had two sons who "were scoundrels who had no respect for the Lord" (1 Samuel 2:12). They denied their flesh nothing, and Eli did little to stop them.

To think that we would repress our children's ability to express themselves by giving them boundaries for their behavior: this would give them a wrong definition of love (Hebrews 12:6). What's more, refraining from saying the word "no" does not protect our children from the unpleasant things in life; rather, it leaves them unprotected. As Proverbs 25:28 says, "A person without self-control is like a city with broken-down walls."

Maturity isn't measured by how old we are or how much we know, but in our response to adversity. Just as an athlete or artist focuses on the benefits of discipline while understanding its cost, we should look for opportunities to tell our children "yes" without avoiding the times we need to say "no."

—Regina Franklin

seeing potholes

read>
1 Kings 11:1-13
He had warned Solomon specifically about worshiping other gods, but Solomon did not listen to the Lord's command (v.10).

more>
What does Hebrews 10:22 tell us about how to deal with the guilt of our sin? Read Luke 6:45 and—in the light of Jesus' words—consider what's hidden in your heart.

next>
How have you been isolating yourself from God and others? What will you do to come out of isolation and walk in "integrity and godliness"? (1 Kings 9:4).

Potholes can be a pain. If a car tire hits a deep one, we're talking some serious damage. That's why the idea of Italian engineering students Domenico Diego and Cristina Corradini is so bright—*literally!* The duo, noting that many potholes in Europe aren't repaired due to lack of funding, came up with something called the Street Safe initiative. Their creative plan called for potholes to be painted bright yellow, an inexpensive way to help drivers avoid big pits in the pavement.

God knew the "potholes" that Solomon needed to avoid—things that could bring his kingdom down. "He had warned [him] . . . but Solomon did not listen to the Lord's command" (1 Kings 11:10). Instead, the king who was known for wisdom unwisely withdrew into isolation with his "many foreign women" (v.1). God had warned His people against marrying such women, for "they will turn your hearts to their gods" (v.2; Exodus 34:12-17).

Solomon saw the potholes and still caved. And this happened even after God had warned him on three occasions to obey Him (talk about "bright yellow paint"!): "Follow Me and obey My commands" (3:14); "Obey all My decrees" (1 Kings 6:12); "Follow Me with integrity and godliness" (9:4). Turning from God to the isolation of his private pleasures and folly, Solomon chose sin, and God's subsequent discipline resulted in his kingdom being taken from him (11:11).

When we turn from God—isolating ourselves from Him and godly friends—we're headed for destruction. Sometimes we think we can cuddle with sin or keep it hidden, but God's bright warnings can't be avoided. Eventually, guilt will sweep over us as God brings "our secret sins" to light (Psalm 51:2, 90:8).

Don't fall into the pothole of isolation. Open up and let God and godly friends help you repent of your secret sins. —Tom Felten

"what would be a healthy response to the guilt and remorse I feel over my past sins?"

As you look back over your life, you may be filled with guilt and remorse over sins you've committed, either as an unbeliever or a backslidden or immature Christian. It's important to remember that your sin and backsliding or immaturity isn't unique. Israel as a nation was often unfaithful to her covenant relationship with God. Peter denied Jesus, wept bitterly, and later was publicly restored (Matthew 26:69-75; John 21). The Lord also reproached the believers in Ephesus because they had left their first love, and He urged them to remember, repent, and return (Revelation 2:1-7).

Even though the Bible tells us we receive a new life when we believe, we are still influenced by the "old nature," the law of sin within us (Romans 7). The old nature is still part of us and continues to affect us (1 Corinthians 3:1-3; Ephesians 4:22).

I doubt that anything you have done is worse than the acts committed by two of the greatest men of faith, King David and the apostle Paul.

The more spiritual vision we gain, the more we sorrow over the wrongs we've done. Accordingly, there are three facts to consider:

First, I doubt that anything you have done is worse than the acts committed by two of the greatest men of faith, King David and the apostle Paul. David not only committed adultery, but he had a good man killed to conceal his sin. Paul persecuted and murdered Christians. Yet both Paul and David were forgiven, though their past sins caused them legitimate sorrow. Our salvation has nothing to do with the extent of our past sins. It is entirely based on the infinite suffering of the Son of God Himself, who fully and willingly bore the consequences of all our evil.

Second, sorrow over past sins has an important function. It softens the heart and engenders humility and compassion, qualities essential to the work of the kingdom. Consider the words of the prophet Ezekiel, who wrote, "I will give you a new heart, and I will put a new spirit in you. I will take out your stony, stubborn heart and give you a tender, responsive heart" (Ezekiel 36:26). All of us need to realize how foolish we were before we were willing to surrender our hearts to Jesus.

Third, don't overlook the power of God's grace. Even if we can't repair the damage we've caused, God is able to bring healing and restoration in ways that would be impossible for us to anticipate. We can still pray for the healing and restoration of those we've injured.

Remember the parable of the prodigal son (Luke 15:11-32). God is always ready to welcome us as long as we're willing to humble ourselves and turn towards home.

—Dan VanderLugt

Adapted from Answers To Tough Questions *© 2010 RBC Ministries.* *Read more helpful articles like this one on the Web at Questions.org*

celebrating a loss

read>
2 Corinthians 5:18–6:2
God made Christ, who never sinned, to be the offering for our sin, so that we could be made right with God through Christ (5:21).

more>
- Romans 8:35-37
- 1 Corinthians 15:51-58

next>
What has been your biggest loss? Did victory come out of that loss? How does Jesus' victory over sin and death give you assurance?

As time ticked away at Hull City's beautiful KC Stadium in the UK, an appreciative and raucous crowd stood in anxious anticipation. At game's end, hundreds of fans scurried onto the field to celebrate. Their beloved Tigers had just gone toe-to-toe with legendary Manchester United and . . . lost?

The TV commentator explained, "Hull City may have lost this battle, but they've won the relegation war." By losing "only" 0-1, Hull avoided relegation from England's vaunted Premiership and the dreaded banishment to an inferior league.

Clearly, not all losses are created equal. The greatest loss of all time occurred when Jesus was crucified. He had come to live on this earth. He walked among us, ate our food, breathed our air, healed our sick, and offered eternal life to any who would accept it. What did He get for His trouble? The religious leaders of His day conspired to put Him to death.

Yet Jesus didn't lose; He won! When Bono sings in *Sunday Bloody Sunday,* "to claim the victory Jesus won," he's singing about this victory. Jesus went willingly to the cross as a sacrificial Lamb to pay the price for our sins and to defeat sin and death. He who had never sinned became "the offering for our sin," says 2 Corinthians 5:21. And the very next portion of Scripture makes this crucially important appeal: "We beg you not to accept this marvelous gift of God's kindness and then ignore it. For God says, 'At just the right time, I heard you. On the day of salvation, I helped you'" (6:1-2).

Because of Christ's victory, we aren't relegated to live a dreary life of addiction to our sins, waiting for life's final whistle. Jesus conquered death. In Him, ultimate and overwhelming victory is ours (Romans 8:37). His loss became His greatest victory—and demands our praise and celebration of Him. —Tim Gustafson

what our world tells us

read>
Psalm 19:1-6
The heavens proclaim the glory of God (v.1).

more>
O Lord, our Lord, Your majestic name fills the earth! (Psalm 8:9).

next>
What spiritual encounter have you had when surrounded by nature's beauty or ruggedness? How can you train your eyes and ears to hear and see God's wonder?

Dr. Clyde S. Kilby, longtime English professor and noted devotee/interpreter of C. S. Lewis, formulated and passed along 11 life resolutions. The tasks he strived to do every day were designed to keep his heart open to imagination and his eyes open for God. One of his resolutions reads: "Once every day I shall simply stare at a tree, a flower, a cloud, or a person. I shall not then be concerned at all to ask what they are, but simply be glad that they are." Kilby's lifelong belief was that wonder lies all around us, if only we have the eyes to see it.

Scripture tells us that God's wonder and majesty are woven into all of creation. Wherever we turn, wisps of glory and bits of beauty announce to us that God is near. The psalmist announces that "the skies display [God's] craftsmanship" (19:1). And these skies (and all that lies beneath them) tell a story. Oh, how they tell a story! "Day after day they continue to speak; night after night they make Him known" (v.2).

The fact remains, however, that we have to be listening; we have to be looking. The voices echoing all around us, in every yellow daffodil and rippling creek and whispering willow, are strange voices. They do not yell. They do not shout and struggle to capture our attention. Rather, they "speak without a sound or word" (v.3).

A beautiful mystery: Creation always speaks, yet never says a word. And the name always spoken, though never uttered, is God.

Elizabeth Barrett Browning captures the spirit of the psalmist: "Earth's crammed with heaven. And every common bush afire with God. But only he who sees takes off his shoes. The rest sit round it and pluck blackberries."

—Winn Collier

hands free

read>
1 Samuel 17:19-23, 41-51
So David left the sheep with another shepherd and set out early the next morning with the gifts, as Jesse had directed him (v.20).

more>
- Psalm 144:1
- Proverbs 20:24
- Matthew 4:19-22

next>
Why is it difficult to entrust the things we value to someone else's care? Is there anything in particular God is asking you to lay down so your hands can be free?

Around our house, I am lovingly known as "the pack mule." I have an incessant desire to carry everything from the car in one load. Whether I'm walking across the grass or trying to haul an entire shopping trip in two hands, I always look for the shortest distance between two points. Heaven forbid that I should have to make multiple trips. More than once, I've discovered the inconvenience (and groceries-damaging practice) of trying to unlock the door with full hands.

Detailing David's battle with Goliath, 1 Samuel 17 takes us from his home to the frontlines. In the story, two phrases often get overlooked for their simplicity. Verse 20 says, "So David left the sheep with another shepherd," while verse 22 tells us, "David left his things with the keeper of the supplies."

When thinking about facing a Goliath, we want to know what the battle will demand. Will we have the faith to stand as David did? (vv.45-47). Will we have the confidence to reject man's ideas in order to use the weapons the Lord chooses? (vv.38-40). Our actions away from the battlefront hardly seem relevant.

But for David, victory wouldn't have come without his willingness to leave his sheep and his belongings behind. Imagine going to war with a flock and baggage in tow. Though he was not looking for a fight, David's ability to leave the right things behind made him ready.

Though the battle looks different for us, the principle is the same: God may ask us to leave what we're doing so that we can carry out His new assignment (v.20).

When Goliath shows up, will you be ready? —Regina Franklin

postcard secrets

read>
Psalm 32
Finally, I confessed all my sins to You and stopped trying to hide my guilt. I said to myself, "I will confess my rebellion to the Lord." And You forgave me! All my guilt is gone (v.5).

more>
If we claim we have no sin, we are only fooling ourselves and not living in the truth. But if we confess our sins to Him, He is faithful and just to forgive us our sins and to cleanse us from all wickedness (1 John 1:8-9).

next>
What sin is weighing heavily on your heart today? Why?

Some years back, Frank Warren handed out 400 blank postcards bearing his address to strangers and asked them to send their untold secrets to him. Warren began receiving confessions like: "I haven't spoken to my dad in 10 years, and it kills me every day" and "Everyone who knew me before 9/11 now believes I'm dead." Today, Warren's Post-Secret project receives over 1,000 postcard secrets every week.

Since then a plethora of online confessionals have followed. Many of the confessions posted are fabricated. But many are heartfelt—like the woman who confessed to cheating on her boyfriend and then wrote: "I'm sorry. I don't believe in a god, but I feel I need to finally tell someone the truth, even if it is just the Internet."

The human soul longs to confess its guilt. Three thousand years ago, King David wrote in a song: "When I refused to confess my sin, my body wasted away, and I groaned all day long" (Psalm 32:3). We don't know what sin was on his mind, but we know how he felt before he came clean: "Day and night your hand of discipline was heavy on me. My strength evaporated like water in the summer heat" (v.4).

David finally confessed his sin to God and discovered the power of divine pardon. "And You forgave me!" he sings heavenward in relief. "All my guilt is gone" (v.5).

Confessing our wrongs on a postcard or Web site may be partially therapeutic, but it doesn't go far enough. It's not just confession we need, but cleansing. The Internet doesn't "hear" our confession. A postcard can't "pardon" our sin. But the personal God of the universe can do both.

"Therefore," David sings on, "let all the godly pray to You while there is still time" (v.6). Confess and be clean, for the God of forgiveness is listening.

—Sheridan Voysey

leave the dead alone

read>
Deuteronomy 18:9-14
You must be blameless before the Lord your God. The nations you are about to displace consult sorcerers and fortune-tellers, but the Lord your God forbids you to do such things (vv.13-14).

more>
- Leviticus 19:31
- Isaiah 8:19-20

next>
As you seek answers to life's questions, what can you do to protect yourself from deception? What can you do to make loving contact with the living for the purpose of sharing the good news about Jesus?

There's a growing fascination about life after death. Thousands of so-called psychics around the world claim to contact the spirits of the dead. And online, people can visit with psychics, spirit guides, and experts in reincarnation. There are nearly 16,000 witchcraft sites, 13,000 reincarnation sites, 12,000 psychics sites, and more than 1,000 sites dedicated to talking with the dead.

God told Moses to warn Israel that deliberate involvement with contacting the deceased was forbidden by Him (Leviticus 19:31; Deuteronomy 18:9-14). Talking to mediums, seeking spirits, practicing sorcery and divination to try to contact the dead was forbidden because these practices prevented Israel from being a peculiar people—a people who would be a blessing to all nations (Leviticus 20:6-8). How could she influence her neighbors if she was imitating their evil behavior? So, why did people attempt to contact the dead? They were:

- desperate for guidance (1 Samuel 28:3-15)
- disobedient to God (1 Chronicles 10:13-14)
- deceived (2 Corinthians 2:10-11; 11:3)

For believers, these practices are forbidden as well. These practices are not motivated by the Spirit, but are the fruit of the sin nature (Galatians 5:19-21). Any believer who seeks out psychics, horoscopes, and mediums, for the purpose of contacting the dead, is choosing to follow Satan. They aren't being peculiar and cannot please God.

Instead of having a fascination with contacting the dead, we should initiate loving contact with the living. That way we can tell them about God who—through His Son—loves them and can secure their eternal life. —Marvin Williams

mistaken motives

read>
1 Samuel 17:24-32
You just want to see the battle (v.28).

I once sent a hurting person an anonymous note that included the reference for this verse: "Why are you scheming against the Lord? He will destroy you with one blow; He won't need to strike twice" (Nahum 1:9). Why send that verse, you ask? Well, I thought I was citing Nahum 1:7, "The Lord is good, a strong refuge when trouble comes. He is close to those who trust in Him." I cringe every time I remember my slip-up. I wanted to encourage this individual, but reading that Scripture verse probably made her doubt my motives.

Mistaken motives were at the heart of a verbal scuffle between David and his oldest brother Eliab. David had been inquiring about the reward for fighting Goliath—showing his interest in facing the giant. But Eliab accused him of voyeurism, claiming, "You just want to see the battle" (1 Samuel 17:28). David replied, "I was only asking a question!" (v.29), and then he skedaddled. He didn't waste his time explaining himself to someone who was looking for a fight.

Like David, we can respond by simply stating the facts when our motives are questioned. We can also adopt his laid-back attitude as we allow our noble actions to speak for themselves. David didn't let his brother's doubt deter him from advertising his interest in fighting Goliath. "He walked over to some others and asked them the same thing" (v.30).

When Saul and David finally discussed David's wartime wishes, I'll bet David was happy he hadn't used up his emotional energy arguing with Eliab. David knew that God alone "examines the motives of our hearts" (1 Thessalonians 2:4; 1 Samuel 16:7), and that was enough for him. We too can rest knowing that God sees our hearts, and He will never mistake our motives.

—Jennifer Benson Schuldt

more>
- Proverbs 16:2
- Jeremiah 17:10
- Hebrews 4:13

next>
How will you respond if your motives are misjudged? Why is it reassuring to know that God understands all of our motivations—even better than we understand ourselves?

cleaning our catch

read>
Mark 1:16-20
Jesus called out to them, "Come, follow Me, and I will show you how to fish for people!" (v.17).

more>
• Luke 5:1-11

next>
What has Jesus taught you about fishing for people? What "cleaning" does God do in people who receive salvation? How do we help people grow in purity and holiness?

One of the worst parts of fishing is cleaning your catch. It's a messy, stinky, dirty job that requires a strong stomach, but someone has to do it. In my family, that someone is usually—well actually always—me.

I'll never forget the time my wife and I had a successful deep-sea fishing day. It was one of those trips where everything clicked. Fish after fish struck our bait. By the end of the day, our arms ached from fighting and landing dozens of keepers. I was in a fisherman's paradise—until it came time to clean our catch. Back at the dock, the fun was over and the "reel" work began. Early in His ministry, Jesus invited a few commercial fishermen to trade in their nets, follow Him, and learn how to "fish for people" (Matthew 4:18-22). Most of us aren't anglers by trade. Still, His call to share the good news with others is our mission as well.

As an avid angler, I know that one of the best things Jesus has taught me about the job of fishing for people is that I don't have to "clean" my catch. God handles the job of cleaning (1 John 1:9). Yes, I may be called to play the role of encourager or confronter or mentor. At times, I've had to mercifully say hard things to those who were young in the faith—speaking the truth in love. But it's never my job to force anyone to change. Transformation is God's business.

We sometimes have the firsthand privilege of seeing someone place his or her faith in Christ. But it's liberating to realize that we don't bear the responsibility to "clean" them up. Letting go of that burden frees us to help others become the people they were called to be—more like Jesus (Romans 8:29). —Jeff Olson

anxious times

read>
1 Peter 5:6-11
Give all your worries and cares to God, for He cares about you (v.7).

more>
Give your burdens to the Lord, and He will take care of you (Psalm 55:22).

next>
How have you been trying to handle your anxious thoughts and spirit? What will happen if you choose to act and acknowledge today?

My friends were dealing with a daughter who was struggling physically and emotionally. Unable to determine the source of her problems, they were getting stretched thin. Not surprisingly, as their precious girl struggled with her anxiety—that invisible foe with physical manifestations—they too started to become anxious.

The world events over the past few years have led many people to experience anxious times. And while anxiety has different degrees of severity, with some people needing professional help, the apostle Peter has given us a prescription for dealing with it: "Give all your worries and cares to God, for He cares about you" (1 Peter 5:7).

Peter's two-pronged plan leads us to:

• *Act.* We can actively release our concerns to Jesus. The verb give, in verse 7, literally means "to throw upon." By "tossing" our worries to Him, we can experience a release from the anxiety that's threatening to take us down (Matthew 6:25-34).

• *Acknowledge.* We can be encouraged and sustained by the recognition that "He cares about [us]" (1 Peter 5:7). Instead of staying in emotional turmoil, we have the uplifting opportunity to look to the One who cares and provides for us (Philippians 4:19).

One of Peter's traveling companions, the apostle Paul, expresses some similar thoughts: "Don't worry about anything; instead, pray about everything. Tell God what you need, and thank Him for all He has done" (4:6). Both men faced "high anxiety" situations in which their faith was tested, so their words come from real experience.

Take Peter and Paul's words to heart if you're feeling anxious today. By taking action (giving your troubles to God) and acknowledging God's care for you (looking to Him, not to your own resources), you can find rest and restoration (1 Peter 5:10). —Tom Felten

childhood again

read>
Psalm 116:1-14
The Lord protects those of childlike faith (v.6).

more>
Anyone who becomes as humble as this little child is the greatest in the kingdom of heaven (Matthew 18:4).

next>
How does your faith today parallel or differ from the confidence you had early in your walk with God? What needs to change for you to return to your childlike faith?

I once thought Davy Crockett was merely a fictitious raccoon hunter. But that changed when I read a Crockett biography to my 6-year-old son and 5-year-old foster child.

With the two small boys sitting by my side, I learned that though many myths surround the "King of the Wild Frontier," beneath the coonskin cap lived a real American hero—a longstanding member of the United States Congress, and a legendary soldier.

Among the most exhilarating gifts that accompany raising children are the opportunities that we, as adults, have to learn and discover. Through children, we have opportunities to master subjects we once considered dull, relish the messages in fairy tales, and delight in simplicity. In terms of faith, though, God doesn't suggest that we return to thinking and reasoning as a child (1 Corinthians 13:11). But He does exhort us to return to "childlike faith" and to simply trust in Jesus.

He longs for our expressions of faith to echo those of the psalmist who declared, "I love the Lord because He hears my voice and my prayer for mercy. Because He bends down to listen, I will pray as long as I have breath!" (Psalm 116:1-2).

The same God who "bends down to listen" to us experiences pleasure when we look up to Him. "O Father, Lord of heaven and earth, thank You for hiding these things from those who think themselves wise and clever, and for revealing them to the childlike. Yes, Father, it pleased You to do it this way!" (Matthew 11:25-26).

God desires that we once again view Him with credence versus skepticism, with trust instead of fear, and with hope rather than apprehension.

—Roxanne Robbins

numero uno?

read>
Luke 22:24-27
But among you it will be different. Those who are the greatest among you should take the lowest rank, and the leader should be like a servant (v.26).

more>
- Matthew 20:20-27
- Luke 9:46-47
- Philippians 2:3-8

next>
Revisit the dinner scenario in today's article. Where would you be sitting? Would you be sitting on Jesus' right—in the place of honor? Why or why not?

Consider this scenario. You've invited the 10 most important people from church to dine with Jesus, people whom you would consider VIPs—your pastor, elders, deacons, or lay leaders, for example. As host, you're in charge of the seating arrangement. Assuming you have a round table that seats 12 people, where will Jesus sit? And since Jesus' left- and right-hand sides are places of highest honor, whom would you assign to sit next to Him?

As the disciples entered the upper room to eat the Passover meal, they were all intent on sitting in the places of honor. This was not the first time they had fought over who was numero uno (Matthew 20:20-24; Mark 9:33-35,10:35-37; Luke 9:46). And the jostling surfaced yet again in the midst of the Passover meal (Luke 22:20,24), barely hours before Jesus was crucified.

It was not uncommon for Jesus' disciples to vie with one another over who would sit at His right and left. But as Christ's followers, we're to be different. Those who are truly great Christian examples take the lowest rank and become like a servant (v.26). Jesus Himself "got up from the table, took off His robe, wrapped a towel around His waist, and poured water into a basin. Then He began to wash the disciples' feet, drying them with the towel He had around Him" (John 13:4-5). Paul later commented, "Though He was God . . . He gave up His divine privileges; He took the humble position of a slave" (Philippians 2:6-7). Jesus showed us what it takes to be truly great.

When people look at you, do they see a leader in high position exerting authority? Or do they see a servant serving in humility? —K.T. Sim

hedging bets

read>
1 Kings 18
Then Elijah stood in front of them and said, "How much longer will you waver, hobbling between two opinions? If the Lord is God, follow Him! But if Baal is God, then follow him!" (v.21).

more>
I am the Lord; that is My name! I will not give My glory to anyone else, nor share My praise with carved idols (Isaiah 42:8).

next>
How can you know when something such as science or money has taken the place of God, instead of being used to serve Him? Why does God take such drastic measures to end idolatry?

Millions of people say they believe in God, but to guarantee the good life they also put their trust in capitalism, science, or immoral pleasures. Recently, however, we've seen further proof that these gods cannot deliver. Free markets have collapsed, sending the economies of most countries into deep recessions. Scientific breakthroughs have produced cloning and greenhouse gasses. And the sexual revolution left us with AIDS and increased divorce.

Our predicament is not unlike Old Testament Israel, which hedged its worship of Yahweh by betting on Baal, the god of fertility. Baal was the storm god who, with lightning in one hand and thunder in the other, promised to send rain on the Israelites' fields and make them rich.

God responded by striking Israel at their point of compromise. You worship Baal for the rain he provides? Then "there will be no dew or rain during the next few years until I give the word!" (1 Kings 17:1).

After 3 years of drought, the parched Israelites agreed to meet Elijah on Mount Carmel for a faceoff between Baal and Yahweh. The prophets of Baal shouted and cut themselves, but they couldn't persuade Baal to drop a lightning bolt and burn their sacrifice. Elijah scoffed that perhaps the pagan god was "daydreaming" or "relieving himself," "Or maybe he is away on a trip, or is asleep and needs to be wakened!" (1 Kings 18:27).

When the exhausted Baal worshipers had finally given up, Elijah called down fire on his waterlogged sacrifice, a fire so intense that it consumed even the stones of the altar. Then Elijah seized the prophets of Baal and slew them.

Capitalism, science, and sex are good gifts from God. But if we put our trust in them (instead of Him), He may use these very things to destroy us.

—Mike Wittmer

uncertainties

read>
Philippians 4:6-9
You will experience God's peace, which exceeds anything we can understand. His peace will guard your hearts and minds as you live in Christ Jesus (v.7).

more>
You will keep in perfect peace all who trust in You, all whose thoughts are fixed on You! (Isaiah 26:3).

next>
Do you lack peace in some area of your life? What will happen if you fix your thoughts on what is true, honorable, right, pure, lovely, admirable, excellent, and worthy of praise?

Due to an economic downturn, the university my brother-in-law attended no longer provided any paid academic teaching or research opportunities for students who had been in the program for more than 5 years. This change affected him big-time. He was set to graduate with his doctorate degree that year. But now new plans had to be made.

At the time, my sister referenced Romans 8:28 as she wrote in an e-mail: "Though these are uncertainties, we have peace in our hearts as we know that God works for the good of those who love Him."

It's evident that believers in Jesus can have peace in the midst of uncertainties. But how? In Philippians 4:6, Paul tells the believers in Philippi not to worry about anything but to pray about everything. Why? The heavenly Father loves His children and cares for their needs (Matthew 6:25-34). We can bring all our concerns to Him with an attitude of thankfulness—trusting Him to meet our needs.

To say the peace of God surpasses all understanding reveals that we can't explain it, but we can experience it as He guards our hearts and minds (Philippians 4:7). The word *guard* means to set up a sentinel or "to watch over." God not only guards our hearts from anxiety, He also guards our minds from spiraling downward.

In verses 8 and 9, Paul gives us 10 things to focus on and do that replace worry. We are told to "fix our thoughts" on them, and to "keep putting [them] into practice."

Our peace comes from being confident that God is in control. He alone provides the peace that settles our nerves, fills our minds with hope, and allows us to relax even in the midst of changes and challenges. —Poh Fang Chia

right in front of you

read>
James 1:22-27
Don't just listen to God's Word. You must do what it says. Otherwise, you are only fooling yourselves (v.22).

more>
- Matthew 25:31-46
- Malachi 3:5

next>
How well are you respecting the elderly and caring for the needy? Is it time to step out of your comfort zone and visit a nursing home? What child in your life could use some time and help?

When the economy went bad, many sensed impending disaster. Pastor Bob Johnson saw opportunity. He had been on mission trips, and he'd seen some of the vital work going on in various corners of the world. But he wanted his church to make a difference in their community. This was the chance.

He scheduled a meeting with his city's mayor and asked, "What can we do to help you?" The mayor was astounded. Usually, people came to him for help. Together, the mayor and the pastor came up with five ways to provide assistance. In one local county, more than 20,000 seniors went an entire year without a single visitor. The church could definitely do something about that.

Foster care presented a dire need as well. Hundreds of children needed a family to take care of them. And many kids with a mom or a dad still needed tutoring that their parents couldn't provide. Some needed more substantial, one-on-one mentoring to help them stay out of gangs and out of trouble. And the community had numerous military families that needed assistance when Mom or Dad was deployed.

It's telling that the writer of James singled out widows and orphans as objects for the attention of the church. "Pure and genuine religion in the sight of God the Father means caring for orphans and widows in their distress and refusing to let the world corrupt you" (1:27). It's reminiscent of Jesus' words in Matthew: "When you did it to one of the least of these My brothers and sisters, you were doing it to Me" (25:40). He was speaking of those who had helped the needy, not knowing they were really helping Christ Himself.

Don't stress out about the endless needs in our world. Put your Christianity into practice. Do something about the need right in front of you. —Tim Gustafson

the joy in (not) being God

read>
1 Samuel 2:1-10
There is no one besides You; there is no Rock like our God (v.2).

more>
O Lord, there is no one like You. We have never even heard of another God like You! (1 Chronicles 17:20).

next>
Why is it vital that you understand that you're not God? How does recognizing that God is above you bring joy and freedom?

In her novel *Gilead,* author Marilynne Robinson lets us in on the letter an aged Anglican priest named John Ames writes to his young son. The entire narrative is actually one long—almost rambling—letter. Married in his sixties to a much younger woman, Ames finds himself in poor health and realizes he will soon be dead. As the letter's pages turn, we hear this dying father attempting to do what every father should—help his son know his own identity, who he is.

We all need to know who we are, whether we have a dad to help us or not. The first step to knowing who we are, though, is to know who we aren't. We are not God. And for most of our history, we humans have struggled with this point. In Eden, Adam and Eve sinned because they failed to believe there was a fundamental difference between God and them (Genesis 3:1-4). Later, when God gave Israel the Ten Commandments, He intended these directives to be the primary principles for them to understand their base identity. It's important to note, then, that the initial four commandments centered on declaring how God was "other" than them, above them—and must be reverenced as such (Exodus 20:1-11).

We hear this truth again when Hannah rejoiced because God did the impossible. He gave the infertile woman a son. She knew she was helpless to fix herself, that her hope was based in a God who was far greater than she was (1 Samuel 2:2).

Scripture invites us to declare God as our sovereign Lord. Once we rest in the conviction that we are not God, we begin to discover in turn who we actually are—and we find joy in our dependence on God's kindness and mercy.

—Winn Collier

anger danger

read>
Jonah 4
This change of plans upset Jonah, and he became very angry (v.1).

more>
- Proverbs 14:29
- Ephesians 4:31
- Colossians 3:8

next>
Why is controlling our anger a challenge? How can seeing yourself as Christ's messenger help you keep your anger in check?

"You can keep your overnight bag!" Frustrated that she had missed her flight, the irate woman tossed the proffered package at the customer service agent and marched away. The rest of us who were in line watched the employee shrug his shoulders and shake his head with disinterest. Left to appease customers for decisions that had not been his, he had obviously seen many like her. Detachment had become his way of handling the anger and insults.

Though rarely a productive option, the opportunity to get mad presents itself daily—misunderstandings, unrealized goals, hurt feelings. The temptation to get angry can come from something as superficial as another car cutting us off as we drive down the road or to the deep wounding of someone walking out of our lives. But we were not created to walk in wrath. While we know that Jesus experienced anger (Mark 3:5, 10:14), Ephesians 4:26-27 tells us, "Don't sin by letting anger control you. Don't let the sun go down while you are still angry, for anger gives a foothold to the devil." Most often, the wrath we experience is not a righteous indignation but an overflow of our self-centered sin nature.

While Jonah was angry that he had lost his shade, he was also mad that God didn't destroy the people of Nineveh. Rather than being concerned for this nation that would be lost if they didn't hear and receive God's message, Jonah chose to be bitter over His compassion for them.

Jesus taught us to live in such a way that others would see the light of truth (Matthew 5:16). People have difficulty seeing the love of Jesus in us, however, when they're too busy picking shrapnel from our angry explosions out of their eyes (James 1:19-20). —Regina Franklin

longing for a guiding voice

read>
John 10:11-16, 27-30
My sheep listen to My voice; I know them, and they follow Me. I give them eternal life, and they will never perish (vv.27-28).

more>
- Psalm 23
- Isaiah 40:11
- Ezekiel 34:11-16

next>
How have you tried to find guidance for your life without God? When was the last time you were quiet enough before Jesus to hear His voice?

My wife told me about a single colleague of hers who went to consult with the local fortuneteller one weekend. She was looking for guidance. *Where's my life heading? Will I always be lonely?*

So many people continue to look for guidance in wrong and hazardous places. For instance, a few years ago, more than 65,000 women visited the five Australian *Mind Body Spirit* festivals held here. One of the most popular features of the event was the Reading Room, where 60 psychics gave attendees all kinds of guidance on love, money, and happiness. In addition, 20 million people around the world took part in the online course Oprah hosted with popular new age author Eckhart Tolle. And once I stood with 5,000 others who braved pouring rain to hear what the Dalai Lama had to say. (He needs Jesus too!) Millions are searching for spiritual guidance, but I believe there is one Voice they're searching for.

"I am the Good Shepherd," we hear this Voice say (John 10:11)—this Shepherd who is gathering a flock from all nations (v.16). "I sacrifice My life for the sheep," this Voice says (v.15)—this Shepherd who protects when others run and hide (v.12). "My sheep listen to My voice," we hear Him declare (v.27)—He knows them and guides them to the richest of lives (Psalm 23).

"I give them eternal life," we hear Him promise (v.28)—He offers a destiny to those willing to follow.

Thousands of years ago God promised that He would personally come and shepherd His "sheep"—those who had fallen into enemy captivity (Ezekiel 34:11-16). In Jesus, God did that, and today He calls us out of our captivity of confused spiritual searching.

This Voice holds life, love, and the future in His hands. Listen. Follow.

—Sheridan Voysey

giving thanks

read›
Colossians 3:12-17
Always be thankful. . . . And whatever you do or say, do it as a representative of the Lord Jesus, giving thanks through Him to God the Father (vv.15,17).

more›
Be thankful in all circumstances, for this is God's will for you who belong to Christ Jesus (1 Thessalonians 5:18).

next›
What has caused you to complain recently? For whom and for what do you need to give thanks? Why can you still give thanks to God when you face pain, hardships, and unfortunate circumstances?

During winter in my part of the world, we don't often get warm, sunny days. God blessed us with one of those days earlier this season. As I left the office to go home, a man said, "What a wonderful day we're having. This is a gift from God." I replied, "Yeah, but there's going to be a major snowstorm later this week." Oops. What an ugly display of ingratitude. To change my ways, I'm on a quest to build a life and theology of thanksgiving. The apostle Paul, in his letters, is helping me get there.

Paul mentioned the subject of thanksgiving in his letters more often—line for line—than any other Greek author (pagan or Christian). Here are a few lessons he taught us about thanksgiving:

• *Thanksgiving should be primarily directed to God.* People are created by God, and Paul gave thanks to Him for their growth, love, faith, risks, receiving and accepting the Word, and more (Romans 16:4; 1 Corinthians 1:4; 1 Thessalonians 1:2).

• *Thanksgiving should be given always—unceasingly.* This meant that he regularly carved out time to make sure that thanksgiving played a prominent role in his prayer life (Colossians 3:15).

• *Thanksgiving flows from a heart changed by God.* Grace, God's favor and salvation through Jesus, leads to the response, "God, thank You" (vv.12-15).

• *Thanksgiving is given through Jesus, for everything* (Ephesians 5:20; Colossians 3:15,17).

• *Thanksgiving is an important part of praise and worship* (vv.16-17).

• *The ultimate goal of thanksgiving is to glorify God* (2 Corinthians 4:15).

Let's ask God to help us realize all He's done for us, and respond with gratitude. —Marvin Williams

Sorry too worried to wed

read>
1 Peter 3:1-12
All of you should be of one mind. Sympathize with each other (v.8).

more>
- Ephesians 5:21-30
- Colossians 3:18-19
- Titus 2:3-5

next>
How do you think God wants us to respond to the fear of commitment? How do biblical guidelines for marriage help to ease anxiety over the altar?

Wang Guiying was 107 years old and looking for love. Born in the southern Guizhou province of China, she had steered clear of marriage because she grew up watching her uncles criticize and abuse their wives. According to the centenarian, "All the married people . . . lived like that. Getting married was too frightening."

Like this woman, the idea of commitment is enough to make many of us cower. God's ideas about marriage, however, make us brave when we hear wedding bells.

A big part of this courage comes from remembering that God is our ultimate source of love, provision, and protection—even within marriage. Due to our humanness, we will inevitably disappoint our spouse and our spouse will disappoint us, but God will never let us down. Maybe that's why Peter praised women who "trusted God and accepted the authority of their husbands" (1 Peter 3:5).

If you're a woman, that "male authority" thing might have you running scared. Fortunately, God's plan for marriage includes mutual submission (Ephesians 5:21). Building on that foundation, Paul tells wives to submit to their husbands "as to the Lord" (v.22). Guys are supposed to honor their wives, to love them (vv.28-29), and "never treat them harshly" (Colossians 3:19). And all believers in Jesus are supposed to "be of one mind. Sympathize with each other. Be tenderhearted, and keep a humble attitude" (1 Peter 3:8).

Still, many of us have witnessed just the opposite within marriage. Bad marital behavior, however, carries consequences.

God takes marriage seriously. With His help, we can fight the fear that makes us too worried to wed. —Jennifer Benson Schuldt

unpopular

read>
Matthew 5:11-14
God blesses you when people mock you and persecute you and lie about you and say all sorts of evil things against you because you are My followers (v.11).

more>
This is a trustworthy saying: If we die with Him, we will also live with Him (2 Timothy 2:11).

next>
Check your heart to make sure any persecution you might be under is not self-inflicted by your self-righteous behavior. How do Jesus' words encourage you in the likely event of persecution in the days ahead?

Have you ever noticed how people tend to like firefighters more than police officers? Every day, these brave souls are willing to face the flames and put their lives on the line for us—and they don't issue speeding tickets or take us to jail.

Police officers in Joseph Wambaugh's novels often say something like this to each other: "Well, if you really wanted people to like you, you should have been a fireman." While we definitely want the police to be present if someone's threatening our well-being, we don't always appreciate seeing their flashing lights in our rearview mirror.

In a similar way, following Jesus doesn't always draw the admiration of others. While He doesn't call us to be the world's moral police force, part of the path that Jesus summons us to walk will cause others to dislike us.

The New Testament warns us, "Everyone who wants to live a godly life in Christ Jesus will suffer persecution" (2 Timothy 3:12). As His followers, we will suffer for advancing His kingdom. In fact, some of the very people we are trying to rescue from the kingdom of darkness and invite into the kingdom of light will despise us.

If you find yourself taking a lot of grief for your Christian beliefs, you're in good company. Jesus emphasized to His disciples, "If the world hates you, remember that it hated Me first. The world would love you as one of its own if you belonged to it, but you are no longer part of the world. I chose you to come out of the world, so it hates you. . . . Since they persecuted Me, naturally they will persecute you" (John 15:18-20).

Following Jesus may not make you popular, but suffering for His sake is a part of the blessing of becoming more like Him (Philippians 3:10). —Jeff Olson

de-baptism?

read>
Matthew 3:13-17
Then Jesus went from Galilee to the Jordan River to be baptized (v.13).

more>
We died and were buried with Christ by baptism. And just as Christ was raised from the dead by the glorious power of the Father, now we also may live new lives (Romans 6:4).

next>
What has baptism meant in your life? Why is it so important for believers in Jesus to be baptized?

Have you known people who wanted to backtrack on their baptism? Not long ago, the National Secular Society in London created "certificates of de-baptism" that could be downloaded from the Web site. The certificates were originally created to "mock the practice of baptizing infants," but atheists and those who no longer hold to Christian faith began downloading them to the tune of 1,000 per week. *Sad.*

Jesus made it as clear as fresh water that baptism is an important step of obedience for all believers. Before being baptized by John the Baptist, he said, "It should be done, for we must carry out all that God requires" (Matthew 3:15). So at the very start of His ministry, Jesus was baptized out of obedience to His Father.

It's evident that baptism shows our desire to obediently and publicly identify with Jesus in His death (symbolized by our being immersed) and His new life (portrayed by our rising from the water). Baptism does not, however, lead to salvation: "To all who believed Him and accepted Him, He gave the right to become children of God" (John 1:12); "We are made right with God by placing our faith in Jesus Christ" (Romans 3:22); "God saved you by His grace when you believed" (Ephesians 2:8).

To avoid the unthinkable occasion of even considering being de-baptized, it's vital that we prayerfully, solemnly consider what we're committing to prior to being baptized. As we're immersed in the waters and come forth again, we're declaring to God and to other believers that—by grace through faith—"My old self has been crucified with Christ. It is no longer I who live, but Christ lives in me" (Galatians 2:20).

Baptism is God's beautiful way to show that we will love and follow Jesus our whole lives—with no option for de-baptism. —Tom Felten

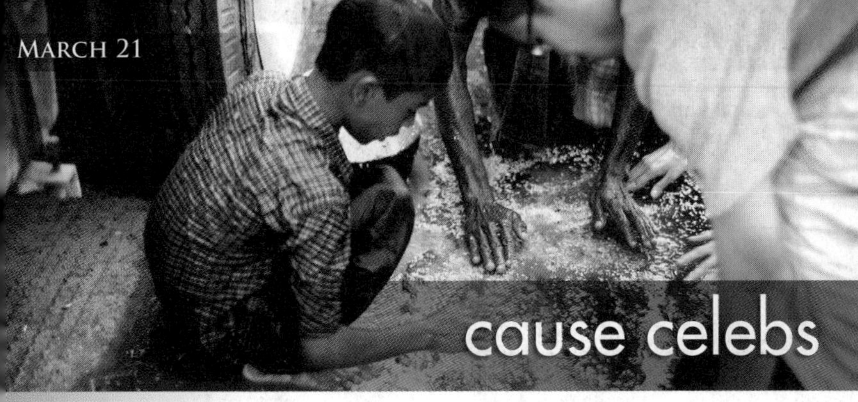

cause celebs

read>
Romans 12:9-18
If you help the poor, you are lending to the Lord—and He will repay you! (Proverbs 19:17).

more>
If someone has enough money to live well and sees a brother or sister in need but shows no compassion—how can God's love be in that person? (1 John 3:17).

next>
Ask God to align your heart with empathy and compassion. What prevents you from reaching out to others with God's love?

A majority of today's celebrities have a cause. Whether it's cancer research, animal rights, human rights, global warming, or a myriad of other charitable undertakings, countless high-profile actors and professional athletes have sought to use their platform of popularity to evoke change.

Instead of considering the impetus behind these stars' good deeds, however, let's look at our motivation and the reasons we may not be personally involved in serving others. With that in mind, how much are you like Job (chapter 29:11-17) who:

- Assisted the poor in their need and the orphans who required help?
- Caused the widows' hearts to sing for joy?
- Wept for those in trouble, and grieved for the needy?
- Served as eyes for the blind and feet for the lame?
- Was a father to the poor and assisted strangers?

In contrast, how much do you epitomize Jerusalem's "younger sister" Sodom (Ezekiel 16:49-50) who:

- Was arrogant, overfed, and unconcerned?
- Did not help the poor and needy who suffered right outside her door?
- Was haughty and did detestable things before God?

Now consider these ways to love others as Jesus loves:

- Be genuine in loving and honoring other people (Romans 12:9-10).
- Be hospitable and humbly enjoy ordinary people (vv.13,16).
- Rejoice with those who rejoice. Mourn with those who mourn (v.15).

Our motivation to do good works should flow from our love for God. Today, ask Him to align your heart with empathy and compassion and to propel you into a life of sacrificial and deeply fulfilling devotion to Him and to others.

—Roxanne Robbins

go ask mom

read>
Deuteronomy 6:1-9
We will not hide these truths from our children; we will tell the next generation about the glorious deeds of the Lord, about His power and His mighty wonders (Psalm 78:4).

more>
- Exodus 12:24-27
- Deuteronomy 31:12-13
- Ephesians 6:4

next>
Is Bible reading a part of your family activity or routine? How have you communicated your faith in Jesus to your children? What spiritual legacy are you leaving behind for them?

The story is told of an unmarried (and childless) professor of child psychology who taught a seminar that he confidently called, "Ten Commandments for Parents." Then he got married and became a father. After a year of fatherhood, he changed the seminar title to "Ten Guidelines for Parents." Three years later, a second child came. The seminar was once again renamed: "Some Suggestions to Parents." After his third son was born, the professor stopped teaching the seminar altogether.

God didn't give us children then leave us with no direction as to what to teach them. The foundation of being a good parent begins long before we actually become one (Deuteronomy 6:1-5). We begin by loving and fearing God (v.5) and by wholeheartedly obeying His commands (v.6). God has made the family home the place for teaching His Word. You're to "repeat [God's Word] again and again to your children" (v.7). More than just teaching the Bible to children, parents are to live out its truth before their kids (vv.7-9).

If we don't know God's Word (Deuteronomy 17:19, 31:12-13), we won't be able to teach it. If we don't love and fear God, we can't model that to our children. We simply can't give what we ourselves do not possess (2 Timothy 1:13-14; Titus 1:9).

One day a child might ask you: "Where is God?" or "Who is Jesus?" Answers like, "Go ask your mom" or "I don't know" won't do. We need to be ready to talk with our children about God (Deuteronomy 6:7-9) and to tell them the story of how God saved us from our sin (vv.21-23). Leading your own children to believe in Jesus is the duty and privilege of every parent.

—K.T. Sim

give it a rest

read>
Matthew 11:25-30
Then Jesus said, "Come to Me, all of you who are weary and carry heavy burdens, and I will give you rest" (v.28).

more>
- Job 6:14
- Proverbs 18:24
- 1 Corinthians 13:4-7

next>
Consider the people you most enjoy. Do you like them for their good looks, skills, wealth, or something else? How can you become what you appreciate in them?

Harold J. Ockenga, friend of Billy Graham and first president of Fuller Seminary and the National Association of Evangelicals, was one of the founding fathers of American evangelicalism. But like most great leaders, Ockenga was not perfect. His problem was sarcasm.

The same brilliant mind and quick tongue that enabled Ockenga to shine in the pulpit also wreaked havoc on his friendships. He wrote in his journal that his tendency to denigrate others "follows me wherever I go, which causes people to not like to be with me." His friends confronted him, and his girlfriend threatened to break up with him, but he never completely conquered his penchant for the put-down.

How different was Jesus! Although He is the perfect person, Jesus never used His excellence as an excuse to be critical of others. He didn't take cheap shots and exaggerate the weaknesses of others for effect. Jesus didn't mock James and John as "Mama's boys" or call Peter "Mr. Motormouth." He didn't even think He had to win every argument. When a Gentile woman rebutted His statement that "It isn't right to take food from the children and throw it to the dogs," Jesus replied, "Good answer!" and healed her daughter (Mark 7:27-30).

Jesus used His perfection and power to inspire others. He released an adulteress to "go and sin no more" (John 8:11), announced to a repentant tax cheat: "Salvation has come to this home today" (Luke 19:9), and invited bumbling disciples to "take My yoke upon you. Let Me teach you, because I am humble and gentle at heart, and you will find rest for your souls" (Matthew 11:29).

It doesn't take talent, beauty, or money to be a friend like Jesus. Friends will find you if you listen, care, and provide a safe place to rest. —Mike Wittmer

wasted gift

read>
2 Peter 1:3-10
Work hard to prove that you really are among those God has called and chosen. Do these things, and you will never fall away (v.10).

more>
I press on to reach the end of the race and receive the heavenly prize for which God, through Christ Jesus, is calling us (Philippians 3:14).

next>
Are you pursuing the qualities God desires for your life? How can you press on and get to know Jesus more intimately and become more like Him?

The poet Samuel Taylor Coleridge possessed a tragic lack of discipline. He left Cambridge University to join the army; he left the army because he couldn't rub down a horse; he returned to Oxford and left without a degree. He started a weekly newspaper that made it to just 25 issues before he ceased publishing it. It's been said of him: "He lost himself in visions of work to be done, that always remained to be done." Coleridge had many gifts, but he lacked an important one—the gift of sustained and concentrated effort.

Every believer in Jesus has great potential to complete the tasks God gives us, based on divine gifts. In 2 Peter 1, we read that "by His divine power, God has given us everything we need for living a godly life" (v.3), and He has given us "great and precious promises" that enable us to share in His divine nature and escape the world's corruption (v.4).

God has given us everything! We lack nothing in growing to become useful and productive people as we serve Jesus (v.8). One thing, however, is required: We must respond to God's promises (v.5).

How do we do this? Verses 5 to 7 contain a list of character qualities that every Christian should strive to attain by God's strength. They include moral excellence, knowledge, self-control, and patient endurance. If we choose not to pursue these things, then we're set for spiritual failure (v.10).

Let's strive to grow as believers in Jesus who possess strong character and the ability to finish what He calls us to do within His perfect plan. The sovereignty of God should never be an excuse for passivity or inactivity; rather, His sovereignty is our basis for sustained and concentrated effort toward spiritual growth.

—Poh Fang Chia

God stands here

read>
John 20:11-31
Jesus was standing there among them! (v.19).

more>
- John 1:1-18
- Philippians 2:5-11

next>
Where have you seen Jesus come and stand with you? Where is the place you most need Jesus to meet you right now?

Shusaku Endo, widely acclaimed as Japan's finest modern novelist, penned *Silence*, a haunting story raising questions about Western religious assumptions concerning Jesus and the gospel. Emerging from his dual (and unique) identity as a Japanese Catholic, Endo used his novels and essays to push forward these core beliefs: Jesus' story was not imprisoned by the West, and essential to the gospel is its power to embody anew Japan's people, and all people. "Unless there is in [Christianity] a part that corresponds to Japan's mud swamp," said Endo, "it cannot be a true religion."

Though Endo wrestled with the implications (and though not all agree with the way Endo worked it out), he insisted on one of Christianity's most elemental assertions: the incarnation, the fantastic belief that God came and lived as a human. Jesus met us in ways we could comprehend. Jesus became, for us, a God we could touch.

When Jesus appeared in first-century Palestine, He didn't come as a mist or mirage. He was not some form of alternate consciousness. Rather, Jesus came as a man with a name; and He came to particular people—other human beings with names and stories all their own.

Jesus was most often found with people, participating in their life: attending parties (John 2), eating with the hungry (Luke 9), telling stories to anyone who cared to listen (Mark 4). Then, when Jesus met His friends after the cross, He (again) "was standing there among them," as He always had (John 20:19). Even more, "He showed them the wounds in His hands and His side" (v.20). Physical. *Present.*

Along with Endo, Christians proclaim that Jesus comes to all people. We believe in—and have experienced—a Jesus who comes near, a Jesus standing here, with us. Right beside us. —Winn Collier

letting go

read>
Philippians 3:8-16
No, dear brothers and sisters, I have not achieved it, but I focus on this one thing: Forgetting the past and looking forward to what lies ahead (v.13).

I've never been a particularly fast writer, but when it came to texting, my speed was somewhere in the range of "turtlelike." While receiving a second or third text, I was still responding to the first. So when it came time for a new cell phone, I chose one with a QWERTY keyboard in hopes of gaining speed. As much as I love my keyboard, though, one feature came as a pleasant surprise. I can erase my inbox in a nanosecond. It's nice to hit that "ok" button and see my screen become a clean slate.

As believers, our spirit takes on new life at the point of salvation. Our minds, however, require continued renewal (2 Corinthians 10:5). Romans 12:2 teaches that we are not to conform to the "behaviors and customs of this world" but to allow the Lord to change us as our minds are renewed in Him. While this Scripture applies to our putting aside the world's values, we can take on worldly thinking in more ways than one.

Left to our flesh, our minds will replay the past, especially in regard to our regrets. What "was" becomes "our here-and-now" when we allow our desire for a do-over to dominate. Wanting to keep us from moving forward, the enemy lies by telling us the past is not only unforgettable, it's unforgivable.

Thankfully, God's Word speaks differently. He has forgiven and does not remember our blood-covered sins (Isaiah 43:25). We cannot be defined by what does not exist. Paul had it right—to go forward we must let go of the past (Philippians 3:13). After all, it's hard to run a race looking back. Though it requires more than hitting the "ok" button on a cell phone, forgetting the past begins by believing it's possible. Moving forward depends on it. —Regina Franklin

more>
Because of our faith, Christ has brought us into this place of highest privilege where we now stand, and we confidently and joyfully look forward to sharing God's glory (Romans 5:2).

next>
Are there regretful events or things in your past that keep coming to mind? What has God said about these things? How can focusing on the past keep you from reaching for what God has set before you today?

a noun or a verb

read>
John 13:31-38
So now I am giving you a new commandment: Love each other. Just as I have loved you, you should love each other (v.34).

more>
Don't be selfish; don't try to impress others. Be humble, thinking of others as better than yourselves. Don't look out only for your own interests, but take an interest in others, too (Philippians 2:3-4).

next>
How would your relationships be different if you loved others with Jesus as your standard? What do you need to do to start loving others just as Jesus loves you?

A recent movie portrayed a teenage girl who got pregnant and had to decide what to do with her baby. Her relationship with her boyfriend wasn't working out, her dad's first marriage had failed, and the couple to whom she decided to give her baby was having major marital issues. With broken relationships as the backdrop, she said some profound words to her father: "I guess I wonder sometimes if people ever stay together for good—like people in love. Dad, I just want to know that it's possible for two people to stay happy together forever."

More than 2,000 years ago, hours before He died, Jesus gave the secret to having an enduring love relationship with another human being. He gave His disciples a new, unused, unheard of command: "Love each other" (John 13:34). Was this really a new command? Hadn't they heard it before? Maybe the new part of the command was changing love from an emotional noun (something you feel) and making it an active verb (something you do). Maybe the new part of the command was the standard of the command: "Just as I have loved you, you should love each other" (v.34).

Prior to this, the standard for loving their neighbors was a love for themselves (Leviticus 19:18). Now the standard was Jesus. In order for His kingdom to advance into the world, His band of followers would have to set aside personal competition, selfishness, and pride. They would need to wash one another's feet, sacrifice for one another, submit to one another (Ephesians 5:21), and even be willing to die for each other (John 15:13).

The love that Jesus commands His followers to have for one another isn't based in sappy emotion. It's a love of service, duty, humility, sacrifice, and affection. —Marvin Williams

maximum sentence

read>
Proverbs 6:32-35
But the [one] who commits adultery is an utter fool, for he destroys himself (v.32).

more>
Since they are no longer two but one, let no one split apart what God has joined together (Matthew 19:6).

next>
How can you guard your heart and marriage against adultery? Why do you think the Bible is so opposed to breaking the covenant of marriage?

South Korean courts sentenced actress Ok So-ri to 8 months in jail for cheating on her husband. During court proceedings, So-ri fought to stay out of prison, claiming the 1953 law against adultery was an invasion of privacy. The courts upheld the law, but suspended her sentence for 2 years.

Even though most countries don't recognize adultery as a criminal offense, God is offended by this sin (Exodus 20:14). Unfaithfulness carries a maximum sentence that none of us can escape.

This penalty includes public disgrace. Even if an affair never hits the front pages, believe me—word gets around. The Bible claims that cheaters will "be wounded and disgraced. [Their] shame will never be erased" (Proverbs 6:33). This shame not only permanently trashes a person's reputation, but it scars children and extended families as well—not to mention the other individual involved in the affair.

The Bible warns, "Sexual immorality is a sin against your own body" (1 Corinthians 6:18), and "the [one] who commits adultery is an utter fool, for he destroys himself" (Proverbs 6:32). Adultery can destroy us through disease, emotional entanglement with another person, and a messed-up marriage.

Once a relationship is polluted by unfaithfulness, the jealous spouse "will be furious and . . . will show no mercy when he [or she] takes revenge" (v.34). Divorce, neglect, reciprocal affairs, and even murder are all forms of revenge that stem from the business of betrayal.

God asks us to "remain faithful to one another in marriage" (Hebrews 13:4). As both our advocate and judge, He wants us to avoid the maximum sentence that adultery carries. —Jennifer Benson Schuldt

hold on loosely

read>
Philippians 2:4-8
Don't look out only for your own interests, but take an interest in others, too (v.4).

more>
You have been called to live in freedom, my brothers and sisters. But don't use your freedom to satisfy your sinful nature. Instead, use your freedom to serve one another in love (Galatians 5:13).

next>
In what way might you be holding too tightly to a relationship? How does Jesus' example help you to hold on loosely?

I stopped at a fast-food restaurant for a quick bite to eat. I placed my order at the drive-thru, picked up my beverage and chicken sandwich (minus the sauce), and was all set for an uneventful meal—or so I thought. A minute later, as I went to take a sip of my soft drink, the plastic lid on my paper cup popped off. Instinctively, I squeezed the cup to minimize the mess, but it only made things worse.

Along with again being certain I was born to spill things, the incident reminded me how much can go wrong in a relationship when we hold on too tight. If we turn into the clingy smothering type where it becomes all about us, we'll end up squeezing the life out of those we claim to love.

The New Testament speaks about a more balanced approach to relationships: "Don't look out only for your own interests, but take an interest in others, too" (Philippians 2:4). We're talking mutual consideration. Without it, relationships often become one-sided and oppressive.

If we feel as if the lid is coming off a friendship, dating relationship, or marriage, putting the squeeze on others is anything but mutually thoughtful. Conversely, the lyrics of a 1980s song encourages listeners to "hold on loosely," but not "let go," Not bad advice. In our close relationships, we need to always give the other person "someone to believe in" and lots of room "to breathe in."

Even Jesus exhibited the importance of holding things loosely in relationships. The Bible says, "Though He was God, He did not think of equality with God as something to cling to" (Philippians 2:6).

Everyone has legitimate needs. But if we're after healthy and Christlike relationships—let's remember to "hold on loosely" by thinking of what's best for others. —Jeff Olson

faith and fear

read>
Matthew 14:22-36
"Don't be afraid," [Jesus] said. "Take courage. I am here!" Then Peter called to Him, "Lord, if it's really You, tell me to come to You, walking on the water." "Yes, come," Jesus said (vv.27-29).

more>
But thank God! He gives us victory over sin and death through our Lord Jesus Christ (1 Corinthians 15:57).

next>
In what sense is faith the opposite of fear? Do faith and fear cancel each other out, or is it possible to have both at the same time?

Death scares me. I love my life, and I don't want it to end. There's also a part of me that wonders what the afterlife is really like. What if it's different from what the Bible says?

Some people might think that my fears are unchristian and a threat to my faith. On the contrary, I think that they're not only normal—who honestly isn't afraid of the great beyond?—but they also play an important role in my faith. Fear doesn't prevent me from having faith; fear actually presents the possibility for great faith.

It was no great thing for Peter to walk on land, but to lower himself over the side of the boat and splash through whitecaps toward our Lord—that took faith. We can, of course, allow fear to overwhelm us to the point of losing faith. But we can also channel our fear into Peter's desperate cry as he began to sink, "Save me, Lord!" (Matthew 14:30).

Having faith does not mean that we're not afraid. It gives us the courage to stand tall and to hang on in the middle of our fears. And the greater our fears, the stronger our faith can become.

We place our faith in Jesus, whose resurrection has defeated death. If we minimize death and claim that it's no big deal, then we inadvertently also cheapen Christ's resurrection that conquered it. But if we honestly admit that death is the enemy that terrifies us, then we can begin to appreciate the unparalleled power of the resurrection.

Faith isn't about suppressing fear and pretending that everything is okay. But it does allow us to swallow hard—with shaky knees and sweaty palms—and cling to God's promise that we will live again. Death is frightening, and for that reason it provides the ultimate test of our faith. —Mike Wittmer

count the cost

read>
Luke 14:25-35
If you do not carry your own cross and follow Me, you cannot be My disciple. But don't begin until you count the cost (vv.27-28).

more>
For His sake I have discarded everything else, counting it all as garbage, so that I could gain Christ (Philippians 3:8).

next>
What are the costs of being freed to follow Jesus fully? How does He provide what we need to make surrender to Him a reality?

When world-renowned tenor Luciano Pavarotti was a youth, he became the pupil of a professional tenor in Italy. Later, he studied music education in college. Upon graduating, he asked his father, "Shall I be a teacher or a singer?" "Luciano," his father replied, "if you try to sit on two chairs, you will fall between them. For life, you must choose one chair."

In Luke 14:25-35, Jesus presented a similar message to a large crowd of people who were following Him. His "sermon" made it clear that He wanted single-minded commitment. He wanted men and women who had truly counted the cost of discipleship and were prepared to follow Him. So He listed the demands (vv.26-27), decisions (vv.28-33), and distinctiveness (vv.34-35) of discipleship.

In His message, Jesus gave illustrations of two people who start a project without counting the cost. The consequences of failing to do so include shame and humiliation.

While counting the cost implies that time and thought are required when one considers becoming a disciple of Jesus, no one has the resources to follow Him on his or her own. He gives us what we need to follow Him. Counting the cost, therefore, is not about evaluating whether we have what it takes to do what He commands; rather, it indicates a real commitment to let go of anything that could come between Jesus and us. We must choose to place Him before family and possessions, and to take up our cross daily. We are then freed to follow Him fully in complete allegiance and dependence.

It's been said that there are only two ways to take a thing seriously—either reject it or risk everything for it. Discipleship begins by recognizing the high price required, and—without reserve—casting ourselves upon the sustaining grace and strength found in Jesus alone. —Poh Fang Chia

inside information

read>
Luke 18:31-34
Taking the twelve disciples aside, Jesus said, "Listen, we're going up to Jerusalem, where all the predictions of the prophets concerning the Son of Man will come true" (v.31).

more>
- Deuteronomy 29:29
- Romans 16:25-26
- Ephesians 3:2-6

next>
If you had been one of the disciples, how would you have responded to Jesus' words about the coming events? How has Jesus prepared you for the future?

Tiptoeing mischievously toward me, my son leaned down and placed something near the base of the chair where I was sitting and then scampered away. Looking down, I smiled at his childlike belief in my supposed ignorance. There on the floor was the homing unit to his spy gear listening device. Though he would hear little more than the turning of pages or tapping of the keyboard, he remained unaffected in his resolve to listen in and get some "inside information." He simply loved the mystery of being able to be somewhere without really being there.

Preparing for His crucifixion and ascension, Jesus told the disciples some inside information pertaining to what was coming and how they were to respond (John 16:4). They tried to make sense of God's plan based on what they could see, however, and "failed to grasp what He was talking about" (Luke 18:34). Even Peter—the one whom Jesus named "the rock"—boldly questioned the methods through which the Messiah would be revealed (Mark 8:31-33). The death of Jesus wasn't in their plans.

If we're honest, most of us want to see what's ahead so we can be prepared. Desiring control, we want God to tell us where we're going and when we'll arrive.

Jesus didn't give the disciples the pieces of the puzzle ahead of time so they could be comfortable. He gave them inside information for a purpose outside of themselves. He knew they would be the ones who would turn the world upside down.

The gospel is indeed a great mystery, and God has placed us as believers at its core (Ephesians 1:9). We may not know tomorrow's exact events, but God has revealed His heart to us. Likewise, our hearts are revealed by our response to the information He gives us. —Regina Franklin

baby, not so grand

read>
Ephesians 6:1-4
Do not provoke your children to anger by the way you treat them (v.4).

more>
Fathers, do not aggravate your children, or they will become discouraged (Colossians 3:21).

next>
What does godly discipline accomplish? How does God discipline you in love?

When one of my sons was a young boy, he carved some words into a pristine piece of wood. Unfortunately, the beautiful board was part of our baby grand piano. Needless to say, my wife and I were not delighted with his newly honed woodworking "skills." He soon discovered that the destruction of another person's property leads to being disciplined. You might say he had to "face the music" for defacing our music maker!

God's Word plainly states that to discipline a child is vital for their growth and maturation: "Those who love their children care enough to discipline them" (Proverbs 13:24). We also read that God disciplines us for our own good and because of His love for us (Deuteronomy 8:5; Hebrews 12:6). To imitate His example means that the disciplining of our children isn't an option—it's required.

So how can we do it in a way that honors God and provides the right kind of correction for our kids? The apostle Paul provides some great insight with a little negative and positive "reinforcement" found in Ephesians 6:4:

The Negative. "Do not provoke your children to anger by the way you treat them." This teaching was radical for the *patria potestas* (absolute father authority) society of Paul's day. It called for fathers to be considerate of their children's feelings. "Provoking" children leads them to become resentful and unwilling to receive correction. A Christlike parent will encourage and discipline in love.

The Positive. "Bring them up with the discipline and instruction that comes from the Lord." Children should be tenderly corrected and instructed at home—being brought up in ways that reflect the way our loving God delights and disciplines us.

Children need discipline. They need to face the music. Just make sure you're providing loving correction, not provoking them to destruction. —Tom Felten

lonely places

read>
Mark 1:32-36
Before daybreak the next morning, Jesus got up and went out to an isolated place to pray (v.35).

more>
Listen to my voice in the morning, Lord. Each morning I bring my requests to You and wait expectantly (Psalm 5:3).

next>
Are you trying to spin too many plates in life? How will you rework your schedule to spend more time with God?

A performer who spins plates on sticks never ceases to fascinate me. He takes a stick and spins a plate on the tip of it. He then adds a second and a third plate. By the time he gets several plates spinning, the crowd is clapping and shouting encouragement. The more plates he spins, the louder the applause. When he has set 20 or more plates in motion, the crowd is up on their feet. They're thinking, How does he keep all those plates spinning without any of them crashing? Check it out—the performer is moving like mad, frantically shifting from one stick to another as he keeps all the plates doing their thing!

Every day, large crowds came to hear or see Jesus (Mark 1:32,45; 2:2,13; 4:1)z. He was so busy ministering to people—shifting from one to another—that it became difficult and almost impossible for Him to be alone. People kept coming from everywhere to be with Him (1:45).

On one occasion, despite having ministered late into the night (v.32), Jesus got up before daybreak the next morning. If I had been there, I wouldn't have skipped getting my zzz to get up at 4 a.m.! But Jesus got up and went out to an isolated place to pray (v.35).

Jesus often withdrew from the crowd and deliberately sought out solitary places. It was a habit with Him (Luke 5:16, 6:12; Matthew 14:23). Why? He had a deep need to talk and fellowship with His Father. Jesus needed some time alone because He was human.

Being alone with God is an essential part of our life, and it also reveals our humanness and weakness. When we skip our time with God, we're telling Him that we can keep all those plates—all the stuff of life—spinning perfectly all by ourselves.

Instead, let's find a lonely place and spend some much needed time with our heavenly Father. —K.T. Sim

that special

read>
Luke 18:9-14
Those who exalt themselves will be humbled, and those who humble themselves will be exalted (v.14).

more>
God opposes the proud but favors the humble. So humble yourselves under the mighty power of God, and at the right time He will lift you up (1 Peter 5:5-6).

next>
Why is it detrimental to criticize others and exalt ourselves? How does humility acknowledge our brokenness before God?

My mother is one of the most quotable people I know. Her quips usually make us laugh while poking us with a bit of truth. For example, when one of us spouts off about a minor achievement or takes on a me-first attitude, my mom is sure to say (with a smile), "You're not *that* special."

Jesus had a similar message for a group of listeners "who had great confidence in their own righteousness" (Luke 18:9). He told them about a Pharisee who barged into God's presence with this so-called prayer: "I thank You, God, that I am not a sinner like everyone else. . . . I'm certainly not like that *tax collector*!" (v.11).

Picking on the tax collector and bragging about his goodness backfired on the religious leader because Jesus said, "Those who exalt themselves will be humbled" (v.14).

I don't know about you, but I don't want God to look at me and think, *Hmm . . . she needs to be humbled today.* I'm so thankful that Jesus also said "those who humble themselves will be exalted" (v.14). The tax collector in Jesus' story knew how to humble himself. Beating his chest in sorrow, his prayer went like this: "O God, be merciful to me, for I am a sinner" (v.13). Christ noted that this man was the one who returned home forgiven by God.

It's no mistake that Jesus used the context of prayer to contrast humility with pride. When we pray like the Pharisee, our self-importance prevents us from connecting with God. The Bible says, "If God does not answer [people], it is because of their pride" (Job 35:12).

The good news is that humility opens God's ears to our prayers. Those tearful, chest-beating encounters with God over our sin matter deeply to Him. But our brokenness is essential. As we bow low before Him, He can lift us up and assure us, "You *are* that special." —Jennifer Benson Schuldt

NORMAL

the new normal

read>
1 Corinthians 15:1-11
Let me remind you, dear brothers and sisters, of the Good News I preached to you before. . . . It is this Good News that saves you if you continue to believe the message I told you (vv. 1-2).

more>
- Ecclesiastes 3:18-21
- Matthew 5:3-10
- Romans 10:8-9

next>
Which story are you living out: the good news or "what you see is what you get"? How might living the good news change your attitude, decisions, or actions today?

Life. You grow up, go to school, get a job and get married, have 2.4 kids, buy a house, save for retirement, and enjoy an occasional vacation and dinner out. Along the way you learn the rules. It takes money to get what you want, and that requires skill, preparation, and befriending the right people. If you play it smart—with timely moves—you can forge a career replete with promotions and a retirement right on schedule. And then you die, leaving a surprisingly sizable inheritance to your heirs. That's life—the same for you as for everybody—as far as the eye can see.

But what if we aren't limited to our sight, but can hear a Word from God that teaches us a different way to live? Paul said that "faith comes from hearing, that is, hearing the Good News about Christ" (Romans 10:17). This good news is that "Christ died for our sins, just as the Scriptures said. He was buried, and He was raised from the dead on the third day, just as the Scriptures said" (1 Corinthians 15:3-4).

The good news is the great game changer. Jesus entered our world, died on the cross, and rose again to defeat sin, death, and Satan. After His resurrection, He was seen in a variety of places by hundreds of witnesses (vv.5-8). Due to Jesus' world-changing words and existence, life as we know it has turned upside down. The rules have changed.

Here's our new life: "Love your neighbor as yourself" (Matthew 22:39); "It is more blessed to give than to receive" (Acts 20:35); "Be humble, thinking of others as better than yourselves" (Philippians 2:3); and when we return—and Christ's resurrection means that we will return—"those who are humble . . . will inherit the whole earth" (Matthew 5:5). —Mike Wittmer

the God-Shepherd

read>
John 10:11-18
The Lamb on the throne will be their Shepherd (Revelation 7:17).

more>
- Isaiah 40:11
- Ezekiel 34:11-16

next>
The Good Shepherd may know you, but how well do you know Him? How can you make sure that it's the Shepherd's voice you're hearing?

SARS in 2003. Bird or avian flu (H5N1) in 2004 and 2006. And the H1N1 or swine flu in 2009. It looks like the world is set for more flu outbreaks and potential pandemics. In 2006, surveys were conducted to determine if healthcare workers would abandon their workplace during a flu pandemic. One survey in Singapore revealed that nearly 26 percent of the medical professionals felt they should not be forced to care for patients during an outbreak. Thirty percent of German medical personnel stated that it would be acceptable to abandon their workplace. In a US survey, an alarming 50 percent of healthcare workers said they might bolt from the workplace during a pandemic.

While every job has its occupational hazards, no employee wants to die in the course of his or her work. A soldier strives to stay alive in order to carry out his duties. A shepherd will reluctantly die for his sheep. Except for the Good Shepherd, that is.

Twice, Jesus says, "I am the Good Shepherd" (John 10:11,14). This is one of the seven "I am" sayings in John's gospel (John 6:35, 8:12, 10:7, 10:11, 11:25, 14:6, 15:1). "I am" is the language of deity (Exodus 3:14). Jesus is the Divine Shepherd. He's the God-shepherd.

Three times Jesus says He "sacrifices His life for the sheep" (John 10:11,15,17). Why? Because the sheep belong to Him (v.12) and He really cares for them (v.13). The Good Shepherd knows His sheep by name (vv.3,14; 2 Timothy 2:19). Jesus knows us intimately. He knows our idiosyncrasies, strengths, weaknesses, failures, and hurts. He knows us inside out (Psalm 139:13-16).

Jesus speaks of His deity and His duty. He is the God-shepherd who sacrificially lays down His life for His sheep. He's the Good Shepherd who is there and truly cares. —K.T. Sim

the pilot seat

read>
Deuteronomy 11
You will be blessed if you obey the commands of the Lord your God (v.27).

more>
Obey Me, and I will be your God, and you will be My people. Do everything as I say, and all will be well! (Jeremiah 7:23).

next>
Have you turned over the controls of your life to God? What does that include?

An F16 fighter jet is an amazing aircraft with incredible capabilities. But there's one thing that a jet pilot requires above all else: The F16 must respond to his control.

God has much to say in Deuteronomy about why He must be at the controls of our life. The book is the story of Israel's renewed covenant with God—one that would guide the nation to His blessings. In chapter 11, Moses outlined the motivations for obedience:

- Obedience is the appropriate response for those who have experienced the discipline of the Lord and have seen His greatness (vv.1-7).
- Obedience to God—and only obedience—leads to real life, helping us soar past empty pursuits (vv.8-12).
- Obedience allows us to enjoy God's blessings (vv.13-15).

Next, Moses warns us to avoid flying headlong into the trap of thinking that . . .

- There is no consequence for disobedience (vv.16-17).
- There is no reward for being obedient (vv.18-21).
- There is no one to watch over us, so we need to fight for our rights. Instead, Scripture reveals that God will "drive out" our enemies, "stretch" out the land before us, and "cause the people to fear and dread [us]," as we follow Him (vv.22-25).
- There is little difference between choosing obedience or being disobedient (vv.26-32).

A. W. Tozer wrote, "The true follower of Christ will not ask, 'If I embrace this truth, what will it cost me?' Rather he will say, 'This is truth. God help me to walk in it, let come what may!' "

Obedience to the God who "pilots" our ways and days is the key to a life of joy and excellence. —Poh Fang Chia

an unlikely route to life

read>
John 20:1-9
For until then they still hadn't understood the Scriptures that said Jesus must rise from the dead (v.9).

more>
When you put a seed into the ground, it doesn't grow into a plant unless it dies first (1 Corinthians 15:36).

next>
What do you need to die to today as you choose life in Jesus? How does Jesus' resurrection affect your view of the present and the future?

The first Easter morning didn't start out well for the disciples. The one thing they knew for sure, when they woke up that day, was that Jesus was dead. The precious Master and Friend they had followed for three years, hanging on His every word, was gone—having been brutally executed on a Roman cross. His death must have been a crushing blow. Imagine their emotions. Disbelief. Disillusionment. *Despair*.

Until that morning, the disciples had operated from the understanding that normally death was final. That's the way the program worked. It wasn't until the disciples saw the empty tomb that they finally "believed" and understood "the Scriptures that said Jesus must rise from the dead" (John 20:9).

Suddenly, Old Testament passages such as Psalm 16:10, which predicted Christ's death and resurrection, made sense. Weeks after Resurrection Sunday, on the day known as Pentecost, Peter quoted that very passage to a crowd in Jerusalem as he testified to the dramatic turn of events surrounding Jesus (Acts 2:22-32).

Speaking of His own impending death, Jesus said, "I tell you the truth, unless a kernel of wheat is planted in the soil and dies, it remains alone. But its death will produce many new kernels" (John 12:24). In other words, death is the way to life.

Yes, it's a paradox that death can be an unlikely route to life and joy. Only Jesus could lay down His life "as a ransom for many" (Matthew 20:28). Our path to experiencing His life involves daily crucifying anything that would lead away from Him.

Lord, help us to see what needs to die in us so that Your life can be our all.

—Jeff Olson

ultimate allegiance

read>
John 8:31-58
Are You greater than our father Abraham? He died, and so did the prophets. Who do You think You are? (v.53).

more>
- John 3:30
- 1 Corinthians 1:12-13
- 1 Corinthians 3:4-11

next>
Which religious heroes are you prone to idolize? How have your thoughts, words, and actions revolved around them rather than around Jesus?

Read the first 8 chapters of the gospel of John and you get the distinct impression that inaccurate views of two men—Moses and Abraham—stood in the way of many first-century Jews believing in Jesus. For instance:

- *Jesus heals a lame man on the Sabbath* (5:8-10). The Pharisees charge Jesus with breaking the Mosaic Law (vv.10,16,18). Moses remained their authority even though the Lord of the Sabbath had come (Luke 6:5).
- *Jesus calls the Jews to believe in Him* (John 6:29). "Show us a miraculous sign," they reply. Moses had given them manna from heaven—"What can you do?" (vv.30-31). They clung to the bread of Moses when the "bread of life" was right there (vv.32-36).
- *Jesus calls for followers whom He will set free* (8:31-32). "But we are descendants of Abraham," the people reply. "We have never been slaves to anyone" and so need no release (v.33).
- *"Anyone who obeys My teaching will never die!" Jesus says a few moments later* (v.51). "Are You greater than our father Abraham?" the Jews retort (v.53).

In case after case, misinterpretation and misunderstanding of Moses and Abraham blurred their vision to the One to whom these very heroes were pointing (5:46). Did you catch that? The two men were not the problem—Jesus commended their examples (8:39). But the inaccurate view of any religious hero can keep us from accurately seeing Jesus.

Who are your religious heroes? Lutherans might say Martin Luther. Methodists might say John Wesley. Reformed folks might say John Calvin. How many theological battles have been fought between the modern-day followers of each? When others are raised as ultimate heroes, Jesus is eclipsed.

Christian leaders are God's gift to us (Ephesians 4:7-13), but wholehearted devotion belongs to Jesus alone. —Sheridan Voysey

help the weak

read>
1 Thessalonians 5:12-28
Brothers and sisters, we urge you to warn those who are lazy. Encourage those who are timid. Take tender care of those who are weak. Be patient with everyone (v.14).

more>
I have been a constant example of how you can help those in need by working hard. You should remember the words of the Lord Jesus: "It is more blessed to give than to receive" (Acts 20:35).

next>
What struggling person in your life will you help today? When you assist the weak, how does that reflect the heart of Jesus?

On April 25, 2003, 13-year-old Natalie Gilbert was singing the United States National Anthem for a National Basketball Association (NBA) playoff game. Shortly into the song, nerves got the best of young Gilbert and she completely blanked on the words. That's when "Mo" Cheeks, the coach of the Portland Trail Blazers, intervened.

Even though Cheeks couldn't carry a tune in a bucket, he quickly came alongside the struggling youngster and helped her finish the song. Before it was over, all of the players and fans joined in to pull her through. Later, the relieved singer commented, "He totally saved me . . . I tried to start over again, but the words wouldn't come."

As I watched "Mo" Cheeks and the others come to her aid, it reminded me of the kind of help Paul had in mind when he wrote, "Share each other's burdens, and in this way obey the law of Christ" (Galatians 6:2).

As he wrapped up his first of two letters to the church of Thessalonica, Paul reiterated this same idea to his readers: "Take tender care of those who are weak" (1 Thessalonians 5:14).

Those who are weak and floundering are in need of help. And those who are in a position of strength have an opportunity to help. So when you see someone struggling under a heavy load, be open to intervene with whatever resources God has given you. Lend a hand. Offer a shoulder to cry on. Help a neighbor finish a project, or pay a bill for a friend who lost his job.

Helping out those in a weakened state is a powerful way to share Christ with others. Come alongside and sing along with them! —Jeff Olson

learning to be content

read>
Philippians 4:11-19
So if we have enough food and clothing, let us be content (1 Timothy 6:8).

more>
Be satisfied with what you have. For God has said, "I will never fail you. I will never abandon you." So we can say with confidence, "The Lord is my helper, so I will have no fear. What can mere people do to me?" (Hebrews 13:5-6).

next>
What has God been teaching you about contentment? What ends contentment?

For nearly a year, I was disturbed by a passage in Philippians in which the apostle Paul claims to possess unwavering contentment. "I have learned how to be content with whatever I have," Paul said, adding, "I know how to live on almost nothing or with everything. I have learned the secret of living in every situation, whether it is with a full stomach or empty, with plenty or little" (Philippians 4:11-12)

Night after night I'd lie awake comparing myself with Paul, my friends, and other believers. Each time, I felt like an utter failure—a pathetic, impostor Christian. While no storm, beating, or prison term could rattle Paul's contentment; all it took to bring me down was a little bad weather or a slow day at work.

If I'm really a new person in Christ, I wondered, why am I so easily dissatisfied? Why can't I embrace challenges instead of concluding in the midst of them that God is neglecting me?

Perhaps one of the most freeing moments in my Christian journey came the night I was fretting over Philippians 4:11, and a phrase—that I hadn't paid much attention to before—jumped out at me: "I have learned . . . ."

It was then that I grasped that Paul didn't achieve lasting contentment the instant he entered into his relationship with Christ. To the contrary, Paul reached a state of steady contentment only after a lengthy and excruciating learning process.

Like Paul, you and I can achieve increased contentment by drawing upon Jesus' power and strength (v.13) and depending on God's perfect provision (v.19). As we become more and more satisfied with what God has given us, we'll be able to say with confidence that the Lord is our helper in all situations. We will become *content.* —Roxanne Robbins

no condemnation

read>
Romans 7:25–8:1
So now there is no condemnation for those who belong to Christ Jesus (8:1).

more>
- John 3:17-18,36
- John 5:24
- Ephesians 2:1-10

next>
Since your good performance didn't secure your salvation and your failure can't cause you to lose your salvation, why should you live differently? How will you praise God this day for His "no condemnation" proclamation?

The Thirteenth Amendment that abolished slavery in the United States was ratified by the necessary number of states on December 6, 1865. So, how many slaves were there in the US on December 7? Technically, there were none. Although the law had been passed, there were many who did not know the truth and continued to live like slaves. There were many others who knew they were free but doubted the reality of their freedom.

This seems to be true of many believers in Jesus today. An "amendment of freedom" has been passed by the death of Jesus, but many doubt the reality of their freedom and continue to live like slaves to sin. This is precisely what Paul spoke of in Romans 8.

He begins the chapter with "So now," a phrase that referred to the earlier themes of Romans: freedom from sin, justification by faith alone, friendship with God, and assurance of salvation and eternal life—all which were achieved through Christ.

Paul reminded his readers, "There is no condemnation for those who belong to Christ Jesus" (v.1). This means that there is absolutely no eternal punishment or estrangement for those who place their trust in the finished work of Jesus. Their sins are forgiven and covered. The war is over and they are no longer enemies of God. No accusation against them will stand. In this verse, Paul communicated that we're no longer condemned under the penalty of sin, and there's no condemnation or peril that could ever separate us from the love of Christ (vv.31-39).

At times, sin and failure cause us to doubt the reality of the freedom that Jesus has provided for us. Let's remember that He alone has secured and sustained our salvation. It's all about Him, not our performance. —Marvin Williams

handle with care

read>
2 Timothy 3:10-17
You have been taught the holy Scriptures from childhood, and they have given you the wisdom to receive the salvation that comes by trusting in Christ Jesus (v.15).

more>
Put on salvation as your helmet, and take the sword of the Spirit, which is the Word of God (Ephesians 6:17).

next>
What do you enjoy the most about studying the Bible? When it comes to using God's Word, in what areas do you feel intimidated or inadequate? What will it take to increase your confidence?

Various vacations have taught me that jet skis and boulders don't go together. Neither do 3-wheelers and thin ice.

My motorized mishaps began when, as a kid, my family spent the afternoon visiting friends. Willing to accommodate my need for speed, their son let me use his go-cart. He showed me the gas pedal but assumed I would find the brake. So when my friend and I realized we were headed for the highway at full throttle, we jumped off to avoid crashing into any cars. *Ouch!* It's so important to be properly trained in how to use expensive recreation vehicles!

Much more important than just a means of entertainment, the Word of God is both a weapon and a tool. Just as a soldier is trained to use his weapons in battle and a builder learns how to use his tools, believers in Jesus must be trained in how to handle the Word.

In recounting the temptation of Jesus, Matthew demonstrates how even Satan used Scripture (4:1-11). Manipulative, the enemy was interested in his own selfish purposes and not in truth. Because God is serious about His Word, we need to understand:

- Keeping our hearts pure before the Lord enables us to receive instruction from the Holy Spirit (Proverbs 4:23; Matthew 5:8).
- Wielding the sword includes accepting our inability to know everything, while being willing to learn (1 Timothy 4:12-16).
- Learning how to handle the Word develops us as people who are unashamed and ready to share it (2 Timothy 2:15, 4:2-4).

Scripture tells us that in the end days, deception will grow stronger (Mark 13:22). God wants us to be master swordsmen, trained and ready to communicate His truth. Let's do what it takes to learn. —Regina Franklin

no looking back

read >
Luke 9:51-62
Anyone who puts a hand to the plow and then looks back is not fit for the kingdom of God (v.62).

more >
Jesus said to His disciples, "If any of you wants to be My follower, you must turn from your selfish ways, take up your cross, and follow Me" (Matthew 16:24).

next >
What does it mean to follow Jesus with no looking back? How does His example inspire you?

During World War I, Oswald Chambers came to a crossroads. Should he continue to oversee the Bible Training College he had started, or go where God was leading—to serve and minister among the British troops in Egypt? The man whose teachings and insights are found in *My Utmost for His Highest* chose to follow God. He wrote, "I give it up because I believe I do so in answer to Thy call." Oswald Chambers never looked back. He went and selflessly served God for 2 years in Egypt, until a ruptured appendix led to his death at age 43.

Jesus was in Galilee when He made a "no looking back" decision to make the 3-day journey to Jerusalem. He "resolutely set out" for the city (Luke 9:51), knowing that opposition from Samaritans (who were hostile to the Jews) would make for a thorny trek to Jerusalem—the city where He would ultimately be crucified on a cross. His mission to provide salvation for all who would believe in Him had to be accomplished (Romans 3:25-26).

As He made His way along the dusty roads, Jesus called out to a man, "Come, follow Me" (Luke 9:59). He says the same thing to you and me today. The decision to follow Him is the most important decision we will make, for it leads to eternal life. Without His salvation, we're destined to eternal suffering in hell (Matthew 10:28). When we follow Jesus, we experience "a rich and satisfying life" in Him (John 10:10). But it is also a life, like Jesus' own experience on earth, that will likely be filled with opposition and great difficulty.

Jesus said that a person must leave it all behind to follow Him. "Anyone who puts a hand to the plow and then looks back is not fit for the kingdom of God" (Luke 9:62). Let's follow Him today and not look back. —Tom Felten

groundhog day

read>
Ecclesiastes 1:1-10
Whenever we have the opportunity, we should do good to everyone—especially to those in the family of faith (Galatians 6:10).

more>
- Galatians 6:9-10
- Hebrews 13:15-16
- 1 Peter 3:10-17

next>
Complete this sentence: My purpose in life is ________________.
What's one good deed you can do for a colleague, friend, or neighbor this week?

Groundhog Day, one of my favorite movies, is a comedy featuring Phil Connors, a self-centered, arrogant TV weatherman. After being forced to take on a much-hated assignment—covering the annual Groundhog Day event in Punxsutawney—he suddenly finds himself caught in a time loop, repeating the same day over and over again. At first, he pursues every hedonistic escape he can think of. But eventually he begins to reevaluate his priorities, to better himself, and to think of others' needs.

Thousands of years earlier, Solomon had carefully observed the circular repetition of human activity. The sun rises, you wake up, have breakfast, send the kids to school, and then off to work you go. Many hours later, you leave the office and come home. And you repeat the same routine over and over again. For some people, this routine couldn't be more mundanely repetitive and monotonous. The endless cycle never produces anything "truly new" (Ecclesiastes 1:9). In frustration, Solomon concludes: "Everything is meaningless, completely meaningless" (v.2).

Like Phil Connors, we need to reexamine our life and priorities. Instead of seeing himself as a prisoner of life's repetitive cycles, Connors began to use his knowledge of how the day would unfold to help people. Knowing that a child would fall from a tree at a certain time, he made it a point to be there and catch the child every time. He befriended a dying, homeless man. In helping others, he found meaning and purpose in life.

We too can find purpose and meaning in life. Who is one person we can help today? Solomon advises "I know that there is nothing better for men than to be happy and do good while they live" (Ecclesiastes 3:12 NIV). Life may be monotonous at times. But it is never without purpose or meaning. —K.T. Sim

adoption option

read>
Matthew 5:13-16
In the same way, let your good deeds shine out for all to see, so that everyone will praise your heavenly Father (v.16).

more>
Be careful to live properly among your unbelieving neighbors. Then even if they accuse you of doing wrong, they will see your honorable behavior, and they will give honor to God (1 Peter 2:12).

next>
If you can't adopt a child, perhaps you can provide prayer, financial, and family support to those who do. What will you do today for needy orphans?

In his *Apology* (AD 197), Tertullian argued that the Roman government should stop persecuting its best citizens. He said that Christians not only prayed for the emperor and the empire, but they also sacrificed for the sake of their neighbors. He said they pooled their money "to feed the poor and to bury them; for boys and girls who lack property and parents; and then for slaves grown old and ship-wrecked mariners; and any who may be in mines, islands, or prisons." They didn't use their cash to fund lavish banquets as the Romans did.

This "trust fund of piety" was so successful that when a new emperor named Julian the Apostate wanted to return Rome to its pre-Constantinian, pagan ways a century and a half later, he discovered that paganism had been thoroughly discredited by the charity of the Christians. Julian complained that he could not turn people from the Christian faith when "the impious Galileans [Christians] support not only their own poor but ours as well."

A similar opportunity exists today. James 1:27 states, "Pure and genuine religion in the sight of God the Father means caring for orphans and widows in their distress." Christians are rightly known for opposing abortion. What if we were also known for supporting adoption?

What would happen if our churches were lovers of orphans; if our church directories were as diverse as the world; if we made disciples of all nations in part by adopting their most at-risk members; and if mothers considering abortion chose life because they knew they could give their child to any number of Christian homes?

We would be imitators of God, who has adopted us into His family, and we would generate praise from non-Christians who witness our good works. They just might become followers of Jesus; but if not, they would at least understand why someone would. —Mike Wittmer

real success

read >
2 Chronicles 26:4-16
As long as the king sought guidance from the Lord, God gave him success (v.5).

more >
Remember the Lord your God. He is the one who gives you power to be successful, in order to fulfill the covenant He confirmed to your ancestors with an oath (Deuteronomy 8:18).

next >
What does success look like from God's perspective? How can you guard against pride?

Not long ago, one of my good friends was at the Cannes Film Festival with her husband. Their film had been nominated for the prestigious Golden Camera award. Another close friend was named number 6 in the Top 10 Copywriters in the World as presented in "The Big Won" (a survey of the world's best marketing communicators as measured by the quantity and quality of awards won). Wow!

Depending on the Bible version you use, the word *success* appears around 50 times in the Scriptures. Several Bible verses reveal that it isn't wrong to ask God for success. For example, we read in Psalm 90:17, "May the Lord our God show us His approval and make our efforts successful."

God wants us to take pleasure in our achievements. It's a gift from Him, for His glory (Ecclesiastes 5:18-19). However, we need to keep an eye on our ego. Just ask King Uzziah. In 2 Chronicles 26:6-15, we read of his impressive achievements. But the reason for his success is found in verse 5: "As long as the king sought guidance from the Lord, God gave him success."

Uzziah forgot, however, that God was the One who had helped and blessed him all along. This led to his destruction. God's Word puts it plainly: "But when he had become powerful, he also became proud, which led to his downfall" (v.16).

Think about it: Who gave you the skills that have allowed you to experience success? Perhaps you've worked hard. But others have tried just as hard and didn't make the grade. This leads to the realization that God deserves the credit for any success that comes our way. Let's celebrate Him and remain humble when we taste success. —Poh Fang Chia

lost

read>
Jeremiah 50:1-10
My people have been lost sheep (v.6).

more>
I am the way (John 14:6).

next>
Where do you feel most lost right now? How is Jesus asking you to look to Him to be your way "home"?

Soon after Charles Lindbergh completed his monumental transatlantic flight in the *Spirit of St. Louis,* the US Ambassador to Mexico asked Lindbergh to make another flight in order to foster positive US-Mexico relations. Taking off from Washington DC on December 13, 1927, Lindbergh began the 24-hour flight to Mexico City. After navigating through dense fog, Lindbergh lost his bearings. With only land markings and a makeshift map, he flew low, attempting to follow road signs. However, he was confused by the repeated signs that read, *Caballeros.* How could so many towns have identical names? Eventually, he determined that the signs were for *men's restrooms.* Embarrassed, Lindbergh finally found his way.

All of us have been lost at one time or another. Our marriage may be in shambles or our career may be a mess. All of us have faced (or will face) seasons when we either can't see any signs pointing the way forward—or when the signs we're following seem to lead nowhere.

On multiple occasions, Israel was lost, adrift from God's intent for them. Worse, their spiritual leaders were the ones leading them in the wrong direction. "Their shepherds have led them astray," Jeremiah said. Their situation seemed irreparable: They "have lost their way and can't remember how to get back" (50:6). Thankfully, God never abandons His people. He never leaves us groping in despair or without hope. God declared that Israel's dire predicament was not the last word. The people will return home "seeking the Lord their God" (v.4).

We start to find our way whenever our heart begins to yearn again for our God, for our true home. Our "way" forward isn't actually a direction, but a Person: Jesus. —Winn Collier

an indifferent spouse?

read>
2 Timothy 2:11-13
If we are unfaithful, He remains faithful, for He cannot deny who He is (v.13).

In the film *The Painted Veil,* an unhappily married couple—Walter and Kitty Fane—trek into China's rural Guangxi Province where cholera is decimating the locals. Their visit is hardly altruistic. Walter has caught Kitty in an affair and this trip is her punishment.

While Walter, a bacteriologist, fights the disease, Kitty offers her services to the Catholic-run hospital. One day the nun overseeing the hospital speaks of her own troubled "marriage": "I fell in love when I was 17—with God," she says. "Over the years my feelings have changed. He's disappointed me. Ignored me. Over the years we've settled into a relationship of peaceful indifference."

Surrounded by cholera and feeling disappointed by God, the nun vows faithfulness. A honorable stand?

A young pastor named Timothy once faced his own hardships. His church was being persecuted, some of his church leaders were teaching falsely (1 Timothy 1:3), his confidence was shaky (4:12-16), and his mentor was imprisoned (2 Timothy 1:8). So the apostle Paul sent him some song lyrics as encouragement (2:11-13). The song unequivocally calls for perseverance (v.12). Like the nun in *The Painted Veil,* Timothy was called to stay with God when the joys of faith dissipated.

But Paul adds a vital point: God is faithful to us when we disappoint Him (v.13). The God who faithfully helps us persevere (1 Corinthians 1:8-9), fight temptation (10:13), and face spiritual attack (2 Thessalonians 3:3), is by very nature faithful (Exodus 34:6).

The nun's comments ring with pride—painting the picture of a faithful follower who abides when the moody God ignores her. The apostle Paul challenges this theology. God is no indifferent heavenly spouse, but a Lover who cannot be anything but faithful to us—His bride. —Sheridan Voysey

more>
Your unfailing love, O Lord, is as vast as the heavens; Your faithfulness reaches beyond the clouds (Psalm 36:5).

next>
When have you felt most disappointed with God? How has God shown His faithfulness to you, even when you were unfaithful to Him?

godly wisdom

read>
James 3:13-18
But the wisdom from above is first of all pure. It is also peace loving, gentle at all times, and willing to yield to others. It is full of mercy and good deeds. It shows no favoritism and is always sincere (v.17).

more>
God has made the wisdom of this world look foolish. Since God in His wisdom saw to it that the world would never know Him through human wisdom, He has used our foolish preaching to save those who believe (1 Corinthians 1:20-21).

next>
Which type of wisdom do you exhibit the most—godly or ungodly? What do you need to do to live out the wisdom of God?

Yogi Berra, former Major League Baseball player and manager, demonstrated the linguistic gymnastics that earned him eight entries in *Bartlett's Familiar Quotations,* when he addressed graduates at Montclair State University with these gems: "First, never give up, because it ain't over 'til it's over." "When you come to a fork in the road, take it." "Remember that whatever you do in life, 90 percent of it is half mental." How's that for some confusing common wisdom?

James, the brother of Jesus was one of the most prominent leaders in the early church. Under the power of the Holy Spirit, he demonstrated his writing skills and uncommon wisdom when he penned 5 chapters in the greatest book in the world—the Bible. In chapter 3, James defined two types of wisdom—spiritual and godly; unspiritual and ungodly. According to verses 14-16, being bitterly jealous and selfish is the epitome of being unwise. James' readers would have understood what his words meant: Having ill will toward others, creating cliques, measuring yourself by your own standards, and denying what God says about you are all characteristics of an ungodly and a devil-motivated wisdom.

In verses 17-18, James presents some characteristics of godly wisdom: walking in integrity with God and others (purity); refusing to awaken and incite anger in other people (peace loving, planting seeds of peace); valuing and accepting other people's feelings, opinions, and suggestions (gentle, yielding to others); forgiving others' mistakes and sins (merciful); and being transparent about my weaknesses (sincerity).

Jesus is the wisdom of God (1 Corinthians 1:30). When we stay connected to Him (John 15:5), His values and very life will be formed in us and His wisdom—from above—will flow through us. —Marvin Williams

divine tripping

read>
2 Chronicles 25:1-9
If you let them go with your troops into battle, you will be defeated by the enemy no matter how well you fight. God will overthrow you, for He has the power to help you or to trip you up (v.8).

more>
No discipline is enjoyable while it is happening—it's painful! But afterward there will be a peaceful harvest of right living for those who are trained in this way (Hebrews 12:11).

next>
Where has God tripped you up? How will you respond to His loving discipline?

In 2 Chronicles 25 we read about the reign of King Amaziah, the twelfth king of Judah who took over the throne after his father was assassinated. For the most part, Amaziah was a good king who "did what was pleasing in the Lord's sight" (vv.1-2).

As he worked to restore order to his country, the king assembled an army among the men of Judah. He also hired the services of an additional 100,000 soldiers from Israel for a serious pile of silver—3¾ tons to be exact (v.6). Before going off to war, however, an unnamed "man of God" warned Amaziah not to let the hired troops fight with Judah because the Lord was no longer with Israel. So, no matter how bravely his men would battle, Judah would ultimately lose because God has the "power to help you or to trip you up" (v.8).

Breaking the coalition with the soldiers from Israel was complicated. The new king had invested a lot to enlist their services, but it was an unholy alliance. So rather than wait for God to topple his house of cards, he cut his losses—trusting that God could make up for much more than he had invested (v.9).

There's a lot to take away from this story, but what sticks with me is that—when necessary—God will "trip" us up. In other words, He can disrupt any unholy alliance that threatens to undo us.

Now, God is not out to ruin us. But He will destroy what could ruin us. So when it seems as if God isn't cooperating with your agenda, consider the possibility that He's trying to save you from *yourself*. Sometimes He mercifully frustrates our best-laid plans for own good. —Jeff Olson

pushed away

read>
Galatians 6:1-10
Share each other's burdens, and in this way obey the law of Christ (v.2).

more>
Cursed are those who put their trust in mere humans. . . . But blessed are those who trust in the Lord and have made the Lord their hope and confidence (Jeremiah 17:5,7).

next>
How have you been too dependent on people? What happens when we place our security in another person and not in God?

I don't remember exactly how old I was, but it was a moment I've never forgotten. Cooling off after a hot summer day, my family had gone swimming at a friend's house. Because I didn't know how to swim, I was trying to maneuver the water wearing a life jacket that awkwardly grazed my chin. Looking for security, I lunged for my mom as she swam by. When my fearful grasps took her under, she pushed me away to catch her breath. Upset, I didn't understand what she knew—the life jacket would keep me afloat.

As the body of Christ, we're called to be in relationship with one another. Galatians 6:2 tells us, "Share each other's burdens, and in this way obey the law of Christ." But, in our humanity, we often reach for the tangible person next to us rather than depending on God—our Creator—to sustain us. An unhealthy dependence on another person can stifle us spiritually.

We may convince ourselves that we can't go forward without others—always needing someone with us or needing another person's approval. But this leads to a spiral of hopelessness and away from our security in God. For when we seek ultimate safety in another person, we're trusting in someone just as full of faults as we are. Psalm 146:3 states: "Don't put your confidence in powerful people; there is no help for you there."

We won't fully depend on Jesus when we're holding on to others. Proverbs 29:25 says, "Fearing people is a dangerous trap, but trusting the Lord means safety." Restoring our relationship with God, Jesus was "beaten so we could be whole" (Isaiah 53:5). When it comes to finding our sense of security, the cross should be the first and only place we look. —Regina Franklin

tattoos aren't new

read>
Romans 6:1-11
We are no longer slaves to sin (v.6).

more>
Those who have been born into God's family do not make a practice of sinning, because God's life is in them. So they can't keep on sinning, because they are children of God (1 John 3:9).

next>
How well are you living out your identity as a slave of Jesus and no longer a slave to sin? What needs to change?

You might think that tattoos are a recent phenomenon. Not true. The ancient Romans would tattoo (or brand) slaves and criminals. Later, during the fourth century AD a Christian sect called the Montanists tattooed themselves as slaves of God (Revelation 7:2-3). And Coptic Christians have been tattooing crosses and other symbols on their hands for more than 1,200 years. Many Coptic (Egyptian) Christian villagers still sport cross tattoos today. For them, the tattoo reflects their commitment to Jesus, whose scars will forever be reminders of His sacrifice for us (John 20:19-28).

Paul, in Romans 6, reveals what should be the mark of a true believer in Jesus today. "We are no longer slaves to sin," he wrote (v.6). Unlike the slaves branded by the Romans, giving them a permanent identity as a criminal, believers in Jesus choose to be "a slave of Christ Jesus" (1:1). Jesus transforms us from the inside out and calls us to "live new lives" that show "we were set free from the power of sin" (6:7).

As we turn from sin and embrace the holy life to which Christ calls us, we bring glory to Him and present a picture of what Christianity is all about. Paul put it this way: "We know that our old sinful selves were crucified with Christ so that sin might lose its power in our lives" (v.6).

Whether or not tattoos of a cross are a good idea may be a disputable matter. But all of us who are true believers in Jesus will reveal our faith in Him by turning from sin. He has broken the power of sin over us, setting us free to live "for the glory of God" (v.10).

You don't have to get a tattoo to show your faith. A life of pure devotion to Jesus, radiating His power to resist sin, will show the world you belong to Him. —Tom Felten

crashing down

read>
Obadiah 1:1-21
"You have been deceived by your own pride. . . . I will bring you crashing down," says the Lord (vv.3-4).

more>
- Proverbs 15:25
- James 4:6

next>
How has your position and power, like Edom's, given you a false sense of security and invulnerability? How will you humble yourself before God this week?

Years ago, Charles Haddon Spurgeon wrote in *Sermons on Sovereignty*: "There are two sins of man that are bred in the bone, and that continually come out in the flesh. One is self-dependence and the other is self-exaltation. It is very hard, even for the best of men, to keep themselves from the first error. The holiest of Christians, and those who understand best the gospel of Christ, find in themselves a constant inclination to look to the power of the creature, instead of looking to the power of God and the power of God alone."

Hundreds of years after Esau and Jacob's birthday, God expressed His holy anger and condemnation toward the Edomites' pride (Obadiah 1:1-2). They had attacked the Judeans during the Babylonian crisis, instead of assisting them (vv.10-14). They delighted in bringing disaster to God's people. This greatly displeased God. He also condemned their pride of heart that made them think they were indestructible (v.3).

The Edomites lived in the mountainous region east of the Arabah, with elevations up to 5,000 feet above sea level. Their inaccessible location had given them a false sense of security and feeling of invulnerability. The sins of self-dependence and self-exaltation were bred in their bones and were continually coming out in their words and actions. Edom asked a rhetorical question: "Who can ever reach us way up here?" The Lord answered: "I will bring you crashing down" (v.4).

God still opposes the proud and arrogant. Every human effort at self-security will ultimately fail and be made small before God. What God desires from His people is humility—an attitude of submission and obedience, grounded in the acknowledgment of our true needy status before Him.

—Marvin Williams

saved to sin?

read>
1 Corinthians 6:15-20
You do not belong to yourself, for God bought you with a high price. So you must honor God with your body (vv.19-20).

more>
- Psalm 74:2
- Romans 6:15-18
- Revelation 5:9-10

next>
The Lord Jesus Christ wants to restore every aspect of what we think, choose, feel, and do. What area of your life still needs saving? Commit it to Him now.

A Christian leader accepted my invitation to deliver an address at the seminary where I teach. During his talk, the preacher distinguished between goodness as moral purity and goodness as acts of service. He illustrated the difference by saying that if you resist going into a pornographic shop, that is moral purity, and if you give five dollars to a panhandler, that is an act of service.

When I wrote to thank him for his speech, I jokingly asked whether giving five dollars to a panhandler is really an act of kindness, or have you just bought that fellow a drink? The man responded in kind, saying that Jesus healed a blind man without wondering whether he would use his newfound sight to look lustfully at women.

He intended it as a joke, but it made me think. I had never considered what it would have been like to be tempted in the very area that had been healed by Jesus. *Would a former blind man think twice before using his redeemed sight to sin?* If I were that person, I think I would.

Then it struck me that I am that blind man. Augustine wrote that our sin natures were as broken as the traveler on his way to Jericho who was beaten by robbers and left for dead (Luke 10:30). And as that helpless man was rescued by the Good Samaritan, so also our corrupted wills have been restored by Jesus.

Just as it would be unthinkably inappropriate for that rescued victim to launch an attack on Samaritans, or a healed blind man to use his restored sight to lust, or a former mute to use her tongue to slander others, so it is wrong for us to use any redeemed part of our body for sin. "You were bought at a price," says Paul. "Therefore honor God with your body" (1 Corinthians 6:20 NIV). —Mike Wittmer

chutzpah

read>
Matthew 15:21-28
"Dear woman," Jesus said to her, "your faith is great. Your request is granted." And her daughter was instantly healed (v.28).

more>
- Matthew 7:7-11
- Luke 18:1-8
- 1 Thessalonians 5:17

next>
How have you demonstrated your faith through chutzpah in prayer lately? What prayers have you seen answered as you've persisted in calling on God?

When I was growing up, my father kept one can of WD-40 in the house and another in his car. It seemed it was the be-all and end-all for almost every mechanical problem. But what is WD-40? It literally stands for Water Displacement 40th attempt.

In 1953, chemist Norm Larsen was attempting to concoct a formula to prevent corrosion—a task which is accomplished by displacing water. Larsen's unyielding tenacity and persistence paid off when he perfected the formula on his 40th try.

Matthew introduces us to a Gentile woman who had this same kind of persistence. Her daughter was violently and cruelly demon-possessed (15:21). She had no hope of ever seeing her daughter normal again, until she heard that Jesus was in town. She had heard about Jesus' power and the miracles He had worked in the lives of others, and she believed He could help her too. So she approached Jesus boldly and persevered with unyielding tenacity, even when everything and everybody seemed to be against her. Her race, religious background, gender, the disciples, Satan, and even Jesus seemed to be against her (v.24).

Despite these seeming obstacles, she did not give up, but pushed her way through the dark corridors of her desperate need. She had *chutzpah* (khoot-spuh), a Jewish/Hebrew word for headstrong persistence, unyielding tenacity, bold determination, and raw nerve. Jesus complimented her chutzpah and rewarded her faith by healing her daughter (v.28).

Sometimes we pray, and if we don't get an answer the first time, we give up. That's not chutzpah! Chutzpah is having the raw belief, the deep trust, and the confident hope to be persistent with God, believing that He is good, just, and loving, and that He desires what's best for us. —Marvin Williams

buyer's remorse

read>
Genesis 3:1-7
At that moment their eyes were opened, and they suddenly felt shame at their nakedness (v.7).

more>
Christ made us right with God; He made us pure and holy, and He freed us from sin (1 Corinthians 1:30).

next>
What lies of the world have you bought into? How will you live out the righteousness of Jesus today?

Have you ever experienced buyer's remorse? I have. I wonder why I buy half the clothes hanging in my closet.

Just prior to making a purchase, I feel the positive emotions that come with getting something new. Afterwards, having bought the item, a wave of remorse crashes over me. I become more aware of the negative aspects of my shopping.

In Genesis 3, history's first buyer's remorse is recorded. The whole thing began with the crafty serpent and his sales pitch. He persuaded Eve to doubt God's Word. She even ends up misquoting what God had said to her and Adam: "You must not eat it or even touch it; if you do, you will die" (v.3). Allen Ross in *The Bible Knowledge Commentary* writes, "Either Eve did not know God's command very well or did not want to remember it."

Satan then capitalized on the waffling woman's uncertainty by casting doubt on God's character. He mixed the truth with a lie to make it more palatable.

So Eve ate. Adam ate. And sin entered the world. But the first man and woman got more than they bargained for. Their eyes were opened all right, but they didn't become "like God" (v.5). In fact, their first act as enlightened sinners was to hide from God (vv.7-8).

This account in Genesis 3 teaches us that sin has dire consequences. It always keeps us from God's best. Because of His grace, however, Genesis 3 is filled with more than just bad news. For God took innocent animals and shed their blood. He clothed Adam and Eve in garments made from the animals' skins.

This was a foreshadowing of what Jesus Christ would do for us by dying on the cross for our sins. His blood was shed so that we might be clothed with His righteousness—with no buyer's remorse! —Poh Fang Chia

so we may live

read>
Deuteronomy 30:1-10
So that you will love Him with all your heart and soul and so you may live! (v.6).

more>
Live in a way that pleases [God], and love Him and serve Him with all your heart and soul (Deuteronomy 10:12).

next>
Are you merely surviving or truly living? What changes do you need to make in order to embrace God's plan for you to live well?

"We decided we had to move or freeze to death." Eleven-year old Norman Ollestad uttered these harrowing words to a newspaper reporter soon after being rescued in the San Gabriel Mountains. The small Cessna plane he had been traveling in had smashed into one of the range's jagged peaks. Norman was the lone survivor—his dad and the pilot died immediately, his dad's girlfriend a bit later. Norman's book *Crazy for the Storm: A Memoir of Survival* recounts the remarkable tale.

While the crash was center stage, Ollestad's story is about more than surviving that cruel day—it's about his emerging from trauma as a man who, in the aftermath, has learned to live.

In Deuteronomy, God laid out a framework for Israel that would govern their corporate identity. He provided numerous regulations about their diet and their worship and the way they would govern themselves. Underlying it all, however, was the subtext of God preparing them for the long days when they would be in foreign lands and under foreign rule. Whenever they would find themselves "living among the nations," God knew it would be vitally important for Israel to be able to survive, to maintain their unique identity and their unique story and purpose (30:1).

However, these structures and instructions were about much more than mere holding themselves together. God intended this way of life to guide them into (or at times return them to) a deep love for Him. And this love for God was not a technique to help them merely survive, but an invitation to life—to experience the joy and bounty of all God would give them (v.6).

God's kind intentions toward us are more delightful than we can imagine. His plan is for us to live well, taking deep pleasure in all the goodness He provides.

—Winn Collier

the source of life

read>
Matthew 11:25-30
Then Jesus said, "Come to Me, all of you who are weary and carry heavy burdens, and I will give you rest" (v.28).

more>
No one has ever seen God. But the unique One, who is Himself God, is near to the Father's heart. He has revealed God to us (John 1:18).

next>
If you knew Michele, how would you respond to her comments? Have you allowed any "rituals and recitations" to get in the way of your relationship with God?

An Amazon message board comment caught my attention. "I have a zillion books in my library," Michele said in a discussion on New Age spirituality, "books on the Kabbalah, Golden Dawn books, The Zohar, books on the Tetragrammaton, Ernest Holmes books, Dalai Lama books, Ascension books, Christian Science books, Theosophical books, and on and on." Michele's vast reading left her confused. "I couldn't assemble [their teachings] into a bottom line if my life depended on it. If the ultimate communion with Source relies somehow on endless ritual and recitation, all is lost to me."

Michele longed to commune with the "Source"—with God—but felt disheartened by the contradictory teachings her mystical authors gave about how to do so. She was weary. Burdened.

Jesus addressed people like Michele. Many years before He came to earth, another Jesus—Jesus ben Sira—had called people to find soul rest by taking on the "yoke" of the Jewish Law through study and reflection (Ecclesiasticus 51:23-27). By Christ's time, legalistic teachers had distorted that Law, adding long lists of rules to it. This "yoke" (originally a device worn on the shoulders to make a load easier to carry) now crushed the faithful (Matthew 23:4). The people longed for God, but were burdened with "rituals and recitations."

Jesus gave an extraordinary invitation to these weary folks. "Come to Me," He said. "Take My yoke upon you . . . and you will find rest for your souls" (11:28-29). With those shocking words Jesus claimed that He was the ultimate source of soul rest—not the teachers' rituals or even the Law itself.

Jesus is the ultimate source of life (John 1:4). Come to Him today.

—Sheridan Voysey

enough for me

read>
Matthew 14:13-21
They all ate as much as they wanted (v.20).

more>
- Psalm 112
- 2 Corinthians 9:6-11
- James 2:14-16

next>
Where do you struggle the most with generosity toward others? Where, this week, can you follow Jesus' example of selfless giving?

Author Peter Rollins offers a jolting retelling of Jesus' feeding of the 5,000. Rollins recounts how the swarming crowds thwarted Jesus' efforts to find solitude in a boat. As the crowds poured into this remote location, it became obvious that they needed food. The disciples could only scrounge up five loaves of bread and a few fish, Jesus miraculously multiplied the meager supplies, producing piles of food. Here Rollins turned the biblical story in a disturbing direction, concluding that "Jesus and His disciples ate like kings" and "what was miraculous . . . was that when they finished this massive banquet," there wasn't a crumb left for the starving people.

Of course, this was not at all the way the story actually ended, which is precisely Rollins' point. In the biblical telling, 5,000 men (plus women and children—probably 10- to12,000 in all) ate their fill; and with everyone stuffed, Jesus' disciples gathered up "twelve baskets of leftovers" (Matthew 14:20).

Nothing in the biblical story could be further from Rollins' parable of selfishness and greed. At the beginning of the narrative, the gospel writer Matthew noted that Jesus felt intense compassion for the throngs that overwhelmed Him (v.14). This compassion moved Him to first "heal their sick" even before He began to fill their bellies (v.14).

Rollins' ending is not intended to raise questions of Jesus—but questions of us. If we consider it scandalous that Jesus and His disciples would hoard food from the hungry crowd, do we consider it just as scandalous if we do the same?

While Jesus provided generous food for everyone, I'm often consumed with making sure there is just enough for me. I can't say I follow Jesus if I hoard God's generosity for myself. —Winn Collier

what's the purpose of sex?

Of course, sex is necessary for the propagation of the race. But while we are to "be fruitful and multiply" (Genesis 1:28), sex is not merely limited to the procreation of the human species.

Sexual intimacy is designed to reflect the beautiful mystery and intimate union between God and His people (Ephesians 5:25). God gave us sex to arouse and satisfy our innate craving for intimacy, for union (Genesis 2:24-25). A couple that enjoys emotional, relational, and spiritual intercourse with one another will be drawn to celebrate their love through sexual intimacy. That's why sexual intimacy is exclusively reserved for marriage. Sexual experiences outside of marriage mar our enjoyment of the beauty of sexual intimacy in its proper context as God intended.

The Bible describes the sexual experience within marriage as honorable (Hebrews 13:4). Some of the most beautiful erotic literature ever composed is found in the wisdom literature of the Old Testament. For some, the idea of verbally inspired erotic literature is difficult to accept. Yet God has frankly recorded for us His view of the delights of sexual intimacy between a married couple in poetic verse (Proverbs 5:15-19).

In the Song of Solomon, the husband's description of his bride's body (4:1-15) and her description of his (5:10-16) reveals the joy of love and sexual intimacy that God extols for a married couple. While sexual intimacy between a couple is not to be observed by anyone outside of the relationship, God, the One who sees and knows all, must smile with delight when He sees two of His children enjoying the good gift of sex He has given to them.

God intended sex to be far more than mere pleasurable sensations. He designed it as the intimate union of body, soul, mind, and spirit exclusively shared between a husband and wife. It's about being open, exposed, naked, and unashamed in the presence of our spouse who finds us desirable and yearns to draw close to us. That's how God captures our hearts. Being

captured by our lover will give us a taste of being caught up in Christ's love in a way that we feel deeply enjoyed without shame. In essence, sexual intimacy within marriage should draw us to deeper worship of God who initiated sexuality for His glory and our delight.

Enjoying sex with one's spouse is always to be viewed as a part of the whole marriage relationship. Sex is never to be singled out as some isolated aspect of our being that is disconnected from the rest of the relationship. Rather, sexuality is a vehicle for expressing our identity as a man or a woman made in the image of God. Sexuality pulsates throughout a godly marriage and is not exclusively reserved for the bedroom experience.

A devastating assault on our ability to enjoy sexuality is the perpetuation of the myth, "Sex is just sex. It's just another biological urge demanding satisfaction." But that's not true. God didn't make sex as a mere physical act. Whether we're willing to acknowledge it now, or we face the pain of admitting it after the fact, sex is always woven into our view of ourselves, one another, and God. Each of us distinctly reflects the image of God through the lens of our sexuality as either male or female. How we handle this good gift of sex will either enhance the glory of God's image in us or will mar that glory.

If anyone should be enjoying sexuality, Christians should. We should know better than anyone else that sex was never intended to be an end in itself. It is intended to be a joyous celebration of the intimate love that a man and woman share together in the covenant relationship called marriage. It is designed to be a reflection of the intimate love relationship between Christ and His church (Ephesians 5:25-33).

—Tim Jackson

Adapted from What's the Purpose of Sex? (Q & A) © 2009 RBC Ministries. Read more helpful articles like this one on the Web at helpformylife.org

telling the truth

read>
Exodus 20:1-17
You must not testify falsely against your neighbor (v.16).

more>
- Psalm 119:29
- Proverbs 30:8
- Ephesians 4:15,29-32

next>
In what situations are you tempted to color the truth with falsehood? In what area of your life do you need the most help in living out the ninth command? How will you let the Holy Spirit lead you in telling the truth?

Professional integrity and a commitment to excellence are the working philosophies which guide us on a daily basis." This is one of the introductory sentences from a Web site designed to provide fictional explanations, fake employment references, and verification for unexcused absences. A more accurate sentence would be "professional lying and commitment to providing false testimony are what guide us daily."

The ninth commandment was designed to protect the Israelite community from such falsehood (Exodus 20:16). When Moses said, "You must not testify falsely against your neighbor," he was telling them not to deceive a close community companion. The primary idea of "false testimony" was meant to color a situation with something other than the whole truth. The Israelites were to avoid coloring a situation with falsehood to protect themselves, such as lies that ruined reputations, half-truths, and boastful exaggerations.

The immediate context of this commandment was fairness and honesty toward those with whom we have close or even occasional contact. The basic truth of this instruction was personal integrity in our relationships. This command was so important because behind all truth we find the Lord's character, which cannot be false. Likewise, God wanted His covenant community to deal truthfully with one another. The consequences of not obeying this command were a diluted, weak community and, ultimately, God's judgment (Psalm 5:6).

How do we live out this commandment today? It begins with developing a deeper reverence for the character of God (Exodus 20:20). Our fear of God helps us to remain truthful and blameless. We must teach others to tell the truth as we submit our heart and tongue to the power and control of the Holy Spirit (Ephesians 5:18-21). —Marvin Williams

MAY 2

get up and pray

read>
Luke 22:39-46
Get up and pray, so that you will not give in to temptation (v.46).

more>
Pray in the Spirit at all times and on every occasion. Stay alert and be persistent in your prayers for all believers everywhere (Ephesians 6:18).

next>
What keeps you from praying for strength? How can you grow a daily dependence on Jesus?

"Draw strength from God—because you'll need it!" That's how I would paraphrase Luke 22:40 where Jesus told His disciples, "Pray that you will not give in to temptation." The call to pray is so urgent that Jesus repeats the plea in verse 46. The reason for this repetition is found in the warning, "so that you will not give in to temptation."

Prayer strengthens us when we face temptation. Someone said: "Lead me not into temptation—I can find it myself." We all struggle with our human tendencies and desires. Temptation stirs the blood and inflames the imagination. Only God can keep us from its charms and help us to see temptation for what it is.

The prayerlessness of the disciples is a reminder of our sinful inclination towards a lack of prayer. And in these same verses, we see also the perfect example of a prayer for strength. The Savior met the coming crisis the way He met all others—prayerfully.

Jesus called out to the Father "in such agony of spirit that His sweat fell to the ground like great drops of blood" (v.44). The words "agony of spirit" communicate the idea of wrestling. Jesus the Son wrestled with God the Father concerning the "cup" that included His unthinkable separation from the Father. It also meant accepting the full wrath of God for all sins committed by us. Jesus was tempted in His full humanity not to go to the cross.

Yet, the heart of His prayer was clear: "Your will be done." He submitted to the will of the Father. And we read, "an angel from heaven appeared and strengthened Him" (v.43). Jesus was then able to turn away from the possibility of taking the way of the crown without the dark passage of the cross. And because of His submission, we can now be redeemed, cleansed, and justified.

—Poh Fang Chia

does anyone care?

read>
Lamentations 3:19-24
The faithful love of the Lord never ends! His mercies never cease. Great is His faithfulness; His mercies begin afresh each morning (vv.22-23).

more>
- Job 38:12-13
- John 11:35
- Hebrews 4:15

next>
Thank God for three ways that He provides for you. How can you be a channel of God's love to someone today? Who is needing His love as displayed through you?

Those who have suffered severe loss often lament that their day of tragedy seemed like a normal day for everyone else. On the day they were fired, learned of their cancer, discovered their spouse was unfaithful, or held a child as she died—on that very day other people went about their business as usual. *My divorce is final! My beloved is gone!* they silently scream. *How can you go to work, eat out, and catch a movie as if nothing has changed? Don't you care?*

Worse, their disastrous day seemed normal for God as well. The sun shone, clouds rolled by, night fell, stars appeared. Doesn't God care either?

The book of Lamentations captured Jeremiah's anguished cry as he considered the suffering of his people. Life was bad. Jerusalem had been destroyed and its citizens carried off to Babylon. Those left behind had resorted to cannibalism—mothers eating their own children to survive (2:20). Jeremiah laments that his suffering "is bitter beyond words," but he grasps a glimmer of hope when he remembers that "the faithful love of the Lord never ends" and "His mercies begin afresh each morning" (3:19-23).

Actually, the Lord's mercies don't merely begin each morning, they *are* each morning. Psalm 104 praises God for faithfully tending His diverse creation. The routine events of nature—are all directed by God's powerful hand. "When You give them Your breath, life is created, and You renew the face of the earth" (v.30).

The clockwork consistency of nature on your worst day is a reminder that God cares. Take it as a sign that God loves you. He's not debilitated by His grief for you, but is preserving your life until the morning when His mercies will begin afresh. —Mike Wittmer

listening

read>
Luke 10:38-42
Mary sat at the Lord's feet, listening to what He taught (v.39).

more>
- Psalm 95:6-7
- John 10:22-30

next>
What distractions are keeping you from hearing Jesus? What do you think Jesus is saying to you right now?

Our youngest son, Seth, is very active. About the only time I've seen him still for more than a minute or two is when he's asleep. He's constantly moving, spinning, jumping, running in circles, doing cartwheels and handstands, or diving off something. One time, Seth sat on his pillow and flung himself down our stairs—riding the soft cushion like a rollercoaster—down to the first floor. Keeping his attention is nearly impossible. Most often, when I want him to hear me clearly, I have to hold his face in my hands and draw him close. "Listen," I say.

In the account Luke provides of Jesus' visit to Martha and Mary's house (10:38-39), it seems that Jesus needed to hold Martha's face in His hands and say, "Listen, please. Now! Stop and be quiet so you can hear Me and be with Me."

Martha had invited Jesus and His followers into their home, and she began to prepare a meal for them. Preparing dinner for her guests was a good thing. The Hebrew tradition at that time had much to say about welcoming strangers into your home and offering them generous hospitality. However, even good things—at the inappropriate time—become hindrances. In this case, Martha's myopic devotion to her work caused her to miss another opportunity . . . a better opportunity. "Martha was distracted by the big dinner she was preparing," Luke tells us (v.40).

Her distraction kept her from "the one thing worth being concerned about," which was listening to Jesus (v.42). For all of us, the one central thing—whether we're working or resting, filled with joy or burdened by sadness—is to hear what Jesus is saying to us. As John Ortberg says, "That one thing is the decision to live so continually in Jesus' presence as to be always covered with the dust of the Rabbi." —Winn Collier

sinners alike

read>
Romans 1:16–2:3
You may think you can condemn such people, but you are just as bad. . . . When you say they are wicked and should be punished, you are condemning yourself (2:1).

more>
A man leaves his father and mother and is joined to his wife, and the two are united into one (Genesis 2:24).

next>
How has the church at large responded to those struggling with same-sex attraction? How can God use your testimony to reach someone involved in homosexuality?

As my husband and I sat with our children watching some fireworks, two lesbian women sat nearby with their young toddlers. Expressive in their affection for each other, what they perceived as liberty, God's Word defines as bondage. I remembered a young woman I had sat with a month earlier. Listening, I grieved with her as she shared her struggles. Longing for acceptance, her wounds had led her to homosexuality.

Today's society tells us homosexuality is a normal part of being human, even defending one's sexual orientation as predesigned by God. On the other extreme, stand those who define homosexuality as a sin more egregious than others.

While Paul teaches that sexual sin affects our bodies differently than other sins (1 Corinthians 6:18), any standard different from God's brings spiritual death.

Spiritual bondage to sin ensues anytime we choose to follow our flesh instead of what God has commanded in Scripture. If we worship the created over the Creator, we will live contrary to God's design (Romans 1:21). With blurred vision, we view our sin as acceptable and even normal (vv.22,25).

Paul reminds us, however, "This good news tells us how God makes us right in His sight" (Romans 1:17). The body of Christ must lovingly choose to:

- Respond to homosexuality as we would any sin in our own lives (Galatians 6:1-2).
- Demonstrate how God's heart of love can change and transform us when we call on His name (1 Corinthians 6:9-11).

We're surrounded by people who struggle with sexual identity. As living proof of God's forgiveness, we must remember that only His grace and truth provides the path to righteousness. —Regina Franklin

less than 1 percent

read>
Judges 7
When Gideon heard the dream and its interpretation, he bowed in worship before the Lord (v.15).

more>
Be strong and courageous! Do not be afraid or discouraged. For the Lord your God is with you wherever you go (Joshua 1:9).

next>
What current challenge in life has made you feel small and powerless? What will it take for you to press on in God's strength?

The movie *Rudy* tells the true tale of Daniel "Rudy" Ruettiger, a smallish, walk-on (nonscholarship) player who tried to make the powerhouse University of Notre Dame's football team. He didn't have the size. He didn't have the athleticism. But he had the heart to make the team and even went on to play in a game!

Gideon was also a "shrimp" who didn't seem to stand a chance against the imposing Midianite army. In fact, when the angel of the Lord told him that he would lead the attack, he squealed, "How can I rescue Israel? My clan is the weakest in the whole tribe of Manasseh, and I am the least in my entire family!" (Judges 6:15). Gideon was feeling mighty wimpy.

That's when God totally blew his mind. In the span of just six verses, God winnowed Gideon's Israelite army—already outnumbered four to one—from 32,000 men to just *300!* (7:2-7, 8:10). We're talking less than 1 percent of the original number of soldiers. If he had been allowed to, Gideon would have likely bolted with the 22,000 guys who left on the first day of downscaling due to their serious case of knee-knocking fear.

Why did God mini-size the Israelite army? To keep Gideon and his guys from thinking it was all about them! (v.2). He wanted them to know that the battle would be won by His strength alone. And it was—the "half-pint" army of 300 was used by God to destroy the mammoth Midianite forces (vv.22-25).

When you feel small standing before the mountainous task that God has called you to, remember these words: "[God] chose things that are powerless to shame those who are powerful" (1 Corinthians 1:27). His "power works best in weakness" (2 Corinthians 12:9).

Follow God's lead and watch Him receive the glory when the battle is won by *His* strength! —Tom Felten

the kingdom of things

read>
Revelation 21:1-22
So he took me in the Spirit to a great, high mountain, and he showed me the holy city, Jerusalem, descending out of heaven from God (v.10).

more>
May Your kingdom come soon. May Your will be done on earth, as it is in heaven (Matthew 6:10).

next>
In what ways are you pursuing the wrong "kingdom"—seeking affluence, possessions, and wealth for yourself? How should the values of God's kingdom guide your dreams, career choice, and lifestyle today?

Since 1993, sales of luxury cars in my country—Australia—have doubled. Since the 1950s, Australian homes have doubled in size, yet the average family has decreased by a third. We've been on a pilgrimage to the "kingdom of things." But, on arrival, we haven't found fulfillment. Thirty percent of us take some form of mood-enhancing substance (like drugs, alcohol, sleeping tablets, or antidepressants) to get through the day.

I'm grateful that there's another kingdom to which we can make our pilgrimage. The apostle John saw it as a gleaming city descending from heaven (Revelation 21:2); a place where humanity's deepest longings are fulfilled in relationship with God (v.3); a place where wounds are healed and tears forever cease (v.4); a place of radiant beauty (vv.11,18-21) that reflects the beauty of its Creator (4:3).

Eight hundred years earlier, the prophet Isaiah also saw this kingdom. A place where the blind see, the deaf hear, the lame leap, and the mute sing for joy (Isaiah 35:5-6); a place where weapons become farm implements, (2:4), where justice is brought to His people (65:21-23), and where the deserts will blossom (35:1).

Then a Man from Galilee appeared on the scene who made blind folks see and lame men leap; who said "the kingdom of God has arrived," as He healed and cleansed and delivered (Matthew 12:28).

Luxury cars will rust, and the "kingdom of things" will collapse. Jesus told us to seek the kingdom of God instead (Matthew 6:33) and to pray and work for its reality on earth (Matthew 6:9-13). Will we invest in that kingdom and resist the temptations of the "kingdom of things"? —Sheridan Voysey

childlike

read>
Luke 10:1-24
Thank You for hiding these things from those who think themselves wise and clever, and for revealing them to the childlike (v.21).

more>
Pride goes before destruction, and haughtiness before a fall (Proverbs 16:18).

next>
Read Jesus' prayer in Matthew 11:25-30. What does this say about Jesus? What does Mark 10:13-16 say about faith and children?

Popular culture reveres pride. Celebrities bathe in their narcissism, only to gain even more fans. Kids on the playground imitate the self-promoting celebrations of their favorite athletes. Arrogance masquerades as "confidence," while meekness becomes a dirty word.

But if personal pride is such a good thing, why is it that no one likes to live close to a proud person? Jesus showed us a radically different way. As He commissioned 72 disciples to do some advance work for Him, He pushed them out of their comfort zone. He hinted that they might face rejection (Luke 10:10). Yet they were to take nothing extra with them. Instead, they were to rely on the kindness of the people they visited (vv.3-7). Jesus left no room for self-sufficiency.

His followers enjoyed great success stating, "Even the demons obey us when we use Your name!" (v.17). But Jesus replied, "Don't rejoice because evil spirits obey you; rejoice because your names are registered in heaven" (v.20).

Jesus is always taking us out of our comfort zone. As He does, it nurtures our complete reliance on Him. But when we find success, we naturally gravitate toward personal pride in "our" accomplishments. This is not the reaction Jesus wants. He desires our gratitude for belonging to the Lord of heaven and earth. "O Father," He prayed, "thank You for hiding these things from those who think themselves wise and clever, and for revealing them to the childlike" (v.21). "The kingdom of God belongs to those who are like these children," said Jesus on another occasion (Mark 10:14). That's a far cry from the "mature" pride our society esteems.

Pride is something we all need to work on giving up—for good. —Tim Gustafson

how soon we forget

read>
Matthew 15:29-39
Do this to remember Me (1 Corinthians 11:24).

more>
Always remember that Jesus Christ, a descendant of King David, was raised from the dead. This is the good news I preach (2 Timothy 2:8).

next>
What's important about remembering Jesus' sacrifice for us? Which memories of what God has done in your life do you cherish most?

The New Testament records the day Jesus fed 4,000-plus people with only seven loaves of bread and a few small fish. That's some serious sushi!

For 3 days, droves of people brought their sick and crippled to the Savior for healing (Matthew 15:29-31). When they ran out of food, Jesus pulled His disciples aside and pointed out the situation. He was concerned that the people would collapse if they tried to go home hungry (v.32). Not a problem for the Man from Galilee. He fed every last one of them, "as much as they wanted" (v.37).

One of the remarkable parts about this all-you-can-eat wilderness buffet was the disciples' first reaction to the prospect of feeding all those people: "The disciples replied, 'Where would we get enough food here in the wilderness for such a huge crowd?' " (v.33). One thing was certain. It would take a miracle.

Apparently, however, the disciples forgot that Jesus already pulled off a nearly identical feat when He used less bread and fish to feed 5,000-plus hungry people (Matthew 14:13-21). One would think that it would have been a day to remember, but apparently it slipped their minds.

It could be just me, but I'm fairly certain that forgetting what God has done on our behalf is a problem we must all contend with. It's the kind of foe that sneaks up on us and takes over without our even knowing it. That's why the Bible tells us over and over again to "remember" (Exodus 13:3; Luke 22:19). It's the reason Jesus instructed His followers to practice the sacrament of communion on a regular basis: "Do this to remember Me" (1 Corinthians 11:24,25).

If we don't pause to remember, it's only a matter of time before we forget what Jesus has done. —Jeff Olson

unclean, ungrateful, unusual

read>
Luke 17:11-19
One of them, when he saw that he was healed, came back to Jesus, shouting, "Praise God!" (v.15).

more>
- Isaiah 12:2-6
- Psalm 86:7-13
- Psalm 105:1-5

next>
There were 10 unclean men—nine who were ungrateful and one who had faith and gratitude. What about you? How can you be more faithful and grateful today?

The husband and wife were desperate. Their only son had been in a coma for 2 months. The doctors weren't sure what was slowly taking his life. Their brother-in-law, a believer in Jesus, brought them to his home church. The distressed couple heard the message of salvation and professed their belief in Jesus. They then asked the church to pray for the healing of their son. Much to the amazement of the doctors, the deathly sick young man's condition began to improve. Two weeks later, he was discharged from the hospital. But soon after, the couple stopped going to church.

There were once some men afflicted with leprosy who failed to follow God after being healed by Jesus. If infectious, lepers had to be quarantined from the community (Leviticus 13:45-46). Ceremonially unclean and socially despised, 10 lepers were helpless and hopeless until they saw Jesus. They cried out, "Master, have mercy on us!" (Luke 17:12).

Jesus told them to go and show themselves to the priests (Luke 17:14; see Leviticus 13:9-10), in itself an act of faith, for they had not yet been healed. "And as they went, they were cleansed of their leprosy" (Luke 17:14). Their obedience was evidence of their faith.

It would not be unreasonable to expect all 10 men to run to Jesus to thank Him for a new start in life. But only one did (Luke 17:17), and he was a foreigner, a Samaritan (vv.16,18). All the men had faith, but only one had faith and gratitude. Gratitude is even more rare than faith. Often, we're quick to pray but slow to praise. We enjoy the gift, but soon forget the Giver. All the lepers received the gift of good health, but only one received the gift of eternal life (v.19).

Physical healing is a great blessing, but it still ends at death. The blessing of salvation lasts forever. —K.T. Sim

leaving your edges

read>
Deuteronomy 24:17-22
When you are harvesting your crops and forget to bring in a bundle of grain from your field, don't go back to get it. Leave it for the foreigners, orphans, and widows (v.19).

more>
- Ruth 2
- James 1:27

next>
In what way can you leave the "edges of your fields" for those in need? How can you invite the poor to glean from the edges of the grace, salvation, and redemption found in Jesus, our Savior?

Bono, the lead singer for the band U2, is a humanitarian par excellence. He headlined the humanitarian efforts of Band Aid and Live Aid to fight poverty in Ethiopia two decades ago. He continues to make a clarion call to all nations to stand as one as they fight poverty and AIDS in our world.

Long before Bono called for people to stand as one to fight poverty, however, God through His servant Moses called His people, Israel, to stand as one to protect and provide for the orphan, widow, and the foreigner. Moses commanded the people not to withhold justice from these groups of people because they were landless and represented the most vulnerable in the land (Deuteronomy 24:17). Remembering their own years spent in slavery in Egypt—a time when they were vulnerable, helpless, and persecuted—was to motivate the Israelites' sensitivity to and proper treatment of the poor (vv.18,22).

One practical way they could meet the needs of the poor was through leaving the edges of their fields unharvested (vv.19-21). The edges provided food for the poor in the land. It was a way of showing generosity to the poor and gratitude to God for blessing the land. If they cared for the poor in this way, God would continue to bless their agricultural efforts, and it would express one aspect of holiness and their imitation of God (Leviticus 19:2).

As followers of Jesus, we're called to stand as one to protect and provide for the poor in our churches, neighborhoods, cities, and world. We can do that by volunteering our time and skill, opening our homes and lives, repositioning our financial resources, and leveraging our influence to satisfy the needs of the poor in our world. When we care for those in need in this way, we reflect the heart of our heavenly Father. —Marvin Williams

virtuous

read>
Ruth 2:1-22
Everyone in town knows you are a virtuous woman (3:11).

more>
The righteous Lord loves justice. The virtuous will see His face (Psalm 11:7).

next>
How has Scripture renewed or corrected your understanding of what being virtuous means? What could prevent you from living a virtuous life?

So, when was the last time you heard someone being complimented for being virtuous? In Ecclesiastes 7:29, we read, "God created people to be *virtuous*." So, what does this word mean? The Hebrew word for virtuous is *chayil*, which means "strength." Throughout the Old Testament, we find that in the majority of cases this word refers to soldiers, to fighting men, to armies. When used to describe a woman, it means that she possesses noble character (Proverbs 31:10-31).

Ruth was described as a virtuous woman (Ruth 3:11). What did she do to earn that reputation? In chapter 1, Naomi knew that her two daughters-in-law, Orpah and Ruth, would face a bleak future if they returned with her to Bethlehem. She released them from their obligation to her. But Ruth made the life-changing decision to stay with Naomi. Her incredible loyalty was seen in the price she paid. First, it meant leaving her family and homeland. Second, it meant, as far as Ruth knew, a life of widowhood and childlessness. Third, it meant going to an unknown land and living among people of different customs. Fourth, she made a commitment never to return home, not even after Naomi would die (v.17). And the most amazing commitment she made to Naomi was, "Your God will be my God" (v.16).

In Ruth 2, we read that the young widow was gleaning in the field. Not only was it backbreaking work where women were often abused, it was also uncertain work. Yet Ruth was out in the sun, trying her best to provide for Naomi.

Ruth embraced God in spite of her circumstances. And she did her best with a joyful disposition. From Ruth's life, we see that a virtuous person is one committed to God and to doing what's right. Let's follow her example and pursue a virtuous life in Jesus! —Poh Fang Chia

small and large

read>
Luke 13:10-21
What is the kingdom of God like?. . . It is like a tiny mustard seed that a man planted in a garden; it grows and becomes a tree, and the birds make nests in its branches" (vv.18-19).

more>
- Proverbs 19:17
- Matthew 10:42
- Matthew 25:40

next>
How do the reactions to the crippled woman by the synagogue leader and Jesus differ? What does this teach us about the difference between religiosity and true religion?

How big is the kingdom of God? Jesus said it begins small, like a mustard seed or a pinch of yeast, and it grows until it permeates "every part of the dough" (Luke 13:21). It's large enough for birds to nest in. But it's not so big that it overlooks details. Just as our immense sun illumines every corner of Earth, so God's kingdom transforms every aspect of life. The kingdom is both small and large.

The sheer scope of the kingdom means that Jesus noticed little things, like a stooped-over woman. How many of us even remembered that Jesus healed her? This was definitely not His most famous miracle. Yet Jesus observed that her crippling disease was the work of Satan. And since God's kingdom extends as far as the curse is found, He said "Dear woman, you are healed of your sickness!" (v.12).

One problem. Jesus healed her in the presence of a small man. Not in height, but in *heart*—much like the Grinch in Dr. Seuss' famous tale, whose heart was "two sizes too small." This leader of the synagogue rebuked the woman—who was now standing straight and tall—for coming forward. " 'There are six days of the week for working,' he said to the crowd. 'Come on those days to be healed, not on the Sabbath' " (v.14).

Jesus replied: "Isn't it right that she be released, even on the Sabbath?" (v.16). Even meaning "especially on the Sabbath." Israel rested on the Sabbath to commemorate her deliverance from Egypt (Deuteronomy 5:15), so there was no more appropriate day to deliver "a daughter of Abraham" from the curse of sin.

The kingdom of God is too large to be petty and too big to ignore the smallest burden. Lend a hand in Jesus' name, and your small kindness will be gathered into something mighty and massive—the kingdom of God. —Mike Wittmer

laughter

read›
Genesis 18:1-15
Sarah was long past the age of having children. So she laughed silently to herself (vv.11-12).

Chuck Shepherd oversees the Web site News of the Weird that reports all the strange, unbelievable stories crossing the newswires. Shepherd's site will leave you scratching your head at the improbable or ludicrous happenings. The site boasts the tagline: "Proof that true stories are weirder than made-up stories."

Often, people put God's words in the same category. *Are you kidding me? That sounds preposterous. Can't be true.* God offers a new way to live, a new way to see and hope and love; and His kingdom often seems entirely out of touch with the world we know.

When God came to Abraham (old, withered, 99-year-old Abraham) to tell him he would father a son, Abraham couldn't help himself: "He laughed to himself in disbelief." And He chuckled in amazement, saying, "How could I become a father at the age of 100?" (Genesis 17:17).

Abraham's wife Sarah, "long past the age of having children" (a kind way of saying Sarah was older than dirt), had exactly the same response (18:11). She laughed (v.12). The notion was comical.

"Why did the two . . . laugh?" asked Frederick Buechner. "They laughed because they knew only a fool would believe that a woman with one foot in the grave was soon going to have her other foot in the maternity ward." But 9 months later, Isaac arrived. And, appropriately, his name means "laughter." This was a different laughter, an irrepressible laughter of joy and beautiful hope-come-true.

Perhaps this is a good sign that we've heard God correctly—we laugh at the seeming impossibility of it all. God says we are forgiven and loved, that He will make our world right, no reason to fear—and we can hardly believe it. Without God, it *is* impossible and laughable. —Winn Collier

more›
Eight days after Isaac was born . . . Sarah declared, "God has brought me laughter. All who hear about this will laugh with me" (Genesis 21:4-6).

next›
What God-words have seemed impossible to you? Where have you seen God make good on His preposterous truths?

at His feet

read>
John 11:17-37
When Mary arrived and saw Jesus, she fell at His feet and said, "Lord, if only You had been here, my brother would not have died" (v.32).

more>
He will give a crown of beauty for ashes, a joyous blessing instead of mourning, festive praise instead of despair (Isaiah 61:3).

next>
Is there any loss in your life where you have struggled to trust the Lord? In what ways has God been your Comforter?

Today I drank a peach milkshake and cried.

Far from being emotional over ice cream, I was flooded with memories. Though my dad has been gone nearly 2 decades, I still miss him. So when my kids and I went to get milkshakes, I couldn't stop the tears as I sipped bits of peach through my straw. When he was in the final stages of renal cell carcinoma, peach milkshakes were among the few pleasurable foods my dad could tolerate. I bought him one the day he died in an attempt to ease his discomfort. Like our time together, it remained unfinished.

Few things redefine our lives like the death of someone we love. John's account of Lazarus' death brings the compassion of Christ into sharp focus. Jesus knew that Lazarus would live again (John 11:11), but He still wept as He saw him lying in the tomb (v.34).

Overcome by their loss, Martha and Mary (in separate instances) say to Jesus when He finally arrives: "Lord, if only you had been here, my brother would not have died" (vv.21,32). One distinct difference, however, marks their responses. Scripture tells us, "When Mary arrived and saw Jesus, she fell at his feet" (v.32). Because she had been willing to sit at Jesus' feet in sweet fellowship (Luke 10:39), Mary had no trouble falling at His feet in her moment of crisis.

Two women—the same question, but dramatically different postures. Intimacy defined the difference.

God doesn't ask us to embrace our loss with gladness. Confident of His love for us, we are to trust His goodness in spite of our pain. Matthew 5:4 says, "God blesses those who mourn, for they will be comforted." When we choose to worship despite our loss, He becomes our comfort, the very presence of peace in our lives (Isaiah 9:6). —Regina Franklin

in control

read>
Luke 22:47-53
Jesus said, "No more of this." And He touched the man's ear and healed him (v.51).

more>
Jesus came and told His disciples, "I have been given all authority in heaven and on earth" (Matthew 28:18).

next>
What do you learn about Jesus in how He chose to use His power? How do you see His love and compassion even in this bitter scene of betrayal?

Flight 1549 was in trouble. After taking off from New York's LaGuardia Airport on January 15, 2009, the jetliner struck a flock of geese. Some of the birds were sucked into its twin engines, causing them complete failure.

Captain Chesley "Sully" Sullenberger didn't allow the chaos of the moment to overwhelm him. He didn't lose control. The veteran pilot chose the safest course—a water landing in the Hudson River. Due to his cool head, the lives of all 150 passengers and five crewmembers were saved.

In Luke 22, as Jesus faced betrayal and an unjust arrest that would lead to His crucifixion, He remained calm and in control. He said to Peter—who had just used his sword to slash off the ear of the high priest's slave—and the others, "No more of this" (Luke 22:51; John 18:10). Then, showing His divine power, Jesus reached out and touched the man's gaping wound and "healed him" (Luke 22:51).

The Master chose to use a gentle touch and calming words to still the chaos of the moment (v.51). As He confronted the leading priests, captains of the temple guard, and elders who had come to bind Him and take Him away, He coolly stated, "But this is your moment, the time when the power of darkness reigns" (v.53).

Jesus knew the horrors that awaited Him as He laid down His power in order to allow the "power of darkness" to reign for a time. Earlier, He had told His disciples, "No one can take My life from Me. I sacrifice it voluntarily. For I have the authority to lay it down when I want to and also to take it up again" (John 10:18).

Out of love for you and me, Jesus willingly was led away in chains. But make no mistake—He was still in control. —Tom Felten

the longing of God

read>
Revelation 21:1-4
I heard a loud shout from the throne, saying, "Look, God's home is now among His people! He will live with them, and they will be His people. God Himself will be with them" (v.3).

more>
- 2 Samuel 7:23
- Matthew 18:12-14
- Luke 15:22-24

next>
How do you view God? The "You will be My people" statements are often in the context of God's disobedient people repenting. How can this encourage you when you repent of your sin?

Blaise Pascal once said the now-famous words: "There is a God-shaped vacuum in the heart of every man which [can] only be filled by God." St. Augustine once prayed, "Our hearts are restless until they find their rest in You." In Revelation 21 we see the end of human longing—the heart at rest in relationship with its Creator in His eternal kingdom.

Something we spend less time thinking about, however, is the longing that God has—a longing that will also be fulfilled on that great day. Now, to be sure, an omnipotent, self-sufficient God doesn't lack anything. We don't meet God's needs. But throughout biblical history, God has expressed His longing for us: "You will be Mine."

- "I will claim you as My own people, and I will be your God" (Exodus 6:7).
- "I will be your God, and you will be My people" (Leviticus 26:12).
- "I will put My instructions deep within them, and I will write them on their hearts. I will be their God, and they will be My people" (Jeremiah 31:33).
- "You will live in Israel, the land I gave your ancestors long ago. You will be My people, and I will be your God" (Ezekiel 36:28).

For thousands of years, God has had one desire—a people drawn to Himself. This longing has fueled His missionary endeavors: sending prophets to call back His straying people, sending His Son to find His straying sheep (Luke 19:10). In the kingdom of God, His desire will finally be fulfilled: "I will be their God, and they will be My children" (Revelation 21:7).

God is our King and Judge, that's true. But we often miss His Father heart—a heart that longs for our free, loving, devoted allegiance to Him; a heart that awaits that longing to be fulfilled. —Sheridan Voysey

teach us to pray

read>
Luke 11:1-13
Jesus said, "This is how you should pray" (v.2).

more>
- 1 Chronicles 16:4
- 2 Chronicles 7:14
- Matthew 6:10

next>
Pray the Lord's Prayer throughout the day today. Journal about what God teaches you in response.

"My biggest problem with 'The Lord's Prayer,' " wrote Helen in response to an online post, "is knowing which version we're using. . . . It's always assumed we know it by heart, but I first learned *trespasses*, then learned *sins* and now am confronted by *debts and debtors*. So, when 'we will now say the Lord's Prayer' is announced, instead of being able to pray and mean it, I'm nervous and wondering which version to use, which rather defeats the point of saying it together aloud."

Like Helen, you might find your mind and heart distracted from the essence of prayer for any number of reasons. Be it choice of words, varying Bible translations, or conflicting philosophies about liturgical readings, the topic of prayer, particularly the Lord's Prayer, garners much discussion and theological debate.

By taking a closer look at Luke 11:2-4, we can see that much confusion over this passage stems from Jesus' preamble, in which He tells His disciples, "This is how you should pray." Many interpret His instructions to mean this is the only way you should pray. To the contrary, throughout the New Testament Jesus builds on His suggested framework of prayer. In the gospel of Luke, for example, He directs us to:

- Pray for those who hurt you (6:28).
- Pray continually and with persistence (18:1-5).
- Pray that you will not give in to temptation (22:40,46).

Scripture emphasizes that there is power in prayer. Respectively, Jesus wanted His disciples and wants you to experience deeper fellowship with the Lord through an enriched prayer life.

Ask God to give you renewed appreciation for the Lord's Prayer, to grant you fresh insights into the verses, and to help you find joy as you meditate on the words and lift them up to God. —Roxanne Robbins

the humanitarian veterinarian

read>
Philippians 2:1-11
Though He was God, He did not think of equality with God as something to cling to (v.6).

more>
- John 13:1-16
- 2 Corinthians 12:8-10
- Hebrews 12:1-4

next>
What's the worst situation facing you right now? How can Jesus use it to show others His humility through you?

Steve Goldsmith is a veterinarian who performs humanitarian work in difficult locations around the world. It's humanitarian work because in poverty-stricken regions healthy animals can spell the difference between life and death for the people!

A few years ago, Dr. Goldsmith went on a medical mission to war-ravaged Afghanistan. One family cow didn't take kindly to being stuck with a needle. The bad-tempered beast managed to kick free of her handlers. In the process, she kicked up a helping of—you guessed it—fresh fertilizer. The flung dung splattered across the vet's face. *Yuck!*

The crowd of curious kids that had gathered found this highly amusing. And Dr. Goldsmith? He laughed heartily with them. "I won them over with that," he recalls. "It broke down the barriers."

The classic example of barrier-breaking is Jesus Himself. Author Philip Yancey notes that when Jesus came to earth, "He played by the rules." Yancey means that Jesus didn't come as divine royalty but as a humble baby, totally reliant on His mother, fully vulnerable to life's pain. The apostle Paul writes of Jesus: "He gave up His divine privileges; He took the humble position of a slave and was born as a human being" (Philippians 2:7). Jesus did this to rescue us from the penalty of our own willful disobedience. "He humbled Himself in obedience to God and died a criminal's death on a cross" (v.8).

Our first reaction to unpalatable situations is to preserve our own comfort and dignity. Jesus offers a stunning contrast. "Because of the joy awaiting Him, [Jesus] endured the cross, disregarding its shame" (Hebrews 12:2). We all face things we'd rather avoid. Remember, we serve One who has endured far worse for our sakes. —Tim Gustafson

God's patience

read>
Luke 20:1-19
Everyone who stumbles over that stone will be broken to pieces, and it will crush anyone it falls on (v.18).

more>
- Isaiah 5:1-7
- 1 Peter 3:20
- 2 Peter 3:9-15

next>
Jesus will come back again as Judge. Are you ready to meet Him? Have you presumed on God's grace and patience, or are you living a pure and blameless life? (1 Peter 3:16).

Nearly one-third of the recorded teachings of Jesus in the Gospels are parables. It's said that a parable is "an earthly story with a heavenly meaning." Jesus was the Master teacher who taught with simplicity, clarity (Matthew 13:54), and great authority (7:28-29). So much so, that the leading priests, teachers of the law, and elders asked Him, "By what authority are you doing all these things?" (Luke 20:2). Jesus responded by telling a parable of the evil tenant farmers (Matthew 21:33-46; Mark 12:1-12). Jesus spoke of:

- *The sinfulness of humanity* (Luke 20:9-15). Jesus drew from Isaiah 5:1-7, where the vineyard refers to the nation of Israel (v.7). The Jews, despite their favored nation status, had rejected God's authority. The tenant farmers are a vivid representation of man's rebellion and rejection of God.
- *The long-suffering patience of God* (Luke 20:10-13). Despite the cruel treatment of all His messengers, the landowner relentlessly reached out to the tenants. He even sent His cherished son. For He is "the God of compassion and mercy . . . slow to anger and filled with unfailing love and faithfulness" (Exodus 34:6). The landowner is a clear picture of God's patient endurance with people (2 Peter 2:9, 3:15).
- *The severity of God's judgment on those who reject the Son* (Luke 20:13-16). There's a mistaken idea that a loving God can't get angry. But God said, "My Spirit shall not strive with man forever" (Genesis 6:3 NKJV). There is such a thing as "the wrath of the Lamb" (Revelation 6:16). This is a warning of judgment on everyone who rejects the Son.

The teachers and leading priests knew that Jesus was telling the story against them—they were the wicked farmers (Luke 20:19). What was Jesus saying to you and me in this tale? —K.T. Sim

shared happiness

read>
Genesis 2:18-25
All the believers devoted themselves to the apostles' teaching, and to fellowship, and to sharing in meals (including the Lord's Supper), and to prayer (Acts 2:42).

more>
Your love has given me much joy and comfort, my brother, for your kindness has often refreshed the hearts of God's people (Philemon 1:7).

next>
How do the relationships within the Trinity inspire you in your relationships? Why is going it alone a bad decision in God's eyes?

The 2007 film *Into the Wild* tells the true story of Chris McCandless. Upon graduating from college in the early 1990s, McCandless had become disillusioned with his conventional life. Without saying a word to his family, he sold all his belongings, disappeared into the back country of the western United States, and eventually ventured deep into the Alaskan wilderness—alone.

McCandless underestimated the rigors of the Alaskan wilderness and was found dead months later. Before his tragic death, he appeared to have a change of heart regarding his decision to live alone. These were his final words scrawled in his journal: "Happiness only real when shared."

Being a loner is not what it's cracked up to be. It was one of the first experiences God spotted as unhealthy—"Then the Lord God said, 'It is not good for the man to be alone'" (Genesis 2:18).

God wired us with a dual need for companionship with Himself and with other human beings. Sustaining healthy relationships with family and friends is a central part of being created in the image of a Triune God who enjoys a level of togetherness that's beyond our comprehension. We can't escape how our Creator made us. The truth is, there can be no real joy in life outside of relationships.

The early church had this down. The book of Acts states, "They worshiped together at the Temple each day, met in homes for the Lord's Supper, and shared their meals with great joy and generosity" (Acts 2:46).

God meant for us to share life with others. As Paul wrote, relationships were a source of great joy to him (2 Timothy 1:4). The only thing worse than dying alone is living alone. Share your life with others. —Jeff Olson

being sure of the cause

read>
Luke 22:1-38
It has been determined that the Son of Man must die (v.22).

more>
God called you to do good, even if it means suffering, just as Christ suffered for you. He is your example, and you must follow in His steps (1 Peter 2:21).

next>
Compare Jesus' plans with the plans of the Jewish leaders. As you examine Jesus' plan, what impresses you about the Savior?

John Calvin once said, "All the exhortations which can be given us to suffer for the name of Jesus Christ and in defence of the gospel will have no effect if we do not feel sure of the cause for which we fight." Jesus, in Luke 22, was absolutely sure of the cause for which He was fighting.

Luke's account of Jesus' passion opens with the Jewish leaders, aided by Judas, plotting to put Jesus to death (vv.1-6). Judas' collusion with the Jewish opposition brought the Savior ever closer to the great suffering and ultimate fulfillment of His mission—redeeming humanity. He faced His passion with confidence, awareness, humility, and faithfulness. Knowing His death was imminent, Jesus made plans to celebrate the Passover meal with His disciples (v.8). During the meal, He predicted His painful death (vv.15-16), using the bread and wine to give the disciples a way to remember Him and His sacrifice (vv.19-20). Jesus also announced His betrayal (v.21), taught that greatness is found in serving others (v.26), appointed 11 of the disciples to future authority (vv.29-30), and predicted Peter's denial (v.34).

The Savior was completely aware of what was unfolding, and He trusted God the Father in the process. Although He predicted His suffering, He understood what was at stake—redemption and hope for all mankind. It was all part of God's plan, and He was willing to humbly, obediently submit to it. Jesus exemplified the walk of the innocent and righteous before a hostile world, initiating the New Covenant between God and His people (Jeremiah 31:31-34).

As followers of Jesus, we will engage the world and face great opposition. Like Him, we're not called to withdraw or be afraid but to face suffering head-on—for His glory. —Marvin Williams

who needs relationship?

read>
Romans 15:1-7
Accept each other just as Christ has accepted you so that God will be given glory (v.7).

Emperor Frederick carried out an isolation experiment to try and determine humanity's original language. He reasoned that infants would eventually speak the natural tongue of humans if they were sheltered from the sound of the human voice. The infants never heard a spoken word. Wet nurses, sworn to absolute silence, were employed. Within several months, the babies all *died*.

We're made for relationships, and we need them to survive. In Romans 14–15, Paul addresses the essence of what it means to live in community. Christians were criticizing each other over various practices related to Old Testament law, and Paul told them to accept each other and to look to Jesus' example of self-giving love as the model to emulate.

In Romans 15:1, Paul says: "We who are strong must be considerate." The word *must* means more than just "we should." It means "a debt." The strong—those who feel free to engage in certain disputable matters—have a debt to bear the weaknesses of those who don't share the same views.

Following Christ's example, the strong are not to please themselves, but to please the neighbor for his good, his edification. When Paul says "accept each other" (v.7), these words mean, "Keep on accepting or receiving one another." Just as Jesus receives us—although we're not perfect—we need to receive others. Why? So they can also bring glory to God.

The churches of the New Testament were imperfect—made up of imperfect people. But they regularly gathered together because of their need for their perfect Savior and Lord—and for one another. So even though we may rub each other the wrong way at times, don't withdraw. —Poh Fang Chia

more>
The eye can never say to the hand, "I don't need you." The head can't say to the feet, "I don't need you." In fact, some parts of the body that seem weakest and least important are actually the most necessary (1 Corinthians 12:21-22).

next>
Is there someone in your church you need to learn to accept? How can you show consideration toward him or her?

choose love

read>
Proverbs 5:15-23
Let your wife be a fountain of blessing for you. Rejoice in the wife of your youth (v.18).

more>
- Philippians 2:3-11
- 1 Peter 2:21
- 1 John 4:10-12

next>
What steps can you take to protect your marriage from the selfish and promiscuous messages of our age? Do something tangible—either for your spouse or a close friend—that demonstrates your commitment.

The actress Cameron Diaz explained why none of her romantic relationships have led to marriage. "I think that what I've found . . . is that you always find the person you're meant to be with at that time in your life. And what I've also found is that you have to move on from those people at certain times, because that's the way it happens. . . . A lot of people find themselves trapped in something they've outgrown and are unhappy. And they don't know how to get out of it because they think they're supposed to make it happen."

This attitude may be acceptable when dating, but too many people bring it into their marriage. "Till death do us part" becomes "You're the person I want to be with at this period in my life," and they quickly discard their spouse when they've "outgrown the relationship" or the chemistry is no longer working. Then, in a futile quest to "find themselves," they tear apart their family and ruin the lives of everyone in it (Proverbs 5:15-17).

But what if love doesn't mean "what makes me happy or meets my needs this very moment"? What if we replaced this thin view of love with the muscular love of God? "God loved the world so much that He" . . . what? Tingled with happiness? Got wobbly in the knees? Used the world to find Himself? No. "God loved the world so much that He gave His one and only Son" (John 3:16).

The cross is the greatest act of love, not because it filled God with warm feelings, but because God put us ahead of Himself and chose to die for us.

How about you? Will you chase Hollywood's idea of happiness, or will you commit to spend your life with your spouse? (Proverbs 5:18). Choose love.

—Mike Wittmer

refusing to play the fool

read>
Proverbs 1:1-7
Fools despise wisdom and discipline (v.7).

more>
I have seen that fools may be successful for the moment, but then comes sudden disaster (Job 5:3).

next>
How are you looking to (or refusing to look to) God for wisdom? Where in your life do you most need God's wisdom right now?

Israeli media reported on the frenzied scene in garbage dumps around Tel Aviv, as people searched for one million dollars stuffed in an old mattress that had been accidentally discarded. A woman identified only by her first name, Anat, told a local radio station that she didn't realize her elderly mother had the money stuffed into the beat-up bedding. After she made the discovery, the garbage truck had already picked up the trash-turned-loot. Perhaps sticking a million dollars in your mattress without telling anyone is not the wisest choice.

We make both wise and foolish choices every day. Some decisions yield good dividends, some are costly. Some choices weigh heavy, while others prove to be inconsequential. Most of us, however, would prefer to live according to wisdom. We'd like to make healthy and fruitful choices for our lives, careers, friendships, finances, and marriages.

Scripture tells us that God desires to give us wisdom, to bless us with the kind of knowledge that allows us to live with joy and integrity (Proverbs 1:2). In fact, God Himself is the wellspring for this freeing wisdom. The "fear of the Lord is the foundation of true knowledge," says the Bible's wisdom writer (v.7). If our lives already reflect wise direction, we can take in God's wisdom and "become even wiser" (v.5). If we're struggling with learning how to live well, God's wisdom will teach us how to "do what is right, just, and fair" (v.3).

The opposite choice, of course, is to ignore wisdom, to ignore God. Tragically, disaster and heartache will always result from this foolish choice. As Bob Dylan once sang, "Gonna change my way of thinking, make myself a different set of rules. Gonna put my good foot forward and stop being influenced by the fools."

God alone provides wisdom to keep us from playing the fool. —Winn Collier

rich

read>
1 Timothy 6:6-12,17-19
True godliness with contentment is itself great wealth (v.6).

more>
- Proverbs 11:25
- Matthew 6:24
- James 1:27

next>
What needs in your life are consuming your attention and focus right now? In what ways are you investing in the kingdom of God through your time, money, and skills? Why is it important to see any gift to others as a gift to the Lord?

Their fatigue and discomfort blended with the barren landscape as the group walked through the dirt streets. Trash littered what could hardly be considered front yards. This arid area of Choluteca known as "The New City" exists in denial of its name. Unclothed children, wild dogs, and a few large pigs ran through the streets with little purpose or focus beyond survival. For the mission team members, accustomed to green grass and a ready source of water, this view of Honduras was a stark reminder of their ultimate purpose to proclaim that Jesus gives new life found in wells that never run dry.

The suffering of others often eludes our glance because we're caught up in the pace of everyday life. Surrounded by deadlines, family issues, and various trials, we are easily drawn into self-centered living. Our hearts aren't hard; they're distracted by the noisy, consuming world in which we live.

Warning against self-absorption, Paul teaches that contentment is not a circumstantial condition. Satisfaction comes only as we position ourselves to be consumed with nothing but God (Matthew 5:6). In reminding us of our temporary stay, Paul writes, "We brought nothing with us when we came into the world, and we can't take anything with us when we leave it" (1 Timothy 6:7).

God doesn't want us to live feeling guilty for the blessings and material things we've been given. He does challenge us, however, to live with both His justice and His mercy in view (Micah 6:8). When we "walk humbly with our God" and live toward this end, what we possess becomes a means for the advancement of His kingdom (Matthew 14:15-21).

Whether we sit in need or in abundance, we must regularly assess if our time, money, and energy are being used for what is everlasting or for what will never satisfy (Isaiah 55:1-2). —Regina Franklin

one, two, three . . .

read>
Luke 18:15-30
The kingdom of God belongs to those who are like these children. I tell you the truth, anyone who doesn't receive the kingdom of God like a child will never enter it (vv.16-17).

more>
- Luke 5:20
- John 1:12-13
- John 3:16

next>
Why does Jesus celebrate childlike faith? What will it take for you to trust in Him this way?

When my son was a toddler, I played a game with him that made a big splash—literally. As I stood in the water, just a few feet from the edge of the pool, I would reach out my arms and encourage him to leap from the safe *terra firma* to me. I would count, "One . . two . . . THREE!" and with a giggle he would launch himself into my arms. To add some excitement, I would let his feet splash in the water just a bit.

Jesus reached His arms out to the "little children." Though His disciples felt that the children were a "bother," the Savior highly valued them and their faith (Luke 18:16-17). Unlike the pious and proud (v.9), they possessed a childlike faith marked by openness and trust. As Jesus lovingly embraced some kids, He said, "Anyone who doesn't receive the kingdom of God like a child will never enter it" (v.17).

In contrast, Luke then records Jesus' interaction with a rich religious leader. The man testified that he had kept God's "commandments since I was young" (v.21). Like the apostle Paul prior to his conversion, this man had been diligent in keeping the letter of the law (Philippians 3:6). But Jesus zeroed in on the rich leader's heart and told him to sell all his possessions and "follow Me" (Luke 18:22).

Does Christ ask every person to jettison all they own? No. This was simply a way of showing the man that he'd have to take the step of faith he desperately needed. The goal was for him to have a trusting, humble, childlike faith in the Savior.

Today, Jesus calls to you with arms outstretched. Humbly receive Him with childlike trust. Ready? *One . . . two . . . three!* —Tom Felten

fighting the good fight

read>
1 Timothy 6:11-16
Fight the good fight for the true faith (v.12)

more>
- John 15:18-19
- 1 Timothy 1:18
- 2 Timothy 2:3-4

next>
What attacks from your unseen enemies have you been experiencing? What do you need to do to be better prepared for spiritual warfare?

Jacqueline's eyes flash fury and fire. She's the embodiment of the hot-tempered, angry, fight starter described in Proverbs 15:18 and 29:22. It's not surprising then that rather than pleading with her landlord for more time to pay her delinquent rent, she beat him up and gave him two broken ribs.

The landlord was not the first person to suffer Jacqueline's wrath. She has slugged both strangers and neighbors alike, and once she hit her husband so hard he ran off—never to return. Despite her behavior, Jacqueline was the direct beneficiary of two of my friends' generosity. She was so touched by their kindness—something she hasn't extended or received much of in her lifetime—that she decided to give up physical combat. Jacqueline has now gone a long time without throwing a punch.

While "right hooks" aren't highly regarded in Scripture, we're nonetheless called to engage in a lifetime of tenacious fighting against opposition and temptation that aims to hinder our walk with Christ.

In his first letter to Timothy, Paul explained that we must "fight the good fight" as we remain true to the faith (1 Timothy 6:12). In another letter, the apostle says we're to approach spiritual warfare as an athlete would approach a competition, with discipline and with the goal of obtaining an "eternal prize" (1 Corinthians 9:25).

Finally, Paul wrote, "Be strong in the Lord and in His mighty power. Put on all of God's armor so that you will be able to stand firm against all strategies of the devil. For we are not fighting against flesh-and-blood enemies, but against evil rulers and authorities of the unseen world" (Ephesians 6:10-12).

The ultimate enemies we face are not human. Let's choose today to prayerfully, carefully battle against our unseen enemies as we lift up the truths of Jesus. —Roxanne Robbins

no limits

read>
Luke 10:25-37
"You must love the Lord your God with all your heart, all your soul, all your strength, and all your mind." And, "Love your neighbor as yourself" (v.27).

more>
If a stranger dwells with you in your land, you shall not mistreat him. The stranger . . . shall be to you as one born among you, and you shall love him as yourself (Leviticus 19:33-34 NKJV).

next>
What keeps you from caring for those who are not like you? How did Jesus live out the truths of the Good Samaritan parable?

A couple of years ago, I spotted a man in a wheelchair rocking back and forth on a street corner. One of his front wheels was stuck in a crack on the curb, and he was struggling to get loose. Moments later, a kind man came along and gave him a push to set him free.

Many of us would refer to the man who offered assistance as a "Good Samaritan." We borrow the label from a well-known story Jesus told (Luke 10:30-35).

The story centers around a man who was robbed and left for dead on a remote road to Jericho (v.30). His attackers left him badly beaten and in need of major assistance. Amazingly, two separate Jewish travelers completely ignored the man's plight. Then a Samaritan man came along and went out of his way to help (vv.33-34).

The point of Jesus' story is obvious: Be a neighbor to anyone who is in need, even those who are unlike you. It's a point He stressed in response to questions from a Jewish lawyer who was out to minimize and limit God's call to love one's neighbor: "The man wanted to justify his actions, so he asked Jesus, 'And who is my neighbor?' " (v.29). But when the hero of the story turned out to be a Samaritan, long considered to be a lowlife by the Jewish establishment, it became painfully clear to him that no such limits exist for those who truly love God.

We live in a world where prejudices run deep. But there's no place for a follower of God to be a choosy kind of neighbor. The story of the Good Samaritan reminds us that a sincere lover of God is merciful and compassionate to all, not just certain people. As Jesus said, "Now go and do the same" (v.37).

—Jeff Olson

oscar ewolo's transformation

read>
John 3:1-21
Anyone who belongs to Christ has become a new person (2 Corinthians 5:17).

more>
Don't copy the behavior and customs of this world, but let God transform you into a new person by changing the way you think. Then you will learn to know God's will for you, which is good and pleasing and perfect (Romans 12:2).

next>
Can you say your life is truly transformed? Are you missing the joy possessed by Oscar and his mother? What simple prayer—imitating Oscar's—will you offer to God?

Born in the Congo and raised in France, Oscar Ewolo dreamed of playing in the World Cup. Today, as captain of Congo's football team, he has a chance of realizing that dream. But when Oscar was 14, his father died, and his life had begun to disintegrate. "It was as if my whole family was dying on the inside," Oscar said.

Then someone told his mother about Jesus, and she opened her heart to the Savior. Oscar recalls the transformation. "I saw it and was astonished. I saw a woman who had lost her joy start to find a different joy." Eventually Oscar started reading the Bible for himself. He prayed this simple prayer: "Yes, Jesus, I want to follow you. I want to walk with You. Give me the strength to live a Christian life." And Oscar too began to change.

The young soccer star's transformation is a living example of what Jesus told Nicodemus, the religious leader who came to see God's Son: "Unless you are born again, you cannot see the kingdom of God" (John 3:3). Nicodemus didn't understand. So Jesus explained, "Humans can reproduce only human life, but the Holy Spirit gives birth to spiritual life" (v.6).

Jesus further explained that He was the One who had come down from heaven to win back His creation—a creation that had rejected Him. "God's light came into the world, but people loved the darkness more than the light, for their actions were evil" (v.19). It doesn't have to be that way. "Everyone who believes in Him [Jesus] will have eternal life" (v.15). And "those who do what is right come to the light so others can see that they are doing what God wants" (v.21).

The label *Christian* is understood by many in solely a cultural context. But to be a follower of Christ means a total transformation. —Tim Gustafson

i am who?

read>
Luke 20:41–44
Then He [Jesus] asked them, "But who do you say I am?" Simon Peter answered, "You are the Messiah, the Son of the living God" (Matthew 16:15-16).

more>
- Matthew 16:13-16
- Mark 12:35-37

next>
What do you think of Jesus? Who is He to you?

Jesus rode into Jerusalem on a donkey the week before His crucifixion. On that day, which we now call Palm Sunday, the crowd proclaimed Him to be the Son of David (Matthew 21:9). On the following Tuesday in the temple, Jesus asked the Pharisees a question: "What do you think about the Messiah? Whose Son is He?" They replied, "He is the Son of David" (Matthew 22:41-42). From the Old Testament, they knew that the Messiah would be a descendant of David, their greatest king (2 Samuel 7:13-14; Psalm 132:11; Isaiah 9:7; Jeremiah 23:5).

Jesus drew their attention to Psalm 110:1, a prophetic verse written by David and the Old Testament Scripture most referred to in the New Testament (Acts 2:34; 1 Corinthians 15:25; Ephesians 1:20-21). David wrote, "The Lord said to my Lord" (Luke 20:42). To paraphrase, he was stating, "The God of Israel said to the Messiah." David calls the Messiah "my Lord" and declares that He is exalted to the highest place of honour (vv.42-43).

If the natural order is that a father is superior to his son, Jesus confounded them with this question: "Since David called the Messiah 'Lord,' how can the Messiah be his son?" (v.44). Jesus implies that the Messiah was more than just David's son. The Messiah is God's Son. The Messiah is David's Lord, who is the Lord of all. In revealing His true identity, Jesus declared His authority, superiority, and deity.

Earlier, Jesus had privately asked His disciples, "But who do you say I am?" (Matthew 16:15; Luke 9:20). To which Peter declared, "You are the Messiah, the Son of the living God" (Matthew 16:16).

Today, Jesus is asking us this same question: "But who do you say I am?" Your salvation and eternal destiny depends on what you think of Christ. —K.T. Sim

God's unobstructed view

read>
Psalm 33
The Lord looks down from heaven and sees the whole human race. From His throne He observes all who live on the earth (vv. 13-14).

more>
I trust in the Lord. I will be glad and rejoice in Your unfailing love, for You have seen my troubles, and You care about the anguish of my soul. You have not handed me over to my enemies but have set me in a safe place (Psalm 31:6-8).

next>
Reflect on a time when God saw you in a difficult situation and helped you through it. How does this change your view of current challenges you face?

Every Sunday I drive an overloaded car full of former street kids to church. While I try to navigate the crazy Kampala roads, the boys are constantly demanding my attention.

"Look over there, Auntie Rox!" one shouts, "That's where we used to find scrap to sell." "See those men?" adds another. "They beat me and stole my shoes!" "I used to sleep on that sidewalk," a third boy shares. "The (Ugandan) President often comes down this road. I thought if he saw my condition, he would do something about it."

The third boy's longing to be seen—so that his circumstances might improve—struck me profoundly, reminding me of people throughout Scripture who believed that God's awareness of their situation was mandatory for their deliverance. King David, for example, when his own son Absalom was trying to kill him, said to his advisor and servants, "Perhaps the Lord will see that I am being wronged and will bless me because of these curses today" (2 Samuel 16:12).

Then there's Hezekiah who, when the pressure mounted, pleaded, "Bend down, O Lord, and listen! Open Your eyes, O Lord, and see!" (Isaiah 37:17). Nehemiah cried out to God for mercy, exclaiming, "Look down and see me praying night and day for Your people Israel" (Nehemiah 1:6). And, Daniel, who found himself and the Israelites in yet another tight spot, lifted up a similar petition. "O my God, lean down and listen to me. Open Your eyes and see our despair" (Daniel 9:18).

Even though David, Hezekiah, Nehemiah, and Daniel didn't sense God's eyes upon them, He was perfectly aware of their trials (Psalm 33:13-14). In His intentional and flawless timing, He brought them from tough situations to places of safety and rejoicing. Give Him your challenges today. —Roxanne Robbins

hannah's adversary

read>
1 Samuel 1:1-20
I was pouring out my heart to the Lord. . . . For I have been praying out of great anguish and sorrow (vv.15-16).

more>
- Psalm 4:1
- Matthew 5:44
- Romans 12:12

next>
How have you been responding to the attacks of your adversary? How can prayer be the right response for your situation?

Caroline Petrie was suspended without pay. Her offense? She offered to pray for an elderly patient to whom she was giving care. When the married mom of two was informed of her discipline, she expressed sadness and surprise—but she didn't lash out at her accuser or those who suspended her.

Her response reminds me a lot of Hannah's in 1 Samuel 1. Her husband, Elkanah, had unwisely (and against God's plan for marriage—Genesis 2:24) married another woman—possibly so that he could have children (v.2; see also Genesis 16:1-3, 30:3-10). This led to some ugly behavior. Peninnah—wife no. 2—taunted Hannah, gloating in the fact that she had borne Elkanah children while Hannah had none (v.6).

So how did Hannah respond to these attacks? Did she mount a counterattack and send back a volley of insults, including the fact that Elkanah actually loved her more than Peninnah? (v.5). Scripture reveals that she chose something else. She chose to *pray*.

Sobbing and groaning in raw, emotional pain (v.10), she poured out her heart to God (v.15). Instead of dwelling on her adversary, she chose to rest in the arms of her Advocate. And God heard her and chose to bless her with a son. She named him Samuel, for she said, "I asked the Lord for him" (v.19).

Will God always give us the desire of our heart? No. But we know He is good and that He will bring about the good works in our life that we need (Romans 8:28).

In Caroline Petrie's life, God chose to restore her job after she chose to call on Him rather than curse her adversaries. Call on God as you face your adversary. He *is* listening. —Tom Felten

more than a medal

read›
Philippians 3:8-10
All athletes are disciplined in their training. They do it to win a prize that will fade away, but we do it for an eternal prize (1 Corinthians 9:25).

more›
I have fought the good fight, I have finished the race, and I have remained faithful. And now the prize awaits me—the crown of righteousness, which the Lord, the righteous Judge, will give me on the day of His return (2 Timothy 4:7-8).

next›
If we become one with Christ by faith, why does Paul also say that we achieve this prize through effort and exertion? (see 1 Corinthians 9:27; Philippians 3:12-14). Is union with Christ a gift, a reward, or both?

The apostle Paul appealed to the Christians in Corinth by comparing their lives to the races of the Isthmian games. As the runners conditioned their bodies to win a perishable wreath, so the Corinthians should strive to win a crown that will last forever (1 Corinthians 9:25). When I first read this verse, I thought that Paul was being naïve. *Who cares about winning a wreath or a crown?* The athletes in Corinth didn't train so they would have something to wear on their heads. Like our Olympic athletes, they toiled for the pride, fame, and wealth that came from winning gold.

Then it struck me that Paul's argument was brilliant. While athletes race for more than a wreath that will wither or a medal that will tarnish, even the renown and money that accompany these trophies will eventually fade. Can you name any of the winners of the Isthmian games? How many Corinthian coins do you have?

As the Isthmian games delivered trophies that were more than a wreath (and yet nearly as short-lived), so the race we're running rewards us with an everlasting prize that is much more than a mere crown.

Paul told the church in Philippi that this prize is to "gain Christ and become one with Him," for "everything else is worthless when compared with the infinite value of knowing Christ Jesus my Lord." He wanted "to know Christ" so that He might receive Jesus' righteousness and resurrection power (3:8-10). According to John Calvin, "as long as Christ remains outside of us . . . all that He has suffered and done . . . remains useless and of no value to us." But when we are one with Jesus, all of His benefits become ours.

Our goal is not crowns but Christ. It's to know and love Jesus, and to be known and loved by Him. —Mike Wittmer

no babbling

read>
Matthew 6:1-13
When you pray, don't babble on and on as people of other religions do. They think their prayers are answered merely by repeating their words again and again (v.7).

more>
- Ephesians 1:15-21
- Ephesians 3:14-19
- Colossians 1:9-12

next>
From the prayers found in the "more>" section, what can we learn about the God to whom we pray? How do your prayer practices need to change?

The Lord's Prayer is well-known and often quoted (Matthew 6:9-13). It has become, however, a victim of its own popularity. While it's often recited, it's also poorly understood. Our familiarity with it hasn't resulted in a deeper appreciation of its meaning. Ironically, it's typically used in the very same way that the Lord warned us not to use it—vain repetition (vv.7-8).

Jesus gave two examples of unacceptable ways to pray. First, "don't be like the hypocrites who love to pray publicly on street corners and in the synagogues where everyone can see them" (v.5). We're not to use our perceived piety as a platform to show off how religious or spiritual we are (v.1). Second, Jesus said, "don't babble on and on . . . by repeating [our] words again and again" (v.7).

Instead, we're to pray simply, sincerely, privately (v.6), and confidently. For our Father knows exactly what we need even before we ask Him (v.8). And we're promised a reward from God when we deliberately do not showcase our prayer life (v.6).

What does Jesus mean when He says, "Pray like this"? (v.9). Does it mean that we pray in the exact words of Matthew 6:9-13?

The Lord's Prayer serves as a guide or blueprint for what true prayer can be. From it, we learn how to talk with God and how and what to ask of Him giving direction to our own adoration, confession, thanksgiving, and supplication. It's a model for us, just like many other recorded prayers in the Bible (1 Chronicles 4:10; 2 Chronicles 6:14-21; Daniel 9:3-19; Nehemiah 1:4-11).

The Lord's Prayer is God's Word, so there's nothing wrong with memorizing and reciting it. It's important that we don't simply babble memorized words, however, but pray what we mean and mean what we pray. —K.T. Sim

correct change

read>
Leviticus 19:9-13
Do not steal. Do not deceive or cheat one another (v.11).

more>
- Proverbs 11:24
- Luke 6:38
- Ephesians 4:28

next>
What are some ways you're tempted to steal? What happens when you justify taking something that doesn't belong to you?

Making decisions while shopping has never been one of my strong points. I take forever to settle on a purchase, and then all the way from the checkout line to my house, I still question whether or not I got the best deal. One time, after finishing my shopping, I realized after leaving the store that the cashier had rung up the lamp base and shade together instead of separately as they were priced. When I returned to the store, the customer service clerk seemed surprised that I was correcting an issue that had been financially in my favor.

In our "it's all about me" society, the lines often get blurred between right and wrong. Rather than asking what God expects or how we would like to be treated, we look for the most expedient means to get our needs met. While we wouldn't consider blatantly stealing, we don't mind keeping extra change from the cashier or sneaking in our own snacks to the local theater.

In Leviticus 19, however, God teaches us that if we're going to serve Him—to be His holy people—then we must be willing to do things His way, even if it seems to put us at a disadvantage. Frugality is desirable, but not at someone else's expense.

Proverbs 11:25 says, "The generous will prosper; those who refresh others will themselves be refreshed." Being faithful stewards doesn't begin with not stealing. It begins with *giving*. God commanded the Israelites to leave the outer edges of their fields and portions of their fruit unharvested (Leviticus 19:9-10). We can see how doing so helps the less fortunate, but what we often miss is the benefit to us (2 Corinthians 9:6-8).

A heart willing to give won't take what it doesn't rightfully own. That's a change you can bank on. —Regina Franklin

guess who's coming to dinner?

read>
Luke 14:16-24
So his master said, "Go out into the country lanes and behind the hedges and urge anyone you find to come, so that the house will be full" (v.23).

more>
The Lord isn't really being slow about His promise, as some people think. No, He is being patient for your sake. He does not want anyone to be destroyed, but wants everyone to repent (2 Peter 3:9).

next>
How have you been passionately inviting others to God's table of forgiveness? Why is it important that "all" people are invited to come to the feast?

Five to ten times a year, I receive invitations to attend breakfasts, luncheons, and dinners, and to partner with various organizations. Some of these invitations spark no interest in me, while others are so compelling and close to my heart that I respond with an enthusiastic, "Yes!"

Jesus once used an illustration to talk about a dinner invitation that deserves a hearty "yes" from everyone. In Luke 14, a wealthy man sent out invitations to a dinner party he was hosting. To get a personal invitation during this age signified distinct honor. When the dinner was ready, he sent his servant out to notify all the guests (v.17). That's when the unthinkable happened.

His guests showed no respect for His invitation by making excuses as to why they could not attend the dinner (vv.18-20). You would think the host would cancel the dinner, but he didn't. He sent out *more* invitations (v.21). This time, he sent his servant to the streets and alleys of where the outcasts of Israelite society were found, and to the country lanes and behind the hedges where the Gentiles lived. In short, the servant was sent to persuasively invite the unwanted, the unfit, and the unworthy of society to the feast, until the tables were full of guests (v.23).

This brief but important story reveals a wonderful truth about God: He values *all* of humanity—particularly the less fortunate in our world. Moreover, this story reveals a truth about the gospel. The message of salvation is fundamentally an invitation to everyone, but it is especially good news to the less fortunate in our world.

How can we live this out? By passionately, unconditionally, and extravagantly loving everyone—especially the marginalized in our world. Let's invite them all to the wonderful feast of God's love. —Marvin Williams

revenge

read>
Genesis 50:15-21
You intended to harm me, but God intended it all for good. He brought me to this position so I could save the lives of many people (v.20).

more>
God blesses you when people mock you and persecute you and lie about you and say all sorts of evil things against you because you are My followers (Matthew 5:11).

next>
How have you seen God bring good out of something hurtful that happened to you? Why should revenge be left to God?

I ran across a Web site that instructs you in ways to take revenge. Later, I was stunned to find many online sites that are dedicated to getting even. From "thepayback.com" to "makehimpay.net," they feature stories and tips on how to get even with people who rub you the wrong way. The sites are obviously put together by folks who live by the saying, "I don't get mad. I get even."

If there was ever someone who had the chance to get even, it was Joseph. After his jealous older brothers sold him into slavery and staged his death (Genesis 37), they thought they were done with him. But that wasn't the last time they would see the kid with the multicolored coat. Joseph eventually landed in Egypt, where his life took a number of divine twists and turns. In fact, by the time Joseph was just 30 years old, Pharaoh had put him in charge of the whole land of Egypt (41:41-43).

Joseph proved to be a wise ruler. During some good crop-growing years, he stored up huge quantities of food to get the people through the years of famine that were to come (vv.47-49). Later, during the famine years, Joseph's brothers traveled to Egypt to buy food. This presented a golden opportunity for him to get revenge. But rather than get even, Joseph showed mercy (50:15-22).

In the end, he demonstrated a level of forgiveness that could only be of God (ch.45). Joseph recognized that he was involved in something much larger than himself—something bigger than even his own mistreatment (v.5).

Have you been wronged by someone? Seek God instead of revenge. He can use hurtful things to bring about a larger good (45:7-8). —Jeff Olson

chameleon

read>
John 7:37-52
Is it legal to convict a man before he is given a hearing? (v.51).

more>
Be strong and very courageous. Be careful to obey all the instructions Moses gave you. Do not deviate from them, turning either to the right or to the left. Then you will be successful in everything you do (Joshua 1:7).

next>
What keeps you from speaking up for Jesus? Are you afraid of what others will think? When was the last time you did something that overtly identified you as believer in Christ?

Nicodemus is a man I can relate to. You may recall him as the religious leader who came to see Jesus "after dark one evening" (John 3:1-2). Some scholars say the time of his visit is simply how meetings were done back then. Others say he wanted to keep the meeting hidden from his colleagues, men who saw Jesus as a threat to their power base. I agree with the latter. Here's why.

In John 7, we read the fascinating account of a heated confrontation between Jesus and the religious leaders. Full of misguided anger and envy, the men wanted to kill Jesus. So they sent the temple guards to arrest Him.

When the guards returned empty-handed, the leaders were indignant. "Is there a single one of us rulers or Pharisees who believes in Him?" they demanded (v.48). Well, apparently there was, for Nicodemus spoke up. "Is it legal to convict a man before he is given a hearing?" he asked (v.51). It was a simple, sane defense of the Man I believe Nicodemus had already come to believe in.

At this point, Nicodemus may have been a "chameleon" disciple, operating undercover. But here, in the face of the full rage of his fellow leaders, he found the courage to speak. Not much later, he would find even more courage. After the Romans crucified Jesus, Nicodemus openly helped bury Him (John 19:39-40).

Nicodemus had graduated from a timid searcher for truth to one who decided that Jesus was "the way, the truth, and the life" (14:6). Somewhere along his spiritual journey, he had become a courageous Christian. He left behind a chameleon façade for full-fledged faith.

Where are you in your spiritual journey? Is your faith wilting in the heat or growing in courage and power? —Tim Gustafson

intimacy with God

read>
Exodus 24:1-15
Inside the Tent of Meeting, the Lord would speak to Moses face to face, as one speaks to a friend (33:11).

more>
Everything else is worthless when compared with the infinite value of knowing Christ Jesus my Lord (Philippians 3:8).

next>
If you were living in Moses' day, where would you be on that mountain? Why? Pray, "O God, the Triune God, I want to want Thee; I long to be filled with longing; I thirst to be made more thirsty still. Show me Thy glory, I pray Thee, that I may know Thee indeed" (*The Pursuit of God*, A. W. Tozer).

As we look at the Christian landscape, only a portion of believers in Jesus appear to enjoy an intimate, vibrant relationship with God. Are they God's favorites? Is it possible that there are some people who have "qualified" for a deeper intimacy with Him?

In Exodus 24, we read about people who were at four different levels of intimacy with God. The first level contained the Israelites who Moses led out of the camp to meet with God at the foot of the mountain (Exodus 19:17). This group worshiped God from a distance.

The second level was attained by "Aaron, Nadab, Abihu, and seventy of Israel's elders" (24:1). They ascended the mountain and actually "saw the God of Israel" (vv.9-10). In fact, they ate and drank in His presence! (v.11).

The third level was realized by Joshua and Moses who "set out" to receive God's commands inscribed in stone (v.13). Why did Joshua receive this honor to accompany Moses? In Exodus 33:11, we catch a glimpse into his heart. Joshua desired intimacy with God. He preferred to be in God's presence, to be identified with Him.

The fourth level was reached solely by Moses with whom the Lord spoke "face to face, as one speaks to a friend" (Exodus 33:11).

Oswald Sanders, in his sermon on Exodus 24, concluded: "Every one of us is as close to God as we have chosen. It is not as close as we would like to be, or what we sometimes want to be." God will not drag us up the "mountain." But He sees the desire of our heart as displayed in our choices, and as you "come close to God, . . . God will come close to you" (James 4:8).

Don't confuse familiarity with intimacy. Familiarity is *knowing about* God; intimacy is *knowing* God. —Poh Fang Chia

from eden to here

read>
Genesis 1:1-28
Be fruitful and multiply. Fill the earth and govern it (v.28).

more>
- Genesis 12:7
- Acts 2:42-47

next>
Where does your heart most long for God to create this kind of new world? Where do you sense God inviting you (with your unique passions and desires) into His creative work?

My young son, Seth, came running into the room. "Daddy, you have to teach me a superpower." Apparently, Seth's older brother Wyatt had convinced Seth that I had already bequeathed to him a superpower—how to be invisible. Now, here Seth stood, waiting for his own bit of the birthright.

Each of us desires to have a unique purpose. We want to make an impact. We want what we do to matter. Good news! All of these things can be realized as we accept God's invitation to join Him in His redemptive work.

God invited humans into His work of multiplying, filling, and reigning over all He had made (Genesis 1:28). This work to be done by Adam and Eve was pretty straightforward. They would build homes, craft utensils, raise sons and daughters, and enjoy the perfection of God's creation.

Even when sin darkened Eden, God's vision for His creation went unabated. God called out a people, Israel, who were to be—by their living and their loving—a "blessing to others" (12:2). As with Adam and Eve, much that God had for Israel to do sounded like simple details—how to butcher their meat, what kind of material to include in their clothes, and what work could be done on what days. These appeared to be unremarkable instructions. But they were precisely the particulars needed to grow a new kind of people in a new kind of world.

It's the same for us. Paul says we are agents of God's vision to continue this work of creating a "new people" (Ephesians 2:15). Like Jesus' first followers, we do this in simple ways. We share meals and build friendships. We work diligently in our areas of industry. We create beauty by our art and passions and laughter. We join God's work, the work from Eden to here. —Winn Collier

ken cooper's kitten

read>
2 Corinthians 3:7-18
All of us who have had that veil removed can see and reflect the glory of the Lord. And the Lord—who is the Spirit—makes us more and more like Him as we are changed into His glorious image (v.18).

more>
- Ephesians 4:22
- Colossians 3:9

next>
How legalistic are you? Do you believe that your allegiance to God's law will make you good? What sin or weakness will you offer to Jesus today as you seek to be transformed into His character?

In 1983, Ken Cooper's 3-year career as an armed felon ended when he was sentenced to 99 years in Florida's infamous prison—The Rock. With just five guards controlling 900 inmates, The Rock was a hell hole of knifings, beatings, murders, and rape. But while there, Ken Cooper heard the gospel through a brave prison chaplain and became a follower of Jesus. Soon some of Ken's cellmates did too, and their lives began to change.

One day Ken and his friends adopted a kitten that they named Mr. Magoo. Mr. Magoo's back had been broken and his eyes had been blinded by acid—cruel acts committed by other inmates. But Ken and the other kind inmates held Mr. Magoo each day, took turns feeding him, and even prayed for his sight to return. Mr. Magoo was lavished with love. And his sight did return!

The justice system could punish Ken and his cellmates, but it couldn't change their hearts. The kindness shown to Mr. Magoo revealed the transformation taking place inside them.

The apostle Paul once lamented that many of his fellow Jews rejected Jesus for the Old Testament law. Paul's response was that while that law was good (Romans 7:12,14) and glorious (2 Corinthians 3:7), it could only condemn when we broke it (v.9). Like the civil law that judged Ken Cooper, the law exposes our bad deeds and sentences us.

In contrast, Jesus, by His Spirit, offers inner transformation. He enters our lives and starts restoring our souls to make us "more and more like Him as we are changed into His glorious image" (v.18). We are freed and changed (v.17).

For Paul, the good-but-condemning law was no match for the good-and-transforming Spirit (v.8). Ken Cooper would concur, for God's grace turned hardened criminals into kitten-loving gentlemen. —Sheridan Voysey

legacy

read>
2 Timothy 1:3-9
I thank God for you—the God I serve with a clear conscience, just as my ancestors did. Night and day I constantly remember you in my prayers.

more>
- Genesis 15:6
- Joel 1:3
- Romans 10:5-15

next>
What steps can you take to pass on your faith in Christ to future generations? What is the legacy of your life in Jesus so far?

I'm writing from Karamoja, a vast plain located in northeast Uganda. This region is home to the Karamojong, a tribe whose dress, religion, and traditions represent a vestige of pre-colonial Africa.

The Karamojong are fierce warriors, guided by their deep-seated belief that all cattle belong to them by divine mandate. In other words, if anyone else owns a cow, they stole it from the Karamojong.

To repossess their animals, the tribe stages violent raids on neighboring villages in Uganda, Sudan, and Kenya. The brutal attacks leave hundreds of people dead and a large number of homes destroyed each year. But such retaliation is justifiable in the minds of the Karamojong. Though their claim is without legal merit, the tribe's elders have passed their belief down from generation to generation.

The faith of Timothy is an example of a more positive legacy that is endorsed by the Bible. The apostle Paul, writing about this true son in the faith, declared, "I remember your genuine faith, for you share the faith that first filled your grandmother Lois and your mother, Eunice. And I know that same faith continues strong in you" (2 Timothy 1:5).

In the Old Testament, Abraham showed true belief and trust in God (Genesis 15:6). His rock-solid faith was based in the promise God had given Him—including the revelation that he would become the father of many nations (17:5-8). Today it's the responsibility of fathers and mothers to teach their children God's truth "so that they too might believe and obey Him" (Romans 16:26).

It's vital that we carefully consider what messages, values, and beliefs we're conveying to others. What legacy are you leaving behind for the next generation? —Roxanne Robbins

trumping tradition

read>
Matthew 15:1-9
Their worship is a farce, for they teach man-made ideas as commands from God (v.9).

more>
You cancel the Word of God in order to hand down your own tradition. And this is only one example among many others (Mark 7:13).

next>
How has tradition trumped your fellowship with other believers? Why must God's Word always supersede tradition?

It's tough when tradition trumps family. Daman Rao knows this bitter reality only too well. Born in a small South Asia village to a family steeped in superstitious tradition, he was despised and mistreated by them for simply being the fifth child and a boy.

Fortunately, as Daman grew into his teens, he was befriended by believers in Jesus and received the Lord as His Savior. His new family in Christ loves him and is helping him grow in his faith.

Jesus voiced some strong words about man-made practices to some religious leaders of His day. He questioned, "Why do you, by your traditions, violate the direct commandments of God?" The Pharisees and religious teachers had asked Jesus why their elaborate hand-washing routine had been ignored by the disciples as they headed to the buffet table (Matthew 15:2-3).

Jesus' potent question blew away their smokescreen and revealed two things:

• The religious leaders' adherence to futile human laws and tradition versus God's commands (they were not honoring their parents, v.4; Exodus 20:12).

• The leaders were acting nice and righteous, but they lacked a real heart of worship for God (Matthew 15:8-9). This latter point was driven home by Jesus as He quoted Isaiah 29:13—a passage familiar to His audience in which God condemned His people for being all about man-made, legalistic rules, but not His commands.

Traditions can be important. But when we begin to confuse them with what Scripture actually teaches, we've crossed a line. When we start to love them more than God Himself, we're in trouble spiritually. Let's strive to honor God with our actions and worship Him with all our hearts (Matthew 15:8-9). —Tom Felten

the slippery slope of sin

read>
James 1:1-16
Temptation comes from our own desires, which entice us and drag us away. These desires give birth to sinful actions. And when sin is allowed to grow, it gives birth to death (vv.14-15).

more>
Let us strip off every weight that slows us down, especially the sin that so easily trips us up. And let us run with endurance the race God has set before us (Hebrews 12:1).

next>
What do you need to change to avoid being led deeper into sin? Why is it significant that most passages on perseverance come near the end of the Bible?

My friend had been a loving mother who put her Bible degree to good use by teaching Sunday school and participating in several Bible studies. But then she informed her husband that she recently had two affairs and is open for more. After I recovered from the initial shock, I marveled at how quickly a person can destroy her marriage, family, reputation, and her fellowship with God. A lifetime of faithful obedience can be trashed in a single moment.

Or can it? While my friend's meltdown came as a surprise to us, her self-destruction was the conclusion of a number of smaller compromises that snowballed down the slippery slope to adultery (James 1:14). A desire to be admired produced a hunger for male attention, which led to a lingering conversation, then a touch.

Large failures are the result of smaller sins (v.15). Jonah didn't start out in the belly of a big fish. He landed there because he hated his enemies, which led him to run away from God, which forced God's hand to get his attention (Jonah 1:3). If Jonah had put his feelings aside and obeyed God at the outset, all of his trouble would have been avoided.

Are there signs that you are open to temptation? Do you crave attention from members of the opposite sex? Do you go out of your way to talk with a particular person? Are you weighing the odds of getting caught if you fudge your taxes or cheat your employer? Has it been a while since you made time to pray?

We can walk with God for 30 years and then throw that sweet fellowship away in a flash. But we won't if we check the smaller sins that are leading us there. Which direction are you running: toward God or away from Him?

—Mike Wittmer

passion and pigtails

read>
1 Corinthians 9:11-23
Yet preaching the Good News is not something I can boast about. I am compelled by God to do it. How terrible for me if I didn't preach the Good News! (v.16).

more>
- Matthew 9:35-38
- John 4:34-38
- John 20:21

next>
How do you reveal your passion for sharing the gospel? What change will help you better spread the good news?

In 1853, 21-year-old Hudson Taylor left Liverpool for China. His ship arrived in Shanghai, one of five treaty ports China had opened to foreigners following The First Opium War with England. Soon after arriving, Taylor made a radical decision (at least for Protestant missionaries of his day). He decided to wear Chinese clothing and grow a pigtail (as Chinese men commonly did).

Eighteen hundred years earlier, the apostle Paul lived out a similar missions philosophy: "When I was with the Jews, I lived like a Jew to bring the Jews to Christ" (1 Corinthians 9:20-21). It's likely that Paul would have insisted on wearing a Chinese "chang pao ma gua" complete with pigtail too.

While recuperating in England because of a sickness, and troubled that believers had little interest in China, Taylor wrote: "Can all the Christians in England sit still with folded arms while these multitudes [in China] are perishing—perishing for lack of knowledge—for lack of that knowledge which England possesses so richly?"

Taylor began the China Inland Mission, later called Overseas Missionary Fellowship, with a number of distinctive features: Its missionaries would have no guaranteed salaries nor could they appeal for funds; they would simply trust God to supply their needs. Furthermore, its missionaries would adopt Chinese dress and spread the gospel into China's interior.

Paul also felt compelled to preach the gospel to as many people as he could (vv.16,22). Though he could have asked (vv.11-15), Paul restrained from seeking support from the people to whom he was ministering. He wanted to preach the gospel without charge (vv.15,18). Both the apostle Paul and Hudson Taylor were men consumed by one singular passion: "I do everything to spread the Good News and share in its blessings" (v.23). What's your passion? —K.T. Sim

expansion

read›
Isaiah 54:1-8
Enlarge your house; build an addition. Spread out your home, and spare no expense! (v.2).

more›
I am placing a cornerstone in Jerusalem, chosen for great honor, and anyone who trusts in Him will never be disgraced (1 Peter 2:6).

next›
Is God calling you to expansion in a particular area of your life? What costs will you need to pay in order to move forward?

Looking out my back picture window, the normally peaceful view had become a bit of a wasteland. Scraps from our now nonexistent deck lay stacked against the fence, twisted sprinkler pipes poked out at varied angles from the red clay, and the once green grass now bore the violent claw marks from a backhoe. We had entered into an entirely new phase of our lives called "home renovation."

Whether we're referring to a physical building, our emotional landscape, or even our spiritual growth, expansion requires moving beyond what has been to what will be. Stirred by visions and dreams, we may willingly step into new territory with our hearts wide open and our expectations high. As hidden costs bubble up from beneath the flow of activity, however, questions fill our minds. Later, when back-to-back delays set in, discouragement threatens to derail the entire endeavor.

Dull, gray cement foundation blocks stand like unfeeling sentinels around the gaping hole where our hopes can be seen only by faith. In the chaos, we come face to face with the reality that we didn't expect growth to be this . . . messy. *Surely*, we reason, *if God were in it, shouldn't it look better?* As we look around, desperate for green pastures and quiet waters, we figure we must be somewhere in the valley of the shadow of death (Psalm 23:4).

A specialty of God, however, is bringing life from death. Pointing to places we thought were long past producing, God calls us to prepare for new growth (Isaiah 54:1). We are charged to "enlarge," "build," and "spread out" (v.2). Our role is to obey; His is to make it happen. When we make Him the Master Designer, we can rest assured that our plans do not go forth in vain (Psalm 127:1, 138:8). —Regina Franklin

run the race

read>
Philippians 3:12-21
Forgetting the past and looking forward to what lies ahead, I press on to reach the end of the race and receive the heavenly prize for which God, through Christ Jesus, is calling us (vv.13-14).

more>
So all of us who have had that veil removed can see and reflect the glory of the Lord. And the Lord—who is the Spirit—makes us more and more like Him as we are changed into His glorious image (2 Corinthians 3:18).

next>
How could Paul's past failures and present successes prevent him from running a good race? What kind of race are you running for Jesus?

One of my favorite television programs is *The Amazing Race*. This reality show takes up to a dozen couples (people in pre-existing relationships) and places them in a foreign country where they race—via trains, buses, cabs, bikes, and feet—from one point to the next, gaining instructions for the next challenge. The goal is to get to the designated finishing point before everyone else. The last couple to make it to each finishing point is eliminated. And the couple who wins the race receives one million dollars.

Paul said that he was in a race too. He presented this word picture in Philippians 3. The apostle admitted that he had not fully developed as a Christian and that there was room for improvement in his walk with Jesus (v.12). He was in a race, making progress, racing toward the finish line of being conformed to the image of Jesus and having perfect fellowship with Him forever. As he ran the race, Paul didn't allow his past failures and successes to prevent him from making progress. He didn't let his past failures make him feel guilty or his present successes make him complacent. He didn't look back, but he moved forward despite his failures because he knew that Jesus had forgiven him (v.13).

As believers in Jesus, we're also running a race. We're in process, striving to make progress in our spiritual life. If we want to make it to the finish line, we must be in a constant state of growth in Christ. We must also forget the past and focus on the future. We can move forward despite our failures, knowing that we have been forgiven.

We're racing, not for a million dollars, but for the ultimate prize of being more like Jesus. Let's "press on to reach the end of the race" (v.14). —Marvin Williams

a good investment

read>
Proverbs 8
Listen as Wisdom calls out! Hear as understanding raises her voice! (v.1).

more>
Getting wisdom is the wisest thing you can do! And whatever else you do, develop good judgment (Proverbs 4:7).

next>
What unwise decisions have you made lately? What wise words from God's Word will you focus on today?

In a time when financial and housing markets around the globe have taken a beating, good investments can be hard to find. Some urge, "Buy gold. It's an inflation beater that will always be worth something." Others suggest that a corrected real estate market is a good place to park your money. Many recommend traditional long-term investments in mutual funds.

The book of Proverbs points us to an even better investment. It claims investing in "wisdom" is "more profitable than silver" and produces a better return than gold—figuratively speaking, of course (Proverbs 3:14). Wisdom is the exercise of good judgment and common sense. It helps us to discern the way to go and prevents us from making immature mistakes.

When God gave a young King Solomon the chance to ask for anything he wanted, he requested "a discerning heart" (1 Kings 3:9 NIV). Somehow, Solomon was wise enough to know he was sunk without it.

Solomon would go on to rave about the value of wisdom. In Proverbs 8, personifying wisdom, he wrote, "And so, my children, listen to me [wisdom], for all who follow my ways are joyful. Listen to my instruction and be wise. Don't ignore it. Joyful are those who listen to me, watching for me daily at my gates, waiting for me outside my home! For whoever finds me finds life and receives favor from the Lord. But those who miss me injure themselves" (vv.32-36).

Perhaps one of the best things about wisdom is that God wants to give it to us. In the New Testament, we're told to "ask our generous God, and He will give it to you. He will not rebuke you for asking" (James 1:5).

We all could use more wisdom. Let's seek it today. Past performance *is* indicative of future results! —Jeff Olson

he walls come tumbling down

read>
Ephesians 2:11-18
[Jesus] broke down the wall of hostility that separated us (v.14).

more>
For God was in Christ, reconciling the world to Himself (2 Corinthian 5:19).

next>
What is the wall that separates you from another person right now? What steps do you need to take for Jesus to tear that wall down?

If you perform a Google search for the Rwandan genocide, you'll encounter thousands of disturbing stories and graphic images. The most disturbing emerge from a church building in Nyarubuye, where between five and ten thousand Tutsis were murdered. The visual depiction of such gruesome violence in the one place where the victims thought they would be safe is horrific. BBC writer Fergal Keane viewed the scene and described "the rotting bodies . . . twisted terribly, faces frozen in the last terrible expression of violent death." Keane finished with the question we all ask: "How could men do this?"

We do this, the Bible tells us, because we are sinful and are tempted toward the vile bent to crush others who seem different from us or who are offensive to us.

In Ephesians, Paul wrote a letter bursting with overarching themes of sin, mercy, and grace (Ephesians 1:2-9). After painting broad brushstrokes of God's redemptive activity, however, Paul specifically stated how God's people were to live in His world.

The central social issue of Paul's day was the bitter conflict between the Jews and the Gentiles. This was not mere dislike—but true hatred. One first-century Jewish theologian stated this extreme view: "The Gentiles were created by God to be fuels for the fires of hell." And the Gentiles abused Jews at every opportunity. "But now," says Paul, "you have been united with Christ Jesus" (v.13). Because of Jesus, the wall separating human from human has come crashing down.

Jesus intends to do this to every wall sin erects. The wall of resentment between husband and wife. The wall of anger between daughter and dad. The wall between Israelis and Palestinians, between Hutus and Tutsis, between rich and poor. Everywhere we find a wall of division, the mercy of Jesus will one day arrive with a wrecking ball. —Winn Collier

complete integrity

read>
John 1:43-50
Now here is a genuine son of Israel—a man of complete integrity (v.47).

more>
Joyful are people of integrity, who follow the instructions of the Lord. Joyful are those who obey His laws and search for Him with all their hearts. They do not compromise with evil, and they walk only in His paths (Psalm 119:1-3).

next>
How does the essence of your life line up with Nathanael's? What do you need to do to establish a life of "complete integrity"?

If Jesus were to identify one thing He appreciates about you, what would it be? Nathanael, whom some scholars say was also known as Bartholomew, heard the following words from Jesus, "Now here is a genuine son of Israel—a man of complete integrity" (John 1:47).

What is a "genuine son of Israel"? Romans 2:29 states, "A true Jew is one whose heart is right with God. . . . It is a change of heart produced by God's Spirit. And a person with a changed heart seeks praise from God, not from people." This type of person possesses "complete integrity"—consistent in both public and private life. In short, Jesus gave Nathanael a stunning compliment. It's little wonder then that Nathanael—who had never met the Lord—was filled with amazement. He asked, "How do you know about me?" (John 1:48).

Something in Jesus' answer convinced Nathanael that He was the Son of God. For He couldn't have known where Nathanael had been unless He was omniscient (all-knowing).

Jesus knew that Nathanael had been under a fig tree. Some scholars think that he had been studying the Scriptures there.

But, aside from today's Bible passage, little is known about this "genuine son of Israel." Matthew, Mark, and Luke mention him only once—when they list all 12 apostles. But early church records suggest that after Jesus' death and resurrection, Nathanael ministered in Persia and India and took the gospel as far as Armenia.

As an example for all believers in Jesus, Nathanael apparently lived out his faith with passion and confidence. He simply followed Jesus with "complete integrity" as he sought to bring more sons and daughters of God into the kingdom. Could the same be said of us? —Poh Fang Chia

idols

read>
Deuteronomy 4:9-20
You must not make for yourself an idol of any kind or an image of anything in the heavens or on the earth or in the sea (Exodus 20:4).

more>
- Exodus 3:1-15
- 1 Kings 19:11-13
- John 12:28-29

next>
What do I worship? What takes priority in my life over God?

I knew of a young couple living in Togo, West Africa. As followers of Jesus, they occasionally encountered disapproval from family members who still practiced the old tribal rites.

One day the husband was tragically killed in a traffic accident. It was then that the clash between faith and tradition came to a head. At the funeral, the wife's family urged her to take part in tribal ceremonies. It would "make her free," they said. Despite the intense anguish of the moment, she courageously refused. Her decision was a simple, grace-filled statement to the community that Jesus was sufficient in her grief.

Having lived in the West for much of my life, I have seen how Western followers of Jesus tend to spiritualize these words from the apostle John: "Dear children, keep away from anything that might take God's place in your hearts" (1 John 5:21). Another translation renders it this way: "Little children, keep yourselves from idols" (NIV). An idol is anything we adore or worship that turns us away from God. But John was writing to an audience that would understand this to be a literal idol—a physical representation of a false god. Millions still worship this kind of idol.

God feels so strongly about us not having representations of a false god, that he etched it in stone. "You must not make for yourself an idol of any kind," reads one of the Ten Commandments (Exodus 20:4). When we do "see" God in Scripture, He is elusive and mysterious: a flame; a gentle whisper; a voice thundering from heaven; a rushing wind; a helpless baby; the light that dispels the darkness.

It takes courage to live out your faith in Jesus in a culture that denies Him. But, by His strength, let's continue to worship the God who transcends culture and defies description. —Tim Gustafson

waiting patiently

read>
John 11:1-44
Although Jesus loved Martha, Mary, and Lazarus, He stayed where He was for the next two days (vv.5-6).

more>
Wait patiently for the Lord. Be brave and courageous. Yes, wait patiently for the Lord (Psalm 27:14).

next>
What are you waiting for God to do in your life? How is God shaping your character while you wait?

While I've been a Christian for many years, there are some aspects of Jesus' life that I've only recently come to wonder about. Like what His Galilean accent really sounded like, what mannerisms He picked up from Joseph and Mary, and who His best friends were. Actually, today's passage sheds light on that last question. While Jesus called His disciples "friends" (John 15:15), it was Martha, Mary, and Lazarus who we're told that He "loved" (11:5,36).

It's funny how Jesus treats those He loves.

These two sisters—Jesus' best friends—once sent Him word: "Lord, Your dear friend is very sick" (v.3). Far from dropping everything to come to their aid, Jesus stayed where He was, seemingly ignoring their cry for help. And when He did come, He arrived at Lazarus' funeral late! (vv.17-19). The sisters understandably expressed their grief: "Lord, if only You had been here, my brother would not have died" (vv.21,32).

Surely, this is no way to treat those you love.

But Jesus had made a comment that Martha and Mary had not been privileged to hear. "Lazarus' sickness will not end in death," He'd said on receiving news of the illness. "No, it happened for the glory of God" (v.4). When He arrived, He wept (vv.33-35). As He wept, He approached the tomb. And as we know from reading the story, Jesus' mighty cry brought the beloved Lazarus out of the tomb (vv.43-44). The sisters indeed saw the glory of God (v.40).

Ever felt ignored by God? Like your cries have gone unnoticed?

Could it be you didn't understand His good intentions for your crisis?

Could it be that He weeps as He sees your pain?

Could it be that as you wait patiently for His arrival, you will see the glory of God? —Sheridan Voysey

true view

read>
Romans 5:1-11
Now we can rejoice in our wonderful new relationship with God because our Lord Jesus Christ has made us friends of God (v.11).

more>
- Matthew 16:25
- Philippians 1:21
- Revelation 6:9-11

next>
How did Jesus both live and die for life? How can you daily surrender your life more fully to Him?

Researchers Christian Smith and Melinda Lundquist Denton have coined a term for the religious beliefs of many teens—*Moralistic Therapeutic Deism*. Their view of God and faith—shared by a good portion of adults as well—is *moralistic* in that they think life is all about getting people to "be good." *Therapeutic* stands for the reality that the teens feel that faith is solely to make them happy and feel good. And *deism* defines their view of God as the One who created the world but isn't really involved in our lives today.

The apostle Paul had a very different view of God and our goodness. In Romans 5 he states that we were not born good, but dead in our sins (vv.6-8). Striving to "be good" will not work, for we can only be "made right in God's sight by the blood of Christ" (v.9).

Paul describes life as not being all about happiness, for we will face "problems and trials" (v.3). These challenges bring about helpful development of our character and hope in Jesus (vv.4-5). We may not always be happy, but we can "rejoice" because of what God has done and is doing in us (v.3).

Finally, Paul states: "We can rejoice in our wonderful new relationship with God because our Lord Jesus Christ has made us friends of God" (v.11). The intimacy and relationship seen in the apostle's inspired words are a far cry from a distant God who isn't really involved in our lives. He *loves* us and His Spirit *lives within* us (v.5).

Do Paul's views of God and belief in Him jibe with your own? A true view of God and His active, redeeming work in our lives is essential for a transforming faith—one that glorifies and accurately reveals Him to others. —Tom Felten

foundations

read›
Ephesians 2:19-22
Together, we are His house, built on the foundation of the apostles and the prophets. And the cornerstone is Christ Jesus Himself (v.20).

more›
- Isaiah 28:16
- Luke 6:46-49
- 2 Timothy 2:19

next›
Do you know and love Jesus more today than yesterday? Can you point to one example where you obeyed Him even when you didn't want to? In what ways do you still need to submit your will to His?

A nearly finished 13-story apartment building in Shanghai toppled over like a lone domino pushed by an invisible hand. An engineer on site said, "When we arrived on the scene, we were very shook up. In my 46 years of work, I've never seen or heard of such a thing." When they investigated, the engineers discovered that excavators had undermined the building when they dug out dirt for an underground parking garage. Even the sturdiest of buildings needs a foundation in order to stand.

So it is with *us*. We may build an impressive ministry for God, but we never grow so tall that we can afford to neglect our foundation. With that said, our foundations are:

- *Jesus Christ* (1 Corinthians 3:11)—It's good to serve in church, care for the poor, and follow doctrinal discussions. But knowing and loving Jesus is our first call.
- *The Word of God* (Ephesians 2:20)—It's good to read Christian books, attend Christian concerts, and download sermons from our favorite preachers, but none of these should replace our diligent study of God's Word.
- *Obedience*—Jesus said that a wise man builds his house upon a rock when he "listens to My teaching and follows it" (Matthew 7:24). It's good to know the Word of God, but if we ignore His will and do what we want, we're foolishly building our lives on sand.

The higher we grow, the deeper we must go. The wider we branch out, trying new ministries and attempting great things for God, the more important our foundation becomes. Don't coast on your reputation or past success. Your life will crash if you ever stop loving Jesus and obeying His Word. —Mike Wittmer

sock puppet and frenemy

read>
Genesis 3:1-7
Even Satan disguises himself as an angel of light (2 Cor. 11:14).

more>
- Acts 17:11
- 2 Cor. 11:3-4, 13-15
- 2 Timothy 2:15

next>
How have you been carefully studying the Scriptures to verify that what you've been taught is the truth? (Acts 17:11). Why is it vital that we don't mishandle God's Word?

Do you use a *sock puppet* to secretly keep track of your *frenemies*? Plan to spend your *staycation* watching *vlogs* and *webisodes*?" If you're not sure what all that means, turn to the latest edition of the *Merriam-Webster's Collegiate Dictionary*. The book of words has just added more than 100 new ones. Two entries caught my attention: *sock puppet* and *frenemies*. A "sock puppet" is a false online identity used for deceptive purposes. A "frenemy" is someone who acts like a friend but is really an enemy.

The words *sock puppet* and *frenemy* definitely describe Satan. The evil one came to Eve as a frenemy, telling her what a friend might say. "Did God really say you must not eat the fruit from any of the trees in the garden?" (Genesis 3:1). *Don't worry about the consequences. God is exaggerating. You won't die! (v.4). God is withholding something better from you!* (v.5).

The sock puppet misquoted God's words to subtly cast doubt on His goodness. God's command applied to only the "tree of the knowledge of good and evil" (Genesis 2:16-17)—not to *all* trees. "You won't die!" was a direct challenge to what God had emphatically warned: "You are sure to die" (v.17). Soon Eve, too, felt it was okay to modify God's clear instruction: "You must not . . . even *touch* it" (3:3).

Totally deceived, Adam and his wife chose to disregard God's instructions and warnings. Their actions created eternal consequences for all creation—the birth of evil, the presence of sin, and death.

Satan is no friend. He's a sock puppet and a frenemy. Speaking from personal experience (Luke 22:31-34), Peter warns: Satan is your great enemy. He prowls around like a roaring lion, looking for someone to devour. Stay alert. Watch out! (1 Peter 5:8). —K.T. Sim

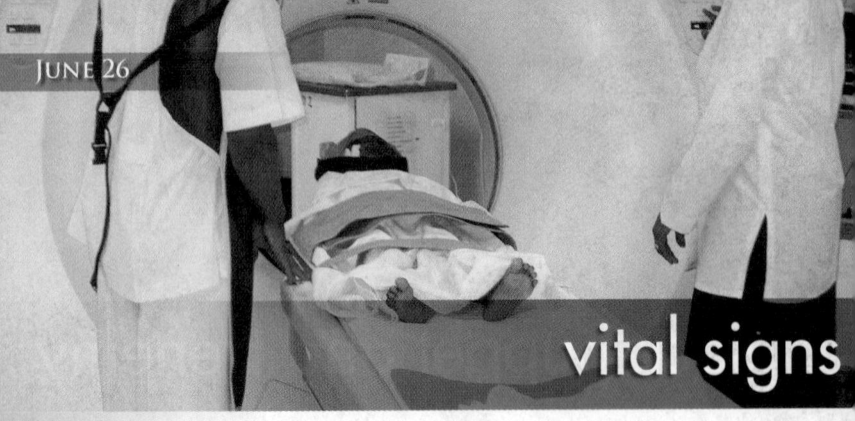

vital signs

read>
2 Samuel 12:1-13
Then David confessed to Nathan, "I have sinned against the Lord" (v.13).

more>
- Proverbs 3:7-8
- Ecclesiastes 7:5
- James 5:16,19-20

next>
Why do we sometimes see others as self-righteous when they point out a sin issue in our lives? What person in your life challenges you to live according to God's Word? How are you viewing your spiritual health through your eyes and not God's?

Quietly reading her magazine, she waits to hear her name. Upon her turn, she follows the nurse back to the examination room. When the doctor enters, the woman amiably proceeds to tell him everything's going just fine and that she's expecting him to write her a clean bill of health. Unprepared for the truth, she stands up abruptly and walks out when he tells her she needs medical intervention. Six months later when she needlessly dies from something that was treatable, the doctor can only shake his head in dismay.

While the above scenario might seem ridiculous, let's consider what happens when people choose consumer Christianity instead of genuine relationships that sharpen and challenge us spiritually. There are great consequences when believers refuse accountability because church life has become more social than redemptive. We find it increasingly difficult to leave behind the sin that "so easily trips us up" if we're unwilling to let others tell us the truth (Hebrews 12:1).

Leaders in the church often face the challenge of trying to confront sin while dealing with individuals who think their appearance at church meetings entitles them to a clean bill of spiritual health. They care little about real treatment for the hidden disease of sin.

Willing to deal in truth, David saw Nathan's confrontation for what it was: a call from the heart of God (2 Samuel 12:7). As we live in relationships with other believers, we need to recognize that accountability has a twofold purpose:

- To restore our relationship with the Lord (Psalm 51:12).
- To restore health to the body of Christ (Ephesians 1:4).

If you hear the hard truth from a "Nathan," recognize that it isn't a putdown. It's a sign of great love (Hebrews 12:6). —Regina Franklin

put your feet on the rock

read>
Isaiah 28:14-22
This is what the Sovereign Lord says: "Look! I am placing a foundation stone in Jerusalem, a firm and tested stone. It is a precious cornerstone that is safe to build on" (v.16).

more>
Simon Peter answered, "You are the Messiah, the Son of the living God" (Matthew 16:16).

next>
Where do people look for stability when their lives are crumbling? What are some ways we can trust Jesus more completely today?

During a leaders' gathering, my friend Chad watched intensely as his daughter, Hannah, climbed up a rock wall. Hannah was making progress, until she began slipping a bit. Chad called out to her, "Put your feet on the rock!" He wanted his daughter to understand that she could find stability on the hard stone that was near her. Isaiah had the same idea in mind when prophesying about the coming Messiah in Isaiah 28.

The prophet gave us a beautiful picture of the coming Messiah. He described Him as the rock on which God's people should place their feet (v.16). According to Isaiah, in what ways is Jesus like a rock? Check these out:

• *The stone was tested.* As a foundation stone, it had been carefully inspected to determine its strength. What's more, this "cornerstone" was prepared by the master mason to be placed at the start of the building process—determining the course of the entire structure (Psalm 118:22; Mark 12:10). The Messiah would be the perfect One—the perfect fit—for God's plan of salvation (Mark 12:6), and a proven foundation for those who believe in Him.

• *The stone was Jesus Christ, the Messiah.* He lived a perfect life; and He was crucified, buried, and raised again from the dead. All who put their faith in Him will not be disappointed because He alone can save and provide a firm foundation in life. Faith in Him is what makes the difference during unstable and difficult times. He's been tested and proven for strength, and His strength can handle the weight of our sin, broken relationships, negative and ungodly habits, and spiritually sick souls.

Let's stand on the Rock—Jesus Christ. —Marvin Williams

worn out?

read>
Exodus 17:8-16
As long as Moses held up the staff in his hand, the Israelites had the advantage. But whenever he dropped his hand, the Amalekites gained the advantage (v.11).

more>
I commend to you our sister Phoebe, who is a deacon in the church in Cenchrea. Welcome her in the Lord as one who is worthy of honor among God's people. Help her in whatever she needs, for she has been helpful to many, and especially to me (Romans 16:1-2).

next>
Who are the allies you can turn to when you feel worn out? How has God given you hope today?

I'm just so tired." It's a common phrase that I've heard from people in my counseling office over the years. Sometimes they say the words to play the "pity me" card. Others are unknowingly lying to themselves—falling deeper into discouragement and depression. But in many cases, they're voicing a legitimate cry of an exhausted heart.

At a time when Israel was still growing as a nation, Moses found himself going through a difficult situation where he was physically and emotionally spent (Exodus 17:8-16). Journeying through the wilderness on their way to the Promised Land, the newly freed slaves came under attack by an experienced army of desert nomads known as the Amalekites.

During the battle, God instructed Moses to stand on top of a hill and hold up his staff (a symbol of God's power). As long as Moses held the staff high, the Israelites won. When the staff became heavy and his arms started to lower, the Amalekites got the upper hand.

Over the course of the day, Moses started to tire. So the people rolled a rock underneath him to provide some support. A couple of men also stood next to Moses and held his weary arms up in the air until the battle was won (v.12).

As the story unfolds, it's almost as if God intentionally put Moses in an impossible situation to teach him some important lessons. He and the people still had a lot to learn about living a new life of freedom. One of the things God wanted Moses to understand is this: *When we run out of gas, we need help from others to get through.*

Are you tired? Do you feel worn out? Learn from Moses and seek help from God and an earthly ally or two. —Jeff Olson

even in the dark

read>
Psalm 139:1-17
Lord, You have examined my heart and know everything about me (v.1).

more>
God showed His great love for us by sending Christ to die for us while we were still sinners (Romans 5:8).

next>
What are you attempting to hide from God? How would you find freedom by shining God's loving light in your dark places?

Joining the rash of reality television shows in the United States, *Dating in the Dark* hit the airwaves a few years ago. Each week, three guys and three girls got together for a week of dates—in a darkened room. They all made the rounds, talking and sharing meals as couples. But they never actually *saw* what one another looked like. At the end of the experiment, each of them picked the one they were most attracted to. Then, in a nerve-wracking encounter, they received glimpses of the other—discovering whether or not physical appearance ruined their attraction.

The whole enterprise preys on one of our most personal fears—*if someone sees who we really are, they will want nothing to do with us.*

This fear is why I find Psalm 139 to be so amazing. David tells me that there is absolutely nothing about me that God does not see. It's out in the open, bright as the sun. No matter where I go, whether "I travel [or] rest at home," God sees (v.3). He knows my actions even before I think to do them (v.2). My most private thoughts echo in God's ears. God hears "what I am going to say even before I say it" (v.4) There isn't a single thing we can hide from God, no matter how hard we try.

Knowing this could make me fall down and cower before God. *If God sees all my impure motives and my lustful thoughts and my shadowy desires, surely He finds me despicable. Surely God will push me aside with disgust.* Stunningly, David says just the opposite. "How precious are Your thoughts about me, O God. They cannot be numbered!" (v.17).

God's kindness toward us flows with pure, undeserved generosity. We are free to come out of the dark because God already sees and knows us—and loves us *anyway.* —Winn Collier

the embrace of God

read>
John 14:15-26
Jesus replied, "All who love Me will do what I say. My Father will love them, and We will come and make Our home with each of them" (v.23).

more>
- John 1:12
- Romans 8:14-16
- Ephesians 3:14-17

next>
The day you felt most abandoned, were you ever really alone? How will you express your love and obedience today in response to God's embrace?

Adrian Edwards was separated from his parents as a toddler, passed along from institution to foster home, and introduced to a life of crime at a young age. As a teenager, he was convicted of armed robbery and spent time in Western Australia's Fremantle jail. There, in a strange twist of fate, he met his father who was serving time for murder. Adrian was released but longed to see his father again.

Father and son did meet again when Adrian was convicted a second time. Adrian served his sentence and was released, but he desired to be with his father.

Finally, a string of armed robberies had Adrian back in the courts. "He is looking forward to spending a long period of time incarcerated with his father," his lawyer informed the judge. A long sentence followed. Adrian's plan to be with his dad was finally fulfilled.

Orphans long for their parent's embrace and will do extraordinary things to receive it. Thankfully, there's a God who longs for His children and goes to extraordinary lengths to embrace us.

"I will not abandon you as orphans," Jesus once told His disciples (John 14:18). They had met their Creator-incarnate (1:3) and would soon lose Him for a time (14:1-2), but they were not to fret. He was going to prepare their heavenly room and would return to collect them (v.3). He was sending them the Holy Spirit, who would "never leave." (v.16). And as the Spirit was received into the disciples' obedient hearts, Jesus said something extraordinary would happen: Father, Son, and Spirit together would come and live within them (v.23). The disciples would be wrapped in the embrace of God—in intimate union with Jesus and the Father (v.20).

This promise stands for all—for Adrian Edwards and for us. Love the Son, receive the Spirit, and be embraced in the Father's arms. —Sheridan Voysey

How can our family set standards for the movies and TV programs we watch?

Here are some standards to apply to your entertainment viewing:

The Reality Test — Even in comedy, unrealistic plots and stereotyped characters often indicate a warped moral perspective. Movies and programs that don't depict the painful consequences of wrong actions distort reality. Just as we shouldn't spend our lives aimlessly associating with evil people and fools (1 Corinthians 15:33), we shouldn't invest valuable time watching immoral and frivolous stuff.

Every family member should learn to be a critical viewer, ready to switch off "junk" productions that are done in poor taste. We all should be willing to explain our viewing choices to other family members.

The Value Test — Relaxation is a legitimate need, but some kinds of relaxation are better than others. Even recreational time shouldn't be squandered.

Can we justify the time we spend watching particular movies or shows as compared to other more active or edifying forms of recreation—like reading, visiting with friends, playing a game with the kids, taking a walk, or tending a garden? Does the time we spend viewing entertainment make us more productive and balanced people, or is it draining our vitality and undermining our creativity?

The Morality Test — We live in a fallen world. Consequently, all good art acknowledges the reality of evil. Art that ignores evil has no depth. The greatest writers and playwrights of the ages have always grappled with evil. But they portrayed evil without glamorizing or sensationalizing it.

Sometimes actors need to play roles portraying immorality. But a good program distinguishes between acting and exhibitionism. We should keep in mind the simple insight that fornication "acted out" by professional actors and recorded on film for public entertainment is still fornication. Human sexual intimacy is too precious to be prostituted by the media under the guise of "realism" or "artistic freedom." Similarly, both the testimony of common sense and academia affirm that media violence, even when simulated, has the effect of desensitizing viewers, lowering their inhibitions, and creating an appetite to see more. It often exploits evil rather than exposing it, gaining viewers by inflaming their passions.

Your use of the media says a lot to your family and friends about your values, priorities, goals, and dreams. Choose wisely. —Dan Vander Lugt

Adapted from Answers To Tough Questions © 2009 RBC Ministries. Read more helpful articles like this one on the Web at Questions.org

simple

read>
2 Chronicles 15:16–16:9
The eyes of the Lord search the whole earth in order to strengthen those whose hearts are fully committed to Him (16:9).

more>
- John 16:33
- 2 Corinthians 12:1-10
- James 1:2-4

next>
In what ways have you been too self-sufficient to ask God for His help? How is pride keeping you from a deeper relationship with Jesus?

Life seems so much simpler in the Old Testament. *Obey God = get blessed. Don't obey Him = expect trouble.* It's a simple theology that satisfies our craving for justice.

The story of King Asa offers a textbook example of this apparent cause-and-effect relationship with God. Asa was an excellent leader who turned his people from worshiping false gods (2 Chronicles 15:8). But late in his reign, he depended on his own strength and judgment instead of on God (16:2-7). Eventually, Hanani the prophet told Asa: "The eyes of the Lord search the whole earth in order to strengthen those whose hearts are fully committed to Him" (16:9). Asa's heart was evidently not fully in tune with God, for the balance of his life was marked by war and disease (v.12).

It's easy to look at this story and say that people get what they deserve. But we don't always see that happen in life. Good people often suffer. Bad people sometimes get away with murder.

A closer look at Scripture reflects these deeper nuances accurately. Even in the Old Testament, we see how the wicked seem to prosper while heroes of the faith suffer terribly. Joseph, an innocent man, languished in prison for years (Genesis 39:19–41:1). Asaph lamented that the ungodly seemed to prosper, before concluding that justice would eventually prevail (Psalm 73). In raw honesty, Jeremiah actually accused God: "You misled me" (Jeremiah 20:7).

Does God care? Yes, He does! The greatest injustice in all of history took place when Jesus suffered and died on the cross. God permitted His innocent Son to pay the horrid penalty for our sins. Is there justice in that?

"God helps those who help themselves," some say, But the truth is, God helps those who are fully dependent on Him. —Tim Gustafson

fooling ourselves

read>
Obadiah 1:1-9
You have been deceived by your own pride because you live in a rock fortress and make your home high in the mountains (v.3).

more>
Because you are stubborn and refuse to turn from your sin, you are storing up terrible punishment for yourself. For a day of anger is coming, when God's righteous judgment will be revealed (Romans 2:5).

next>
What repentance of sin have you delayed? Is there any sin in your life that you ought to turn from before it's too late?

Almost 30 years ago, according to a magazine story, an unusual work of modern art was put on display—a chair attached to a shotgun. It was to be interacted with by sitting in the chair and looking directly into the gun barrel. The gun was loaded and set on a timer to fire at an undetermined moment sometime in the next hundred years. Amazingly, people lined up so they could stare right into the shell's path! They all knew the gun could go off at any moment, but each one took the chance that the fatal blast wouldn't happen during his or her minute in the chair.

Yes, it was foolhardy. Yet many people who wouldn't dream of sitting in that chair live a lifetime gambling that they can get away with sin. The book of Obadiah brings this foolhardiness to the fore.

In chapter 1, we read that the Lord sent a messenger among the nations to stir them up to war against Edom (v.1). The people of the nation of Edom thought they were indomitable. In order, to attack them, foes had to enter through a narrow rocky passage. So even if you had a million-man army, you could still only enter one soldier at a time.

God was against Edom for her pride and her sin against Judah—His people. And He had spoken, so destruction was certain. It was to be so thorough that nothing of value would be left (vv.5-6)

Sure enough, in 553 BC the king of Babylon burned down the cities of Edom. And between 600 to 400 BC, the nation was infiltrated and displaced by Arab tribes.

In the end, Edom symbolizes people who know that their sin is against God, yet who still try to get away with it. God has one word for them: Fools (Proverbs 1:32). —Poh Fang Chia

tossing it back

read>
1 Timothy 6:1-12
True godliness with contentment is itself great wealth (v.6).

more>
- Philippians 4:11-12
- Hebrews 13:5

next>
What's the difference between being content with what you have and simply being lazy and lacking motivation? How will you work on being more contented with what God has given you?

During a Major League Baseball game between the Philadelphia Phillies and the Washington Nationals a few years ago, a man named Steve Monforto caught a foul ball as he sat in the bleachers. Since fans are allowed to keep balls hit into the stands, Monforto handed the prize catch to his 3-year-old daughter Emily. But instead of treasuring the gift, she innocently tossed the ball back on the field!

As fans gasped and laughed, Steve simply hugged Emily and let her know that "she didn't do anything wrong." Fortunately for the smooth-fielding father, a Phillies representative brought him a new baseball to take home.

Just as little Emily didn't see the value in the baseball, you and I sometimes don't value what God has given us. Paul addressed this issue in 1 Timothy 6 as he implored his young protégé to be content. After warning Timothy about false teachers who are more interested in making a buck than blessing others (vv.3-5), he wrote, "True godliness with contentment is itself great wealth" (v.6). The word *contentment* in this context literally means "a perfect condition, not lacking anything."

Does that describe you and me? Instead of being grateful for the gifts our heavenly Father has placed in our lives, sometimes we toss them away and grasp for useless stuff that we *think* we need. Paul nailed it when he wrote, "If we have enough food and clothing, let us be content" (v.8).

If we keep seeking stuff that "we can't take" out of this world (v.7), we'll only end up being "trapped by [our] many foolish and harmful desires" (v.9). There's only one thing Paul tells us to "hold tightly"—the eternal life we have in Jesus.

Today, instead of moaning about your meager lot in life—tossing God's good gifts back in His face—thank Him for all He's given you. —Tom Felten

risk takers

read>
Joshua 1:1-9
This is my command—be strong and courageous! Do not be afraid or discouraged. For the Lord your God is with you wherever you go (v.9).

more>
To those who use well what they are given, even more will be given, and they will have an abundance. But from those who do nothing, even what little they have will be taken away (Matthew 25:29).

next>
Where is God calling you to take some risks with Him? What has been holding you back?

One of the saddest accounts in the Bible is recorded in the Old Testament book of Numbers (chapters 13–14). It's the story of the Israelites who had previously been miraculously delivered from a life of backbreaking slave labor in Egypt.

This generation had witnessed the 10 plagues in Egypt and God parting the Red Sea (Exodus 7–14). For nearly 2 years, they journeyed through the wilderness following a pillar of cloud during the day and a pillar of fire at night. And every day God caused manna and quail to fall from the sky (Exodus 16). He even kept their clothes from wearing out as they endured the elements and strain of desert life (Deuteronomy 8:4).

That's impressive!

And now, as we tune into Numbers 13, we see that God finally had His people on the verge of conquering the Promised Land—*and they wouldn't do it.* Outside of Caleb and Joshua, the leaders refused to step up to the challenge. They said that the Canaanites were too big and powerful. They told the people they were like "giants" and referred to themselves as "grasshoppers" (vv.31-33).

As a result, God made them wander aimlessly around the wilderness for 38 years (within a few miles of their God-given destiny) until their generation died off.

How tragic! God had rescued them and led them to a new life in a new land. But they refused to take a risk with Him.

If there is one thing that the stories of the Bible tell us again and again, it is this: Following the God of the universe into the purpose of our lives always involves meaningful levels of risk (Joshua 1:6-9).

Taking a bold and gutsy risk is not the absence of faith. Sometimes it's an expression of our faith in Him. —Jeff Olson

deliverance

read>
Isaiah 63:8-10
In His love and mercy He redeemed them. He lifted them up and carried them through all the years (v.9).

more>
With Your unfailing love You lead the people You have redeemed (Exodus 15:13).

next>
How can you help free innocent boys and girls from commercial sexual exploitation and other forms of slavery and abuse? How does God view these children?

A 10-year-old human trafficking victim is freed from a brothel in Southeast Asia where she had been abused and sexually exploited. Another child, age 9, is released from indentured slavery in India. Meanwhile, across the ocean in East Africa, a 13-year-old orphaned boy is ushered into a residential home for youth after 5 years of struggling to survive alone on the streets.

While removing these children from their respective residences of horror required valiant efforts on the part of their rescuers, one might argue that the greatest work on behalf of the boys and girls has just begun. For, as both biblical and modern-day cases reveal, it's in the aftermath of oppression that some of the most complex obstacles to healing and restoration come to light.

Among the hindrances to a victim's restitution is the ongoing threat of enemies. The Amalekites ruthlessly attacked the Israelites when they were "exhausted and weary" after fleeing slavery in Egypt (Deuteronomy 25:17-18). Today, equally relentless perpetrators seek to recapture children who are weak and vulnerable following their extraction from an abusive situation.

Guilt, stigma, and chronic poverty are additional barriers to a child's lasting deliverance.

What can you do to bring forth positive change on behalf of the hundreds of thousands of girls and boys who are trafficked each year?

- Pray that child traffickers will be arrested and brought to justice.
- Pray that rescued children will receive the ongoing love, care and protection they need.
- Support organizations that are providing holistic aftercare for boys and girls. They're used by God to provide true deliverance (Isaiah 63:9).

—Roxanne Robbins

no money down?

read>
Matthew 19:16-30
If you want to be perfect, go and sell all your possessions and give the money to the poor, and you will have treasure in heaven. Then come, follow Me (v.21).

more>
Don't begin until you count the cost. . . . You cannot become My disciple without giving up everything you own (Luke 14:28,33).

next>
What aspect of your life—a relationship, possession, talent, or activity—do you need to release to Jesus? Empty your pockets and enjoy the fullness of His salvation.

Some people suppose that the offer of salvation is similar to other big-ticket items. Beds, refrigerators, and automobiles cost more than most people can afford, so stores often offer these products for no money down. Customers can enjoy these products for a year or so before beginning the dreaded monthly payments that slowly but surely drain their bank account. Likewise salvation costs nothing up front, but those who receive Jesus as Savior should eventually pay the price of making Him their Lord.

But this is backwards, for receiving salvation is the opposite of purchasing a car or couch. Unlike them, salvation is affordable to all. It does not lie beyond anyone's price range (for Jesus has paid our debt to God), but it does demand that we put all our money down—and everything else that we are and have (Matthew 19:21).

Jesus explained that all who want to follow Him must "turn from your selfish ways, take up your cross, and follow Me," for only those who lose their lives for His sake will save their lives (16:24-25). This makes sense, for it's hard to argue that Jesus is our Savior if He's not also our Lord. How can we claim that He has rescued us from sin if we remain enslaved to it?

Augustine explained the cost of salvation this way: "Give yourself, and you've got it. What are you worrying about? Why are you in such a sweat? You aren't going to have to go looking for yourself, are you, or to go and buy yourself? Look, it's you, who you are, what you are; give yourself for that thing, and you've got it."

The gospel is free, but it doesn't come cheap. It cost Jesus His life, and if we wish to receive His great salvation, it will cost ours too. —Mike Wittmer

embodied

read>
Romans 12:1-5
We are many parts of one body (v.5).

more>
- 1 Corinthians 12
- Ephesians 3:1-6

next>
Where in the world do you see the need for Jesus to act? How might Jesus be asking you to be His voice or hands or feet in that place?

While serving as a professor at the University of Washington, sociologist Rodney Stark wrote his influential book, *The Rise of Christianity*, to answer the riddle of Christianity's explosive growth during the first 3 centuries. How did this upstart faith, originating in a dusty corner of Palestine, expand to a globe-changing movement within a matter of years? Essentially, Stark's answer was that Christians lived their faith in tangible ways. For instance, they treated women better than the broader culture; and when several waves of plague and epidemics ravaged the Roman Empire, it was primarily Christians who stayed, tending to the sick.

This is the very heart of the gospel: Faith as an embodied life, faith that takes on skin and bones, faith—not merely discussed and affirmed—but lived in the way of Jesus. The center of Christianity is not big ideas (though we have many) or overarching systems of belief (and we have these too). The center of our faith is a person, Jesus Christ, who brought God to us. Jesus is God in human skin.

And now, in a remarkable turn, we who claim Jesus as Lord are sent into our world, carrying Jesus with us. We are invited to bring God near to every friend and stranger. We, quite literally, are "the body of Christ." And no believer in Christ is excluded from this identity as Jesus' body; "each of [us] is a part" (1 Corinthians 12:27).

God continues to work in His world to bring justice, to offer mercy, to love the forgotten. And He uses those who form the body of Christ, those He has transformed into new people (Romans 12:2). As Dietrich Bonhoeffer reminded us, "the body of Christ has penetrated into the heart of the world in the form of the church." —Winn Collier

on fire

read>
Leviticus 6:8-13
Remember, the fire must be kept burning on the altar at all times. It must never go out (v.13).

more>
- Psalm 51:10
- Ezekiel 36:25-27
- 2 Timothy 1:6

next>
Do you fervently pray for revival? Are you consumed with God? In what ways is God asking you to prepare your life for the fire of His presence?

When you set yourself on fire, people love to come and see you burn. —John Wesley

Savannah, Georgia, has always been a charming city. Throughout the downtown area, its graceful squares rest quietly with their shady well-established trees, intermittent park benches and surrounding historic structures. Walking through the squares never fails to evoke a sense of the past.

On a recent anniversary trip there, my husband and I went for a walk before heading to dinner. As we entered Johnson Square, we were drawn in once again by the silent—and yet captivating—statue of revivalist John Wesley. With people meandering around us, we wondered how brightly we were "burning."

Revival. The word may evoke different images for each person depending on our spiritual backgrounds. As a movement, though, revival seems a bit elusive in our culture today. We pray for it in our churches, but what exactly are we seeking? Sadly, *Webster's Dictionary* defines *revival*—with its consuming fires from a holy God—as "a period of renewed religious interest" or "an often highly emotional evangelistic meeting or series of meetings."

When the Lord established His tabernacle, He gave clear instructions for the priests to keep the fires of the altar burning continually. The same instructions hold true for us. While we do not take wood to a literal altar, we are a "living and holy sacrifice" placed on the altar of submission (Romans 12:1).

Without question, revival cannot be generated by man but takes place as God pours out His Spirit upon us. As His temple (1 Corinthians 3:16) and His royal priesthood (1 Peter 2:9), however, we are called to prepare and maintain the fire. Are we prepared? —Regina Franklin

Christ comes incognito

read>
John 21:1-14
"Come and have some breakfast!" Jesus said. None of the disciples dared to ask Him, "Who are You?" They knew it was the Lord (v.12).

more>
"[Jesus] asked them, "But who do you say I am?" Simon Peter answered, "You are the Messiah, the Son of the living God" (Matthew 16:15-16).

next>
Can you remember a time when you didn't "see" Jesus, but "knew" He was working in your life—answering a prayer, working through some circumstance? How did you realize that it was Him?

The board game *Articulate* challenges players to help their teammates guess the object, action, or location they're describing without saying it outright. You can't give the first letter of the word or say what it rhymes with, and on "all play" rounds you have to work fast as your description may help another team win.

The way to win *Articulate* is to play with someone you know really well and exploit your shared experience. "We visited this place in 2006," you say. "India!" your wife replies, as you win the point. "When you do this in the kitchen, I always laugh," your wife says. "Dance in my underwear!" you say, and win the point! You win by alluding to what no one else could know.

At the end of John's gospel, we find Peter, John, and some other disciples fishing on the Sea of Galilee. They cast their nets all night but the fish elude them. Then a man on the shore calls out to them (John 21:4). "Throw out your net on the right-hand side of the boat," He says (v.6). They follow directions and can hardly haul in the catch.

Suddenly, a flood of memories fill John's mind. Three years before, on this same sea, Jesus had performed an identical miracle, calling John and his friends to discipleship (Luke 5:1-11). "It's the Lord!" he cries—solving the puzzle, winning the point!

Something similar had happened to Mary Magdalene (John 20:11-16) and to a couple on the Emmaus road (Luke 24:30-35)—Jesus appearing incognito. But with just a word ("Mary") or an action (breaking bread), they suddenly knew who He was.

Jesus can come to us incognito—an oblique figure on the horizon. Yet with a word, an action, an allusion to shared experience, we recognize His ways and cry out, "It is the Lord!" —Sheridan Voysey

overcoming spiritual failure

read>
Joshua 7:1-19
Israel violated the instructions about the things set apart for the Lord. A man named Achan had stolen some of these dedicated things, so the Lord was very angry with the Israelites (v.1).

more>
- Ezra 9:6
- Daniel 9:7
- James 5:14-16

next>
How have your sins weakened your fellowship with God? What sins do you need to confess to God today?

One of the dangers of past successes is that it can lead to complacency. Positive outcomes are exciting, but they can make us feel overconfident and in control. Soon we're humbled and brought back to reality when we experience failure.

This seems to be what Joshua and Israel felt when they went to take Ai (Joshua 7:2-3). God had given them overwhelming victory and success in their previous battle at Jericho. So they must have thought that taking Ai would be a piece of cake, especially since there were so few of them. They were, however, routed and embarrassed (vv.4-5).

What went wrong? They were crushed because a guy named Achan had clandestinely breached the covenant by coveting and taking the devoted things (things dedicated for destruction, v.1). As a result, the Lord's anger burned against the whole community of Israel.

Though it was the act of one man, God's wrath was experienced by all, for the whole nation was in covenant with Him (vv.11-12). God pointed out to Joshua that Israel had violated His covenant, and He instructed him to deal severely with the perpetrator who brought trouble on the entire community. Joshua obeyed God. Achan confessed his spiritual failure, and he and his entire family were severely punished.

Achan's sad story teaches us: (1) Sin will weaken God's people and rob the community of holiness before God. (2) There are always consequences to our sins. (3) When we fail, we need to refocus our lives on God and his glory. (4) We should confess our sins to God and others when they are revealed to us. (5) When we deal with sin, we must eradicate it. (6) Spiritual failure should teach us not to make the same mistake twice (Joshua 8:1). By, God's grace, we can move on. —Marvin Williams

our Father

read>
Matthew 6:9-13
Our Father in heaven, may Your name be kept holy (v.9).

more>
We call him, "Abba, Father." For His Spirit joins with our spirit to affirm that we are God's children (Romans 8:15-17).

next>
What did it cost Jesus to allow you to call God "Abba, Father"? Pray to your "Father in heaven" and praise Him for the intimate relationship you can enjoy with Him.

Bilquis Sheikh, a Pakistani, wrote about her conversion to Christianity in the book *I Dared to Call Him Father*. The title caught my attention. *Dared to call Him Father?* We usually take it for granted that we can address God as "Father." We hardly realize what a great privilege it is anymore! Jesus introduce something completely revolutionary when He told us to call God, "Our Father in heaven" (Mathew 6:9). Considering how dangerous it was for Jesus to call God "My Father" (John 5:17-18), perhaps Bilquis Sheikh was right. We can't take it for granted that we may call God "Abba, Father."

While on earth, Jesus spoke with God with evident familiarity and intimacy, calling God "Father" more than 200 times. Jesus never called God by any other name until—while on the cross, bearing the sins of the world and forsaken by His Father—He cried out in anguish: "My God, my God" (Matthew 27:46). But once His act of ultimate sacrifice was nearing completion, Jesus reverted to calling God "Father." His final, triumphant words were: "Father, I entrust My spirit into Your hands!" (Luke 23:46).

Because of the cross, we now have the privilege and the right to call God "Abba, Father," for we "are all children of God through faith in Christ Jesus" (Galatians 3:26; see also John 1:12). God is our Father, for He has adopted us (Romans 8:15; Ephesians 1:4-5). We dare to call Him "Father" because we have received "the full rights of sons" (Galatians 4:4-7 NIV) through the gift of the Holy Spirit, "the Spirit of sonship" (Romans 8:14-17 NIV). A nonbeliever will never be able to call God "Abba, Father."

Our Father in heaven (v.9) is a name of endearment. God is our "Abba Father" who deeply loves us His children. —K.T. Sim

maybe?

read>
John 10:22-30
I give them eternal life, and they will never perish (v.28).

more>
God loved the world so much that He gave His one and only Son, so that everyone who believes in Him will not perish but have eternal life (John 3:16).

next>
Who do you think Jesus is? Is He simply a good man? Why should you believe in Him?

I sat in the dark atop a mountain overlooking a lost city. Above my head, a Mindanaon downpour assaulted the tin roof of the bungalow I called home. I had just learned that my best friend from high school had died. Along with the torrential rain came a flood of memories, both good and bad.

About the time my friend turned 20, he had trusted in Jesus. But just a couple of years ago, he told me, "I no longer believe in the so-called God." That statement *haunts* me.

I can't vouch for my friend's spiritual beliefs; neither can I vouch for the beliefs of the band Collective Soul. Still, much of their music resonates with my spirit. And on this dark night, their song "Maybe" captured my thoughts precisely:

Where am I to take refuge
when the storms of pain release. Shelter me.
This blessedness of life, it sometimes
brings me to my knees. I call on Thee.
And I have not the words to write
a farewell to you tonight.
Maybe God you found.
"Maybe" is all that you can offer now.

It's that refrain "maybe" that gets me. How much more comforting is another song by Collective Soul! "Once was blind but now I see; salvation has discovered me. This precious declaration means I believe all hope is dead no longer."

I don't know where my friend is. But through it all, *my* faith remains in Jesus, who made this precious declaration: "My sheep listen to My voice; I know them, and they follow Me. I give them eternal life, and they will never perish. No one can snatch them away from Me" (John 10:27-29).

In the end, it isn't about idle words we may say; it's about what Jesus did and said! And it's about our heart-belief toward Him. I've chosen to believe Him. Life is far too short to trust in *maybe*. —Tim Gustafson

none of my business?

read>
Obadiah 1:10-14
Because of the violence you did to your close relatives in Israel, you will be filled with shame and destroyed forever (v.10).

more>
If someone has enough money to live well and sees a brother or sister in need but shows no compassion—how can God's love be in that person? Dear children, let's not merely say that we love each other; let us show the truth by our actions (1 John 3:17-18).

next>
What are some needs of others you are often tempted to turn a blind eye to? How could you step out in love today?

When we first read the book of Obadiah, it's easy to regard its contents as little more than a prophetic tirade in which God's wrath is directed toward Israel's enemies. We see His wrath and the reality that evil does not go unpunished. But the book has far more to say than simply those two truths.

Some other key points include the fact that we should be careful about what we plant, because the time of harvest will come quickly. God is offended by wrongdoing, and He brings justice for the oppressed.

Obadiah details the main reason for the judgment of Edom: "Because of the violence you did to your close relatives in Israel, you will be filled with shame and destroyed forever" (v.10). The details of the violence against Israel are given in the next four verses: They stood aloof and withheld assistance (v.11). They rejoiced over Judah's downfall (v.12). They plundered Jerusalem (v.13). They prevented the escape of Judah's fugitives (v.14).

Edom's sins against Israel progressed downwards. At first their sin was simply indifference, but then it became the promotion of evil and, finally, participation in the evil. This reveals sin's downward path.

While writing this article, I received a text message. A church friend was asking for my help. I was tempted to ignore it, as it would inconvenience me. However, I was reminded that Edom's downfall began with withholding assistance. So I quickly attended to the request.

Often we'd like to think that somebody else's trouble is none of our business, but Galatians 6:9-10 reminds us, "So let's not get tired of doing what is good. At just the right time we will reap a harvest of blessing if we don't give up. Therefore, whenever we have the opportunity, we should do good to everyone—*especially to those in the family of faith*." —Poh Fang Chia

memory before birth

read>
Exodus 20:1-17
You must not murder (v.13).

more>
- Psalm 139:13-16
- Proverbs 31:8-9
- Isaiah 44:24

next>
How has abortion affected society overall? How can we winsomely live out God's view of protecting the life of innocent persons?

Got a good memory? Recent research conducted in the Netherlands and published in the medical journal *Child Development* reveals that babies can remember things quite well—even when they're still in the *womb*! The sonogram-based study showed that at 30 weeks, babies *in utero* display short-term memory. By 34 weeks, they can store information and retrieve it up to a month later.

As scientists continue to study the early stages of human life, one fact shines brightly: Babies in the womb are living, growing *persons*. That's why abortion is a big deal. In Exodus 20, when God gave Israel the words to help them follow His ways, He stated "you must not murder" (v.13). The wanton destruction of another human being is despised by God, for people are made in His image (Genesis 1:26-27, 9:6). Persons, even the tiniest ones, are precious image-bearers of Him.

The Hebrew word for *murder* used in verse 13 is found just 47 times in the Old Testament. Of the seven possible Hebrew words that mean "to kill," it's the one that speaks the strongest of premeditation and intentionality—words that describe the act of abortion.

God allows for the taking of life in certain instances such as killing an animal for food (9:2-3), the execution of murderers by the government (Genesis 9:6), the death of a burglar attempting to rob your home (Exodus 22:2), accidental killings (Deuteronomy 19:5), and certain types of war (Joel 3:9-10). Abortion is not acceptable to God, however, for it involves the killing of innocents—babies who are individual persons created in His image.

By God's grace, those who have been involved in abortions can find forgiveness in Jesus. But today, regardless of the past, each of us should remember that even babies in the womb display memory. They are persons—made in the image of God. —Tom Felten

power isn't happiness

read>
Isaiah 50:10-11
But watch out, you who live in your own light and warm yourselves by your own fires. This is the reward you will receive from Me: You will soon fall down in great torment (v.11).

more>
I have told you these things so that you will be filled with My joy. Yes, your joy will overflow! This is My commandment: Love each other in the same way I have loved you (John 15:11-12).

next>
When have you tried not to care, when you really do? How has self-protection clouded your relationships?

The movie, *Ghosts of Girlfriends Past* (which is a loose adaptation of Charles Dickens' *A Christmas Carol*), is about a hedonistic, womanizing bachelor who despises the idea of love and marriage. The night before his younger brother's wedding, he is visited by ghosts representing his past, present, and future girlfriends. By the next morning, he opens his broken heart to love again.

Personally, I don't recommend the movie—except for maybe the last 10 minutes. In particular, the best man's speech was positive:

"Someone once told me that the power in all relationships lies with whoever cares less. And he was right. But power isn't happiness . . . happiness comes from caring more about people—rather than less."

The "power" referred to above is the power of *self-protection*. You know—those games we play to try not to care too much for someone. And, yes, it may keep a broken heart from getting hurt again, but there is no joy or life in it. It only ends up incarcerating the soul in a prison of fear, emptiness, and selfishness.

The Old Testament prophet Isaiah described the dangers of self-protection. Figuratively speaking, he said that when we try to protect ourselves in the darkness with our own self-generated light, we will end up in torment (Isaiah 50:10-11). Protecting ourselves by deadening our hearts may seem to make sense, but it only makes things worse. It reminds me of the proverb that says, "There is a path before each person that seems right, but it ends in death" (Proverbs 14:12).

Nothing is greater than the power of love. Only the willingness to care and be cared for is what brings us true joy and life and the freedom to be who God made us to be for others. First comes love, *then* comes joy. —Jeff Olson

community or clique?

read>
James 2:1-9
My dear brothers and sisters, how can you claim to have faith in our glorious Lord Jesus Christ if you favor some people over others? (v.1).

more>
- Matthew 11:19
- John 17:20-21
- Ephesians 2:14-15

next>
When did you last share a meal or some time with a Christian individual or family from a different race or social or economic status? Who might God want you to invite into your world? Why?

Birds of a feather flock together. That's why you never see a robin flying wingman in a "V" formation of geese or a crow hanging out with hummingbirds (actually, crows are mean enough that they don't even like the company of other crows).

But we who are filled with the Holy Spirit are empowered to buck this law of nature and follow the example of Jesus. He shared His life with an unusual group of guys who were not like Him or even each other. What do the Son of God, a tax collector, an anti-government zealot, and a handful of fishermen have in common?

This kind of community was not natural, and—sadly—the first generation of Christians began separating over class and racial differences. Jews looked down on Gentiles, masters thought less of slaves, and the wealthy abused the poor. James ordered the church to stop giving preferential treatment to the rich (James 2:1-9) and Paul admonished the Corinthians to eat together rather than divide by class (1 Corinthians 11:33-34). He reminded the Galatians that "there is no longer Jew or Gentile, slave or free, male and female. For you are all one in Christ Jesus" (Galatians 3:28).

Henri Nouwen defined community as "the place where the person you least want to live with always lives." Philip Yancey explains: "Often we surround ourselves with the people we most want to live with, thus forming a club or a clique, not a community. Anyone can form a club; it takes grace, shared vision, and hard work to form a community."

Do you start conversations at church with those who are different from you? Do you invite people to dinner that you don't particularly like? This kind of community is not natural. But it changed the world once, and it can do so again. —Mike Wittmer

disappointed

read>
1 Kings 21:1-16
So Ahab went home angry and sullen because of Naboth's answer. The king went to bed with his face to the wall and refused to eat! (v.4).

more>
God is not a man, so He does not lie. He is not human, so He does not change His mind. Has He ever spoken and failed to act? Has He ever promised and not carried it through? (Numbers 23:19).

next>
How can disappointment affect our relationships with others? What disappointment is troubling you?

Scanning my e-mail inbox, I stopped in excitement when I saw a particular name. As I opened the e-mail, I held my breath in anticipation of what I would see. Waiting to hear about a manuscript I had sent in, I read through the e-mail quickly looking for the publisher's response. Disappointment flooded my thoughts, however, when I read the letter. While the assessment had been accurate—the manuscript still needed a lot of work—I couldn't stop the tears from falling from my eyes. *I had significant work to do if I intended to proceed further.*

Disappointment is a normal, human reaction to an unmet desire. Proverbs 13:12 says, "Hope deferred makes the heart sick, but a dream fulfilled is a tree of life." We were intrinsically designed for hope, but living in a fallen world means facing disappointment. What we do with it makes all the difference.

When Ahab didn't get the vineyard he wanted, his disappointment took over his emotions—and his life (1 Kings 21:4). Mired in his own frustration, Ahab didn't look to the Lord for his answer. He had a pity party. Furthermore, his disappointment didn't affect only him. Vineyard owner Naboth paid a dear price (v.13). Anytime we let disappointment rule our emotions and lives, we're believing that what we want is more important than anything—or anyone—else.

God wants to bring good things into our lives. As proof, He has offered Himself as the unfailing hope (Romans 10:11). The problem comes when:

- We think we deserve something.
- We make our happiness dependent on whether we get what we want.

In contrast, God asks that we live a life surrendered to and dependent on Him (Psalm 37:3-5). —Regina Franklin

a leaning faith

read>
Mark 9:14-29
I do believe, but help me overcome my unbelief! (v.24).

more>
It is impossible to please God without faith (Hebrews 11:6).

next>
Where are you most desperate for God to act for (or in) you? What holds you back from simply leaning toward Him?

When I was 6 years old, I stood atop the neighborhood pool's 12-foot high dive while my parents tried to coax me to take the plunge. I was afraid of heights, and they wanted me to face my fears. So they had encouraged me to climb up and give it a try. However, I stood atop the small tower for 10 minutes, protesting that I simply couldn't. The moment didn't require anything fancy, no triple-flips or corkscrew twists. I really didn't even have to jump. All I needed to do was step to the edge and lean the tiniest bit. Gravity would have taken care of the rest.

Jesus encountered a man whose faith halted at the edge. For years, a demon had terrorized his son. So the desperate father carried his boy to Jesus (Mark 9:17-18). With two sons of my own, I can't imagine the dad's agony, as he watched his boy's body tormented by violent convulsions, constant falls, and "writhing and foaming at the mouth" (v.20).

The father brought his son to Jesus because he knew that He was the only one who could help. None of the religious leaders or healers, despite all their attempts, had been able to do anything for him. As Jesus asked the dad about his son's grim condition, however, the father's answer evidenced his conflicted hopes. His hesitation showed: "Help us if You can," he said.

Pushing back and prodding the man's courage, Jesus answered, "If I *can*?" Immediately, a spark of faith lit in the father. "I do believe; help my unbelief" (v.24 NAS). Such an honest confession—words of faith mixed with doubt. But Jesus' heart quickly responded; and without hesitation, He healed the boy.

While receiving from Jesus requires our faith, this faith is simply an act of openness, a willingness to just lean (even if barely) and allow Jesus to take care of the rest. —Winn Collier

the holy riddler

read>
Matthew 13:24-52
I will speak to you in parables. I will explain things hidden since the creation of the world (v.35).

more>
Let the wise listen to these proverbs and become even wiser. Let those with understanding receive guidance by exploring the meaning in these proverbs and parables, the words of the wise and their riddles (Proverbs 1:5-6).

next>
How quick are you to read over Jesus' "riddles" and parables without really reflecting on them? Which of the parables hold particular significance for you right now?

Mighty, majestic, awesome. Gracious, loving, kind. Such descriptors for God are common, and rightly so. But how many of us would add "playful" to the list? How many of us think of God as the One who toys with us—the holy riddler?

"Son of man," God commands Ezekiel, "give this riddle, and tell this story to the people of Israel" (Ezekiel 17:2). What follows is a warning of judgment couched in a tale of two eagles. "My loved one had a vineyard," sings the prophet Isaiah, with a description of Israel's fruitlessness following (Isaiah 5). The prophet Nathan, led by God, told King David a story about a "little ewe lamb" that exposed the shame of David's infidelity (2 Samuel 12:1-10). The meaning behind such riddles may be dire, but the method is playful—God being coy and indirect with us, using puzzles and parables to see if we have "ears to hear."

"The kingdom of heaven is like a farmer who planted good seed . . . like a mustard seed . . . like a treasure . . . like a fishing net" (Matthew 13:24-52). When the holy riddler took on flesh, He came telling tales of farmers and fishermen, of lamps and tenants (Mark 4:21-23, 12:1-12), of salt and children (Luke 14:34-35; Mark 9:36-37). Jesus taught little without using such riddles (Matthew 13:34) and while His audience was often let in on the riddle's meaning, the practice often frustrated His disciples! (John 16:29).

But the holy riddler delivers His puzzles with a purpose. He speaks in parables to reveal spiritual truth (Matthew 13:35), but also to weed out those who don't truly want to hear (vv.11-15). He throws out a hook to see if we'll bite. Our response to God's riddles shows how much we really want to know of Him. —Sheridan Voysey

give me wisdom

read>
Proverbs 4:1-9
If you prize wisdom, she will make you great. Embrace her, and she will honor you (v.8).

more>
If you need wisdom, ask our generous God, and He will give it to you (James 1:5).

next>
Do three things today that will help in your pursuit of wisdom. (For example: pray, open your Bible to passages about "wisdom," talk to a friend or mentor about steps they've taken to gain godly wisdom.) Why can God's wisdom be trusted?

While driving Ian and Wasswa (two young Ugandan orphans I'm helping to raise) to school one morning, the discussion turned to the boys' future jobs.

Quickly chiming in with his career choice, Ian said, "Me, I'm going to be a doctor!" When I asked Wasswa what he'd like to do, he replied, "Auntie Rox, me, I'm going to ask God to give me wisdom."

Since then, nightly and of their own accord, the boys have prayed out loud, "Dear Jesus, please give us wisdom." Each time they do so, I'm filled with a deep sense of comfort, knowing that their request is preparing them to better know God and what He wants for their lives.

The ultimate example of a child longing for godly wisdom is found in the book of Luke where we're given a glimpse of Jesus' adolescent years. It was then, while living with his parents in Galilee, that Jesus began to stand out from the other boys and girls his age. He would do unusual things, like the time when he was 12 and slipped away from his parents for three days to sit "among the religious teachers, listening to them and asking questions" (Luke 2:46).

As extraordinary as His behavior may have seemed, by opening His young heart and mind to God's Word, "Jesus grew in wisdom and in stature and in favor with God and all the people" (Luke 2:52).

Asking for wisdom pleases the Lord (1 Kings 3:9-11). Receiving wisdom helps us draw nearer to God. This most practical gift also helps us determine the prudent actions we should take to ensure positive outcomes in life.

Let's keep these wise words in mind, "If you become wise, you will be the one to benefit. If you scorn wisdom, you will be the one to suffer" (Proverbs 9:12).

—Roxanne Robbins

cleansing

read>
Exodus 30:17-21
They must wash with water whenever they go into the Tabernacle to appear before the Lord and when they approach the altar to burn up their special gifts to the Lord—or they will die! (v.20).

more>
Create in me a clean heart, O God. Renew a loyal spirit within me (Psalm 51:10).

next>
In the last week, as you ministered before God and people, were you clean or dirty? Why? From what sin(s) do you need to be cleansed today?

Every 12 years, millions of Hindus flock to Allahabad, India, to take a dip in the Ganges River. Scores get hurt as bathers rush to the water. The solution: purification by proxy. A popular Web site, webdunia.com, offers virtual cleansing. "Pilgrims" who want to avoid crowds, chaos, and travel costs can send a passport-size photo to the site, which then provides virtual absolution.

The Old Testament priests who ministered at the Tabernacle couldn't cleanse themselves by proxy or through a dot.com company. They had to physically wash at the bronze laver or basin, which was positioned between the altar and the Tent of Meeting (Exodus 30:8-19).

The priests were required to cleanse themselves by washing their hands and feet. Only then would they be holy and prepared to minister before the Lord and the people. The laver was made of polished bronze (38:8), so the priest could see his reflection in it. This helped him make sure that he had washed away all the blood and dirt. More than likely, the priests washed off the blood that was on their hands and feet from sacrificing at the altar, along with dirt they had picked up from walking from the Tent of Meeting to minister at the altar.

The priests washing at the basin symbolized the removal of ceremonial uncleanness and provided the means to holiness that was required. Like the priests, every Christian should be characterized by holiness. Self-reflection before God helps us to grow in it. For we are cleansed by God through being washed at the laver of the Word (John 15:3; Ephesians 5:26), confessing our sins to Him (1 John 1:9), confessing our sins to one another (James 5:16), and turning from anything that is contrary to God and His commands (Proverbs 28:13). —Marvin Williams

glory and grace

read>
Matthew 6:9-13
Let us come boldly to the throne of our gracious God. There we will receive His mercy, and we will find grace to help us when we need it most (Hebrews 4:16).

more>
- Matthew 7:7-11
- Romans 8:15-17

next>
Memorize the Lord's Prayer this week. Reflect on the relationships that are described in this prayer. Of all the provisions mentioned, which encourages and comforts you the most? Why?

The Lord's Prayer is a relational prayer. And, though it might surprise you, it reveals a lot about our relationship with God. In these well-known lines, He reveals Himself to us—who He is and what He has done for us. The prayer also reveals how we should respond to Him. Its initial focus is on God's glory, affirming His paternity and person (Matthew 6:9), and His program and His purpose (v.10). Then it shifts from a contemplation of the Holy God to who we are—vulnerable children who are totally dependent upon our heavenly Father. The focus turns to God's grace, assuring us of His provision (v.11), His pardon (v.12) and His protection (v.13).

Our Father in heaven, may Your name be kept holy (v.9) affirms the intimacy of the Father-child relationship as we reverently approach our perfect Father. *May Your kingdom come soon* (v.9) speaks of royalty and the loyalty offered to the King by His subjects. *May your will be done on earth, as it is in heaven* (v.10) is a declaration of surrender as we seek to obey our Master.

Give us today the food we need (v.11) reveals our total dependence on God as our provider. With gratitude in our hearts, we receive what He has given. *Forgive us our sins, as we have forgiven those who sin against us* (v.12)—we explicitly ask the Father's forgiveness, even as we implicitly seek a forgiving spirit toward others. *Don't let us yield to temptation, but rescue us from the evil one* (v.13) warns of the dangers and evil of this world, pointing us to the assurance of safety that comes from our Protector.

For Yours is the kingdom and the power and the glory forever. Amen (v.13)—a confident declaration that God's sovereignty and power guarantee that this prayer will be answered in our lives. —K.T. Sim

behaving badly

read>
Romans 7:14-25
The trouble is with me, for I am all too human (v.14).

Evelyn Waugh is the author of such literary classics as *A Handful of Dust* and *Brideshead Revisited*. He possessed a scathing wit, and numerous other personal flaws we won't enumerate here.

After flirting with agnosticism, Waugh converted to Catholicism. Yet he still struggled. One day a woman asked him, "Mr. Waugh, how can you behave as you do and still remain a Christian?" He replied, "Madam, I may be as bad as you say, but believe me, were it not for my religion, I would scarcely be a human being."

Even for those who possess a genuine belief in Jesus, there's no guarantee that they won't behave badly. The classic passage on this internal battle comes from the quill of the apostle Paul himself. "I am all too human," he wrote, "a slave to sin. . . . I don't want to do what is wrong, but I do it anyway" (Romans 7:14,19).

He continued: "There is another power within me that is at war with my mind. This power makes me a slave to the sin that is still within me. Oh, what a miserable person I am! Who will free me from this life that is dominated by sin and death?" (vv.23-24). Paul satisfied his own rhetorical question: "Thank God! The answer is in Jesus Christ our Lord" (v.25).

Followers of Christ are transformed in an instant, but they don't "arrive"—not in this life, anyway. One of Jesus' closest friends, the disciple John, summed it up this way: "We are already God's children, but He has not yet shown us what we will be like when Christ appears. But we do know that we will be like Him, for we will see Him as He really is" (1 John 3:2). —Tim Gustafson

more>
I don't mean to say that I have already achieved these things or that I have already reached perfection. But I press on to possess that perfection for which Christ Jesus first possessed me (Philippians 3:12).

next>
Have you truly taken your struggles to God and asked for His help with them? What might He be teaching you through your weakness? What is the danger of believing that you have somehow "arrived" spiritually?

day of the Lord

read>
Obadiah 1:15-21
The day is near when I, the Lord, will judge all godless nations! (v.15).

more>
So you see, the Lord knows how to rescue godly people from their trials, even while keeping the wicked under punishment until the day of final judgment (2 Peter 2:9).

next>
How would keeping the day of the Lord in view change the way you handle today's trials? What is the source of your hope?

In *The Lord of the Rings,* J. R. R. Tolkien wrote: "There, peeping among the cloud-wrack above a dark tor high up in the mountains, Sam saw a white star twinkle for a while. The beauty of it smote his heart, as he looked up out of the forsaken land, and hope returned to him. For like a shaft, clear and cold, the thought pierced him that in the end the Shadow was only a small and passing thing: there was light and high beauty forever beyond its reach."

In Obadiah 1, the day of the Lord is like the "white star" (v.15). It reminds us that our current pains and hardships are but shadows. They will soon pass. In that day, God will bring full justice to the oppressed and punishment to the oppressors, and it will be the onset of a universal kingdom in which He will rule over all nations.

One major aspect of the day of the Lord will be judgment upon the people who did not obey God. They "will drink and stagger and disappear from history" (v.16). They will drink of God's wrath.

The other major aspect of the day of the Lord is the final deliverance of those who trust God and await His eternal kingdom. On that day, "the people of Israel will come back to reclaim their inheritance" (v.17) and the "Lord Himself will be King!" (v.21).

As we read these prophetic words in Obadiah, let's remember that prophecy is not just important information about what God has done and what He will do in the future. Prophecy is also good for our hearts. It gives us hope that our God is in control, as He says, "Yes, I am coming soon!" (Revelation 22:20). —Poh Fang Chia

dying wish

read>
Joshua 24:1-22
Choose today whom you will serve. Would you prefer the gods your ancestors served beyond the Euphrates? . . . But as for me and my family, we will serve the Lord (v.15).

more>
You must love the Lord your God with all your heart, all your soul, and all your strength. And you must commit yourselves wholeheartedly to these commands that I am giving you today (Deuteronomy 6:5-6).

next>
What's prevented you from wholehearted devotion to God? Why does God want us to love Him with all our heart, soul, and strength?

Last year, Amilcar Hill and Rahwa Ghirmatizion were married at their child's *funeral*. Now before you start to cast stones (instead of rice) at them, realize that they were simply striving to honor their son Asa. Prior to the 7-year-old's tragic death in an automobile accident, he had been repeatedly asking his mom and dad—who had never legally wed—to tie the knot. And so they chose a most unlikely and yet very appropriate time to become husband and wife.

It's interesting what can cause people to do the right thing. Sometimes even death's shadow can lead to good choices. At the close of his life, Joshua presented a choice to the people of Israel. He said, "Choose today whom you will serve." Would they choose their ancestors, the gods of the Amorites or the one true God? His choice? "As for me and my family, we will serve the Lord" (Joshua 24:15).

Joshua was passionately appealing to the people for single-minded devotion to God. But what should this look like? Check out verse 14: "Fear the Lord and serve Him wholeheartedly." When our hearts are filled with reverence and awe (fear) of God, we won't make foolish choices out of fear of man or anything else in this world. When we love God with all our hearts and obey His Word (wholehearted devotion), our lives will glorify Him and testify to others of His reality (v.22).

What will make you choose to fully follow God? What will it take for you to make the right choice? The poignant story of young Asa and his parents is a wake-up call to all of us. Life is fleeting. God is calling us to surrender our hearts, our desires, our *all* to Him. Choose Him today, and begin to truly live. —Tom Felten

genealogies

read>
Matthew 1:1-17
Abraham was the father of Isaac. Isaac was the father of Jacob. Jacob was the father of Judah and his brothers (v.2).

more>
Just as we are now like the earthly man, we will someday be like the heavenly man (1 Corinthians 15:49).

next>
In what ways are others seeing Jesus in you? How will you radiate His truth and love today?

I have a confession to make. Reading through the lists of genealogies in the Bible can be less than scintillating for me. I know. Sure, they're important. They help trace and verify a person's roots. And they often provide essential background information as to why a story or person in the Bible is so relevant and remarkable. But, if you're like me, simply reading a list of names doesn't stir the soul (especially the ones I can't pronounce).

The New Testament Gospels record the genealogy of Jesus twice. Matthew 1:1-17 and Luke 3:23-38 trace His lineage all the way back to Abraham and King David—showing He was the promised Messiah.

The Bible also records another reference to Jesus' ancestry that we can easily gloss over—missing its significance. On many occasions, Jesus referred to Himself as the "Son of man." And there's a lot of meaning packed into that description.

In part, it was a term He used to refer to His own humanity. Jesus was the God-man—fully God and also fully human. "Son of man" was also a phrase intended to show us the kind of humans we are meant to be as well as to point us to the hope that, through Him—the second Adam—we can become as He is (1 Corinthians 15:47-49).

When the disciples saw Jesus on the Mount of Transfiguration, they caught a glimpse of all He is (Luke 9:28-36). He was the same Jesus they knew and loved—*only more so.*

Reading about Jesus helps us view our ultimate destiny. He's the type of person we are in the process of becoming—one day we'll be like Him fully even as we see Him face to face (1 John 3:2). —Jeff Olson

people make the place

read>
2 Samuel 1:17-27
How I weep for you, my brother Jonathan! Oh, how much I loved you! And your love for me was deep, deeper than the love of women! (v.26).

more>
I observed yet another example of something meaningless . . . a man who is all alone . . . yet who works hard to gain as much wealth as he can. But then he asks himself, "Who am I working for? Why am I giving up so much pleasure now?" It is all so meaningless and depressing (Ecclesiastes 4:7-8).

next>
Where did you most enjoy living? How did the meaningful relationships you had there affect your view of that place?

Every romantic movie filmed in Italy includes a classic shot of the Amalfi Coast, where hairpin turns lead wide-eyed sightseers past lemon groves, vineyards, and whole towns built into the side of a mountain. It's one of the most beautiful spots on earth. But I spent 3 days there and *hated* it.

I couldn't enjoy the sights and sounds because I was traveling alone. I was missing my wife and kids, and I longed to leave paradise and return to my snowy Michigan to be with them.

I was lonely, because I am made in the image of a relational God—a Father, Son, and Holy Spirit who thrive in their community of self-giving love (Genesis 1:27). Every person knows that pleasure is meant to be shared. There's little delight in viewing a Renaissance painting if we can't turn to our companion and say, "Look at that!"

David had waited a long time to become king of Israel. Anointed by Samuel while still a boy, David spent a portion of his life dodging the armies of Saul. Along the way, he became best friends with Saul's son, Jonathan, who "loved him as he loved himself" (1 Samuel 18:3). So it was a cruel twist of fate when Jonathan was killed in the climactic battle that defeated Saul and delivered the kingdom to David.

Losing the person he loved the most made winning the palace a tarnished prize. While David's loss seemed inevitable (it might be difficult to persuade Israel that he was king if Saul's sons were still alive), some of us have deliberately sacrificed our relationships on the fast track of success. Remember, the deepest joy doesn't come from where we live or what we do, but who we share our experiences with. —Mike Wittmer

God is coming

read>
Isaiah 35:4-10
Your God is coming (v.4).

more>
God has come to help His people (Luke 7:16 NIV).

next>
What in your life do you feel the most anxiety about right now? How might God be meeting you in the middle of this anxiousness?

Two pygmy sperm whales lay stranded near a New Zealand beach. Though volunteers, led by conservation officer Malcolm Smith, worked tirelessly, they couldn't coax the beached whales back out into the open water. Just as they were about to surrender hope, a local bottlenose dolphin named Moko arrived, made a few shrill noises toward the whales—and immediately led them into the sea. "I don't speak whale, and I don't speak dolphin," Malcolm said, "but there was obviously something that went on . . . [Moko] did what we had failed to do."

Each of us responds to our anxiety and distress uniquely. Some of us go into feverish activity, attempting to scratch a way forward. Some of us turn silent or depressed, overwhelmed with a sense that our efforts will all be futile. However, each of us share the same core need: for someone to approach us where we are and to know how to help us.

Since we are helpless on our own, the prophet Isaiah's instruction may seem cold. "Say to those with fearful hearts, 'Be strong, and do not fear' " (35:4). Don't these words strike you as something odd to say to a person rung out with fear? *Don't be afraid.* Or to a worrier: *Don't worry.* Or to one overcome with loneliness: *Don't be lonely.*

Far from flat admonitions to buck up and change their behavior, however, Isaiah was calling them to look forward, to look up and see that they were in no way alone. A divine rescue was on its way. "Be strong and do not fear," Isaiah said, "for your God is coming . . . to save you" (v.4).

The prophet invites us out of our fear (and out of our worry and loneliness and everything gripping us) because God is here, ready and able to lead us out of our prisons. Will we follow? —Winn Collier

stained

read>
Matthew 26:26-35
This is My blood, which confirms the covenant between God and His people. It is poured out as a sacrifice to forgive the sins of many (v.28).

more>
- Psalm 103:12
- Ephesians 2:13
- Revelation 1:5-6

next>
What value do you place on Jesus' sacrifice? Does your life display the enormity of God's love for you?

It had been one of those days. Busy, disjointed, and generally out of sorts. So I was less than thrilled when I opened the dryer to discover a red marker without its cap among the load of newly washed clothes. Assessing the damage, I sighed heavily as I realized only a few pieces of the large load had been left untouched by crimson stains. Knowing anger would prove fruitless, I grabbed the stain remover and went to work. Later, when the load had finished rewashing, I was thankful to see that all traces of red ink had disappeared.

When it comes to sin, no amount of manmade stain remover will ever work. Like a marker in the laundry, sin becomes visible, marking everything it touches. Our best efforts to make it go away leave us profoundly soiled and without hope (Isaiah 64:6).

We are desperate for Jesus.

Both the Old and New Testaments tell us there can be no removal of sin without the shedding of blood (Leviticus 17:11; Hebrews 9:22). While we attest to this truth verbally by confession, do our hearts grasp the enormity of it?

We are covered by the precious blood of the spotless Lamb of God (1 Peter 1:18-19). Pure, undefiled—undeserving of our sin—Jesus' blood was spilled on our behalf. Not a casual marking here and there. It was a saturation, leaving an indelible mark of love and mercy. For the believer, real life flows from a bloodstained Savior.

His sacrifice demands a response, not because He is demanding, but because His gift leaves us without excuse (Ephesians 1:7). When the magnitude of His sacrifice brings our sin and His hope to light, we realize: Repentance is a way of life (1 John 1:7-9) and our hearts should be filled with gratitude to Jesus for His blood-stain on our lives (Colossians 1:12-14). —Regina Franklin

personal and present

read>
Exodus 3:1-15
God replied to Moses, "I Am Who I Am. Say this to the people of Israel: I Am has sent me to you" (v.14).

more>
Jesus answered, "I tell you the truth, before Abraham was even born, I Am!" (John 8:58).

next>
How important is it that we understand God as being a personal God, rather than simply being an energy, power, or life-force? How significant is it that Jesus called Himself "I Am"?

Author Eckhart Tolle has described God as an "invisible energy field" that animates us and every other thing. For singer-songwriter Annie Lennox, God is "a word to describe the life force that has created all," and for controversial bishop John Shelby Spong, God is the impersonal force behind life, love, and existence.

For some authors, artists, and philosophers, God is a "life-force" God. While I like the idea of divine energy surging through my veins, some questions persist: *If God is an impersonal energy, from where do humans get their individual personalities? If God is an impersonal power, why do humans desire relationship? If God is an impersonal force, where does love come from?* Humans display all these qualities and more, so either humans are greater than the being that created them or God is much bigger than some popularly imagine.

When God revealed Himself to Moses, He presented Himself as "I Am"—*Yahweh* (the Lord)—the personal One who is present to save us (Exodus 3:14). This is a God who *saw* the oppression of His people in slavery, *heard* their cries, was *concerned* for them, and *did* something for them (vv.7-8). And saints and sinners throughout history have found this God to be anything but impersonal. He *feels* happiness (Hebrews 13:16), grief (Genesis 6:6), anger (Exodus 32:10), and compassion (Deuteronomy 32:36). He *planned* our existence and has a plan for each nation (Psalm 139:14-16; Amos 9:7). He *watches* every sparrow (Matthew 10:29-30), *counts* every hair (Luke 12:7), *hears* every cry, and *wipes away* every tear (Revelation 21:4). This is the God who desires a people He can love (Exodus 6:7) and whose invitation has always been for us to seek and discover Him (Jeremiah 29:11-14).

Moses met God in the desert that day. Not a force, but a Person. Not an electrical current, but the Spirit of the living God. —Sheridan Voysey

finishers

read>
Genesis 2
So the creation of the heavens and the earth and everything in them was completed (v.1).

more>
I press on to reach the end of the race and receive the heavenly prize for which God, through Christ Jesus, is calling us (Philippians 3:14).

next>
Are you aware of your God-ordained assignment? What will it cost you to finish what God has given you to do? What will it cost you if you don't finish His work?

Michelangelo was an Italian sculptor, architect, and poet, whose artistic accomplishment exerted a tremendous amount of influence on his contemporaries and on subsequent European art. The sad reality is, however, that he left many of his works unfinished.

Whether or not all His creatures realize it, God, the divine sculptor and architect of the universe, finished His works (Genesis 2:1-2). Having finished creating the world, He evaluated it and said it was good (2:3). Then He rested. Not because He was weary, but because creation was finished.

Not only did God complete His creation, in Jesus He finished the work of redemption. As He was nearing the end of His earthly work, Jesus explained that His nourishment came from doing the will of God and finishing His work (John 4:34). And He did just that! While on the cross, Jesus cried out, "It is finished" (John 19:30). Access to an authentic relationship with God was made available through His sacrificial death. After Jesus finished the work of redemption, He sat down at the place of honor at God's right hand (Hebrews 10:12).

As believers in Jesus, we're called to finish our God-ordained assignments (Colossians 4:17). Our lives are worth nothing unless we give ourselves to doing and finishing the work assigned to us by the Lord Jesus—the work of telling others the good news of God's love and grace.

Let's finish the work assigned to us so we can say, like the apostle Paul, "I have fought the good fight. I have finished the race, and I have remained faithful" (2 Timothy 4:7). —Marvin Williams

heaven

I'm looking forward to long walks with good friends, shared meals without rushing, and endless laughter at no one's expense.

I'm anticipating meaningful work with plenty of time for reading, photography, fishing, and community service. For occasional entertainment, I haven't written off stadiums and ballparks. If my hunch is right, competition between friends will be healthy in heaven. I'm wondering if there might even be hockey without fights, soccer without brawls, and basketball playoffs where losing well is valued as much as winning.

Frivolous speculation? Maybe. Insulting to God? I hope not. I'm trying to imagine a heaven that builds on the good we know while leaving behind the evil. As a child, I feared heaven would be boring. I missed the point of gold streets and pearly gates. As a 10-year-old, what I really liked doing most was playing baseball, collecting fossils, and hunting frogs.

In the years that followed, the deaths of family members and friends changed the way I think about heaven. But I still have questions. What will we do after enjoying long embraces, tears of laughter, and catching up? My mind still locks up like an overloaded computer when I try to weigh imponderable questions about a hereafter that will last forever.

Ironically, what gives me the most peace of mind is not cutting loose my imagination, but rather learning to trust. I find rest in the thought that God doesn't want us to know what He has planned for us. I wouldn't be surprised to hear such a God say something like, "If I told you, I'd have to take you." Or, based on the apostle Paul's experience, "If I told you how good it's going to be, I'd

May Your Kingdom come soon. May Your will be done on earth, as it is in heaven.
Matthew 6:10

have to make life more difficult for you now."

Paul seemed to imply as much when describing what he thought might have been an out-of-body experience. By his own admission, he wasn't sure what happened. But he said he was caught up to Paradise where he heard things he wasn't allowed to talk about (2 Corinthians 12:1-4). Apparently, whatever Paul heard was so exhilarating that it would have distracted him from an ongoing dependence upon the grace of God. So, for the duration of Paul's time on earth, the Lord of heaven let him suffer at the hand of Satan in order to keep him on his knees (2 Corinthians 12:7-9).

I'm convinced that the God who taught Paul to depend on Him one day at a time is now teaching us to rely on Him for an eternity that is beyond our ability to understand. So how much then does He want us to know?

Heaven in the Jewish Scriptures — Moses and the prophets tell us only a little about heaven. Asaph, the worship leader of Israel, tells us as much as anyone when he says to his God, "You guide me with Your counsel, leading me to a glorious destiny. Whom have I in heaven but You? I desire You more than anything on earth" (Psalm 73:24-25).

Later the prophet Isaiah predicts a new relationship between heaven and earth. He foresees a day of international peace, when God will live among His people on earth, when even wild animals will no longer prey on one another (Isaiah 2:4; 65:25). Isaiah envisions the eventual renewal and restoration of earth and sky when he quotes God as saying, "I am creating new heavens and a new earth, and no one will even think about the old ones anymore. . . . And the sound of weeping and crying will be heard in it no more" (65:17,19).

Heaven in the teachings of Jesus — Jesus spoke often of the kingdom of heaven. It was His way of speaking of the realm of God's rule. In prayer, He taught His disciples to say, "May Your Kingdom come soon.

May Your will be done on earth, as it is in heaven" (Matthew 6:10).

Our Teacher, however, described heaven as more than the seat of divine government. He also called it His Father's house. He told His disciples He was going there to prepare a place for them. "I will come and get you, so that you will always be with Me where I am" (John 14:3). This will be a place of happiness and everlasting reward where treasures don't rust, wear out, or get stolen (Matthew 6:19-20).

Heaven in Revelation — The last book in the Bible brings together into one great vision many themes of God's original creation. In Revelation, heaven comes to earth. The city of God descends to us. God lives among His people and wipes away "every tear from their eyes, and there will be no more death or sorrow or crying or pain. All these things are gone forever" (Revelation 21:4).

Now and Forever — So do I still warm to the possibilities I mentioned earlier? Only in a limited sense. Competition where everyone wins might be the equivalent of gold streets or pearly gates. I don't know. I want to hold those lightly. What I'm more sure about is that our God wants us to hold tightly the anticipation of living with Him forever.

I'm convinced that God is planning one surprise after another, and that heaven will be far more than we ever imagined, not less. And whatever it involves will center on the One who assured His friends with the words, "Don't let your hearts be troubled. . . . When everything is ready, I will come and get you, so that you will always be with Me where I am" (John 14:1,3).

Father in heaven, we become confused in the darkness of what we don't understand. Thank You for being so patient with us. Help us to see that the grace You have shown us today is only a taste of Your ability to use all of eternity to surprise us again and again with Your goodness. —Mart De Haan

Adapted from the Been Thinking About article *Heaven* © 2009 RBC Ministries. Read more helpful articles like this one on the Web at beenthinking.org

cement sky

read>
Job 30:16-31
I walk in gloom, without sunlight (v.28).

more>
I waited patiently for the Lord to help me, and He turned to me and heard my cry (Psalm 40:1).

next>
How might the story of Job's life encourage someone who lives under a cement sky? Why does God want us to trust Him, even when life is so hard?

My hometown is nestled between emerald cow pastures, meandering roads, and tree-covered foothills. It's most charming on bright, sunny days, but there aren't many of those. The Finger Lakes region of New York State has one the highest ratios of cloud cover in America. The locals call it "cement sky."

Many of us struggle with cement sky in our daily lives, and I'm not talking about the weather. We can relate to Job, who described his existence like this: "I walk in gloom, without sunlight" (Job 30:8).

Job's bleak outlook was partly because he believed God had ditched him. He said, "I cry to You, O God, but You don't answer. I stand before You, but You don't even look" (v.20). Although I see why Job felt that way, his feelings weren't reality. God is always with us, especially when things look really grim. When we walk through the darkest valley, God is close beside us (Psalm 23:4).

Even if Job had taken refuge in God's presence, he still had another problem. He felt cheated by his life circumstances. Job said, "Did I not weep for those in trouble? . . . So I looked for good, but evil came instead" (Job 30:25-26). Fortunately, God wasn't finished with Job. As his buddy Elihu reminded him, "[God] will bring justice if only you will wait" (35:14).

It's hard to wait when you're restless; and understandably, Job confessed, "My heart is troubled and restless" (v.27). If that sounds familiar, remember Jesus' promise, "I am leaving you with a gift—peace of mind and heart" (John 14:27).

If you struggle with depression and despair, remember that God has not abandoned you, and He is not finished with the story of your life. Only He can replace your restlessness with peace that goes beyond our understanding, like sunlight breaking through a cement sky. —Jennifer Benson Schuldt

justice

read>
Deuteronomy 16:18-20
Let true justice prevail (v.20).

more>
- Isaiah 59:1-15
- Revelation 19:11-16

next>
Where do you see the need for God's justice in your world? What are the ways God may be asking you to be an instrument of His justice?

Two of my neighbors, Eugene and Lorraine Williams, have lived a story we all need to hear. Back in 1958, they bought a house on Ridge Street, and the welcome from their white neighbors wasn't exactly warm—most of them moved away. Soon the Williams family also realized their third-grader Scheryl would be bussed to a black school across town, while the neighbor girl across the street would go to the white school nearby. Eugene and Lorraine wouldn't have it, and they (along with a few other parents) filed suit forcing the local schools to comply with the Supreme Court's decision on desegregation.

We might be tempted to reminisce on the Williams' story and bemoan it primarily as a political quandary or a social ill. Scripture refers to such acts, however, as unrighteousness—*sin*. God's Word has a lot to say about justice, and the word the Bible often translates for justice can also be translated as *righteousness*. So, in the Bible's terms, to do justice is simply to do what is right. To do injustice, then, is to do what is wrong. It's evil.

From the beginning, God intended to form a community of people living out God's just rule. First Adam and Eve, and then Noah and his family (Genesis 1:27, 6:9-10). When the time came to form Israel's society, God provided structures and regulations that would promote justice for the people. Overseeing these structures, God appointed judges and officials who would mediate disputes and ensure equity. God's instructions were clear: Call out leaders who would "judge the people fairly" throughout the land, holding powerbrokers at bay and caring for the weak or oppressed (Deuteronomy 16:18).

God's vision for a just society is part of His response to a world marred by sin. His redemption touches the individual, but redemption also touches the unjust systems of oppression in our world. —Winn Collier

hallowed be Your name

read>
Matthew 6:9-13
Our Father in heaven, may Your name be kept holy (v.9).

In a discipleship class, the participants were asked to monitor their prayer requests in a prayer journal. The purpose was to keep track of things they would present to God. By doing so, they were encouraged to pray beyond their own individual needs.

What are some things we pray for? Good health? Healing? A promotion? More money? It's interesting that Jesus told us to pray, "Our Father in heaven, may Your name be kept holy," or "hallowed be Your name" (Matthew 6:9 NKJV).

Hallow, a seldom-used word, is used four other times in the Bible. What does it mean? To hallow God's name is to:

- *Believe and trust in God.* In Numbers 20, instead of obeying God and speaking to the rock to obtain water, Moses struck it twice. God indicted Moses of sin: "You did not trust Me enough to demonstrate My holiness to the people" (v.12).
- *Fear God more than we fear men.* When we're caught in a hostile situation, God reminds us to make Him "holy in your life. He is the one you should fear" (Isaiah 8:13).
- *Obey God's commandments.* After instructing the people in the importance of holiness (Lev. 17–26), Moses concluded with these words from God, "You must faithfully keep all My commands by putting them into practice. . . . Do not bring shame on My holy name" (22:31-32).
- *Glorify God by living holy lives.* God's glory is present in His holiness (Leviticus 10:3). And God is glorified when we live holy lives. "You must be holy in everything you do, just as God who chose you is holy" (1 Peter 1:15).

Jesus tells us to pray that we will honor, revere, and glorify God as the holy Father. We honor God's name when we trust Him, fear Him, obey Him, and live a holy life. —K.T. Sim

more>
Be careful to live properly among your unbelieving neighbors. Then even if they accuse you of doing wrong, they will see your honorable behavior, and they will give honor to God when He judges the world (1 Peter 2:12).

next>
What is one thing you can do to bring honor and glory to God this week? How will you live a more holy life in Jesus?

receiving and deceiving

read>
Luke 6:27-38
You must be compassionate, just as your Father is compassionate (v.36).

more>
When God our Savior revealed His kindness and love, He saved us, not because of the righteous things we had done, but because of His mercy (Titus 3:4-5).

next>
Have you felt as if someone has taken advantage of your good will? How can you have compassion for those who seem to disregard the sacrifices of others?

My husband and I were leaving a restaurant one evening when a distraught couple approached us. Their story? *Car problems. From out of town. Waiting for their ride.* We responded with compassion, desiring to help them and possibly introduce them to Jesus. We even went to buy two meals and brought them to the hotel where they said they were staying. Arriving at the hotel, we were disappointed when the clerk instructed us to simply leave the meals at the front desk. (We later determined that he was part of the scam) A few weeks later we again saw the couple begging outside another restaurant. We had been deceived.

In such a moment, we might find it hard to see what Paul meant when he said, "God has given us this task of reconciling people to Him" (2 Cor. 5:18). Oftentimes, compassion becomes marked with a sense of romanticism in our minds. Feeling noble, we respond to another's need with the ideal that our response will not only alleviate their suffering but bring redemption to their stories. No wonder the disappointment when we find we've been deceived.

Working from an entirely different value system, God doesn't assess our sacrifices based on whether or not others appreciate what we give. Neither should we. Jesus didn't lay down His life simply for the deserving, the honest, or the thankful. He died for the broken—even for those clothed in spiritual death and persistent in their deceptive endeavors.

To reconcile the world to Christ is to give what is not deserved (Rom. 5:8; Eph. 2:4-9). To exchange kindness for unkindness. To give love instead of hate. To honestly care in the face of dishonesty. In true kingdom fashion, such gentle and humble sacrifices offer great reward. No one can take anything from us, for all that we have has been freely given to us. With whatever measure we give, we receive.

—Regina Franklin

giving to others

read>
Acts 9:36-43
There was a believer in Joppa named Tabitha (which in Greek is Dorcas). She was always doing kind things for others and helping the poor (v.36).

more>
Share each other's burdens, and in this way obey the law of Christ (Galatians 6:2).

next>
Have you committed your life to Jesus? If not, would you consider doing so today? If you have, how would you rate your relationship with Jesus? How can you be rich in good works to others?

Rebekah Rushing, who was a high-level executive assistant at Enron Corporation before it collapsed due to accounting fraud in 2001, demonstrated that ethics is much more than not doing wrong. She went beyond looking out for herself. Rushing, along with two former colleagues, set up a fund at a local bank to help other displaced workers. With $90 of her own money and the help of some publicity, the fund grew into hundreds of thousands of dollars. It was then disbursed to needy former Enron employees. Rushing was quoted as saying: "Things worked out for me and I want them to work out for everyone else." It's easy to see that Rushing is a woman who lives to help others—not just herself.

Luke described a woman in the New Testament who selflessly gave to others as well. Tabitha, a devoted believer in Jesus (Acts 9:36), produced fruits of justifying faith in Jesus Christ. Her good works flowed from her faith in Jesus, and her faith motivated her to perform good works in abundance—particularly by tangibly helping the widows of Joppa (vv.36,39). While serving the poor in her community, however, she became ill and died. Later, she was miraculously brought back to life by God's power (vv.40-41).

Tabitha is a great example of how we should live to serve others. It all begins with a vibrant relationship with Jesus. We can't begin to live beyond our own concerns if we aren't in fellowship with the One who lived and died for us.

As we stay connected to the True Vine (John 15:1-5) and follow Him, He will live His life through us, and that life includes selfless service, generosity, and personal sacrifice. It also includes seeing—not ignoring—the needs of others. And by the grace that flows from Jesus to us, we tangibly give of ourselves to meet those needs. —Marvin Williams

let's make a deal

read>
Exodus 8:20-32
"All right, go ahead," Pharaoh replied. "I will let you go into the wilderness to offer sacrifices to the Lord your God. But don't go too far away. Now hurry and pray for me" (v.28).

more>
- Psalm 51:1-4
- Proverbs 28:13
- Hebrews 12:29

next>
What does full repentance look like? How can you tell if you are truly sorry for what you've done? How might you convince the person you offended that you are genuinely repentant?

I have a friend who admitted to cheating on her husband. But rather than repent and come clean right away, she grudgingly gave up ground only when it was required. She initially hoped that offering to attend counseling would appease her husband. When that didn't work, she eventually agreed to quit her job where she had the affair. Then she floated a vague apology that skirted the numerous ways she had destroyed her family. Her strategy was sad and silly—sad because she had not owned her sin, and silly because she supposed that she could bargain her way out.

Pharaoh tried the same approach. He initially refused to let Israel leave Egypt to worship the Lord, but after the plagues of blood, frogs, gnats, and flies, he pretended to give up. " 'All right! Go ahead and offer sacrifices to your God,' he said, 'But do it here in this land.' " When Moses protested that God had demanded that Israel leave Egypt, Pharaoh bartered, "All right, go ahead. . . . but don't go too far away" (Exodus 8:25,28).

Pharaoh soon changed his mind and refused to let Israel go, but the ensuing plagues of boils, hail, and locusts brought him back to the bargaining table. This time he said that Israel could depart—but only the men. They were to leave the women and children behind as collateral for their return (10:10-11). Pharaoh never did give in completely, for even after he allowed Israel to leave, he chased them all the way to the banks of the Red Sea. There, the Lord finally drowned Pharaoh's army, taking by force what Pharaoh refused to give willingly.

Have you sinned against another person? Don't drag your feet or use whatever leverage you have to avoid making a full confession. And don't even try to bargain with God. As Pharaoh learned too late, God doesn't deal.

—Mike Wittmer

clearing clutter

read>
Philippians 3:3-9
I once thought these things were valuable, but now I consider them worthless because of what Christ has done (v.7).

more>
Let us strip off every weight that slows us down, especially the sin that so easily trips us up. And let us run with endurance the race that God has set before us (Hebrews 12:1).

next>
What's cluttering your relationship with God? How will you remove the clutter?

Have you ever tried to convince a packrat to throw something away? If so, then you know just how difficult it is to get a person who hates to part with anything—even the most unnecessary items—to let stuff go.

Interior designer William Morris suggests, "Have nothing in your home you don't know to be useful and believe to be beautiful." Reducing clutter "isn't a competition to see who has the fewest things," writes the editor of *Simple Living* magazine. "It's about living in a way that keeps your time, money, and energy available for the things that truly matter to you."

In his letter to the Philippians, the apostle Paul discloses that he once had a hoarding problem. While he wasn't necessarily filling his house with *stuff*, we find that Paul was obsessed with keeping the Jewish law. He amassed accolade after superfluous accolade for being a great Pharisee. His self-confidence and legalistic righteousness were overflowing! (3:3-6).

Paul didn't see that what he was accumulating had no good use. "But now," he said after a radical heart conversion, "I consider them worthless . . . when compared with the infinite value of knowing Christ Jesus my Lord. For His sake *I have discarded everything else, counting it all as garbage,* so that I could gain Christ and become one with Him. I no longer count on my own righteousness through obeying the law; rather, I become righteous through faith in Christ. For God's way of making us right with Himself depends on faith" (vv.7-9).

There is a time for everything, our wise teacher King Solomon explains, and that includes: "A time to keep *and* a time to throw away" (Ecclesiastes 3:6).

What should you discard in order to know Christ better? —Roxanne Robbins

human hybrids?

read>
Genesis 1:21-28
Then God said, "Let Us make human beings in Our image, to be like Us. They will reign over the fish in the sea, the birds in the sky, the livestock, all the wild animals on the earth" (v.26).

more>
Through everything God made, they can clearly see His invisible qualities—His eternal power and divine nature so they have no excuse for not knowing God (Romans 1:20-21).

next>
How would you explain your views on human hybrids to a proponent of them? How does human pride affect the way many people discuss what is ethical?

The idea of creatures half-human half-animal has been reserved for fables, folk tales, and fantasy literature. But now, as addressed in a recent *Probe Ministries* article by Heather Zeiger, human hybrids are getting dangerously close to reality. Fortunately, although scientists have tried, no attempt to create such creatures has been successful.

In Genesis 1, the creation account details God's perfect plans for animals and humans. Animals were made by God, and they were to produce offspring of the same kind (v.25; 8:17). Humans were made in God's image (unlike animals), and they were to be "fruitful and multiply" (to bear more human children—1:28).

What's more, God made a clear distinction between the roles of humans and animals on earth. He said, "[Humans] will reign over the fish in the sea, the birds in the sky, the livestock, all the wild animals on the earth" (v.26; also see v.28). The sanctity of human beings (v.26), living persons created by the very breath of God (2:7), is violated by the grotesque formation of part-human part-animal creatures. God's perfect order is cast aside by the very beings He created!

We're talking about the darkness of pride. From the moment that Satan, filled with arrogance, declared he would "ascend to heaven" and "be like the Most High" (Isaiah 14:13-14), rebellion against God became a reality.

As seen in the attempt to create human hybrids and other acts that defy God's sovereignty and authority, people continue to attempt to "play" God. But this leads only to death and destruction (Proverbs 16:18; Romans 1:22-25).

Instead, let's use God's standard as we strive to navigate today's moral and ethical issues. —Tom Felten

beyond sentimental slogans

read>
Romans 12:14-21
Bless those who persecute you. Don't curse them; pray that God will bless them (v.14).

more>
- Matthew 5:43-48
- 1 Peter 3:9-12

next>
Think about a recent conflict when a godly response was difficult. How might you respond differently today? How will you participate with the Holy Spirit to express deep kindness to others?

There's a billboard company in my area that likes to post nice slogans on its signs when it doesn't have paid clients. "Kyoto—Targets Bring Results" declares one environmentally conscious poster. "Knowledge Speaks but Wisdom Listens" reads another. "Love Nature—Love God" says a third. These fill-in billboards are always nice, sweet, and kind.

But a strange thing happened recently. Driving to work one morning, I noticed the billboards had changed—along with their tone. "Don't Buy from [name removed]!" read one sign, taking a shot at one of our large Australian supermarket chains. "[Name removed] Treated Us Badly" read another.

The nice slogans of the billboard operator turned sour when a client disappointed them.

There's a stark lesson in those billboards. Do we really mean the kind words we say? Does *our* facade of niceness melt when we're wronged or disappointed?

According to Scripture, true character is revealed through conflict. "Bless those who persecute you," the apostle Paul told the Romans (12:14). "Never pay back evil with more evil," he wrote (v.17). We're not to take revenge, Paul reminds us, but to conquer evil with good (vv.19-21).

Paul told his protégé Timothy to display love and purity when being persecuted (1 Timothy 4:12) and to oppose false teachers with gentleness and patience (2 Timothy 2:25, 4:2). The apostle Peter encouraged his flock to live such good lives that their accusers' claims would be proven false (1 Peter 2:12,20)—imitating Jesus, who didn't retaliate when He was insulted or threaten revenge when He suffered (v.23).

Sentiments of kindness are mere slogans if they can't withstand the harsh test of conflict. —Sheridan Voysey

pure work

read>
2 Timothy 2:15-22
If you keep yourself pure, you will be a special utensil for honorable use. Your life will be clean, and you will be ready for the Master to use you for every good work (v.21).

more>
God uses [His Word] to prepare and equip His people to do every good work (2 Timothy 3:17).

next>
How can you keep yourself pure so that you can be a special tool for honorable use by God? In what ways are you working hard?

I was 16 when I first discovered *The Pursuit of God* by A. W. Tozer. I reread it recently and my soul was refreshed in a new way. Oh, how I wish I could write like Tozer, with such depth of insight and deft use of words!

Tozer entered the ministry without high school or college education. He trained himself over years of diligent study and prayerful seeking of the mind of God. With no teacher but the Holy Spirit and good books, Tozer became a theologian, a scholar, and a true wordsmith in the use of the English language.

His life reminds me of the truth found in today's Scripture reading. First, Tozer lived out what it means to be a good worker, "one who does not need to be ashamed and who correctly explains the word of truth" (2 Timothy 2:15).

What did Paul mean when he wrote "work hard"? (v.15 NKJV). Some Bible translations render those words as "study." It's been said of Tozer: "He determined to memorize many sections, and succeeded. He wore out many copies as he read and reread the Book."

Second, Tozer endeavored to be a special tool for honorable use by God. How does one do that? Paul gave the answer: "Keep yourself pure" (v.21) by fleeing youthful lusts and pursuing righteousness, faith, love, and peace.

Tozer wrote, "The Bible . . . is a means to bring [people] to an intimate and satisfying knowledge of God, that they may enter into Him, that they may delight in His presence, may taste and know the inner sweetness of the very God Himself in the core and center of their hearts."

Let's continue to pursue God in purity and with hard work. He can use us to reach and train others. —Poh Fang Chia

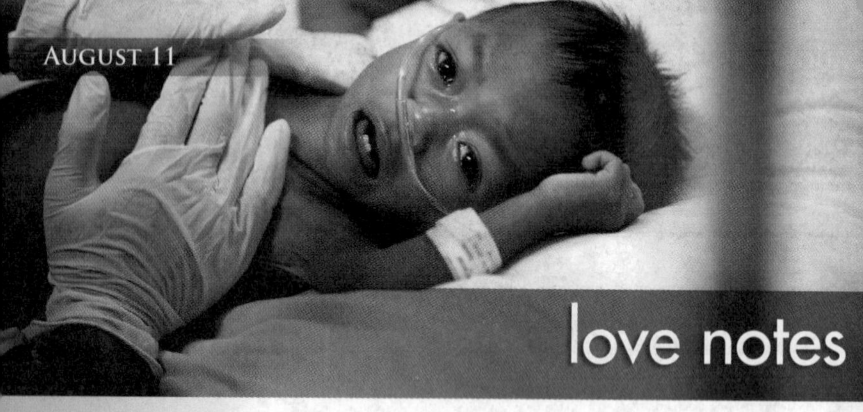

love notes

read>
Psalm 1
They delight in the law of the Lord, meditating on it day and night (v.2).

more>
I have written this to you who believe in the name of the Son of God, so that you may know you have eternal life (1 John 5:13).

next>
What passage of Scripture speaks to you deeply about God's love? What love note will you offer to Him today?

Elena Desserich was nearly 6 years old when she was diagnosed with terminal brain cancer. As the cancer took its toll, her ability to speak was gradually stolen away. But little Elena would not be denied. Wise beyond her years, she continued to communicate and express her love for her family through handwritten notes.

Sadly, cancer took Elena less than a year after her diagnosis. Before she died, however, she apparently began to hide literally hundreds of little love notes and drawings throughout the house for her family to find after she was gone. Her parents would continue to find them intermittently in places like briefcases, among Christmas decorations, and tucked between the pages of old coloring books.

Elena's thoughtful little notes remind me of God's letters to us—the Bible. He left us 66 letters—love notes from a heavenly Father that tell us the story of His care and draws us to His ultimate good for our lives.

Thinking of the Bible in this way takes me to the Psalms, where David penned these lyrics for God, "Your word is a lamp to guide my feet and a light for my path" (Psalm 119:105). He also wrote, "The instructions of the Lord are perfect, reviving the soul. . . . The commandments of the Lord are right, bringing joy to the heart" (19:7-8).

Later, in the New Testament, the apostle Paul reminded us, "Such things were written in the Scriptures long ago to teach us. And the Scriptures give us hope and encouragement as we wait patiently for God's promises to be fulfilled" (Romans 15:4).

Today, take time to read the Bible and find the love notes left for you there. Let each one fall afresh on your heart—reminding you of God's unwavering love that has changed your life forever. —Jeff Olson

coyote wild

read>
Romans 8:2-14
You have no obligation to do what your sinful nature urges you to do (v.12).

I live in a neighborhood where people mow their lawns, plant flowers, and clean up after their dogs. But sometimes at night, we hear eerie noises. I'm not talking about the neighbor's beagle yelping at the moon. This is creepy howling that is totally untamed. For our neighborhood is plagued by *coyotes*.

Sometimes when they wake me up, I lie there and think about the coyote wildness inside us. We all have it—it's part of our spiritual DNA. Paul explained it this way: "There is [a] power within me that is at war with my mind. This power makes me a slave to the sin that is still within me" (Romans 7:23). Paul's transparency helps us see that even Christians who walk with God struggle with unruliness in their souls.

Fortunately, he also reminds us that we have no obligation to do what our sinful nature urges us to do (8:12). If you're like me, you might forget that you have a choice—you don't have to listen to the whispers of your wild side: *A few more glasses of wine won't hurt. . . . Just glancing at that woman is no big deal . . .*

While we do have a choice when it comes to sin, we can't make the right call consistently without the power of the Holy Spirit. As believers in Jesus, we have God's Holy Spirit alive within us, but we have to allow Him to do His job. Paul said, "Let the Holy Spirit guide your lives. Then you won't be doing what your sinful nature craves" (Galatians 5:16).

Untamed, like those coyotes, "the [sin nature] never did obey God's laws and it never will" (Romans 8:7). With the Holy Spirit's help, we can exchange our reckless tendencies for God's peace—a better option than lying awake at night, listening to the call of the wild. —Jennifer Benson Schuldt

more>
- Romans 6:2
- Galatians 2:20
- 1 Peter 1:14-15

next>
How can the Holy Spirit help you defeat your wild side? When was the last time you asked the Holy Spirit to influence your thinking and decisions?

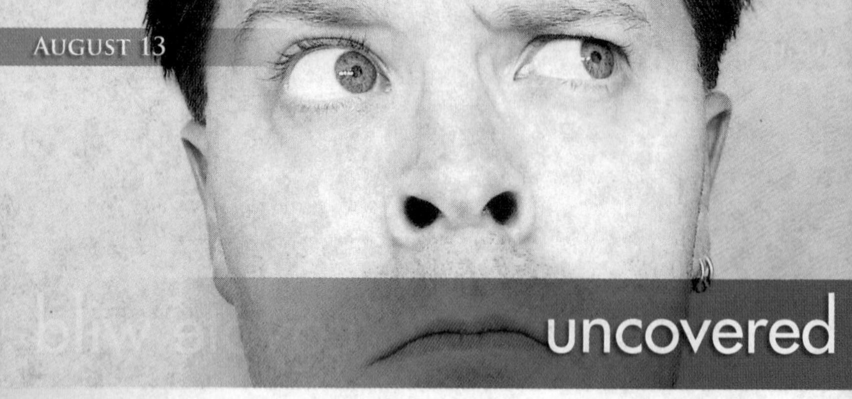

uncovered

read>
John 4:1-30
Come and see a man who told me everything I ever did! (v.29).

more>
Search me, O God, and know my heart (Psalm 139:23).

next>
What are you hiding from others—and trying to hide from God? What do you need to do today to shine God's light into your hiding place?

I remember how nervous he was, how *fearful*. Our friend came in and sat on our couch. He had something to tell us, but he couldn't get the words out. He carried a weight he had held alone, a burden he couldn't hide anymore. The hiding had nearly buried him.

Most of us have something we try to hide, some part of our story we would be horrified for others to know. Jesus met a Samaritan woman at Jacob's well, and she was certainly hiding. John tells us that the woman was drawing water "about noontime." (John 4:6) Because of the heat, the villagers did not come to the well at noon, but she did. She knew how to avoid the other women. She would not, however, be able to avoid Jesus.

Jesus surprised the woman by asking her for a drink. "You are a Jew, and I am a Samaritan woman," she said (v.9). She was accustomed to Jews (particularly men) keeping their distance. But Jesus came near, telling her that He could actually offer her living water so that she would "never be thirsty" again (v.14).

Eager for this living water, she asked Jesus for it; but Jesus made an abrupt turn, telling her to first bring her husband to Him. When the woman protested that she had no husband, Jesus recounted to the flabbergasted woman her five failed marriages—and that she wasn't married to the man she was currently living with.

For a moment, the woman felt panicked. She had been found out, the place of her deepest shame was now in the open. Quickly, however, the shame evaporated. She had encountered love. And she sprinted to the village, breathless with her amazing story. And "the people came streaming from the village to see Him" (v.30). Who wouldn't run to the One who uncovers our darkest shame—and then embraces us? —Winn Collier

Your kingdom come

read>
Matthew 6:9-13
May Your kingdom come soon (v.10).

From the time of the Babylonian Exile (586 BC), the Jews were a conquered people for some 600 years. They were ruled in succession by the Babylonians, Persians, Greeks, and Romans.

When Jesus taught the disciples how to pray (Matthew 6:9-13), the Jews were under Roman rule. God had promised them a deliverer—the Messiah. A Jew praying, "May Your kingdom come soon" (v.10) would have had in mind the end of Roman rule, for the Messiah was to come and establish a new kingdom (Luke 19:11), and for David's descendant to reign as king (2 Samuel 7:12-13; Luke 1:32-33). Today, "May Your kingdom come soon" means:

Commitment. Jesus warned, "Anyone who puts a hand to the plow and then looks back is not fit for the kingdom of God" (Luke 9:62). The disciple must "seek the kingdom of God above all else, and live righteously" (Matthew 6:33). "May Your kingdom come soon" is a prayer of commitment to live for Jesus.

Commission. Jesus was sent to "preach the Good News of the kingdom of God" (Luke 4:43). The committed Christian knows that his commission is a co-mission with Jesus—"As the Father has sent Me, so I am sending you" (John 20:21). "May Your kingdom come" is a prayer for world evangelism, for God's kingdom grows every time a person becomes a Christian (Matthew 21:31-32; Mark 1:15; Luke 16:16).

Coming. The coming of the kingdom is also a future event when Jesus will come again and establish His 1,000-year reign on earth (Daniel 2:44; Revelation 20:1-6). "May Your kingdom come" is a prayer for God's plan to be fulfilled (Isaiah 14:24) and for Christ to be enthroned as King of kings (Matthew 25:31). As we pray those words, we are asking Jesus to usher in the time when we will see Him face to face (Matthew 24:14). —K.T. Sim

more>
- Daniel 7:13-14
- Philippians 2:9-11
- Revelation 11:15-17

next>
Jesus is coming back soon. How well are you prepared for His return? What can you do that will extend God's kingdom?

hopeful

read>
Jeremiah 32:6-17
This is what the Lord of Heaven's Armies, the God of Israel, says: "Someday people will again own property here in this land and will buy and sell houses and vineyards and fields" (v.15).

more>
- Lamentations 3:17-26
- Jeremiah 31:3-6
- Psalm 31:21-24

next>
What desolate places have you experienced lately? What is God teaching you about your level of dependency on Him? When in the position of surrender, do you find yourself angry or hopeful? Why?

Carefully patting the dirt around the base of the seedling, we stepped back to observe our work. Six years old, I was helping my dad plant a small weeping willow in the center of our otherwise barren backyard. When we moved soon afterward, I didn't understand why the tree couldn't go with us. I thought it was for me. Ten years later, when we moved yet again, our new backyard was beautifully landscaped, and in the very center stood—you guessed it—a magnificent weeping willow. It was as if my simple sacrifice years before—leaving that prized willow sapling behind—had somehow been rewarded.

During Jeremiah's prophetic ministry, Jerusalem had been besieged, the land destroyed, and some of its finest taken into captivity. God Himself had told them to settle in for a long haul in a foreign land (Jeremiah 29:4-6). The faithful remnant must have wondered where God was in the midst of the chaos. For few willingly embrace surrender when living in the expectation of a promise.

God, however, remains insistent that we live in His will, not our own. Out of great love, God takes us to places of seemingly no return in order to make us totally dependent on Him (Hosea 6:1-2). In the moment, no amount of posturing or spin can make desolation seem a blessing. And yet, in truth, it is with God.

We can sometimes get drawn into a sense of entitlement. We feel as if God "owes" us. That's why we need desolate places in life. The sacrifices in the journey can often be excruciating, sometimes feeling much like death.

But it is in these places we learn the holiness of surrender. To give up what we wanted to keep—without condition. We learn to hope, believing that God's restoration is greater than any discomfort we may feel today. —Regina Franklin

taking God for granted

read>
2 Samuel 6:1-15
Serve the Lord with reverent fear, and rejoice with trembling (Psalm 2:11).

more>
- Exodus 3:1-6
- Isaiah 6:1-8

next>
In what ways have you trifled with God's holiness? What do you need to change in order to approach God with a greater sense of awe and reverence? How has your obedience led to blessings and freedom?

My wife and I have been married for 2 decades. But, to my own embarrassment, there have been times when I've taken her for granted. I've been so familiar with her presence that I've been insensitive to her needs and wants.

Just as it's not healthy to take our spouses for granted, King David would say it's not healthy to take God for granted. Desiring to unite the nation spiritually, David went to retrieve the ark of God from Kiriath Jearim, where it had been located for over 25 years. They transported the ark on a new cart (2 Samuel 6:3). It must have been classy and convenient. But as they transported the precious piece, the oxen stumbled, and a man named Uzzah reached out—with good intentions—to stabilize the ark. And when he touched it, God's judgment broke out against him and he died (v.7).

David became angry and afraid of God, and he decided to abandon the mission (v.10). Could it be that God had responded with such drastic measures because David had taken Him for granted? Had the king ignored God's standards (Numbers 4:15,20; Deuteronomy 10:8) or failed to inquire how he should transport the ark? David assumed he knew what God would approve. In this failure, David had begun to trifle with God's holiness.

This dramatic episode presents some vital truths:

(1) We must revere God and never attempt to manipulate Him. This narrative reveals how God feels about placing our preferences ahead of His purposes.

(2) Obedience to God's specific will is more important than good intentions. Coming close to doing God's will is not enough.

Let's pay close attention to our relationship with God, not allowing privilege to become presumption. May we approach Him with awe and according to His revealed will! —Marvin Williams

who you are

read>
1 John 3:1-10
See how very much our Father loves us, for He calls us His children, and that is what we are! (v. 1).

more>
The Lord did not set His heart on you and choose you because you were more numerous than other nations, for you were the smallest of all nations! Rather, it was simply that the Lord loves you (Deuteronomy 7:7-8).

next>
Write down words that you or others have said about yourself. Now make another list of what God says about you.

A confused, middle-aged man flagged down a bus driver in Seattle. He wore expensive clothes and spoke French, German, and English, but he did not know who he was. He remembered slices of his life: living in Slovakia, teaching English in China, and last night's sleep in Discovery Park, but he could not remember his own name.

The authorities researched the man's story on the Internet, and within five hours they had discovered that his name was Edward Lighthart. But learning his identity did not get Edward out of the woods. He looked at an old picture and could see beyond a doubt that he was Edward Lighthart, yet he couldn't make the emotional and psychological connection with his identity. He struggled to own who he was.

Many of us can sympathize with his plight. We know intellectually that we are the children of God, adopted by grace into His family, and yet we emotionally relate to our Father as slaves who must earn His acceptance by our own effort. We mistakenly suppose that our integrity or servant's heart attracted God's attention, and so we try harder in a futile attempt to achieve what we can only *receive*.

We hear that we have "become a new person" in Christ so that "the old life is gone; a new life has begun" (2 Corinthians 5:17). We read that our "body is the temple of the Holy Spirit" (1 Corinthians 6:19). We learn that "we died and were buried with Christ" (Romans 6:4). But we look at our sin and can scarcely believe it.

Like Edward Lighthart, we need to continue to look at our true picture. Don't be misled by what you have or have not done. Embrace your true identity. Own it. Then ask God for grace to become what you already are. —Mike Wittmer

compartments

read>
Jeremiah 23:21-32
Am I not everywhere in all the heavens and earth? (v.24).

more>
- Deut. 4:39; 10:14
- Proverbs 15:3
- Amos 9:2

next>
How does it convict you to know that God is always with you? How does it comfort you?

I was talking with a friend the other day about how easy it is to live our life compartmentally. For instance, on Sundays we can enter the compartment of going to church and worshiping God. But the rest of the week we might ease out of church-mode and enter compartments that deny God's presence and His commands.

The prophet Jeremiah, in a strongly worded message condemning false teachers, proclaimed the following truths about God:

- He is "close at hand" (23:23). God is present in the daily events of our lives—all of them.
- He is "far away at the same time" (v.23). God is both *transcendent* (existing beyond the limitations of our material world) and *immanent* (existing in and sustaining our universe).

God declares that He is "everywhere in all the heavens and earth" (v.24). He can't be contained by any compartments we try to lamely create. He's there, and He knows our actions and the words we say (v.31).

In his book *The Knowledge of the Holy,* A. W. Tozer wrote, "The Scriptures teach that God is infinite. This means that His being knows no limits. Therefore there can be no limit to His presence; He is omnipresent. In His infinitude He surrounds the finite creation and contains it. There is no place beyond Him for anything to be. God is our environment as the sea is to the fish and the air to the bird."

I love that thought—God is our *environment.* We live each moment accompanied by Him. Every moment is filled with *Him.* And we can't deny His presence in any place or decision in our life, for He is "everywhere" (v.24).

No compartment can contain God. Let's live today in the comfort and conviction of His presence, for He is "close at hand" (v.23). —Tom Felten

be silent

read>
Zephaniah 1
Stand in silence in the presence of the Sovereign Lord, for the awesome day of the Lord's judgment is near (v.7).

more>
Fear God and obey His commands, for this is everyone's duty. God will judge us for everything we do, including every secret thing, whether good or bad (Eccl. 12:13-14).

next>
What will you bring to God in repentance today? How would remembering the Day of the Lord change the way you live your life?

Recently a friend said to me, "I used to fear how people perceived me. Then I discovered that Satan's deviousness is something even greater to fear. Later, however, I learned that to fall under God's wrath is to be feared the most."

Zephaniah describes the day when God's anger will be poured out as "a day of terrible distress and anguish, a day of ruin and desolation, a day of darkness and gloom, a day of clouds and blackness" (1:15). The prophet's description presents a terrifying picture! Note the descriptive nouns used to characterize this day when God will pour out His wrath on those who have chosen sin instead of Him.

The initial warnings in Zephaniah's message were directed to the people in Judah. They had worshiped God, but only superficially—for they worshiped other gods too. Judah had turned away from following the Lord and failed to seek Him and His guidance (vv.4-6). Though they said they believed in the existence of God, it had little or no impact on the way they lived.

Zephaniah said, "Stand in silence in the presence of the Sovereign Lord, for the awesome day of the Lord's judgment is near" (v.7). What does it mean to be silent before the Lord? It may mean that we should stop making excuses for our sin, or that we cease trying to deny that we're sinners—deserving of God's wrath. Silence is sometimes viewed as a way of admitting one's guilt (Leviticus 10:3). It is also a sign of reverence (Psalm 62:1; Habakkuk 2:20).

After being silent, we must repent by seeking the Lord and following His commands, to do what is right and to live humbly (Zephaniah 2:3). Although God's great day of judgment is coming soon (1:14-16), it's not too late to turn back to God. —Poh Fang Chia

spiritual unity

read>
Ephesians 4:1-6
Make every effort to keep yourselves united in the Spirit, binding yourselves together with peace (v.3).

more>
- John 10:16
- Ephesians 2:14
- Colossians 3:11

next>
How are you keeping your distance from fellow believers who are different from you? Why is it important that believers in Jesus achieve unity?

Segregating ourselves along ethnic and social lines is a common human practice. We're simply more comfortable around "our kind" of people, and we tend to keep our distance from those who seem different from us.

In his letter to the church at Philippi, the apostle Paul addressed the challenges faced by a group of people from mixed backgrounds. Within this particular group, there were people of Asian, Greek, and Roman heritage. The New Testament also specifically mentions a businesswoman who sold expensive cloth to the rich, a slave girl who was demon-possessed, and a prison guard (Acts 16).

Paul's answer to the question of how to blend their multiple ancestries and social classes was the unity they shared in Christ. He wrote, "Above all, you must live as citizens of heaven, conducting yourselves in a manner worthy of the Good News about Christ. Then, whether I come and see you again or only hear about you, I will know that you are standing together with one spirit and one purpose, fighting together for the faith, which is the Good News" (Philippians 1:27).

Unity was at the top of Paul's list for this diverse fellowship. It's the same message he stressed to the church in Galatia: "There is no longer Jew or Gentile, slave or free, male and female. For you are all one in Christ Jesus" (Galatians 3:28). The apostle wasn't denying the value of one's ethnic background or gender. He was, however, lifting up and affirming the spiritual oneness that is found in Jesus. Here's where we share common ground, regardless of our race, social status, or gender.

Ethnicity and social class will always possess the potential to divide. But our shared unity in Jesus has the power to supersede our differences and draw us together for a greater purpose. —Jeff Olson

power-trippers

read›
Nehemiah 6:1-15
They were just trying to intimidate us, imagining that they could discourage us (v.9).

more›
- Psalm 56:11
- Ephesians 6:12
- Philippians 1:28

next›
Does being a Christian mean being a doormat? How can we bring glory to God when we deal with people who want to control us?

Josh Evans never existed. Still, he befriended 13-year-old Megan Meier through an online network Eventually, he sent this message, "I don't know if I want to be friends with you. . . . I hear you're not nice to your friends." Josh posted increasingly cruel notes until Megan committed suicide. As it turned out, "Josh" was actually the mother of one of Megan's friends, posing as a teenage bully.

If you've ever encountered a bully, you understand the fear and humiliation these power-trippers thrive on. Nehemiah understood it too. When he and the Israelites were rebuilding Jerusalem's wall, he said his harassers were "just trying to intimidate us, imagining that they could discourage us" (Nehemiah 6:9).

Sanballat and Geshem sent messages asking Nehemiah to meet with them so they could derail his work. He saw through their device answering, "I am engaged in a great work, so I can't come" (v.3).

After sending their message four separate times, Nehemiah's bullies changed tactics. They threatened to tell the king that Nehemiah was planning a rebellion. Nehemiah replied, "There is no truth in any part of your story. You are making up the whole thing" (v.8). Nehemiah then prayed, "Remember, O my God, all the evil things that [they] have done" (v.14). Like Nehemiah, we need to call on the One who is "glorious in power" (Exodus 15:6), seeking His strength to complete the work He has for us.

Power-trippers are everywhere—at work, at school, and even at the dinner table. They may pick on us for a while, but no one can ultimately thwart the work God has called us to do (Romans 8:31-33). Nehemiah proved it. When he and the Israelites finished the wall, his bullies were the ones who were "frightened and humiliated" (Nehemiah 6:16). —Jennifer Benson Schuldt

small things

read>
Matthew 13:31-46
The kingdom of heaven is like a mustard seed planted in a field (v.31).

more>
Remember, dear brothers and sisters, that few of you were wise in the world's eyes or powerful or wealthy when God called you (1 Corinthians 1:26).

next>
In what ways do you feel small or insignificant? What might God want to do with you in that perceived weakness?

A tech firm in South Africa demonstrated that a carrier pigeon could carry data faster than the nation's premier Internet provider. Unlimited IT strapped a data card to the leg of a pigeon named Winston and sent him off on his 50-mile flight from their headquarters to the coastal town of Durban. At the same time, they began a data download using one of their office computers. Winston arrived in an hour and 8 minutes. The download took two hours and 6 minutes.

Many of us live as though we believe the old cliché, *bigger is better.* The ones who have the most money or power have the most followers—we believe these are the only ones who have an opportunity to make a meaningful impact in our world. Jesus, however, paints a very different picture.

In first-century Palestine, the mustard seed was one of the smallest seeds the farmers knew. A mustard seed represented something diminutive, seemingly insignificant. Yet, Jesus chose this inconsequential speck to explain to His followers God's kingdom. The kingdom of God often begins small, like a tiny seed; yet after it is planted, it "becomes the largest of garden plants" (Matthew 13:32). And after it has finished growing, it offers shelter to all who will accept it. "It grows into a tree, and birds come and make nests in its branches."

Jesus offers this parable as more than a reassuring or comforting story. *Far more.* For this is actually what "the kingdom . . . is like" (v.31). In God's kingdom, size and power and reputation mean little. In fact, God chooses "things the world considers foolish" and taps the shoulder of those who "are powerless" (1 Corinthians 1:27). God is searching for those who will obey Him, not for those who are impressive in the world's eyes. —Winn Collier

healing confession

read>
James 5:12-18
Confess your sins to each other and pray for each other so that you may be healed (v.16).

more>
My son, give glory to the Lord, the God of Israel, by telling the truth. Make your confession and tell me what you have done. Don't hide it from me (Joshua 7:19).

next>
What are some of the risks and rewards involved in confessing our sins to one another? To what mature believer can you confess your sins?

In 2006, confession of sin became an artistic expression. Two artists, Laura Barnett and Sandra Spannan, created an exhibit in a storefront in Manhattan, which allowed passersby to confess their sins. They sat in the storefront, dressed as 19th-century washerwomen. The words on the window read, "Air your dirty laundry. 100-percent confidential. Anonymous. Free." Onlookers were encouraged to confess their sins on pieces of paper. When those who "confessed" walked away, however, the women collected their written sins and displayed them for all to see.

James commanded believers in Jesus to confess their sins to one another (5:16). The context for this verse is praying and caring for the physically sick. Praying for the sick, however, included a command for mutual confession and prayer. James was teaching that all sin, especially unconfessed sin, is a dangerous enemy to the body of Jesus. It leads to the breaking of fellowship with God and others, the building of relational walls and the destruction of community, and the prevention of moral change in the lives of believers. Confession brought healing—physical and spiritual.

Scripture reveals that we should first confess our sins to God (1 John 1:9). Then, despite the risks (rejection, embarrassment), we can and should "confess [our] sins to each other." How? Sin that has affected the body of Christ should be confessed to the body. Sin against a fellow believer should be confessed to that individual. For sin that is not against the body of Christ or a person, we should use wisdom and find a fellow believer to whom we can admit our sins. God gives us divine help as we confess our sins to Him.

There's great power in a community that is serious about mutual confession and prayer. —Marvin Williams

His perfect timing

read>
Mark 6:30-44
Jesus took the five loaves and two fish . . . and blessed them. Then, breaking the loaves into pieces, He kept giving the bread to the disciples so they could distribute it to the people (v.41).

more>
This same God who takes care of me will supply all your needs from His glorious riches, which have been given to us in Christ Jesus (Philippians 4:19).

next>
How can your need be an opportunity to develop a heart of expectation in Jesus? How are you a steward of God's resources?

O*ne hour and 36 minutes until deadline.* Having returned to full-time teaching, I'm learning the complexities of balancing a job along with working with my husband in ministry and continuing my writing. All of which trail the two main roles in my life—wife and mom. Life is far from predictable. Some days—most days—it feels impossible. Tempted to live in the land of "never enough time," I can either become overwhelmed or wait expectantly on the Lord. Only one choice allows my life to become a daily transfer of the impossible to the possible (Luke 1:37).

Because the secular world thrives on a treadmill of activity, we can mistakenly demonize any level of busyness. While we need to be aware of the reasons for our packed schedules and regularly assess their validity, the need for time does not always suggest a lack of order. Sometimes it is the presentation of a divine opportunity.

When Jesus ministered to the multitudes and became aware of their hunger, He didn't chastise them for their lack of preparation (Mark 6:35-37). He fed them. Their need was not a result of sin; it came as a revelation of the kingdom—both in their spiritual hunger and their physical satisfaction (vv.42-44).

God wants to unfold in our lives His principle of kingdom provision—where "not enough" becomes the assurance that He "is able, through His mighty power at work within us, to accomplish infinitely more than we might ask or think" (Ephesians 3:20). Not because we are asking for our own desires, but because we are working for His (James 4:3).

When we've given all we have with the heart of a faithful steward, we have only to wait. He will provide. Present the need to Him and wait on His perfect timing. —Regina Franklin

Your will be done

read>
Matthew 6:9-13
May Your will be done on earth, as it is in heaven (v.10).

more>
I take joy in doing Your will, my God, for Your instructions are written on my heart (Psalm 40:8).

next>
What has God's Word been telling you to do that you've put off or haven't carried out? Don't delay. What will you do to accomplish it today?

The two requests in verse 10 of the Lord's Prayer are two sides of the same coin (Matthew 6). When we pray for God to rule as king, we're also acknowledging that we will obey the King and do His bidding.

God has planned good for us (Jeremiah 29:11; Romans 8:28), so we can pray, "May Your will be done on earth, as it is in heaven." This is a prayer of submission and surrender, in which we ask God to conquer us, to overcome our sinful will and willful resistance, and to align our wills to His perfect one. It's a prayer that says, "We choose to obey God." But what is God asking us to do?

First, God's will for unbelievers is that they believe in Jesus Christ and receive salvation (John 6:40; 1 Timothy 2:3-4). Second, if you're a believer in Jesus, you're already in God's saving will. God wants us to know His good and perfect will (Romans 12:2). He wants us to be holy (1 Thessalonians 4:3) and Christlike (Romans 8:29). He wants us to live honorable lives (1 Peter 2:15) and to suffer for doing good—not evil (1 Peter 3:17, 4:19). He wants us to be thankful in all circumstances (1 Thessalonians 5:18). The list could go on and on, for the Bible provides clear direction for life's decisions (2 Timothy 3:16-17).

The problem, then, is not that we can't know God's will. Rather, we're often unwilling to do what we already know is God's will (Deuteronomy 29:29; John 7:17). That's why it's so important that we pray more and more, "May Your will be done on earth, as it is in heaven. Lord, I want to obey You now. And I pray that the whole world will obey You too." —K.T. Sim

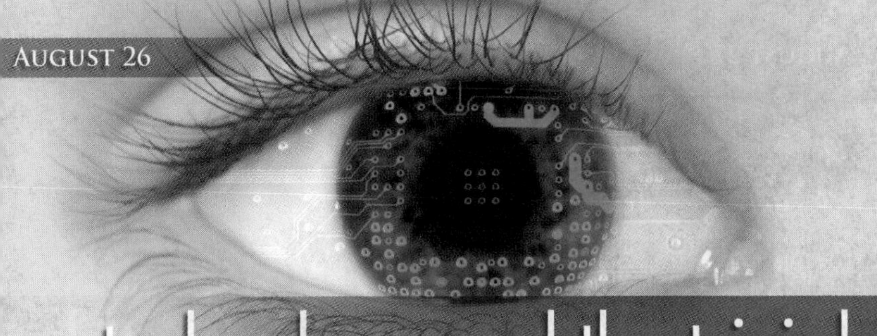

technology and the trivial

read>
Psalm 23
The Lord is my shepherd; I have all that I need. He lets me rest in green meadows; He leads me beside peaceful streams (vv. 1-2).

more>
- Psalm 46:10
- Isaiah 30:15
- Colossians 4:2

next>
Are you using technology or is technology using you? How might the constant diversions of our media influence your ability to think deeply in a single direction, and how might that impact your walk with Christ?

If our technology had existed in Jesus' day, our Bibles might read: "Jesus asked His disciples, 'Who do people say that the Son of Man is?' but they were checking their e-mail and missed the question." Or "A third time He asked him, 'Simon . . . do you love Me?' Peter was hurt that Jesus asked the question a third time, but then his cell phone rang and he replied, 'I'm sorry, Lord, I've got to take this.' " Or on Pentecost, "Peter continued preaching for a long time, and a handful of people believed and were baptized while thousands more texted and sent out tweets on Twitter" (see Mark 8:27-28; John 21:15; Acts 2:40-41).

Technology can stifle our spiritual growth in subtle ways. The first Christians "devoted themselves to the apostles' teaching, and to fellowship, and to sharing in meals (including the Lord's Supper), and to prayer" (Acts 2:42). None of these things come easily in our wired world.

Who has the time or discipline to study the apostles' teaching and pray when cable television and the Internet jangle with unimportant yet interesting diversions? Let's face it, our lives would be little changed if we missed that latest score, review, or celebrity gossip. Yet filling our minds with such minutiae comes at some cost, for we may unknowingly project our reading of the virtual world upon the eternal truths of God's Word. When *everything* is trivial, then *anything* is trivial.

Fellowship and community are thought to be the strengths of our new media, but busy texters ignore us and intrusive phone calls interrupt us. We often sit in the presence of bodies whose minds are elsewhere.

Lest you think I'm simply a hater of today's technology, ask yourself this: When the Good Shepherd leads you beside "peaceful streams," do you "rest in green meadows" or reach for your iPhone? —Mike Wittmer

hagar mistake

read>
Genesis 16:1-16
Sarai, Abram's wife, took Hagar the Egyptian servant and gave her to Abram as a wife (v.3).

more>
Abraham had two sons, one from his slave wife and one from his freeborn wife. The son of the slave wife was born in a human attempt to bring about the fulfillment of God's promise. (Galatians 4:22-23).

next>
Before taking things into your own hands, consider the potential consequences of a Hagar mistake. Why is it vital that we wait on God's timing and provision?

A Christian friend of mine was desperate for marriage and tired of waiting for God to *deliver*. Finally, she entered into an intimate relationship with a man whose character and faith lacked nearly every requisite trait she'd once held dear. When the unhealthy romance finally ended, my friend felt dejected and humiliated. She looked back on the relationship with dismay, questioning her judgment and why she'd allowed her heart to wander so far away from God.

"I made a *Hagar mistake,*" my friend later admitted. A "Hagar mistake" refers to the grievous error Old Testament dame Sarai made when she was unable to conceive. Sarai, in an attempt to rectify a situation which she felt God had ignored far too long, pushed her husband Abram into the arms of another woman—their Egyptian maidservant Hagar (Genesis 16:1-3).

Hagar bore Abram's child, a son named Ishmael. Also born were lethal doses of jealousy and contempt between Sarai and Hagar for years to come. When Sarai took her unfulfilled longings into her own hands, she couldn't see the agony that would follow.

Tony Fetchel, a former Los Angeles pastor whose own *Hagar mistake* nearly cost him his marriage wrote, "Though what we see in our marriages or families may not look how we want it to, when we want it to, we fail miserably when we try and supplement our wisdom for God's. Whether we're trying to satisfy unmet needs, or doing what we think to be the right thing to serve the plan of God, the reality is, our decisions have consequences."

Today and always, remember that you can avoid much turmoil by trusting God instead of yourself! —Roxanne Robbins

your version of joy

read>
John 16:16-24
You will have abundant joy (v.24).

more>
Don't be dejected and sad, for the joy of the Lord is your strength! (Nehemiah 8:10).

next>
What's the difference between happiness and joy? What will it take for you to fully realize the joy found in Jesus?

So I was surfing the Web when the words of an online banner ad caught my eye. "Find your version of happiness now." Interesting, huh? The fine print in the ad explained that it was for Personals—designed to link people in search of dates with other like-minded individuals.

Whether it's finding Mr. or Ms. Right or simply ordering that deluxe pizza with anchovies you've been dying for, happiness waxes and wanes with the events of our lives. It's a fickle and elusive emotion.

Joy, on the other hand, is not found in personals and pizzas. In John 16, Jesus said to His disciples, "You will weep and mourn over what is going to happen to Me, but the world will rejoice" (v.20). He was preparing them for His journey to the cross. They would experience intense grief over His death, while the world would celebrate.

But then Jesus told them, "Your grief will suddenly turn to wonderful *joy*" (v.20). The gloom and darkness of Jesus' passing would be dispelled by His bright and glorious reappearance—by His resurrection from the dead.

We too are recipients of this joy. It flows from the realization that Jesus has died for us—taking the punishment for our sins on Himself—and that He rose again, proving that His promise of eternal life is real. Now *that's* something to rejoice in!

Life is filled with twists and turns, sorrows and happy times. But Jesus tells us that our lives can and should be marked by "abundant joy" (v.24). This isn't our "version of happiness," it's His provision of something real and lasting.

Have you been looking for happiness in all the wrong places? Instead, consider what Jesus has provided. He said, "No one can rob you of that joy" (v.22). —Tom Felten

Our Father's voice

read>
Isaiah 30:18-22
Your own ears will hear Him. Right behind you a voice will say, "This is the way you should go," whether to the right or to the left (v.21).

more>
- John 10:3
- 2 Peter 1:19-21

next>
When was the last time you "heard" the voice of God? How do you think we can discern between His voice and our own thoughts and desires?

I host a live, call-in radio program. One day, we explored the tricky topic of hearing God's voice. "Does God speak personally to people?" I asked listeners. "If so, how? And how can we be sure it's His voice we're hearing and not our own thoughts?" Maryanne was my first caller.

"Fifteen years ago I heard God speak to me—audibly," she said. "I was in the New Age movement, was desperately lonely, and one day called out to God for help."

"What words did you hear this voice say?" I asked. "He told me to visit a particular church," she replied; "the last church I'd have thought of visiting." Maryanne described how she obeyed that voice, visited the church, was introduced to the Bible, and became a Christian.

We can be skeptical of such stories, but doesn't Maryanne's experience ring true to God's character?

Isaiah addressed the Israelites during a time of calamity. They had abandoned God and were now reaping the consequences. Yet God still longed to love them (Isaiah 30:18). "He will be gracious if you ask for help," Isaiah said (v.19). At their earnest cry, the responsive God would speak, His voice guiding them to His side (v.21). As a result, they would reject the idols and spiritualities that had led them astray (v.22). Isn't this Maryanne's story?

God's voice may be heard as thunder (John 12:29), as a thought (Acts 20:22), and even as a human voice (1 Kings 19:12; 1 Samuel 3:4). "I think God primarily speaks to us through the Bible," Maryanne went on to say. "But I will never forget that experience."

As we study the Bible and listen to God (Hebrews 1:2; 2 Timothy 3:16), let's be ready for His voice today—that strong, authoritative, fatherly voice.

—Sheridan Voysey

zealous for Jesus

read>
Romans 12:9-21
Never be lazy, but work hard and serve the Lord enthusiastically (v.11).

more>
I have worked harder than any of the other apostles; yet it was not I but God who was working through me by His grace (1 Corinthians 15:10).

next>
How would you rate your zeal quotient? What does it mean for you to passionately serve God?

All of us are capable of being zealous, regardless of our personality type. Even the most phlegmatic person can be passionate about something. Some people are into soccer, for others it's food. So the issue isn't whether or not one can be zealous, but where a person's devotion lies.

In Romans 12, the apostle Paul provides some instruction that includes being zealous in serving the Lord. John Piper paraphrased it this way: "Do lots of work for Christ, passionately."

The words "never be lazy, but work hard . . . enthusiastically" (v.11) emphasize being earnest and devoted in getting things done. What does that look like? Consider the following questions:

Are we efficient, or do we procrastinate?

Do we work hard to get things done, or do we give up halfway?

Romans 12:11 also contains this idea: Do lots of work for the Lord passionately—not being grouchy. A person passionate about serving the Lord doesn't consider the number of hours he has clocked in for the Lord. He's willing to do more, and he does it without complaint or protest. The reason is simple. Serving Jesus is the highest privilege in the universe for human beings.

In a Billy Graham biography written by John Pollock, there was a conversation recorded between Billy Graham and President Lyndon B. Johnson. President Johnson asked Billy, with whom he had been a friend for years, what position he would like to have in his administration. Billy Graham replied: "Sir, I believe that Jesus Christ has called me to preach His gospel. To me this is the highest calling any man could have on earth."

In view of God's mercy, let's strive to be zealous Christians—passionately serving Jesus. —Poh Fang Chia

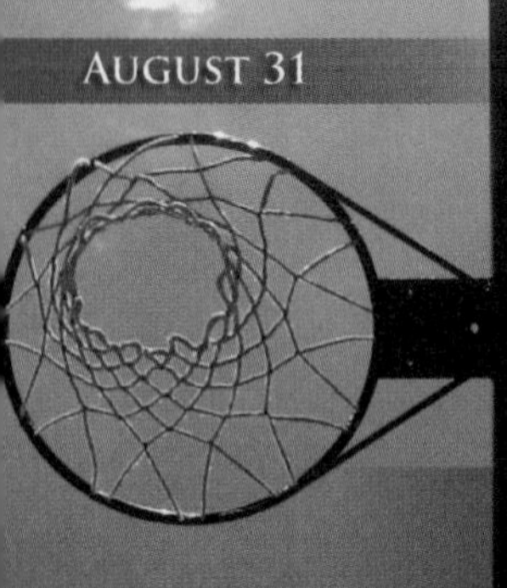

no benchwarmers

read>
Philippians 1:3-11
I am certain that God, who began the good work within you, will continue His work until it is finally finished on the day when Christ Jesus returns (v.6).

more>
God is working in you, giving you the desire and the power to do what pleases Him (Philippians 2:13).

next>
How do you view the significance of your role in God's kingdom? What does God want you to do for the "team"?

I always felt a little sad for the guys on my high school basketball team who were put into a game during the waning seconds when the outcome was already decided. I was glad to see them finally get a chance to play, especially if we were winning, but it always seemed a bit nominal.

Unfortunately, *nominal* is how more than a few Christians view their role in God's kingdom. Many see themselves as nothing but benchwarmers, sitting on the sidelines while others—like pastors or missionaries—do meaningful kingdom work. *If I'm fortunate, they think, maybe God will give me some token playing time near the end of the game.*

That's hardly the way God sees it. Check out what the apostle Paul wrote to a group of Christians in the Roman colony of Philippi: "I am certain that God, who began the good work within you, will continue His work until it is finally finished on the day when Christ Jesus returns" (Philippians 1:6).

In some ways, the Philippians weren't really different from us. They were a diverse group of people who worked and lived and loved. But because of Jesus, they were called up into a greater story that was hardly anything but normal. And Paul was confident that each one played an active role.

The apostle Paul would say a similar thing about another group of believers who lived in the town of Thessalonica: "So we keep on praying for you, asking our God to enable you to live a life worthy of His call" (2 Thessalonians 1:11).

None of us know how much time is left in the "game" before Jesus returns. Whether it's a little or a lot, there are no benchwarmers in God's kingdom. He has cleared the bench and called all of us to join Him in advancing His kingdom.

—Jeff Olson

shalom

read>
Psalm 122
May there be peace within your walls and prosperity in your palaces (v.7).

more>
Lord, You will grant us peace; all we have accomplished is really from You (Isaiah 26:12).

next>
In what area do you need to receive God's shalom? How can we extend God's shalom to the world?

One of my neighbors, who was born in Tibet, has taught me the traditional Tibetan greeting, "Tashi Delek." Whenever I meet him, no matter the time of day, I see his gregarious smile and hear, "Tashi Delek"—and I reply with the same words. The words mean "fine, well" or "all things good." I look forward to seeing him—and receiving his greeting. There is something rich in this ritual.

The Hebrew word *shalom* carries a similar connotation. In English, we translate *shalom* as peace. However, through cultural association and overuse, peace often has a tame sense—denoting some kindly, calm state of passive inner reflection. *Shalom*, on the other hand, is a strong, active word. To offer someone shalom, as the Jews regularly did during Bible times (and still do today), was to pass on a blessing and to evoke God's good intentions for His world. Shalom communicates completeness, wholeness, and human delight. In other words, the notion of shalom speaks of the world as God always intended it to be.

This is why rebellion against God is so destructive. As one theologian put it, "Evil is the spoiling of shalom." When God first created the world, it existed in a state of joy and prosperity (shalom); and He continues to be active in His world, working to bring us back to that good place.

This theme runs throughout the Bible. God is a God of shalom, and He has formed His people to be a people of shalom. We are to work for the "peace and prosperity" of the cities and neighborhoods where we live (Jeremiah 29:7). We are to "search for peace, and work to maintain it" (1 Peter 3:11).

Wherever we go, we carry God's shalom with us. We receive and spread God's peace to the world. —Winn Collier

discover the book

read>
2 Kings 22:8–23:3
Hilkiah the high priest said to Shaphan the court secretary, "I have found the Book of the Law in the Lord's temple!" (22:88).

more>
- Psalm 19:7-11
- Hebrews 4:12

next>
How often do you read the Bible? What part of your life needs to be brought in line with its message? What can you do to renew your commitment to its prominence in your life?

While preaching one Sunday morning, I invited three children to search our church sanctuary for several scrolls with Bible verses written on them. Whenever they found a scroll, I would have them read the words aloud, and then I would give them a prize. You should have seen those kids. They ran, moved chairs, and looked under plants and in purses (they had permission). Their quest for the Scriptures was extremely intense, but exciting. In a similar way, we are to search diligently to discover the importance of the Word of God in our lives.

In 2 Kings 22, King Josiah and the people of Judah also discovered the importance of the Word of God in their lives. When Josiah began taking action against idol worship in Judah, Hilkiah found the Book of the Law (probably referring to the book of Deuteronomy—28:61; 29:21) in the temple. It must have been lost or concealed during the reign of King Manasseh. Josiah did several things after uncovering God's Word.

He had it read to him as he listened intently (v.10). In so doing, he became aware of God's commands. He responded by tearing his clothes in grief (v.11). Then he refined his knowledge by submitting to others who could help him understand it (vv.12-20). Finally, he and the people renewed their commitment to its prominence in their lives by pledging themselves to the covenant written in the Book (23:1-4).

Today, God's Word is not concealed or lost; it's at our fingertips. Yet there's still a need to rediscover its power and prominence in our lives. Let's spend our time reading, responding, refining our understanding, and renewing our commitment to be changed by its message. —Marvin Williams

latest craze

read>
Isaiah 1:1-28
The children I raised and cared for have rebelled against Me (v.2).

more>
- Psalm 51:3
- Isaiah 53:5
- Romans 10:21

next>
Why is it important for rebels to understand God's love for them? What was God's ultimate goal in His relationship with His wayward people?

These days it's hip to hate God. Unfortunately, the fashion industry is cashing in on this anti-Christian cultural trend. One particular brand of jeans is popular because of its satanic logo. The emblem's creator admits that it is "an active statement against Christianity."

While many people think this movement is the latest craze, out-and-out rebellion against God is nothing new. When the Israelites turned away from Him, God said, "The children I raised . . . have rebelled against Me" (Isaiah 1:2). If this statement captures the relationships in your home, check out God's response to His wayward kids. God said, "My people don't recognize My care for them" (v.3). Just like Israel, our rebellious children don't always see our love for them. They tend to reject it in exchange for the acceptance of their friends. It's okay to remind our kids that we care about them, even if they don't mirror our affection.

Loving them does not mean enabling them to go on with their insurgency. Rebellion invites punishment. Isaiah described rebels this way: heartsick, injured, helpless, covered in bruises, plundered, and burned (vv.5-7). Although it's heartbreaking to watch, we can pray that our children's discomfort will propel them back into harmony with God.

Hurting people are often difficult people. That's why we need to be reasonable, even when our kids are unreasonable. Israel's mutiny made God angry, yet His levelheaded approach went like this: "Come now, let's settle this" (v.18).

Sometimes it's hard to know what to say to children who are immersed in a culture that despises God. When we lovingly direct them onto the right path (Proverbs 22:6), they will see that faith in Jesus never goes out of style.

—Jennifer Benson Schuldt

sweet smell of repentance

read>
Hosea 6
Come, let us return to the Lord (v.1).

more>
- Psalm 51:7
- Matthew 4:17
- 1 John 1:9

next>
What stinks in your relationship with God? How would your genuine repentance change things?

As I opened a container that had been neglected at the back of the fridge, a foul odor filled the air and nearly made me gag. Over *way* too many weeks, some leftovers had turned into a repulsive, moldy mass.

In Hosea, we find God holding His nose—being repulsed—as He viewed His people. In a well-known account, He compared unfaithful Israel to Hosea's wayward wife Gomer (1:2–3:5). Something was stinking in the northern kingdom, and a loving God was about to clean house.

As you turn the pages of Hosea, however, you can't miss the relentless love God had for His people (1:7, 2:14). He had made a covenant with His rebellious nation and He compassionately chose not to destroy them completely (11:8-11, 14:4-7). But He did allow them to experience the destruction of their kingdom by Assyria in 722 BC (Hosea 5:13-14). Why? So they would "admit their guilt and turn to [Him]" (v.15)

With those thoughts in mind, the prophet penned, "Come, let us return to the Lord" and "let us press on to know Him" (6:1,3). Hosea cried out to His people to repent and return to God—the One who said, "I want you to show love . . . . I want you to *know Me*" (v.6). God implored them to turn from sin and embrace Him.

When we choose to turn from the Lord and pursue sin, we fall headlong into a state of spiritual death. We take another "lover" into our arms, as Gomer did, and our hearts grow cold. To bring us back, God must lovingly discipline us.

But if we repent, He will replace the stench of our sin with the sweet smell of restored relationship. God's "love will know no bounds" as it fills the air with fresh fragrances like "the cedars of Lebanon" (14:4,6). —Tom Felten

what are you waiting for?

read>
Hebrews 10:32–11:2
Faith is the confidence that what we hope for will actually happen; it gives us assurance about things we cannot see (11:1).

more>
- Psalm 33:17-22
- Isaiah 40:28-31
- Titus 2:11-14

next>
"What are you waiting for?" can mean (1) passively—are you expecting Jesus' return? and (2) actively—what are you doing to anticipate His coming? Why are both elements, and their order, important?

A few years ago, my corner of the world concluded one of the coldest summers on record. Then snowflakes fell early in the fall. My friends and I joke that we don't know about global warming, but we're all for it. We're threatening to buy larger vehicles and any product that comes in aerosol—whatever it takes to expand the greenhouse effect and extend our summers.

Despite our gallows humor, many of our neighbors continue to warn us about the impending danger of climate change and our need to reduce our carbon emissions. Their concerns demonstrate a kind of faith. They may not directly experience rising temperatures, yet their calls for change have led many to conclude that global warming is a future reality which requires action now.

According to Hebrews 11:1, this is the very definition of faith. This verse describes faith as the confidence ("the substance") of "what we hope for" and the assurance ("the proof") of "things we cannot see." Faith brings the invisible facts of the future into the present.

Some see reasons to believe in climate change, but we can all know with certainty that Jesus will return to establish the "new heavens and new earth" (2 Peter 3:13). We may not live to see the second coming, but like the heroes of faith in Hebrews 11, we may die "still believing what God had promised . . . . They did not receive what was promised, but they saw it all from a distance and welcomed it" (v.13).

Our expectations for the future determine how we live now. If we expect Jesus to return, we will live as though He might come back today. The pressing question of the present is all about the future. What are you waiting for?

—Mike Wittmer

never alone

read>
2 Timothy 4:1-18
The first time I was brought before the judge, no one came with me. Everyone abandoned me. May it not be counted against them (v.16).

more>
- Psalm 27:10
- Psalm 73:23
- Romans 8:31-39

next>
Have you ever felt abandoned by someone? How can times of feeling alone strengthen our love for God?

She remembered the day her dad left. Though only a child, she lay in bed and listened to her mother crying herself to sleep in the other room. At 5 years of age, she determined she would never be the cause of her mom's tears. Now 14, she shared how she had determined to be happy and carefree in front of everyone, regardless of whatever pain she felt inside. Still more girl than woman, she had only begun to grieve the lost relationship with her dad.

Romans 8:38-39 tells us that nothing can keep us from God's love. In the "rubber meets the road" of real life, however, we struggle to see God's love for us when someone we love walks away. We may know in our heads that God loves us, but we don't know how to live it out, especially when a close relationship is severed. In their palpable absence, our heart asks: *What about me made them leave?* Our unanswered questions and swirling thoughts threaten to overwhelm us.

The apostle Paul knew what it was like to be forsaken by those close to his heart—people in whom he had invested much (2 Timothy 1:15). He felt the loss, and his calling didn't shield him from loneliness (v.12). Through it all, he remained focused on his true purpose for living and refused to be waylaid by what others said or did (vv.17-18).

We can't live in fear of losing people, and we can't live thinking that our world will fall apart if we're alone. Loneliness is real, and grieving doesn't mean we've lost faith (John 11:35). No matter what we go through, however, we must not lose sight of who loves us most—the One who promised to be there always (Hebrews 13:5). —Regina Franklin

our daily bread

read>
Luke 11:1-4
Give us today the food we need (Matthew 6:11).

more>
- Proverbs 30:8-9
- Matthew 6:25-33
- 1 Timothy 6:6-8

next>
What can you do to help feed the poor and hungry in your community? What can you do with your second loaf of bread?

Both the United Nations Food and Agriculture Organization and the World Food Program report that 1.02 billion people (15 percent of the world population) went to bed hungry in 2009. Every day, 18,000 children under the age of 5 die from hunger-related causes—one child every 5 seconds. The urgent cry of these 1.02 billion people is, "Give us *today* the food we need" (Matthew 6:11).

For Christians living in affluent countries, there will be food on the table tonight. And we seldom buy food for just one day, relying instead on quantities of stored provisions that make our next meal no big deal. Perhaps only in times of economic downturn and job losses do we begin to pray, "Give us *each* day the food we need" (Luke 11:3).

These words teach us that nothing is too small to bring to God. He cares for us intensely because we are His children. As a loving Father, He knows what we need, and no request is too minute for Him to receive (Matthew 6:30-33). So as we pray, we remember:

- *God will provide.* If our earthly parents won't give us a stone when we ask for bread (Matthew 7:9-11), surely our heavenly Father who feeds the birds will also feed us (6:26; Job 38:41; Psalm 145:15-17; Philippians 4:19).
- *We must not be selfish.* Give us (not me) today the food we (not I) need. If my Father supplies me with two loaves of bread, and my brother has none, the second loaf is not for storing in my refrigerator but for sharing with my brother (Deuteronomy 15:7-11; Leviticus 23:22).
- *We need to be content.* Living in a consumerist culture with its insatiable desires, we crave for more and more. We must learn how to be content with what the Lord has already given us (Philippians 4:11-13).

Our daily bread is all we really need. —K.T. Sim

my friends and i

read>
1 Samuel 18
Jonathan made a solemn pact with David, because he loved him as he loved himself (v.3).

more>
There are "friends" who destroy each other, but a real friend sticks closer than a brother (Proverbs 18:24).

next>
How will you selflessly serve your friends today? How does Christlike friendship bring glory to God?

John Chrysostom wrote: "Such is friendship, that through it we love places and seasons; for as . . . flowers drop their sweet leaves on the ground around them, so friends impart favor even to the places where they dwell. . . . It would be better for us that the sun were exhausted than that we should be without friends."

There's no better example of the sweetness of a godly friendship than Jonathan and David's story. The Bible records that "there was an immediate bond between them" (1 Samuel 18:1). Friends share a oneness of spirit.

The two warriors established their friendship after David had killed the giant Goliath in battle. Jonathan also overcame great odds in war (14:6). So they shared the belief that one should risk great odds for a God who could overcome any obstacle.

Their friendship was sustained by the constant renewing of their loyalty to one another (18:3; 20:16,42; 23:18), as well as nurtured by true expressions of concern. These expressions took the form of gifts as well as guidance. Jonathan shared with David gifts of prominence and practicality (18:4), and he also shielded his friend by means of warnings and acts of protection (19:1-2; 20:12-13). *Friends help solve problems and share alternate solutions.*

The apex of Jonathan and David's friendship is found in these words: "Jonathan went to find David and encouraged him to stay strong in his faith in God" (23:16).

Friends help you find strength in God during the low ebb times of life. In a world where most relationships are about what I can get, let's be the type of friend who is focused on what I can give. Jesus, our perfect Friend, told us, "There is no greater love than to lay down one's life for one's friends" (John 15:13). Let's follow His example. —Poh Fang Chia

five mysteries

read>
Genesis 1:26-28
So God created human beings in His own image (v.27).

more>
Thank you for making me so wonderfully complex! Your workmanship is marvelous—how well I know it (Psalm 139:14).

next>
When did you last reflect on the miracle that is your life? In what ways does being made in God's image inspire you?

In his book *Why Us?* James Le Fanu lists five mysteries that a naturalistic view of human origins fails to explain:

Subjective awareness. No scientific theory accounts for how the electrical activity of our brains results in our experiencing so richly and coherently the greenness of grass, the rustling of leaves, and the song of a bird.

Free will. How does our nonmaterial mind influence our physical brain to choose one course of action over another?

Memory. How can we recall millions of experiences even though our brains have changed and developed since the experiences took place?

Reason and imagination. How is it that we can assess truth, imagine scenarios, and empathize with others?

The self. How does the same lump of gray matter in every person's head (our brain) result in our uniquely different personalities?

"Let Us make human beings in Our image," God said at the beginning of time (Genesis 1:26). "So God created human beings in His own image . . . male and female He created them" (v.27).

You and I are more than mere matter. As St. Augustine understood it, the image of God in us is our rational, intellectual soul—a soul made as a reflection of a rational, personal God. That's why we're conscious and aware; that's why our minds control our brains; that's why we can reason and imagine. That's also why we are unique, though made of the same material. The God who saw our unformed bodies and planned our days before birth (Psalm 139:16), knit us individually in our mother's womb (v.13).

James Le Fanu doesn't write from a religious standpoint, so his conclusion that science shouldn't dismiss religion is refreshing. And why not? God is the key to the riddle of human existence. —Sheridan Voysey

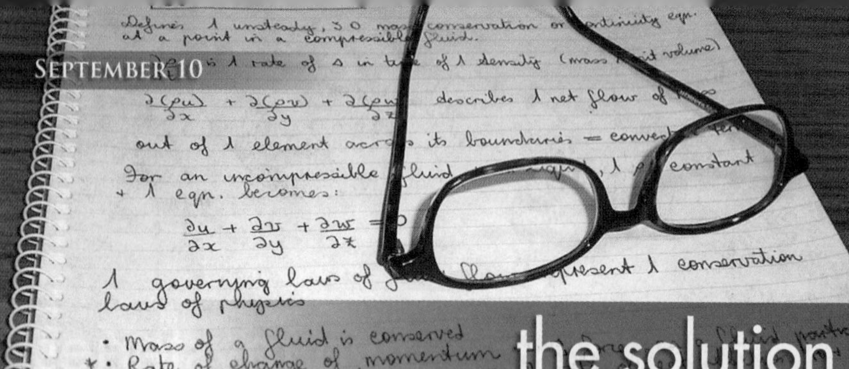

SEPTEMBER 10

the solution

read>
Ephesians 2:1-10
God has now revealed to us His mysterious plan regarding Christ (1:9).

more>
- Ephesians 3:2-12
- Colossians 1:25-29
- 1 Timothy 3:16

next>
What does it mean to you to be "under the authority of Christ" (Ephesians 1:10)? What has God's mysterious plan taught you about Him?

With more than 70 books to his name, Martin Gardner is the world's best-known recreational mathematician. His fun mathematical problems and mind-boggling puzzles have likely introduced more people to the joys of math than anyone in history.

Recently, he said, "If you think about it, everything that distinguishes a modern industrial society from the Greek and Roman period is the ability to solve puzzles."

Unlike math puzzles, scientific discoveries achieved through study, deep concentration, and sudden or gradual insight, biblical puzzles or mysteries can only be answered through God-given revelation.

And no greater revelation has ever been or will ever be given than the solution to the problem of sin. Paul wrote, "God has now revealed to us His mysterious plan regarding Christ, a plan to fulfill His own good pleasure. And this is the plan: At the right time He will bring everything together under the authority of Christ—everything in heaven and on earth" (Ephesians 1:9-10).

The book of Ephesians vividly expresses God's cosmic plan of salvation, and His plan for our daily lives, in a way no human problem-solving capabilities could ever accomplish:

- We were dead in our sins (2:1-3).
- Jesus died for our sins and rose again—showing His power over sin and death (vv.4-7).
- By grace we are saved through faith in Jesus (vv.5,8-10).

Today, thank God for revealing His mysterious plan in Jesus—the solution for your sin—so that you might be saved. —Roxanne Robbins

when the world falls apart

read>
Daniel 11:29-32
But [the king of the north] will vent his anger against the people of the holy covenant (v.30).

more>
[God] comforts us in all our troubles so that we can comfort others. When they are troubled, we will be able to give them the same comfort God has given us (2 Corinthians 1:4).

next>
Where have you encountered suffering? How have you experienced God's presence in that place?

We are obsessed with success. An entire industry revolves around *Guinness World Records,* cataloging stuff like the longest beard, the fastest 40-meter wheelbarrow race, and the most T-shirts worn at once. We have meticulous lists of all the record holders, but nobody remembers the losers.

Unfortunately, this fascination with all things triumphant has corroded our spiritual pursuits. We can begin to believe that God's job is to make us succeed, to clear our path of obstacles, to (always) remove impediments and suffering.

In contrast, the prophet Daniel went to great lengths in warning Israel of a future time of severe troubles. Pushing against any misplaced feelings of entitlement to comfort, Daniel warned that an evil king from the north would descend with his crushing army to "take over the temple fortress, pollute the sanctuary," and unleash his rage on God's people (11:31). Later, Jesus echoed a similarly dreadful prediction to His disciples, essentially warning them that their world would fall apart (Mark 13:14).

Why would God warn His people of coming hardship rather than simply stopping it? And what does this say about us in our places of distress? Is God cavalier about our suffering?

The witness of Jesus teaches us that, amid this world drowning in sin, not all suffering can be avoided. To redeem the world, Jesus had to immerse Himself in it, even at the cost of His own life. Daniel's prophecy pointed toward this long vision of God's activity to rescue the world. And God invites His people to the same perspective, engaging our world in its brokenness. This means that while God will not always remove our suffering, He will always enter our suffering with us. —Winn Collier

serving God leftovers

read>
Malachi 1:6-14
When you give blind animals as sacrifices, isn't that wrong? And isn't it wrong to offer animals that are crippled and diseased? Try giving gifts like that to your governor, and see how pleased he is! (v.8).

more>
- 1 Samuel 2:28-30
- 1 Peter 2:12
- Mark 12:41-44

next>
In what area of your life do you think lightly of God by offering Him leftovers? When are you tempted to offer God less than your best? How can you consistently offer Him your best?

A few years ago, radio commentator Paul Harvey shared a true story about a woman and her frozen turkey. The Butterball Turkey Company set up a telephone hotline to answer consumer questions about preparing holiday turkeys. One woman called to inquire about cooking a turkey that had been in her freezer for 23 years. The representative told her the turkey would be safe to eat, but did not recommend eating it because the flavor would have deteriorated. The caller replied, "That's what I thought. Okay, we'll probably just give it to our church then."

That woman was guilty of serving leftovers to her church. The priests and people of Malachi's day were also guilty of serving leftovers to a holy God. Questioning God's love for them (Malachi 1:2-5), the priests and the people became negligent in their worship. God sent Malachi to scold them for "serving" Him careless worship (vv.6-7). The people were offering defective animals for sacrifice, and the priests, who were responsible for inspecting the animals and offering up unblemished sacrifices to God (Leviticus 22:17-25), were accepting them. The Lord said it was insulting that they were bringing Him—the Great King of the universe—sacrifices that weren't even fit for one of their human authorities (Malachi 1:8).

Are we offering God less than our best? Here are three standards of sacrifices to test our worship and service to God: (1) Are we giving to God first? (2) Are we giving God our best? (3) Are we offering God a sacrifice that costs us something? Let's apply those questions to these areas of our life: our bodies (Romans 12:1-2), our money (Philippians 4:14-18), our praise (Hebrews 13:15), our good works (v.16), and our witnessing to unbelievers. Let's give our best, not simply the leftovers. —Marvin Williams

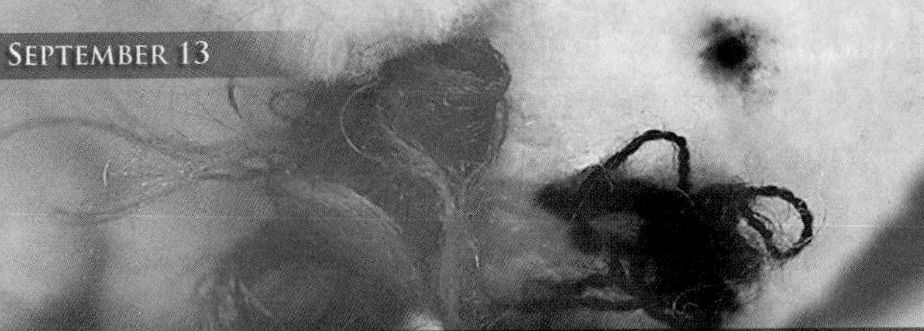

museum of broken relationships

read>
Lamentations 3:19-26
I grieve over my loss. Yet I still dare to hope (vv.20-21).

more>
The Lord is close to the brokenhearted; He rescues those whose spirits are crushed (Psalm 34:18).

next>
Why is it best to turn to God with a broken heart? What might God want to teach us through the pain of heartbreak?

A garden dwarf, a glass house, and a box made of matches. These items and many others are on display at the Museum of Broken Relationships in Croatia. It exists so that everyone who contributes a memento from a shattered relationship has the chance to "overcome emotional collapse through creation."

The Bible offers even more constructive insight on how to mend broken hearts. Jeremiah wrote Lamentations based on his firsthand experience with heartbreak over the nation of Israel. Sorrowfully, he said, "I will never forget this awful time, as I grieve over my loss" (3:20). Jeremiah acknowledged his pain. He didn't bury it or get busy and just try to forget. He expressed his feelings, proving that there is "a time to grieve" (Ecclesiastes 3:4).

Deep in his grief, Jeremiah never lost sight of God's love. He knew, "The faithful love of the Lord never ends!" (v.22). In the Hebrew language, this refers to a kind of love called *chesed* love—translation: *loyal love.* Although people we cherish may break our heart, God's love will never disappoint us.

God's consistent, dependable affection caused Jeremiah to proclaim, "I will hope in Him!" (v.24). The idea of hope here relates to waiting for something, or lingering. While it's tempting to pine away for that guy or girl who just said *sayonara*, it's better to put our hope in God. He "will never abandon [us]" (Hebrews 13:5).

If you're recovering from a splintered relationship, remember that it's okay to take time to mourn the loss. Allow God to comfort you with His faithful love, and wait on Him for emotional healing. Then you can eventually toss out all the reminders of lost love—with no need to keep them on display.

—Jennifer Benson Schuldt

risky business

read>
Ecclesiastes 5:8-20
Money is put into risky investments that turn sour (v.14).

more>
Such is the fate of all who are greedy for money; it robs them of life (Proverbs 1:19).

next>
Does your lifestyle reflect risky business or do you have a heart for God? Why does God hate greed?

A study by the US-based Virginia Tech Transportation Institute reveals that texting while driving is risky business. The study concluded that the risk of being in a collision is 23 times greater for truck drivers who text. The Institute's research team is recommending that texting be banned for *all* drivers.

If Solomon were alive today, he would definitely recommend that we ban a certain risk—dicey investments. He wrote, "Money is put into risky investments that turn sour, and everything is lost" (Ecclesiastes 5:14). Just preceding this verse and setting the context for its instruction, Solomon was condemning the act of "hoarding" (v.13).

The practice of stockpiling stuff out of personal greed can often be a prelude to investing in unwise things. The motives for doing both, along with the character of the individual committing the acts, are tainted.

Jesus condemned this type of greed when He said, "Don't store up treasures here on earth, where moths eat them and rust destroys them" (Matthew 6:19). He then told His disciples to invest instead in something that's not risky—eternal treasure. For "wherever your treasure is, there the desires of your heart will also be" (v.21).

The realization that all our treasures come from God leads us to take these points to heart (Ecclesiastes 5:19):

- *Right investing*—Hoarding and risky investments don't reflect the realization that "we can't take our riches with us" (v.15). They don't reflect the heart of God.
- *Acceptance*—We should accept the material things we receive in life with gratitude and delight in what He has provided (v.18).

Let's avoid texting while driving and steer clear of risky investments. Both lead to devastating results. —Tom Felten

keeping up appearances

read>
Philippians 2:5-11
At the name of Jesus every knee should bow, in heaven and on earth and under the earth, and every tongue confess that Jesus Christ is Lord, to the glory of God the Father (vv.10-11).

more>
- Isaiah 40:18-26
- Matthew 28:18-20
- Revelation 11:15

next>
Can you think of other spiritual ways—such as prayer, offerings, and obedience—where you might be tempted to assert power over God? How have you sometimes used these good things to try to manipulate God into doing what you want?

A young woman was living the high life in Beijing. She resided in a private villa, danced her weekends away, and had her own chauffeur. But she lost it all when new comrades rose to power and threw her father out of his government office. The young woman, however, was not exactly humbled. When friends offered to pay her rent or give her a ride, she would say, "Yes, I will allow you to purchase that for me" or "I grant you permission to do me this favor."

Her feeble attempts to retain a charade of privilege annoyed her friends. They would have preferred a simple, "Thank you, I don't know what I would do without you." It's easy to see that she needed a hefty helping of humble gratitude. But don't you and I act similarly toward God when we say that we *permit* Jesus to be our Lord or we accept Him into our hearts?

We enter this world needy and rebellious—under the curse of sin and death and bound for hell (Romans 3:23, 6:23). When we learn that Jesus gave His life to save us (Philippians 2:8), we sometimes grudgingly announce that we will grant Him this privilege.

Theologian Karl Barth noticed this tendency and explained that our professed "openness" toward God may actually be a spiritual way of remaining closed. We concede that we need God's help. But by granting permission for God to save us, we try to retain the power in our relationship. We refuse to admit that we are "this needy man," and even in our poverty we strive to play "the rich man closed against God."

Like the young woman from Beijing, we're dying to be in control. That's fitting, because our attempt to keep the upper hand is *killing* us. Salvation comes when we confess that Jesus is Lord, with or without our permission (v.11).

—Mike Wittmer

spilled out

read>
Matthew 12:30-37
The words you say will either acquit you or condemn you (v.37).

more>
- Proverbs 10:19
- Proverbs 13:3
- James 3:7-10

next>
Does the Holy Spirit or your flesh control your tongue? How should you respond to a person who has directed harsh words your way? How can you have conversations that are "gracious and attractive"? (Col. 4:6).

As I was grading papers at school one day, I received a text from my husband that read, "we r all n." When I responded "*What?*" he explained that he had spilled half a gallon of paint on the carpeting in our home office. Fortunately, the carpet was old, and we were planning on ripping it up anyhow. Now we were "all in" and there would be no turning back from the upcoming floor project. Meanwhile, until we could afford to remove the carpet, the colored, crusty spot was an ever-present reminder of what spilled paint can do.

Words matter. Whether written or spoken, they have the power to color our world with life or death (Proverbs 18:21). Because we live in a hyper-communicative society, our communication extends thousands of miles in a matter of seconds. From cell phones to Twitter, we have the power to influence others in an instant. Often, we text or e-mail what we refuse to say in person because we feel a measure of safety behind the inanimate keyboard beneath our fingers.

Frustrations are bound to arise when we live in relationship with others. Like paint soaking into carpeting, however, words cannot be gathered up and their effects held back. Crusting over hearts, harsh words continue to speak long after we've had our say—even in the shortest text, the quickest tweet. Wrongfully perceiving electronic communication to be benign, we are still accountable—maybe even more so—for what we write. Erasing our sent box takes only a moment; words we wrote last a lifetime.

We can say we're just venting or even claim our arrows are well-deserved, but the fact remains: If we claim to be religious but don't control our tongue, we're just fooling ourselves, and our religion is worthless (James 1:26).

—Regina Franklin

forgiven & forgiving

read>
Matthew 6:9-15
Forgive us our sins, as we have forgiven those who sin against us (v.12).

more>
- Matthew 18:21-30
- Colossians 3:12-15

next>
Why is it hard to forgive certain people? What will you do today to forgive someone based on God's forgiveness of you?

According to psychologist Abraham Maslow, man's basic needs are physiological—oxygen to breathe and food to eat. According to Jesus, man's basic needs are spiritual—to be forgiven and to forgive.

With the same tenacity and intensity that we ask for God's provisions (Matthew 6:11), we must also seek His pardon. This means asking Him to forgive us of our sins and to enable us to forgive those who have sinned against us. "Forgive us our sins" is an explicit prayer for God's forgiveness. "As we have forgiven those who sin against us" is an *implicit* prayer for a forgiving spirit (v.12).

Commenting on this, Bible teacher Haddon Robinson wrote, "Augustine labeled this request for forgiveness 'the terrible petition,' because if we harbor an unforgiving spirit while we pray to be *forgiven in the same way as we forgive others,* we are actually asking God not to forgive us."

Perhaps that's why Jesus, immediately after teaching His disciples this prayer, stated clearly what was at stake for those who pray it. In fact, this is the only request He elaborated on. He warned, "If you forgive those who sin against you, your heavenly Father will forgive you. But if you refuse to forgive others, your Father will not forgive your sins" (vv.14-15).

While our salvation is not based on our goodness in forgiving others (Ephesians 2:8-9), our personal fellowship and intimacy with God *is* dependent on the understanding that we have been forgiven much (Luke 7:40-47). And one who knows that he has been forgiven much will love much (v.47). Jesus is talking about family forgiveness. Just as the Father has forgiven us, we should forgive our brothers and sisters. For if we are truly forgiven, we will also be forgiving. —K.T. Sim

so close, yet so far

read>
Mark 10:17-31
"There is still one thing you haven't done," He told him. "Go and sell all your possessions and give the money to the poor, and you will have treasure in heaven. Then come, follow Me" (v.21).

more>
Not everyone who calls out to Me, "Lord! Lord!" will enter the kingdom of heaven. Only those who actually do the will of My Father in heaven will enter (Matthew 7:21).

next>
What keeps you from loving God first and foremost? What will you surrender to Him today?

The host of a TV quiz show said, "Come up with the missing word at the end of the phrase and spell it correctly, and you'll win our grand-prize trip to Europe. Are you ready? The phrase is, 'Old MacDonald had a ____.' And remember, you must spell the missing word."

The contestant said, "Old MacDonald had a farm."

"All right," said the emcee, "what you have to do now is spell the word and you win our super-deluxe trip to Europe."

"That's easy," said the contestant. "E-I-E-I-O." *Oops*!

We may laugh at this story, but it illustrates how close we can be to receiving God's blessings, and yet so far away. The rich young man in Mark 10 provides a perfect example of someone in this condition.

We read in verse 17 that he was an earnest seeker. He came running up to Jesus and knelt down. He was undeterred by the opposition of the "religious leader" class he belonged to (Luke 18:18). Next, we find that he had been obeying the commandments to a "T" since his youth. This man had maintained impeccable moral character—even through all the temptations of youth!

Yet he still lacked one thing: He loved riches more than he loved God (Mark 10:22). Jesus had told him that he needed to surrender his all, out of love for God. The rich young man needed to deny himself and love God first and foremost by giving away his money.

Mark records the man's tragic choice. He departed, still possessing his earthly riches, but lacking eternal treasure.

Have you been putting your faith in God or in your material possessions? Unless you've made a personal confession of faith in Jesus Christ—surrendering your all to Him—you're close, yet far away from Him. —Poh Fang Chia

can't stand it

read>
Proverbs 21:19-31
It's better to live alone in the desert than with a quarrelsome, complaining wife (v.19).

more>
- Proverbs 15:18
- 2 Timothy 2:24

next>
What causes you to nag or complain? Have your wishes been driven by selfishness, greed, impatience? How will you make legitimate requests for change without resorting to nagging?

While journeying down the Yangtze River a few years ago, a Chinese ferry crew became concerned when a passenger burst out of his cabin with his hands covering his ears screaming, "I can't stand it any longer!" Crewmembers followed the distraught passenger to the ferry's railing, wondering if he was suffering from an ear injury. As they talked with him, the man's wife rushed up and began to nag him loudly. The man covered his ears again, cried out, "I need a break!" and then jumped over the railing. The fast-moving Yangtze is dangerous and claims many lives each year. Thankfully, the man was later rescued, having battled the raging 2-kilometer-wide river. "I felt I was dying," he reportedly told police, "but even that's better than my wife's nagging!"

According to the book of Proverbs, a wife is a gift from God (18:22), and the "wife of noble character" (31:10 NIV) is to be praised by all (v.28). But Proverbs also laments a nagging, quarrelsome wife. She's like the constant dripping of a leaky tap (19:13). It's better to live in a corner of the attic than to live with her (21:9). Run to the desert to find some relief (v.19). Our Chinese friend would surely agree!

Are women more prone to the sin of quarrelsome nagging than men? I'll leave you to debate that one! Needless to say, the more important issue is what we do with such a sin. "Do everything without complaining and arguing," the apostle Paul reminds us (Phil. 2:14). Our quarrels can be driven by pride (Prov. 13:10), greed, and selfishness (James 4:1-3)—things which are to be "put to death" (Col. 3:5) and replaced with humility, kindness, and patience (v.12).

The quarrelsome person is hard to endure (Proverbs 26:21). Everyone loses in a home fraught with endless complaints. Choose, instead, to lift up and encourage those you love. —Sheridan Voysey

exercising self-control

read>
Acts 24:10-26
Better to have self-control than to conquer a city (Proverbs 16:32).

more>
- Proverbs 5:22-23
- Galatians 5:22-23
- 2 Peter 1:5-7

next>
Write down a "self-control" workout regimen that will help you strengthen your self-control muscle. How does it glorify God when we exhibit self-control?

Here's a secret about self-control: It works like a muscle," says Douglas McKenna, former director of Microsoft's Leadership Development. "With each use, that muscle temporarily loses some strength, leaving you with reduced capacity to handle yourself if the next self-control challenge pops up too soon.

"That's the bad news. The good news is that just like with any other muscle, you can be smarter about how you use it. And you can strengthen it with exercise."

While exercising the self-control muscle may be a new concept to some, this principle has been around for centuries. In the first century, for example, the apostle Paul instructed church leaders and their wives to make self-control *workouts* a regular part of their leadership training regimen. "Exercise self-control," Paul exhorted the group, "live wisely, and have a good reputation" (1 Timothy 3:2; see also v.11 and Titus 2:2).

As with any fitness plan, there will always be slackers like Felix, who badgered Paul for advice and then refused to take it: "As [Paul] reasoned with [Felix and his wife] about righteousness and self-control and the coming day of judgment, Felix became frightened. 'Go away for now,' he replied. 'When it is more convenient, I'll call for you again' " (Acts 24:25).

God calls us to "think clearly and exercise self-control" each moment (1 Peter 1:13) not merely when it's convenient. So set some goals toward strengthening your self-control muscle today. As you do, keep the words of Douglas McKenna in mind: "Small changes to your self-control muscle can make a big difference in your effectiveness as a leader. Don't take my word for it. Try it yourself."

More importantly, take God's word for it! —Roxanne Robbins

party

read>
Deuteronomy 14:22-29
When you arrive, you may use the money to buy any kind of food you want . . . . Then feast there in the presence of the Lord your God and celebrate with your household (v.26).

more>
Come, the banquet is ready (Luke 14:17).

next>
What hinders you from celebrating God's kindness and provision? What kind of kingdom party do you need to throw?

We have friends who don't get very excited about holidays. Our family, however—well, we get downright giddy when a special day pops up on the calendar.

Obviously, we throw a shindig for all the usual suspects (Christmas, Thanksgiving, Independence Day), and we make a big deal out of anniversaries, and any day when one of our boys loses a tooth. In fact, we celebrate birthday-week! One day just isn't enough!

The theme of partying—feasting, rejoicing, laughing—emerges consistently in Scripture. Whenever God's kingdom breaks in, you find people rejoicing. In Deuteronomy, Moses lays out God's instructions for all the details of how the Israelite nation is to structure their community. He offers a blueprint of tithes whereby the people would fund their worship and the livelihood of their leaders and, yes, their parties.

God wanted these parties to be festive and lavish. The people were to bring "the new wine . . . the firstborn males of [their] flocks and herds" (Deuteronomy 14:23). God placed a high priority on the people remembering to throw feasts where they would rejoice and remember—together—that their God is kind and generous and the Giver of all gifts that are "good and perfect" (James 1:17).

When Jesus appeared on the scene, He brought the same message. Jesus' first miracle was at a wedding feast (John 2:1-12), and He was noted as one who "feasts and drinks." The Pharisees even used Jesus' noted attendance at parties as an accusation against Him, calling Him a "glutton and drunkard" (Matthew 11:19).

The message of the kingdom is clear: When Jesus is present, there is reason to party. —Winn Collier

we're not the osbournes

read>
Ephesians 6:1-4
Children, obey your parents because you belong to the Lord, for this is the right thing to do (v.1).

more>
You must commit yourselves wholeheartedly to these commands that I am giving you today. Repeat them again and again to your children. (Deuteronomy 6:6-7).

next>
How faithful are you in taking advantage of the teachable moments God gives you with your children? What should you do differently as a parent or child?

Several years ago, *The Osbournes,* a reality television show that experienced surprising popularity, featured drug-addled rocker Ozzy Osbourne, his wife, and his disobedient and disrespectful children. Every obscenity from the children and parents seemed to attract more and more viewers, making it at one point the second most popular show on cable TV. Ozzie and his dysfunctional family were clearly celebrated by fans.

The apostle Paul encouraged children of all ages in the church at Ephesus to celebrate biblical and functional family life. How? By fulfilling their God-honoring and Spirit-empowered responsibilities (Ephesians 5:18). Paul taught that children have the responsibility to obey and honor their parents. If the offspring fulfill their divine roles, three very distinct characteristics will mark their lives.

First, they will recognize and submit to God-ordained authority. Parents are among God's key representatives of authority on earth, and when children obey them they acknowledge God's authority over their lives. Second, obedience acknowledges God's worth and brings pleasure to Him (Colossians 3:20). Finally, it represents God to a godless culture, repelling its temptations.

Like Paul, let's remind our children that by obeying and honoring parents they play a vital role in family life. We can begin by leveraging every teachable moment during the day to teach our children who God is and what He desires.

When parents fulfill their divine responsibility of teaching their children, and children fulfill their divine role of honoring and obeying their parents, family can reflect "the right thing" to all (Ephesians 6:1). —Marvin Williams

one in ten

read>
Luke 17:11-19
He fell to the ground at Jesus' feet, thanking Him for what He had done (v.16).

more>
Give thanks to the Lord and proclaim His greatness (Psalm 105:1).

next>
Do you spend more time in prayer thanking Jesus, or making requests? What does it mean to God when we express our gratitude?

Clouds of steam poured out from under the hood of my Saab hatchback. I pulled over and made a call for a tow truck. Minutes later, a man approached my car. He wasn't from the towing company, but he said he could fix the problem. Reluctantly, I let the stranger hoist up the hood and peer underneath. He then proceeded to pour water into the car's radiator. It worked!

I jotted down his address, intending to mail him a thank-you note with a gift. To my shame, however, I never followed through.

Jesus wasn't thanked at all by nine of the ten men he healed from leprosy. While on His way to Jerusalem, they spotted Him and shouted, "Master, have mercy on us" (Luke 17:13). With just a simple command, Christ ended their isolation, renewed their flesh, and rescued them from certain death.

When only one of the ten returned to voice his appreciation, Jesus asked him: "Didn't I heal ten men? Where are the other nine? Has no one returned to give glory to God except this foreigner?" (vv.17-18). Apparently, Jesus notices thankless hearts.

Most of us shake our heads and say "tsk, tsk" as we consider the ingrates who took off after being healed. Still, as much as I want to be like the grateful one, I tend to mimic the other nine instead. My lopsided prayer life proves it—it's heavy on requests for mercy and blessings, but light on gratitude.

If you're like me, you may need to focus more on the Giver and less on the good things He supplies. We know that "whatever is good and perfect comes down to us from God our Father" (James 1:17). So let's follow the example of the "one in ten" who fell to the ground at Jesus' feet and give thanks to God today (Luke 17:16). —Jennifer Benson Schuldt

to live and die

read>
Genesis 23:1-11
Please sell me a piece of land so I can give my wife a proper burial (v.4).

more>
Those who follow godly paths will rest in peace when they die (Isaiah 57:2).

next>
How does God view death? What hope do you have for life after death?

During a trip to Singapore, I was fascinated by the variety of cemeteries found there. One featured aboveground crypts with openings at the bottom. When I asked why the holes were there, my host explained that it was due to religious beliefs. The families of the deceased believe that the openings allow the spirits of the dead to move freely from their concrete confines.

Abraham needed a place for the body of his wife Sarah (Genesis 23:1-4). He wasn't concerned about obtaining a crypt with an opening. He simply needed a cave in which to lay his beloved Sarah to rest. During that time, it was expected that people would be buried in the place of their birth. That meant leaving Canaan (Israel) and heading all the way back to Ur (Iraq).

But instead of following that practice, Abraham secured a tomb and buried Sarah in their *new* land—the promised land of God (v.11). This showed that he believed by faith that God had called them to live and die in Canaan.

We also live with a new land in view. The apostle Paul wrote, "As long as we live in these bodies we are not home with the Lord" (2 Corinthians 5:6). When we die, we leave this world behind and our spirit goes to dwell with Jesus (v.8). There will be no looking back to the land of our physical birth, for our eternal "house in heaven" will be beyond compare (2 Corinthians 5:1). Paul penned, "Living means living for Christ, and dying is even better" (Philippians 1:21). For he knew death would lead to being in God's presence forever.

Choose to live today with eternity in mind. There's no need to fear death, for "whether we live or die, we belong to [Jesus]" (Romans 14:8). He has already set our spirit free for all eternity! (Hebrews 2:15). —Tom Felten

how are you?

read>
Hosea 3:1-5
The Lord still loves Israel, even though the people have turned to other gods and love to worship them (v.1).

more>
Return, O Israel, to the Lord your God. . . . "Then I will heal you of your faithlessness; My love will know no bounds, for My anger will be gone forever" (Hosea 14:1,4).

next>
How can you tell when you've turned one of God's good gifts into an idol? What can you do to return this good thing to its rightful place?

How do you respond to the greeting, "How are you?" Most of us simply reply, "Fine. How are you?" Others develop trademark comebacks, such as "Better than I deserve." I know of one fellow who answers, "I'm just the Lord's *prostitute*."

What?! This provocative reply is an inappropriate response to an innocuous greeting—too much information!—but it does make an important point. The fellow is comparing his life to Gomer, the wayward woman whom God told the prophet Hosea to marry to "illustrate how Israel has acted like a prostitute by turning against the Lord and worshiping other gods" (Hosea 1:2).

Israel had been unfaithful from its inception. On its "wedding night"—the very night that Moses was receiving their covenant from God on Mount Sinai—the Israelites melted their earrings into a golden calf and worshiped it. Who commits adultery on their wedding night?!

The Lord was deeply hurt by Israel's adultery, and he told Moses to "leave Me alone so My fierce anger can blaze against them, and I will destroy them." Moses begged God to remember the oath He had made with Abraham, Isaac, and Jacob. And "the Lord changed His mind about the terrible disaster He had threatened to bring on His people" (Exodus 32:10-14). But He wasn't happy. The Lord was as aggrieved as any lover who learns that His spouse has been sleeping with another.

We may not worship a golden calf, but we cheat on the Lord whenever we sacrifice Him or our families and friends on the altar of career, wealth, or pleasure. It comes down to what gives us ultimate worth and security. If it's anything other than Jesus, then we're committing spiritual adultery. We then need to confess our wandering ways, beg Christ's forgiveness, and ask Him to empower us to forsake all others. —Mike Wittmer

alarmed

read>
Ezekiel 33:1-20
If the watchman sees the enemy coming and doesn't sound the alarm to warn the people, he is responsible for their captivity. They will die in their sins, but I will hold the watchman responsible (v.6).

more>
Remember, it is sin to know what you ought to do and then not do it (James 4:17).

next>
Knowing that Jesus' return is imminent, are you speaking the truth in love to those around you? What holds you back from sounding the alarm?

Crouched on the floor amid rows of lockers, the young students lowered their heads to their knees. Barely bothering to kneel, the older students followed the minimal requirement without giving the warning any serious thought. Although they were glad to miss class, the tornado drill was little more than an inconvenience affecting their comfort and rumpling their clothing. In their minds, there was no real threat and thus no need to remain in their protective positions.

Unfailing in its promises, God's Word assures us of Jesus' certain return (John 14:3). For many of us, His coming is greatly anticipated. But not everyone will consider it a joyous reunion (Matthew 7:21-23; 2 Peter 3:10). Like students who see a tornado drill as pointless on a beautiful day, we can easily become lulled into a place of complacency regarding Christ's eventual return. Exposing this age-old temptation, Peter wrote, "The Lord isn't really being slow about His promise, as some people think. No, He is being patient for your sake. He does not want anyone to be destroyed, but wants everyone to repent" (v.9).

Not only must we be diligent to be prepared for "the day of the Lord" (v.10), but as those who find our hope in the cross we also bear a responsibility as watchmen (Ezekiel 33:6). God won't tolerate complacency in our relationship with Him (Revelation 3:15-16). Nor will He overlook our willingness to walk past those lost in spiritual death.

We sometimes buy the enemy's lie that all is well and to be serious about God's business isn't really necessary. Focused on our own comfort, we relax our position in kingdom warfare, and all the while the unseen enemy creeps in without the alarm being sounded. Sound it today—those who will "die in their sins" need to hear. —Regina Franklin

short accounts

read>
Romans 12:9-21
Do all that you can to live in peace with everyone (v.18).

more>
See that no one pays back evil for evil, but always try to do good to each other and to all people (1 Thess. 5:15).

next>
Ask God to show you if you have an old grudge that you've been secretly nursing against someone. How will you learn to keep short accounts that honor Him?

A while ago, I had to make the decision to have our family dog of 15 years put to sleep. It was one of the most heart-wrenching decisions I've ever made. There's a reason why we refer to dogs as "man's best friend." Roger Caras once said, "Dogs are not our whole life, but they make our lives whole."

I'm a better person for having had our "little buddy." Among other things, he taught me the value of forgiveness. I can recall many times when we butted heads (he never fully accepted that he wasn't the alpha male of the home) and found ourselves *doggone* mad at each other. Amazingly, he was always quick to forgive and move on.

My dog didn't realize it, but he illustrated something that Paul stressed as essential for human relationships: "Make allowance for each other's faults, and forgive anyone who offends you" (Colossians 3:13). He urged the same thing when he counseled his readers to "live in peace" whenever possible (Romans 12:18).

During what is often referred to as the "Sermon on the Mount," Jesus stressed that we are far better off if we settle our differences quickly (Matthew 5:25). Theologian Frederick Buechner wrote, "To lick your wounds, to smack your lips over grievances long past, to roll over your tongue the prospect of bitter confrontations still to come, to savor the last toothsome morsel of both the pain you are given and the pain you are giving back—in many ways it is a feast for a king. The chief drawback is that what you are wolfing down is yourself. The skeleton at the feast is you."

Do you have an unresolved, lingering issue with someone? Get it taken care of quickly. Keep short accounts in relationships. You'll be glad you did.

—Jeff Olson

speak the truth

read>
Jeremiah 42:1-22
Today I have told you exactly what He said, but you will not obey the Lord your God any better now than you have in the past (v.21).

more>
Preach the Word of God. Be prepared, whether the time is favorable or not. . . . For a time is coming when people will no longer listen to sound and wholesome teaching. (2 Timothy 4:2-3).

next>
What would happen if all true believers in Jesus began to speak about and live out God's truth winsomely? How can you share the truth with your corner of the culture?

Today, most of us live in a highly pluralistic society. Our next-door neighbor could well be Chinese, Ethiopian, or European. And, in the name of harmony, we're told to respect differing views and opinions.

But when voices of culture state that homosexuality, abortion, and cohabitation are acceptable lifestyle choices, what should believers in Jesus do? When God's truth is replaced by "tolerance," how do we live out our faith?

The prophet Jeremiah lived during a time when truth was spurned. In chapter 42, we find a group of Judean "guerrillas" and the people they had rescued coming to Jeremiah with what sounded like a sincere request for guidance (vv.1-5).

At that time, Jerusalem had been destroyed and Egypt was applying great pressure on the kingdom of Judah to cast their lot with them. After receiving a message from God, Jeremiah delivered God's pronouncement to the people. The substance of God's reply was that they should not go down into Egypt, and that if they did they would be destroyed. The people were intent, however, on going to Egypt, and they rejected Jeremiah's warning (43:4). They called the prophet a liar and added insult to injury by forcing him to accompany them (vv.2,6).

Jeremiah knew his message wasn't what the people wanted to hear. Yet he spoke forth God's Word boldly, instead of trying to make it more palatable for the people.

Today, while we need to be discerning about how to present God's truth to diverse audiences, we should never change what it says. When issues strike at the heart of biblical teaching, we must take a stand and winsomely continue to be God's salt and light to people lost in a declining culture. Let's speak His truth in love. —Poh Fang Chia

rescue us!

read>
Matthew 6:9-13
Don't let us yield to temptation, but rescue us from the evil one (v.13).

more>
- Psalm 37:23-24
- Psalm 121:1-8
- Romans 8:28-39

next>
How are you being tempted? What testing are you going through right now? What are some steps you can take in order to withstand the temptation?

A father and his young son were taking a walk in the country. As they walked down the rough and slippery path, the father cautioned his son to be careful. Suddenly, the son fell and hurt himself. Bruised and in pain, he began to cry. The father picked up the boy and held him close. Amid his tears, the son said to his father, "Daddy, please hold my hand, don't let me fall again." Like that child, we're instructed to cry out to our Father, "Don't let us yield to temptation, but rescue us from the evil one" (v.13).

Words like *temptation*, *rescue*, and *the evil one* tell us that we live in a dangerous and hostile world. The world is not our friend. It wages a war against us (John 15:19-20, 17:14-15; James 4:4; 1 John 2:15-16).

There is a second danger too. Satan, the dark enemy behind evil, prowls around like a roaring lion—ready to tear us apart (1 Peter 5:8). As the prince of demons and ruler of this world (Matthew 12:24; John 12:31), Satan is a "liar and the father of lies" (John 8:44). He's particularly dangerous because he comes to us disguised as an angel of light (2 Corinthians 11:14).

Satan may be powerful, but he's not omnipotent. The plea, "Rescue us from the evil one" affirms that Satan's power is limited to what God has allowed him to have (Job 1:12; Luke 22:31). The words remind us—we who have been wounded in our battles against temptation and Satan—that God is the only omnipotent One.

God picks us up, holds us close, and rescues us from evil and the evil one. He "keeps [us] from all harm and watches over [our] life. The Lord keeps watch over [us] as [we] come and go" (Psalm 121:7-8). —K.T. Sim

universal problem

read>
Romans 2:1-15
Even Gentiles, who do not have God's written law, show that they know His law when they instinctively obey it, even without having heard it (v.14).

more>
The wages of sin is death, but the free gift of God is eternal life through Christ Jesus our Lord (Romans 6:23).

next>
Have you personally accepted this free gift of forgiveness for your sins through Jesus? If not, what's stopping you? If you have, how will you live today to celebrate that fact?

In his book *Human Universals,* anthropologist Donald Brown lists over 400 human behaviors common across all cultures. Some of his findings are touching: All cultures have toys, jokes, dances, and proverbs; they have music, poetry, tickling, and thumb-sucking; the people of each culture develop languages, take names, are wary of snakes, and tie things with string!

Likewise, Brown discovered a number of moral universals across humanity. All ethnic groups have concepts of true and false, good and bad, fairness and equity, and right and wrong. And while vices like gossip, manipulation, and feelings of ethnic superiority are also universal, many are acknowledged to be wrong. All people everywhere, it seems, have some sense of conscience.

The apostle Paul made the same point centuries before Brown. He noted that though God gave the Jews the Ten Commandments to clarify right and wrong, the fact that Gentiles can do the right thing by obeying their conscience shows that God has woven His laws into every human heart (Romans 2:14-15). Ever wonder why atheists can be kind or why cultures without biblical exposure have ethical codes? That's why.

Of course, *knowing* what is right—either through Jewish Law or conscience—doesn't mean that we always *do* what is right. The Gentile senses what is right but still rebels (1:32); the Jew knows the Law but still breaks it (2:17-24). Break those mysterious universal rules and both Law and conscience condemn us, and this is Paul's point. Through the sacrificial death of Jesus, God frees us from the penalty of our rebellion and forgives us for breaking His rules! (3:23-26, 6:23).

Everyone has a conscience, and no one obeys it fully. So everyone has a problem, which only Jesus can solve. —Sheridan Voysey

freedom and God's will

how free are we?

God didn't intend for us to be frozen in anxiety each time we have to make a choice. How free are we? God gave us the freedom to use our own heads to decide what to do. Consider Adam, for example. God put him in the Garden of Eden and told him to name the animals (Genesis 2:19-20). Did Adam get all flustered and say, "But Lord, I want to make sure I name them exactly what You think they should be named"? No, God gave Adam freedom to choose the names that pleased Adam, and it was fine with God.

Another example from Genesis 2 was Adam's choice of food. God had said that Adam could eat from any tree he wanted, except for one. That gave Adam great freedom—even though later he and Eve overextended their freedom and disobeyed God. And therein lies the key. Our God-given freedom extends to those decisions that God's commands and principles have not addressed.

For example, a fish in the ocean is free to swim anywhere it wants to flap its fins. But if it chose to flip up onto land, the decision would be fatal. As human beings, we have freedom to choose among good options that conform to God's standards and His ideas of wisdom. Once we "jump out" of God's standards, however, we make a major mistake.

how does this work in real life?

Will it violate a biblical principle if I buy a BMW instead of a Ford? It would if I trampled all over my wife's feelings on the matter (violation of the principle of Ephesians 5:25-33), or if my decision meant that my children wouldn't have food on the table because my loan payments were too high (violation of the principle of 1 Timothy 5:8). On the other hand, my choice of cars could be an area in which I have a great deal of freedom without violating a biblical principle. There could be several good choices that meet God's standards and reflect a wise use of my God-given mental ability.

if in doubt, is it wise to wait?

If you're standing in line at a fast-food restaurant wondering whether to have a hamburger or a cheeseburger, the outcome of your decision isn't likely to be life-changing. But when the person behind the counter says, "May I help you?" you have to come up with a decision or else get out of line. It would be ridiculous to agonize over such a choice. But what about bigger decisions like proposing marriage, choosing a vocation, deciding whether or not to have risky surgery, or determining how to care for a relative who is terminally ill? At times, it may be wise to wait—if you have the luxury of extra time and if waiting will allow you to find valuable new information or allow for a better analysis of facts already available. Haste isn't a virtue (Proverbs 21:5).

If we're extremely uneasy about a decision, we should take time to evaluate why we feel that way. In some cases, such lack of peace may indicate that our choice is "not from faith" and is a sinful violation of our conscience (Romans 14:23 NKJV). Or a lack of peace may indicate that we haven't expressed our trust in God to meet our needs (Philippians 4:6-7).

We should remember that although God can use our feelings to direct us, what we "feel" may be a result of our emotional makeup rather than a message from God's Spirit. And watch out for the paralysis of analysis, a decision-crippling disease affecting those who procrastinate or who continually fear that some bit of information is yet to be found that will help them know what God wants them to do.

could I flip a coin?

In some cases, yes. Does that sound a bit unspiritual? It isn't if you've acknowledged the Lord, looked for principles in His Word, used common sense, and listened to good advice. However, flipping a coin or making an arbitrary choice, should be a last resort, and only when you are choosing between good options.

In Proverbs 16:33, Solomon said, "We may throw the dice, but the Lord determines how they fall." Casting lots, drawing straws, or flipping a coin fall into the same category.

In the Bible, God worked through such techniques to reveal what He wanted done. For example:

- Aaron cast lots on the Day of

Atonement to select a goat to sacrifice (Leviticus 16:8-10).
• Nehemiah used lot casting to distribute work responsibilities (Nehemiah 10:34).
• Solomon said that "flipping a coin can end arguments" (Proverbs 18:18).
• Jonah was discovered as the villain when a ship captain cast lots (Jonah 1:7).
• Matthias was chosen by lot as an apostle when a replacement was needed (Acts 1:23-26).

When all available information yields no clear direction and a decision is needed, use your God-given freedom of choice or, if you are paralyzed by indecision, simply flip a coin. God can use either choice for His glory. He is in control and He is at work in the lives of those who earnestly desire to please Him. "For God is working in you, giving you the desire and the power to do what pleases Him" (Philippians 2:13).

thinking it over

What kinds of decisions do you make every day without prayer and study to find out what to do? What kinds of decisions give you the most anxiety and tend to paralyze you? Are you exercising your freedom responsibly and in dependence on Jesus?

how does our freedom fit into the bigger picture?

It's important that we see our freedom of choice in the context that God has offered to help us know what He wants us to do. He hasn't left us out in the middle of a wilderness without a compass. He offers help to all who will acknowledge Him as Lord. He has given us reliable guidance in His Word. He has given us rational thinking power to evaluate our options. We have information in the form of advice from people we can trust. And He gives us freedom to choose when the decision lacks any clear admonition or prohibition from Him.

God loves us. He wants us to live for Him. If we desire to honor God, we can be sure that He will not leave us in the dark when we want to know what He wants us to do. Even if we've been foolish or disobedient in the past, we can know and do what God wants us to do—today and tomorrow.

—Kurt De Haan

Adapted from the Discovery Series booklet How Can I Know What God Wants Me To Do?
© 2003 RBC Ministries.

answered

read>
Job 38:1-18
Do you realize the extent of the earth? Tell Me about it if you know! (v.18).

more>
The Lord your God is living among you. He is a mighty Savior. He will take delight in you with gladness. With His love, He will calm all your fears. He will rejoice over you with joyful songs (Zephaniah 3:17).

next>
How can creation speak to you of God's sovereignty? Have you ever wanted to "argue" with God about His decisions? Why?

My young son has always thought way outside of the box. Testing his boundaries, he realizes that while we want him to ask tough questions, not everything we say is up for discussion. It has not been an easy lesson to learn—for him or for us.

How often do we appear like young children to God? Inquisitive, we long to know more. But that same questioning nature that pushes us to search out the mystery of His ways (Proverbs 25:2) can bring us into conflict with His sovereignty. Like a child, we must learn to live with both *wonder* and *trust*.

Few of us question the answers God gives when we're experiencing prosperity and blessing. In heartache and trial, however, the questions tumble over one another and usually resist being neatly tucked away. Later, when we're met with seeming silence from heaven, we become self-righteous, bold—even defiant. All the while, God remains sovereign and completely trustworthy.

Like us, Job couldn't see past the natural world. How interesting that God used nature to remind Job of His absolute power and authority over all things. From Job's experience, we see:

- God is patient with our questions; He too has known suffering (Matthew 26:39; 1 Peter 2:21).
- God's love for us is greater than any trial we may face (Psalm 31:7; Romans 8:35-39).
- God is more interested in our knowing Him than in our simply getting answers (Psalm 27:8; Jeremiah 9:23-24).

Our questions don't keep us from God, but our surrender brings us closer to Him. —Regina Franklin

what matters most

read>
Mark 8:34-37
What do you benefit if you gain the whole world but lose your own soul? (v.36).

more>
- Psalm 39:4-7
- Mark 12:16-21
- 1 Timothy 6:17-19

next>
What matters most to you in life? How does the brevity of life affect your relationship with God? With others?

I'll never forget the time a friend phoned me after he had been diagnosed with terminal brain cancer. He was so pumped about all the things that were becoming clear to him, and he wanted help in writing a book that he could share with others.

My friend could hardly contain his excitement. He was so stoked that it was hard for him to slow down and be specific. That night on the phone, I struggled to get a good read on all he wanted to express. But since his passing, I've come to understand a couple of things that became very clear to him.

First, he seemed to understand as never before what James meant when he said that our "life is like the morning fog—it's here a little while, then it's gone" (James 4:14). While this metaphor applies to a person who lives to be a hundred years old, it is most poignantly understood when someone's life is cut short by a disease or an accident.

Grasping this first point seemed to reinforce a second point—that the goods of life we accumulate are overrated. Or as Jesus put it, "What do you benefit if you gain the whole world but lose your own soul?" (Mark 8:36).

My friend accumulated a lot of cool stuff while working as a fishing and hunting guide in Alaska. But he was the first to say that, while useful, his possessions weren't all that important. What mattered most was having a relationship with Jesus and sharing His love with others.

Looking back, it wasn't that my friend came to see things he didn't already know. He was never one to be consumed with earthly possessions. But facing death sharpened his focus on what is most important. —Jeff Olson

what makes you happy?

read>
Luke 10:25-28
"You must love the Lord your God with all your heart, all your soul, all your strength, and all your mind." And, "Love your neighbor as yourself" (v.27).

more>
- Psalm 1
- Romans 12:9-18
- 1 Cor. 10:24,32-33

next>
Honestly answer this simple question: What makes you happy? How does God view happiness?

In 1937, researchers began studying the health and happiness of 268 Harvard University students. For many decades, the condition of these men was tracked. Featuring many years of data, the research was a serious attempt to answer a simple question: "What makes us happy?" In 2008, Dr. Vaillant, the director of the study, was asked what he had learned about human happiness from his 42 years of poring over the information gleaned. Vaillant's overall conclusion was simple and profound: "The only thing that really matters in life are your relationships to other people." *Relationships* are the key to happiness. "Happiness is love—full stop," he says in a video.

Two thousand years earlier, when asked what makes for a meaningful life (Luke 10:25), Jesus said, " 'You must love the Lord your God with all your heart, all your soul, all your strength, and all your mind.' And, 'Love your neighbor as yourself' " (v.27; Matthew 22:35-40; Mark 12:28-31,33). For believers in Jesus, happiness is loving God and loving other people.

How can you be happy? *Love God.* Fear the Lord your God, live in a way that pleases Him, and serve Him (Deuteronomy 6:1-5; 10:12). Yes, "happy are the people whose God is the Lord!" (Psalm 144:15, NKJV).

How can you be happy? *Love others.* Love one another deeply with all your heart (John 13:34, 15:17; 1 Peter 1:22). Keep on loving (Hebrews 13:1), bearing with one another in love (Ephesians 4:2). Respect, honor, and serve one another in love (1 Peter 2:17; Romans 12:10; Galatians 5:13). It's true. The best way to be happy is to love God and love others. —K.T. Sim

sacred sickness

read>
Isaiah 38:15-16
[God] Himself sent this sickness. Now I will walk humbly throughout my years because of this anguish I have felt (v.15).

more>
Lazarus's sickness will not end in death. No, it happened for the glory of God so that the Son of God will receive glory from this (John 11:4).

next>
What has God taught you through sickness? Why is physical healing less important than spiritual growth?

So here I sit in my sweatpants. Not exactly the corporate casual attire we're supposed to wear in the office. That's because—due to sickness—I've been out of the office the past two days. I picked up a "bug" that my body has been battling. It's not a big deal—far from what I experienced during the three times I've gone toe-to-toe with cancer. Any type of sickness, however, is an unwelcome guest. But it can also be just the bitter visitor we need.

King Hezekiah was afflicted with a sickness that made him "deathly ill" (Isaiah 38:1). Though he had been a good, godly king in Judah for many of his years (2 Kings 18:1-5), he failed by seeking help from Egypt instead of God Himself (Isaiah 31).

God brought some sacred sickness into Hezekiah's life to help him get well spiritually. The steps the king took to get well were just what the doctor ordered:

- *Prayer.* His first response was to pray (38:2). He spent some time with God, pouring out his heart before Him.
- *Humility.* Hezekiah experienced a wake-up call—one that allowed him to see the brevity of life (2 Corinthians 5:1) and his own humble state (Isaiah 38:15). He dropped to his knees before his holy, sovereign God.
- *Acceptance.* He acknowledged that his good God had allowed his illness as a means of pointing him toward renewed service and life (v.16).
- *Praise.* He praised God for His faithfulness, placing his focus and faith firmly on the Great Healer of hearts and bodies (vv.17-20).

God allows sickness in our lives for our good (Romans 8:28). We can grow in our relationship with Him as we call out to Him in prayer, acknowledge our human frailty, accept what He has allowed to take place, and praise Him even in our suffering (Job 1:21). —Tom Felten

strength to spare

read>
1 Kings 18:41–19:8
The Lord gave special strength to Elijah (18:46).

more>
- Isaiah 40:29
- Habakkuk 3:19
- Philippians 4:19

next>
Why is it important to focus on God's capabilities when we're stressed out? How do you typically react when faced with overwhelming personal or ministry demands?

British-born John Evans is a professional head-balancer. He has kept people, books, and other objects teetering on his dome for record-setting times. One of his greatest feats was balancing a MINI Cooper on his head for 33 seconds. Imagine the strain of holding up hundreds of pounds of automobile on your cranium!

Sometimes Christian ministry is a balancing act that requires super-human strength. The emotional, physical, and mental demands can be intense. A vacation may help, but it's not always possible to take a break. Fortunately, God can provide special strength for us—just as He did for Elijah.

After his showdown with Baal, Elijah executed 450 false prophets. Then he climbed Mount Carmel and prayed for the end of a 3-year drought. That's when "the Lord gave special strength to Elijah" (1 Kings 18:46), enabling him to run all the way to Jezreel, about 25 miles away.

Meanwhile, Queen Jezebel had issued an APB for him, so he trekked 100 more miles to Beersheba, before wandering into the Negev desert. Finally, he sat down and prayed, "I have had enough, Lord, . . . take my life" (19:4).

Thankfully, God knows our limits, and He can supply strength in any way He chooses. He might keep us going with a word of encouragement, ministry help, or an insight from the Holy Spirit. In Elijah's case, He sent an angel to provide him with bread and water—*twice*.

While you and I may never slay scores of prophets, it's encouraging to note, "Elijah was as human as we are" (James 5:17). Since God provided strength for Elijah's ministry demands, He can also sustain us as we help others—with strength to spare. —Jennifer Benson Schuldt

designed for relationship

read>
Genesis 1:26-27
So God created human beings in His own image. In the image of God He created them; male and female He created them (v.27).

more>
Dear friends, let us continue to love one another, for love comes from God. Anyone who loves is a child of God and knows God (1 John 4:7).

next>
Do you know someone who needs a friend? What can you do today to love that person?

Human beings are mysteriously designed for relationship. Isolate someone in a room and eventually he or she will become stressed, and confused, and their sleep will be disturbed. The chronically isolated person will become ill more often and have a higher risk of heart disease. In fact, their genes will begin to decay—one researcher likened chronic loneliness to "premature aging." Like flowers without sunlight, we wither without social connection.

But why? Why are we so relationally wired—with food, water, and shelter insufficient to keep us healthy?

Christians believe in the triune God. Scripture stresses that there is only one God (Deuteronomy 6:4), but also reveals that this God is a community of three persons—Father, Son, and Spirit. We see all three members of the Trinity present at Jesus' baptism (Matthew 3:16-17). We are to be baptized in the name of all three (28:19). And looking back, we may even see all three present in the world's creation—Father directing the process (Genesis 1:1), Spirit hovering over the waters (v.2), and Son as the Word of God (John 1:1) through whom creation is spoken into existence (Genesis 1:3-24).

If God Himself is a community, is it any wonder that when God makes humans in His image (1:26-27), He makes them as relational beings? Male and female unite (2:24), and the result is a family (1:28). The siblings born become supports during times of adversity (Proverbs 17:17). Friends become those who sharpen us morally (27:6,17). In origin and function, we are relational to the core.

Loneliness in our homes, churches, and neighborhoods must be remedied by Christian love. In befriending the lonely, we reveal something of the triune God who made us. —Sheridan Voysey

the joy of sex

read>
Proverbs 5:1-23
Drink water from your own well—share your love only with your wife. Why spill the water of your springs in the streets, having sex with just anyone? (vv.15-16).

more>
- Malachi 2:14-15
- Matthew 19:4-6
- Hebrews 13:4

next>
In light of this theology of sex, how does this help you understand why God hates divorce and any sex that occurs outside the covenant of marriage? Whether you're single or married, how can you glorify God in the way you live out your sexuality?

The women's fashion and lifestyle magazine in my mechanic's office flaunted numerous articles about sex. One story, meant to be especially titillating, recounted the exploits of men who made love to multiple partners at once. The article left me sad. These hollow thrill seekers are not just looking for love in all the wrong places, they're looking for love in *too many places*.

The best sex is exclusive. The oneness between a husband and wife—"two are united into one" (Genesis 2:18,24)—is a reflection of the ultimate spiritual oneness shared by the Father, Son, and Holy Spirit. God is a self-giving community of love: Three in One who exist in a perfect relationship. Theologians base our understanding of the mutual indwelling of the Trinity on Jesus' words: "You are in Me, Father, and I am in You" (John 17:21). When we become one with another body, we reflect the God who made us in His image as male and female (Genesis 1:27).

Some popular love songs seem to get it right. Sex can be "almost paradise." It is "knocking on heaven's door," because the companionship and intimacy of marriage echo the love of our triune God. This is why Proverbs instructs married couples to "reserve [sex] for yourselves. Never share it with strangers" (5:17).

When we selfishly use another person for our own physical pleasure—stealing from their body rather than owning and being owned by them—the true joy of sex (that only comes through giving ourselves completely to the one person who has given him or herself to us) is lost.

Any animal can mate. Only humans can know the bliss of being loved by one other—of being naked and vulnerable and still embraced. And that is simply divine. —Mike Wittmer

radical change

read>
Ezekiel 11:14-21
I will take away their stony, stubborn heart and give them a tender, responsive heart (v.19).

more>
Anyone who belongs to Christ has become a new person. The old life is gone; a new life has begun! (2 Cor. 5:17).

next>
What remnants from your old, stubborn life are you refusing to give up? What do you need to do to see God birth new life and bring radical change in you?

In a world where we so easily create virtual identities, we're often tempted to paint ourselves in the best (exaggerated) light and to make ourselves appear as though we're more accomplished or popular than we actually are. And if we want to start over from scratch, we can do so with just a few keystrokes. For instance, Seppukoo.com (with a nod to the ancient Japanese samurai tradition of ritual suicide) allows you to kill off your old Facebook identity. Then, whenever you wish, you can just begin again.

Of course, in the real world, true change requires far more work than clicking a few options on a Web site—and requires much more time (a lifetime usually) to see full fruit.

The prophet Ezekiel wrote to Israel while they were in exile—estranged from their homeland with no power, minimal resources, and little hope for a meaningful future. Spiritually, they were destitute. Even the empire occupying their land saw what had happened. "Those people are far away from the Lord," they said, "so now He has given their land to us!" (Ezekiel 11:15). The entire nation of Israel groveled in a losing life they were desperate to change.

But they couldn't enact the transformation they needed. They couldn't pull themselves out of their mess. Left to themselves, nothing would change. *Ever.* This was true for them, and it's true for us. Locked in cycles of self-destruction and impotent attempts to make ourselves over, we know that we can't bring about the type of renovation we need.

Mercifully, God promised that He would gather His scattered people back together, and that He would "put a new spirit in them" (v.19). God does what we can never do—He takes our old, withered life and gives us new life, full of joy and promise. —Winn Collier

hooks to hang your hopes on

read>
Psalm 91
His faithful promises are your armor and protection (v.4).

more>
- Numbers 23:19
- Psalm 62:5-8
- Isaiah 12:2

next>
Find three additional promises in God's Word to hang your hopes on. Why is it vital that we trust in God's promises?

Pastor Tim Keller says that, in life, "Fifty percent of the reason we get so discouraged and despondent is we're shocked when something bad happens. We say, 'This isn't how it's supposed to be.' "

In other words, we tend to believe that since we've placed our faith in Jesus, and because we've tried to be "good" Christians, a comfortable and problem-free existence should be ours.

New York Giants and New York Yankees Chaplain George McGovern explained the pitfall of such thinking to the professional athletes he works with. He said, "When you hang your hopes on *non-guaranteed promises* rather than on God's *guaranteed promises*, you are destined to experience deep disappointment." Keller adds that with this type of mindset, "You're going to be continually shocked and even overthrown."

Though God doesn't promise us rosy circumstances, worldly success, or the fulfillment of all our "wants," He does present an abundance of promises that, if we cling to them, will help us stand during tough times. His guarantees include: "Forgiveness of sins for all who repent" (Luke 24:47); triumph over sin and death for all who receive God's wonderful gifts of grace and righteousness "through this one Man, Jesus Christ" (Romans 5:17); an Advocate, the Holy Spirit, who will never leave those who love God and accept His commandments (John 14:15-21); "peace of mind and heart" that the world can't provide (v.27); rest for the "weary" who bring their "heavy burdens" to Jesus (Matthew 11:28-30); eternal life through faith in Jesus Christ (Titus 1:1-2).

In a world where people and circumstances disappoint, we can experience true joy by discarding our sense of worldly entitlement and placing our hope in God's promises. —Roxanne Robbins

living counter-naturally

read>
Mark 9:30-37
Anyone who welcomes a little child like this on My behalf welcomes Me, and anyone who welcomes Me welcomes not only Me but also My Father who sent Me (v.37)

more>
- Matthew 25:31-46
- John 13:1-11

next>
What does it mean to welcome someone in Jesus' name? How can you do that in your everyday actions and attitudes?

My family was eating at a mall food court. My middle son couldn't finish all of his food, so he got up to find a take-home box. After being gone for quite a while, he finally returned. When we asked him why it had taken him so long, he told us that customers kept jumping in front of him and that the servers kept looking over him. As I held back my tears, I told him about a child in the Bible that Jesus *didn't* overlook.

Jesus was discussing His upcoming betrayal and death, but His disciples didn't get it. It's likely they failed to grasp Jesus' words due to the fact that they were busy arguing over who was going to be the greatest (Mark 9:34). Sitting down, Jesus taught them a vital discipleship principle—greatness is open to everyone, all who are willing to be last and a slave to all (v.35).

His point was that His kingdom is about position—the lowest one. Then He drove home the point with a powerful and literal illustration. He placed a child—*a culturally helpless, emotionally vulnerable, and socially invisible child*—among the disciples, embraced him, and challenged them to welcome him in His name. In welcoming him, they would be welcoming the Father. Jesus was teaching that greatness in the kingdom of God is all about ministering, especially to those of lower status.

Because Jesus led through suffering and humility, we're called to lead through serving instead of being served. Jesus wants us to embrace humility instead of pride, and to be first to serve the culturally vulnerable instead of the socially powerful. We can live out this counter-natural principle by repenting of our status-consciousness state, entering the world of suffering with the sufferer, embracing the socially invisible, and by serving people intentionally and unexpectedly. —Marvin Williams

love your enemies

read>
Luke 6:27-36
But to you who are willing to listen, I say, love your enemies! Do good to those who hate you (v.27).

more>
God called you to do good, even if it means suffering, just as Christ suffered for you. He is your example, and you must follow in His steps (1 Peter 2:21).

next>
What's keeping you from loving your enemies? How should you live this out in obedience today?

I may not love God as I should, but I'm determined to get a handle on it. I may not love my family the way I should, but I intend to work at it. I may not love my neighbor as I should—but I'll keep trying. But love my enemy? Wow. *That* seems impossible!

Here's why it's so difficult. Enemies scheme, backstab, subject you to mental distress, and can even cause you bodily harm. If you could truly love them, they wouldn't be your enemies anymore, would they? But in Luke 6, Jesus says, "Love your enemies" by doing good to them (vv.27,35).

Love is not mere emotion—it's the decision to do what's right and good for another person. It means blessing those who are against you, praying for them, and responding to their evil with good. And it means helping them even when they don't deserve it.

The three motivations for this kind of love are:

• "Your reward from heaven will be very great" (v.35). Jesus doesn't expand on this statement here, but it's clearly a promise. If we choose to honor Him by loving our enemies, He will reward us.

• "You will truly be acting as children of the Most High" (v.35). As children of the Most High, we can say along with the martyrs throughout the ages, "You can't take my true wealth because it's stored up in heaven. You can't take my real life because it's eternal in Jesus Christ."

• "You must be compassionate, just as your Father is compassionate." We are called to imitate our Father, who is kind even to the "unthankful and wicked" (vv.35-36).

Let's choose love over hatred. No occasion justifies evil for evil; no injustice warrants unjust behavior. Instead, we can follow God's leading by choosing to love our enemies. —Poh Fang Chia

perspective

read>
Matthew 23:5-7,13-28
Outwardly you look like righteous people, but inwardly your hearts are filled with hypocrisy and lawlessness (v.28).

more>
- Psalm 51:6,10
- Ezekiel 11:19
- Matthew 5:8

next>
In what ways have you tried to control what others think of you? What excuses have you used to keep from being transparent with others? What area in your heart do you desire for God to purify?

Still half asleep, I gradually found my way to the bathroom to begin my morning routine. Grabbing my toothbrush, I coated it with toothpaste and sat down on the edge of the bathtub. Because I don't normally sit and brush my teeth, my position afforded me a new perspective of the bathroom sink. Previously hidden from view by the faucet's spout, a fine layer of unidentifiable matter coated the edge where the faucet met the white porcelain. I realized my "working mom" style of cleaning needed some modifications.

Like the unseen grime on a sink, sin thrives in places beyond the view of others. So when we wage war against spiritual enemies, we need help. For our hearts can deceive us (Jeremiah 17:9). Surrounding ourselves with godly people who can speak the wisdom of God's Word into our lives heightens our advantage in the battle (Proverbs 24:6). When we withhold information or spin the truth to make ourselves look good, however, the good counsel we receive can become sullied. Before long, one speck of grime adds to another until our hearts become a musty grave of hidden thoughts and desires.

Sadly, in the past I've whitewashed the tomb of my heart by pushing undesirable responses below others' perceptions. Then, not so strangely, I've wondered why I felt like I could never be good enough. I hadn't yet learned that coating the outside doesn't change the heart. Dressed in layers of self-righteousness, I was naked and blind (Revelation 3:17-18)—desperately needing God's perspective.

True godliness demands the demolition of any manmade construction. Exposing our failings is never easy in the moment; but when we live from the inside out, life becomes real. And our perspective becomes a great deal more accurate.

—Regina Franklin

it feels so right

read>
Proverbs 14:1-12
There is a path before each person that seems right, but it ends in death (v.12).

more>
You must warn each other every day, while it is still "today," so that none of you will be deceived by sin and hardened against God (Hebrews 3:13).

next>
Why can't relationships be trusted simply because they "feel so right"? What good things happen when we abstain from sexual sin?

In 1977, singer Debbie Boone recorded "You Light Up My Life." The song quickly shot to the top of the charts and became one of the biggest hits in the 1970s. While the song was originally written as a romantic love song, Boone claimed to sing it to God.

One of the most familiar lines in the song says, "It can't be wrong when it feels so right." That's certainly true when it comes to our drawing close to the pure presence of our Creator. And it can sure seem right in human relationships too—but that's not always the case. They can most definitely be wrong even though they feel right.

Take King David. I have no doubt that when he watched Bathsheba bathe and then took her into his bedroom, she lit up his life. It felt so "right" and easy to justify enjoying the charms of another man's wife (2 Samuel 11:1-4). That's the deceptive nature of any form of sexual immorality. But the excitement never lasts. In fact, it's like the calm before the storm.

David's infidelity with Bathsheba erupted into a pregnancy, murder, a cover-up, and ultimately the death of an innocent child (2 Samuel 11:5–12:18). In a sexually permissive world where we're bombarded with the message "if it feels good, do it," it's important to remind ourselves and each other of the bigger picture. What makes marital infidelity—and any form of sexual immorality—wrong is its destructive nature. Indulging in it eats away at our hearts and tears apart our relationships. Most important, it's sin in God's eyes.

Now, God isn't trying to take the pleasure out of life when He prohibits sexual sin. Instead, He's a loving Father who is trying to protect His children from doing great harm to themselves and others. —Jeff Olson

inconvenient compassion

read>
Matthew 14:13-21
Jesus saw the huge crowd as He stepped from the boat, and He had compassion on them and healed their sick (v.14).

more>
The Lord is good to everyone. He showers compassion on all His creation (Psalm 145:9).

next>
What keeps you from having a more compassionate heart for those who don't believe in Jesus? How does Jesus' compassion inspire you?

Unlike us sometimes, Jesus didn't allow circumstances to dictate whether or not He chose to act compassionately. We need to take that to heart, for unchurched people are looking for reasons to attend a church and associate with believers in Christ. Nearly 60 percent of non-church-attenders say they would be more likely to step inside if they felt the church "cared for them as a person" (2009 Lifeway survey).

Jesus cared for individuals even when He faced bitter times. John the Baptist, the man God used to "prepare the way" for Jesus and who had baptized Him, was brutally executed by Herod Antipas, the ruler of Galilee (Matthew 14:6-11). When Jesus "heard the news," He experienced sadness and grief and left on a boat to go to a remote place (v.13). His heart was heavy as He dealt with the death of John and perhaps considered His own future sacrifice. During His moments alone on the boat, per His consistent pattern, it's likely He prayed—calling out to His heavenly Father.

When Jesus stepped from the boat, He was greeted by thousands of people. They had left their homes and towns to follow Him. But now they were in the wilderness without food. Though still grieving, "Jesus . . . had compassion on them and healed their sick" (v.14). What's more, He provided for their physical needs by giving them all a miraculous meal (vv.20-21).

To show compassion will often require us to leave convenience far behind. The times we're called to display it may be when our own hearts are heavy or when we're tired. That's the perfect time to call out to our heavenly Father, seeking His comfort and counsel. Then we can pour out Christlike compassion on the people around us who are looking for the reality of Jesus in our words and actions.

—Tom Felten

trials and temptations

read>
Matthew 6:9-13
And don't let us yield to temptation, but rescue us from the evil one (v.13).

more>
• Psalm 119:9-11
• 1 Peter 5:8-10

next>
What trials of life are you going through at this moment? What potential danger to sin exists in these trials? What must you do to overcome the temptations?

Jesus was led by the Holy Spirit into the wilderness to be tested by the devil (Matthew 4:1-11). Each test was a temptation or enticement to sin. It's not a sin to be tempted. But there exists in every trial a potential for us to disobey God. Job, severely tested by Satan (Job 1–2), didn't sin against God (2:10). Mrs. Job, however, responded differently: "Curse God and die," she said (2:9). Her response shows the potential danger in every trial or temptation we face. That's why we need to pray, "Don't let us yield to temptation, but rescue us from the evil one" (Matthew 6:13).

To resist temptation, we need to:

• *Be alert to the dangers of evil around us.* Satan asked permission to test Peter (Luke 22:31). Because Peter did not heed Jesus' warning, he denied the Lord (Luke 22:34,56-62). Jesus said, "Keep watch and pray, so that you will not give in to temptation" (Matthew 26:41).

• *Resist the devil with the Word of God.* In Luke 4, Jesus responded to Satan's temptations by quoting from Deuteronomy 8:3 (v.4), Deuteronomy 6:13 (v.8), and Deuteronomy 6:16 (v.12). Just as Jesus used the Scriptures to overcome Satan and temptation, so should we.

• *Trust in God who is faithful.* God uses the trials of life to perfect us (James 1:2-4; 1 Peter 1:6-8). If these trials couldn't build us up, He wouldn't allow them. Surely, our heavenly Father will be with us in whatever we face. We persevere because He provides us with His all-sufficient grace (2 Cor. 12:8-10).

Our fear of failure is dispelled when we realize that God may place a load on us but will never overload us. He will provide a way out so that we can endure. He is the faithful God we can trust in the midst of any trial (1 Cor. 10:13). —K.T. Sim

textcouragement

read>
2 Thessalonians 1
We proudly tell God's other churches about your endurance and faithfulness (v.4).

more>
When [Barnabas] arrived and saw this evidence of God's blessing, he was filled with joy, and he encouraged the believers to stay true to the Lord (Acts 11:23).

next>
Why do we sometimes let words of encouragement go unsaid? Why does God want us to spur on other believers?

Have you ever received a *textcouragement* message? You know, a little scrap of encouragement sent via a text message? My friend Myrna sent me this one: "Read Philippians 3:1-11 today if you have time. It blessed me." My friend Nicole beamed me: "How is the baby's cough? I've been praying for you."

As Christians, we need to lift up fellow believers. The first chapter of 2 Thessalonians shows how Paul encouraged the church at Thessalonica. The congregation there had trashed their little statues when they turned to Jesus, and as a result the Gentile idol-worshipers were harassing them.

Despite the persecution, Paul noted that the Thessalonians' faith was flourishing. Their spiritual tenacity prompted him to say, "We proudly tell God's other churches about your endurance and faithfulness" (v.4). What an endorsement! If you know some diehard servants of the Lord, give them some good publicity. You'll not only encourage them, but you'll also inspire others to keep going for God.

Another way to spur on our spiritual kin is to remind them that persecution due to our faith is temporary. Paul vowed that God would "provide rest for [those] who [were] being persecuted" (v.7). Allowing people to see trials in light of eternity can help snuff out the misery of the moment.

Finally, Paul assured the Thessalonians that he was praying God would enable them "to live a life worthy of His call" (v.11). Promising to pray for people is great. It's even better when we're specific about the requests we'll make on their behalf!

Christians are supposed to "encourage . . . and build each other up" (1 Thessalonians 5:11). Today, find some ways to let your words "be an encouragement to those who hear them" (Ephesians 4:29). —Jennifer Benson

priceless

read>
1 Kings 21:1-19
"The Lord forbid that I should give you the inheritance that was passed down by my ancestors" (vv.2-3).

more>
- Genesis 25:29-34
- Proverbs 23:23
- Matthew 16:26

next>
What if it's too late, and you have already compromised your integrity or the conscience of someone else? What will you do to receive forgiveness and make things right?

Michael Forbes has lived on the Aberdeenshire dunes in Scotland for more than 40 years. His rustic buildings never bothered his neighbors, but they're an eyesore to Donald Trump, who is building a luxury hotel and golf course nearby. Trump offered Forbes free golf and above market value for his 23 acres, but Forbes replied that he wouldn't leave for any amount of money. He told ABC News, "The place is not for sale. It's never been for sale. And they can't understand that. They think there's a price on everybody. There's not a price on me."

God bless Michael Forbes. He reminds us that some things are priceless, simply because there is no way to estimate their worth. This was Naboth's point to King Ahab (1 Kings 21:3). In essence, he said, "I would love to trade up, but how can I betray the Lord and sell the vineyard which He gave to my family?"

King Ahab cried to Queen Jezebel who executed Naboth on false charges and gave his vineyard to the king. But God had the last word. He sent Elijah to tell Ahab that dogs would lick his blood "at the very place where they licked the blood of Naboth!" (v.19).

Although some situations may end badly for us, we need to be like Naboth. What about us is not for sale? Will we trade our integrity for money, sex for a relationship, or the confidence of our friend to win the approval of another?

We must never be an Ahab—the one who pressures others to sell. Avoid sentences that begin with, "If you love me, you will . . ." "If you're my friend, you will . . ." and "Can't we make an exception just this once?"

Know what is priceless—never to be sold. —Mike Wittmer

OCTOBER 18

surprising life

read>
Ephesians 2:1-6
But God . . . even though we were dead . . . gave us life (vv.4-5).

more>
You can be a slave to sin, which leads to death, or you can choose to obey God, which leads to righteous living (Romans 6:16).

next>
Where in your life do you most sense death—and where do you most need life? How can you open yourself up to God's new life?

Last August in Asuncion, Paraguay, Jose Alvarenga received the worst news a father can hear about a newborn child. The doctors came and told him his son, born prematurely (only 500g / 17.6 oz), was dead. A little over 4 hours after the heartbreaking event, Jose opened the box that held his tiny son's casket so that he could say his goodbyes—and found his son alive.

"I opened it to look at his remains," said Mr. Alvarenga, "and found that the baby was breathing. I began to cry." They rushed the baby back to the hospital where he was stabilized.

Each of us must deal with death on a daily basis. We face death when we bury a parent or a sibling or a friend. We face death when we receive frightening news of cancer or some other medical crisis. Beyond these obvious places, death has sunk its talons into every corner of human existence. Families ruined. Relationships torn apart. Neighborhoods and cities and countries straining under the weight of poverty and crime.

The Bible tells us that this death is due to the rebellion and sin we have committed against our Creator (Genesis 2:15-16). The apostle Paul reiterates this sad reality, declaring that the result of human sin is death—destruction, ruin, and mayhem (Romans 6:23).

Paul starkly presents our situation before God when he states that we're *all* "dead because of [our] disobedience and [our] many sins" (Ephesians 2:1). But God—always one to surprise us with His kindness and generosity—arrives at the moment we're most desperate, most hopeless. He rushes to our aid "even though we [are] dead because of our sins" (v.5). We're dead, lifeless. We are, by all accounts, past hope. Yet God arrives, and immediately everything changes. God gives us life—surprising, beautiful life. —Winn Collier

character that counts

read >
Philippians 1:9-11
May you always be filled with the fruit of your salvation—the righteous character produced in your life by Jesus Christ—for this will bring much glory and praise to God (v.11).

more >
- 1 Corinthians 15:33
- Galatians 5:22
- Hebrews 1:3

next >
Pick two of the character traits in the devo and apply them to a situation you're facing. How does God grow our character? Why?

Rod Handley, director of the ministry Character That Counts, has devoted his life's work to helping people grow in character. He encourages people to, as *Merriam-Webster's* puts it, exude "moral excellence and firmness."

In his book *Team Studies on Character,* Handley lists traits embedded in the essence of 1 Timothy 4:16, which exhorts us to "Keep a close watch on how you live. . . . Stay true to what is right for the sake of your own salvation and the salvation of those who hear you."

Here are some of the traits and what they mean:

Alertness: Being keenly aware of the events taking place around me so that I can properly respond to them.

Benevolence: Giving to others' basic needs without expectations of personal reward.

Forgiveness: Clearing the record of those who have wronged me and not holding past offenses against them.

Generosity: Realizing that all I have belongs to God and freely giving to benefit others.

Holiness: Having no blemish or stain. Being whole with no trace of regret or remorse.

Loyalty: Using difficult times to demonstrate my commitment to others or to what is right.

Responsibility: Knowing and doing what's expected of me.

Self-Control: Bringing my thoughts, words, actions, and attitudes into constant obedience in order to benefit others.

Worship: Honoring God reverently.

Today, consider how you can increasingly implement these character qualities into your life, to the glory of God (Philippians 1:11). —Roxanne Robbins

the grapevine

read>
Proverbs 20:15-19
A gossip goes around telling secrets, so don't hang around with chatterers (v.19).

more>
Be kind to each other, tenderhearted, forgiving one another, just as God through Christ has forgiven you (Ephesians 4:32).

next>
What are some ways you can prevent unwholesome talk from coming out of your mouth? What words can you use to build up and give life to another person this week?

I Heard It Through the Grapevine," a song written by Norman Whitfield and Barrett Strong in 1966, was recorded by Gladys Knight and the Pips and later by Marvin Gaye. It became one of the biggest hits on the Motown label. Its point was that while the telegraph is obsolete, the informal transmission of information, gossip, or rumor from person to person is still going strong.

Solomon said that not only is grapevine gossip wrong, it is dangerous, unwise, and ungodly. The original word for *gossip* meant "birds picking up seed." When applied to a person, it meant one who was an information scavenger, picking up seeds of information (rumors or facts) about others and foolishly or maliciously spreading them around. Solomon not only called this person an information scavenger, but he also categorized him as a fool (Proverbs 10:18).

Grapevine gossip leads to disastrous effects. It separates close friends (16:28), betrays a confidence (11:13), shames and saddles him or her with a bad reputation (25:9-10), perpetually fuels the embers of a quarrel (26:20), and is an indication that the person is not walking obediently with God. Therefore, God condemned grapevine gossip and implemented a zero tolerance policy for it because it tears the fabric of holy communion with Him and holy community with others (Leviticus 19:16).

In our world of e-mail, text messaging, Instant Messaging, Facebook, Twitter, and other communication and social media outlets, it's extremely easy for any of us to become information scavengers and grapevine gossips. We can resist these temptations by avoiding people who talk too much (Proverbs 20:19), asking God for strength to avoid sinning with our words (Proverbs 10:19; Psalm 39:1), talking to God, and saying only what will build up rather than tear down (Ephesians 4:29). —Marvin Williams

single or married?

read›
1 Corinthians 7:25-40
I want you to do whatever will help you serve the Lord best, with as few distractions as possible (v.35).

more›
"I know the plans I have for you," says the Lord. "They are plans for good and not for disaster, to give you a future and a hope" (Jeremiah 29:11).

next›
How could you use your current marital status—whether single, dating, or married—to serve the Lord best, with as few distractions as possible? Why must Jesus be our primary focus regardless of our life situation?

As a single woman, for years my view of marriage was based more on what it takes from a life than what it can add to it. But over time, I've been able to better understand marriage by studying God's Word.

In 1 Corinthians 7:8-9, Paul's general advice is that it's better to stay unmarried because of the opportunities it provides to serve Christ without distraction. The reasons given are: (1) Single people will not have to deal with the unique problems that married people face (vv.25-28). (2) Because the end is near, Christians shouldn't let marriage and the things of the world become their dominant concerns. Their primary focus should be Jesus and eternity (vv.29-31). (3) Since marriage brings earthly responsibilities, singles will be able to devote their lives more fully to serving God (vv.32-35).

But if marriage comes with so many disadvantages, why did God institute this covenant relationship? Here's where the whole counsel of God's Word is vital! While singles may have fewer everyday concerns than married couples, it's also true that two is better than one (Ecclesiastes 4:9). We can see God's blueprint for marriage in Genesis 2:18-25. This passage reveals that, in marriage, the man and wife complement each other in His service.

There's also a selflessness in marriage that one can never attain alone. It's a relationship in which living for another's best interest is put to the test, and yet—at the same time—can be extremely rewarding. A God-honoring marriage is also a strong witness of Christ's love for the church (Ephesians 5:21-33).

Our primary concern should always be our relationship with Jesus—regardless of marital status (Luke 14:26). So whether you're single or married, keep seeking Him and rest in what He deems best for you. —Poh Fang Chia

measured

read>
Galatians 2:11-21
Yet we know that a person is made right with God by faith in Jesus Christ, not by obeying the law. And we have believed in Christ Jesus, so that we might be made right with God (v.16).

more>
- Romans 5:20-21
- 1 Timothy 1:12-15
- 2 Timothy 1:9

next>
How have you wrongly relied on works to assure yourself of God's love for you? If intimacy with God can't be earned, what place should spiritual disciplines have in our lives and why should we practice them?

After a 7-year hiatus of staying home with our children, I finally returned to teaching. Acclimating to the demands of being a high school English teacher, I realized I had not missed grading essays. I love watching students grow in their writing, but the rigor of reading and grading 25 essays at a time can be mind-boggling. To keep from losing sight of the standard I've set, I often use a grading sheet denoting the value for each aspect of the assignment. Rubrics keep me sane as I wade through comma splices and run-on sentences.

While we rarely receive a grade for our varied activities in a day, we are surrounded by performance evaluations. From the movies we see to the cars we buy to our applications on Facebook (and even the devotions we write), we can measure and be measured. Living in a society where ratings determine value, we can mistakenly transfer this mindset to our spiritual growth.

Salvation can't be earned (Ephesians 2:5-9). Understandably though, our humanity gravitates to anything we can control—even the measurable aspect of spiritual disciplines. In Galatians 2, Paul spoke to this issue in his confrontation with Peter. No amount of Bible reading, prayer, or fasting can earn us any part of God's inheritance (Titus 3:7). There exists but one measurement for grace: *We are given what we don't deserve.*

Works don't lead to salvation, but good works should flow from the lives of those who've been saved (Matthew 5:16). If we understand, "He saved us, not because of the righteous things we had done, but because of His mercy," we will then "devote [ourselves] to doing good" (Titus 3:5,8).

Rubrics may provide an earthly standard of measurement, but for our salvation there's just one standard—the blood of Jesus. —Regina Franklin

who's in your five?

read>
Mark 3:13-19
Then He appointed twelve of them and called them His apostles. They were to accompany Him, and He would send them out to preach (v.14).

"Who's in your Five?" was the slogan of a cell phone company which offered its customers unlimited calls to their five favorite people. The advertisements for this plan remind us that we are not vitally important to everyone and that everyone is not equally important to us. We all must choose whom to let into our inner circle. If you could call five people for free, who would they be?

We all have pretty much the same number of essential people. It doesn't matter how large your life becomes. You may be the pastor of a large church, the CEO of a multinational company, even the president or prime minister of an entire nation. Still, you truly matter to only a select group of people. Your death may bring sadness to your fans and followers, but it will be a severe shock only to those who are in your "Fave Five."

Jesus came to save the world, but even He invested His life in a small circle of friends. Jesus chose 12 men to be His disciples, and of these He was especially close to just three. Peter, James, and John accompanied Jesus during His most important moments. They went with Him to the Mount of Transfiguration (Luke 9:28-36) and most of the way into Gethsemane (Matthew 26:36-46).

If the Son of God poured His life into His select group of friends, we should ask how we are caring for our core group. The measure of a life is not riches or respect, power or beauty. It's not even about accomplishing great things for God. No matter your station or status in life, the ultimate test is the same: Who's in your Five, and are they better off for being there? —Mike Wittmer

more>
Timothy, please come as soon as you can. . . . Only Luke is with me. Bring Mark with you when you come. . . . Do your best to get here before winter (2 Timothy 4:9,11,21).

next>
Who's your Fave Five? What can you do to let them know how much they mean to you? How can you help them grow in their faith in Jesus?

jars of water

read>
Hebrews 10:19-25
Our guilty consciences have been sprinkled with Christ's blood to make us clean, and our bodies have been washed with pure water (v.22).

more>
- Psalm 51:10
- John 7:38
- 1 Peter 1:22

next>
What does it mean to be purified by the blood of Jesus? How has God equipped you to bring His purifying power to people you know?

It's cool to see believers in Jesus who reflect His cleansing ways. The band Jars of Clay is a good example. In 2003, they founded a charitable organization called Blood: Water Mission. The goal of Blood: Water was to bring clean water to 1,000 communities in Africa. By early 2011 they had accomplished this goal! The organization also works with partners to establish clinics and provide HIV/AIDS testing and education. These efforts reflect the passon of Jars of Clay to see Africans experience both clean blood *and* clean water.

The writer of Hebrews describes the purification of hearts that Jesus has brought about by His sacrifice on the cross. We can enter "the presence of God with sincere hearts" because we have "been sprinkled with Christ's blood to make us clean, and our bodies have been washed with pure water" (Hebrews 10:22).

Why did our hearts need this deep cleaning? Because each of us is born with a sinful one (Jeremiah 17:9). Only by the blood of Jesus, the sole perfect sacrifice without blemish, could we be set free from the stain and death brought by sin (Hebrews 10:4-10).

Once cleaned and redeemed, however, we're not called to be sparkling statues that portray God's purifying ways. No, He wants us to pick up our jars and pour out fresh water. He wants us to be about the business of cleansing the world in His power and for His glory. A cleansed heart should naturally flow with "acts of love and good works," according to the writer of Hebrews (v.24).

Few of us will be called to initiate something as big as Blood: Water Mission. But each small act that points people to the cleansing blood of Christ is just as profound. What are you doing as a purifying agent for Jesus in your part of the world? —Tom Felten

doxology

read>
Matthew 6:9-13
For Yours is the kingdom and the power and the glory forever. Amen (v.13 NKJV).

more>
- Psalm 100
- Ephesians 3:20-21
- Jude 1:24-25

next>
Why do we often fail to thank God for who He is? What's one thing you can thank God for today?

After making all the petitions for God's glory to be magnified (Matthew 6:9-10) and for God's grace to meet our needs (vv.11-13), *The Lord's Prayer* concludes with a praise item, a doxology: "For Yours is the kingdom and the power and the glory forever. Amen" (v.13 NKJV).

This doxology isn't found in the oldest and most reliable Greek manuscripts. That's why some Bibles have it printed as a footnote. Bible scholars believe that the doxology was added much later—sometime in the first or second century AD.

Now, just because Jesus didn't speak them, this doesn't mean we shouldn't use these words today. There's nothing theologically incorrect about its wording. In fact, King David offered a similar doxology when he dedicated the materials that were collected for the building of the temple (1 Chronicles 29:10-11). Scholars believed that verse 13 is based on David's doxology. In the New Testament, we see the angels in heaven praising God with a similar doxology (Revelation 5:13).

In response to God's gracious provisions (Matthew 6:11), pardon (v.12), and protection (v.13), we offer our heartfelt worship to the Father. "Yours is the kingdom and the power and the glory forever. Amen."

There are three significant phrases in the doxology: *the kingdom, the power,* and *the glory forever*: The kingdom speaks of God's sovereignty—He is King; the power describes our trust in His omnipotence. He is the all-powerful King; the glory forever is a joyful declaration of His Majesty. He is the glorious King.

The doxology beautifully describes the One we pray to and praise. He alone deserves *the kingdom and the power and the glory forever. Amen.* —K.T. Sim

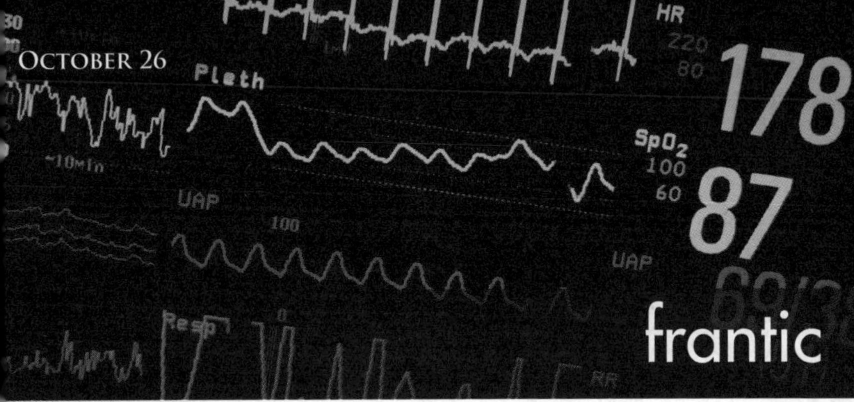

October 26

frantic

read>
1 Samuel 28:1-25
When Saul saw the vast Philistine army, he became frantic with fear (v.5).

more>
God has not given us a spirit of fear and timidity, but of power, love, and self-discipline (2 Timothy 1:7).

next>
Why is it important to practice responding to the Holy Spirit? What other emotions, besides fear, can threaten to take us over? What should we do when we experience them?

I was just a few minutes away from major surgery. Nurses circulated through the room and I was hooked up to all sorts of monitors. Suddenly, a computer screen started blipping wildly. *What was happening? Would I be all right?* A nurse glanced at the readout and announced that it was monitoring my heart rate. I needed to calm down!

I'm not the only one who has experienced anxiety before a big event. One peek at the Philistine army caused King Saul to become "frantic with fear" (1 Samuel 28:5). Fear's influence increased until it controlled the king.

It started out with fear of the Philistines, but then Saul realized that because of some prior disobedience (15:7-26), "the Lord refused to answer him" when he asked for advice (28:6). Silence from God can make a frightening situation even scarier. So, instead of repenting, Saul ordered his advisors to find a spiritist.

Saul's fear was evident as he "disguised himself by wearing ordinary clothing . . . . Then he went to the [witch's] home at night" (v.8). It was against his own law to consult with anyone who summoned dead spirits (vv.3,9), and he was afraid of getting caught!

Still in panic mode, Saul asked Samuel's spirit for advice. Samuel said that the Philistines would trounce Israel, killing Saul and his sons the very next day. Hearing this, "Saul fell full length on the ground, paralyzed with fright" (v.20).

When terror has control of us, it can immobilize us and make us ineffective. That's one reason God doesn't want us to live in the grip of fear. As Christians, we "have not received a spirit that makes [us] fearful slaves" (Romans 8:15). Rather, we're supposed to be filled with the Holy Spirit. Letting God's Spirit control our minds "leads to life and peace" (v.6), instead of frantic feelings.

—Jennifer Benson Schuldt

finding perspective

read›
Proverbs 9:10-12
Fear of the Lord is the foundation of wisdom. Knowledge of the Holy One results in good judgment (v.10).

more›
- Exodus 20:5-6
- Proverbs 29:18
- 1 Peter 5:6

next›
Think of a time when you slipped out of submission to God and lost perspective. What led you there? How will you "bow" before God today?

In London's National Gallery, art critic Robert Cumming stands in front of a classic 15th-century painting by Renaissance artist Fra Filippo Lippi. The painting shows Mary holding the infant Jesus on her lap, with Saints Dominic and Jerome kneeling before Him. The piece is troubling to Robert Cumming. It's a masterpiece, no doubt, but its perspective seems all wrong. Hills in the background look too large; Dominic and Jerome look awkward as they kneel before the child.

Then Robert Cumming remembers something. This painting was never created to hang in an art gallery, but as an altarpiece, to be viewed in a place of prayer. He suddenly realizes what he needs to do. He gets down on his knees and kneels before the painting. From that reverent posture, Robert Cumming sees a different canvas. The mountains ease back into place and saints Dominic and Jerome now appear more settled. On bended knee, he saw a new perspective.

Life can get confusing, and the book of Proverbs is presented to us as a manual on how to find clarity of wisdom (Proverbs 1:1-6). And where does it suggest such clarity can be found? On our *knees*. Fear of the Lord is the starting point (1:7), the reverence of God leading us to make good judgments (9:10). While our lives are to be like a masterpiece painted by God (Ephesians 2:10), they're often distorted by sin and temptation. God's wisdom saves us from greed (Proverbs 1:10-15), lust (ch.5,7), and pride (8:13), those distorting forces that warp our lives. His wisdom keeps our paths and thoughts straight (Proverbs 3:5-8).

Life makes sense only on our knees—a posture of submission that brings life's picture into perspective. —Sheridan Voysey

vipers

read>
Luke 3:1-18
Prove by the way you live that you have repented of your sins and turned to God (v.8).

more>
- Isaiah 1:16-18
- Micah 6:8
- Colossians 3:12-17

next>
If John were speaking to you, what would he encourage you to change? Why do you resist change in that area of your life?

A while back, Tiger Woods' public persona unraveled as one moral failure after another rushed to light. While this sad occasion offered us another opportunity to critique the feeding frenzy of pop journalism as well as the idol status we offer our celebrities (a status they could never live up to), it also provided each of us a sober reminder. If we're honest, the image we present to others is often at odds with the life we actually live.

When John the Baptist appeared, traipsing around in the wild in camel-hair clothes and eating a strange diet, he preached one steady refrain. *Change your behavior—Jesus is coming* (v.4). For their entire history, Israel had looked for the Messiah to come and rescue them. Now, John announced that it was actually happening—the Rescuer was on His way. Israel, however, was in bad shape. They had forgotten God; and if Israel wanted to be ready for Jesus, they had a lot of cleaning up to do.

John wasn't one to mince words. In one instance, he called the gathered crowd a "brood of vipers" (v.7 NIV). A viper was a dangerous, poisonous snake, and John wanted the people to hear plainly that the path they were on (spurning God), was a dangerous way to live. Many heard John's sobering words and asked the most sensible question: "What should we do?" (v.10). John's response was direct:

- If you have extra coats or food, give to those in need (v.11).
- If you're a tax collector, don't cheat anyone (v.13).
- If you're a soldier, don't use your power unjustly (v.14).

John spoke to everyone, from the common person to those with power, and told them to live truthfully, honestly, justly. God is coming, and He is bringing justice with Him. Are we ready? —Winn Collier

turning losses into gain

read>
2 Chronicles 15:1-7
But as for you, be strong and do not give up, for your work will be rewarded (v.7 NIV).

more>
How much better to get wisdom than gold, and good judgment than silver! (Proverbs 16:16).

next>
Go to God and tell Him about a loss you've experienced. What does His Word tell you about how He views you despite the disappointing outcome?

One of the tremendous privileges I've had as a believer in Jesus was serving as an official chaplain for athletes competing in the Olympic Games. Ministering inside the Olympic Village was exciting, but it presented unique challenges. Many times I struggled to find the right words to say as I sat with medal contenders who—away from the glare of spectators and cameras—broke down in tears following disappointing performances.

Losing is difficult. No one wants to experience defeat, especially when we've made great sacrifices and exerted strenuous effort to excel. Ultimately, however, we can respond to loss by seeking God's wisdom and courage to proceed in a manner that brings Him glory. The bitter alternative is to blame God and go our own separate way. (Personally, I've responded both ways on different occasions and can attest, the latter is a miserable way to go.)

In 2 Chronicles 14–17, there's a gripping tale of a father and son, King Asa and King Jehoshaphat, and their respective walks with God. The father, Asa, had run a remarkable race for the Lord until the final 2 years of his 41-year-reign. Sadly, within sight of the finish line, Asa's faith faltered. At that point, even when he developed a serious foot disease, the king who had once walked with God "did not seek the Lord's help" (16:12).

King Jehoshaphat chose not to repeat his father's grievous mistakes. Instead, Jehoshaphat was "deeply committed to the ways of the Lord" *all* the days of his life (17:6). And "the Lord was with Jehoshaphat because he followed the example of his father's early years" (v.3).

How about you? Will you let losses prompt you to turn your back on God, or will you choose to seek Him even in your disappointment? —Roxanne Robbins

going to great lengths

read>
John 4:1-26
He had to go through Samaria on the way (v.4).

more>
When I am with those who are weak, I share their weakness, for I want to bring the weak to Christ. Yes, I try to find common ground with everyone (1 Cor. 9:22).

next>
To what lengths have you gone to reach someone who was far from God? What steps are you taking right now to reach others with the gospel?

Bill Adams, CEO of a large hospital in Virginia, received a frantic call from a woman whose mother had died a few days earlier at the medical center. Prior to her death, the woman had lost her wedding ring somewhere in the hospital. The grieving daughter explained that her parents had been married for 50 years, and that her dad wanted to slip the ring back on his wife's finger before they buried her.

Moved by the woman's story, Bill promised to do all he could to help. The staff did a thorough search, but came up empty. Restless, Bill went to the basement of the hospital and climbed into a bin—amid wet, soggy, dirty laundry. Amazingly, there he found the ring! Bill's up close and personal leadership yielded great fruit.

In John 4, out of divine necessity, Jesus got up close and personal and sorted through some of the cultural "dirty laundry" of His day. He crossed cultural barriers by going through Samaria (Jews considered Samaritans half-breeds) and talking to a woman (it was forbidden for a man, especially a rabbi, to talk to a woman in public). He did this because His mission was to seek and save the lost.

He established common ground with the Samaritan woman (John 4:7), piqued her spiritual interest and curiosity (vv.9-14), was gracious and sensitive as He confronted her sin (vv.17-18), kept the conversation centered on the main issue (vv.19-25), and revealed Himself as Messiah (4:26). Jesus' up close and personal style of evangelism yielded a great harvest of Samaritans who believed in Him as their Savior.

Jesus is calling each of His followers to go to great lengths to help those who are lost in the "dirty laundry" of our culture. He wants us to introduce them to the only One who can satisfy their deepest longings. —Marvin Williams

whose job is it?

read >
Ephesians 4:1-16
As each part does its own special work, it helps the other parts grow, so that the whole body is healthy and growing and full of love (v.16).

more >
A spiritual gift is given to each of us so we can help each other (1 Corinthians 12:7).

next >
How has God gifted you? How can you use your spirtual gifts in ministry and in the building up of the body of Christ?

The story is told about four people named Everybody, Somebody, Anybody, and Nobody. There was an important job to do and Everybody was asked to do it. Everybody was sure that Somebody would do it. Anybody could have done it, but Nobody did it. Somebody got angry because it was Everybody's job. Everybody thought Anybody would do it, but Nobody realized that Everybody wouldn't do it. It ended up that Everybody blamed Somebody when Nobody did what Anybody could have done.

Sound familiar? Sadly, this scenario is lived out in many churches today. Most people in the pews think that the ministry of the church belongs to someone else.

But that isn't God's intent. According to Ephesians 4, the works of ministry (contact with the world) and building up of the body of Christ (maintaining the health of the church) belong to all believers in Jesus! It isn't solely the job of the pastors or the hired staff. The whole congregation is supposed to minister and serve. Anything less than that is a distortion of what God intended the church to be.

"He has given each one of us a special gift through the generosity of Christ" (Ephesians 4:7). God has gifted each of us uniquely to make sure that "the whole body is healthy and growing and full of love" (v.16). In other words, there are no spectators in church. Every person has a part to play.

With hundreds of millions of Christians in the world today, that makes for hundreds of millions of opportunities for the wonderful, life-changing power of Jesus Christ to be presented to people of all levels and classes of society. Let's all do our part in the body of Christ today. It's *our* job. —Poh Fang Chia

oasis

read>
1 Kings 19:7-18
Where two or three gather together as My followers, I am there among them (Matthew 18:20).

more>
We were slaves, but in His unfailing love our God did not abandon us in our slavery. . . . He revived us so we could rebuild the temple of our God and repair its ruins (Ezra 9:9).

next>
What spiritual oasis has God recently provided for you? Why is it important to worship God even in a spiritual desert?

A truck dealership is an odd place to have church. Yet that's what we found when my co-workers and I took in our vehicles for repair because of the damage inflicted by Mindanao's remotest roads. Once in the sparkling showroom, we noticed rows of chairs and a guitarist tuning up. Soon a couple dozen employees exchanged their work posts for worship.

After weeks of work in a rugged location devoid of any church, I craved the companionship of Christians. So when the believers began a praise chorus, I happily joined them. Living away from Christian community had left me feeling like a spiritual lone ranger. Perhaps you've been there too.

The prophet Elijah had been enjoying great success in his ministry. But in a moment, everything dried up. His is a fascinating story of spectacular triumph, suffocating despair, and God's ultimate sufficiency. Threatened by a queen hostile to the one true God, Elijah took her animosity personally and ran for his life. Alone in a cave on Mount Sinai, the very place where Moses had received the Ten Commandments, Elijah sulked. "I have zealously served the Lord God Almighty," he told God. And then he accused the Israelites of killing all of God's prophets. "I am the only one left," he said, "and now they are trying to kill me, too" (1 Kings 19:10).

But God knew that Elijah was far from alone. So He gave the perplexed prophet a fresh set of marching orders, and sent him back to work. He said, "I will preserve 7,000 others in Israel who have never bowed down to Baal or kissed him!" (v.18).

In Mindanao, I left a spiritually dry rainforest to find an oasis in the city. Elijah fled to a lonely place in the desert to find that he was far from alone. We never know where God will provide a spiritual oasis. —Tim Gustafson

even the women

read>
Romans 1:18-32
That is why God abandoned them to their shameful desires. Even the women turned against the natural way to have sex and instead indulged in sex with each other (v.26).

more>
Fix your thoughts on what is true, and honorable, and right, and pure, and lovely, and admirable. Think about things that are excellent and worthy of praise (Philippians 4:8).

next>
How does pornography and promiscuity rob us of the sacred nature of sex? How will you pursue a pure life that honors God?

The mothers in my neighborhood threw a party for the distinctive feature of the male anatomy—one of them even baked a cake in its shape and invited my wife over to see it. My wife politely declined, but the incident reminded us that we're living in an increasingly pornographic world.

Sexual sin is always wrong, but it's particularly troubling when middle-aged women start behaving like junior high boys. Perhaps because sex and pregnancy are particularly personal for women, they have traditionally provided our last line of defense against sexual deviancy. When "even the women" (Romans 1:26) lose all sense of sexual propriety, what hope is there for our men?

We live in an age of pornography. Not long ago, someone who wanted to ogle naked bodies had to make an effort to leave their home and go to the seedy part of town. Now we stumble across pornography while surfing the Web or on television. And few people seem to mind. Some of us remember not being allowed to attend the movie theater because it was "worldly." We scoffed at such legalism, but now the pendulum has swung in the other direction. Most of us are free to go to movies, and there is almost nothing we won't watch. Consider the gratuitous nudity and simulated sex you have seen on television or in a theater, and you'll know what I mean.

God commands us to "give honor to marriage" (Hebrews 13:4). It's hard to do that when we lust after bodies that do not belong to our spouse or use vulgar terms or throw parties that demean the bodies God has given us. God is against porn because He is for sex within the sacred estate of marriage. Don't cheapen His beautiful gift with coarse talk or promiscuity. —Mike Wittmer

old black coat

read>
2 Peter 3:8-18
The heavens will pass away with a terrible noise, and the very elements themselves will disappear in fire (v.10).

more>
- Exodus 34:6-7
- Habakkuk 2:3
- Romans 2:4-5

next>
What do you need to do to get ready for Judgment Day? Why do we sometimes not look forward to the return of Jesus?

I know I should say "bye-bye" to my beloved black coat. It's almost 15 years old and the cuffs are threadbare. The blue satin lining is torn. Still, every time I put it on, it hugs my shoulders perfectly and falls at just the right length. I'll admit it—I'm attached.

Psalm 102 says that the earth and heavens will one day "wear out like old clothing" (v.26), and God will transform the world we know. Peter described this event as the "day of the Lord" when "the heavens will pass away . . . and the very elements themselves will disappear in fire" (2 Peter 3:10).

On that day, "the earth and everything on it will be found to deserve judgment." Even now, God is holding back His judgment because He wants to bring more people to repentance. If you've never established a personal relationship with Jesus, don't miss the urgency of Peter's message: God "is being patient for your sake" (v.9).

Peter instructed those of us who already believe in Jesus to live holy lives while we await the "day of the Lord" (v.11). Specifically, when Jesus returns, He should find us "living peaceful lives that are pure and blameless in His sight" (v.14). Judgment Day should inspire us to make godly lifestyle choices. It should prompt us to ask the hard questions: *Do I want Jesus to find me living with my girlfriend, tangled in sketchy business deals, drunk and polishing off another bottle of booze?*

The "day of the Lord" is a sobering topic. It's no fun to acknowledge that our globe will "wear out"—just like my old black coat. And yet, with the earth's inevitable destruction comes the promise of a worldwide renovation. We can look forward to "the new heavens and new earth . . . a world filled with God's righteousness" (v.13). —Jennifer Benson Schuldt

micro, not macro

read>
Job 12:7-13
Just ask the animals, and they will teach you. . . . Speak to the earth, and it will instruct you (vv.7-8).

more>
With My great strength and powerful arm I made the earth and all its people and every animal (Jeremiah 27:5).

next>
Why is macroevolution accepted by so many people when there is no solid evidence for its existence? How does a person's view of the origin of the natural world affect their view of God? Of other people?

Dr. Fazale Rana, a Christian biochemist, believes in evolution. He notes that there are undeniably at least three types of evolution taking place today: *Microevolution* within a species; speciation, species giving rise to closely related sister species; *microbial evolution,* changes in viruses and bacteria.

What Dr. Rana doesn't see over time, however, is *macroevolution*—the change of one kind of animal into an entirely different kind. He writes, "The absence of transitional forms and the sudden appearances of new organisms in the fossil record fly in the face of the evolutionary framework, yet they are exactly what we would expect the fossil record to look like if a Creator orchestrated its history."

Job had some great insights into God and His creation. In an exchange with a critical buddy named Zophar, Job said, "Ask the animals and they will teach you. . . . Speak to the earth, and it will instruct you" (12:7-8). Though Job was using these words to defend himself—stating that his demise had "come from the hand of the Lord" (v.9), the idea of looking to the natural world for answers jibes with Dr. Rana's approach. And when we "ask the [ancient] animals," we see no sudden appearances of new organisms. When we "speak to the earth," we find that it's silent about any transitional fossil forms.

In Genesis, we read, "Then God said, 'Let the earth produce every sort of animal, each producing offspring of the same *kind*' " (1:24). The Creator made each different type of animal. They didn't just pop on the scene later or mutate from different kinds of creatures.

Job nailed it when he said, "The life of every living thing is in [God's] hand" (12:10). He perfectly designed His creation to change and adapt to climate and environmental change—micro, not macro. Just ask the animals! —Tom Felten

age of grace

read>
Genesis 6:1-8
In the future, their normal lifespan will be no more than 120 years (v.3).

more>
- Matthew 24:37-39
- 1 Timothy 2:3-4

next>
Are you presuming on the patience and grace of God? What do you need to bring to God in repentance today?

Gertrude Baines, a 115-year-old American woman, was the world's oldest person when she died in September 2009. According to the Gerontology Research Group (GRG), the leading authority on "supercentenarians," the world's oldest living person in early 2011 was Eunice Sanborn, a 114-year-old woman from the US. The oldest verified person in history was Jeanne Calment who died in 1997 at the age of 122 years and 164 days old. A GRG spokesperson said, "Anything over 120 is extremely unusual."

Long ago, God said, "In the future, [people's] normal lifespan will be no more than 120 years" (Genesis 6:3). The fact that it's rare for humans to live beyond 120 years today is a reminder of God's judgment on an increasingly corrupt and evil world (vv.5,11).

Some scholars say that the number 120 signifies the gradually implemented new age limit for humans. After the flood, the recorded ages declined steadily—but considerably—from the 900s (5:4-20) to the 120s. Abraham, 10 generations from Noah (11:10-26), lived to be 175 (25:7); Isaac, 180 (35:28); Jacob, 147 (47:28). Joseph lived 110 years (50:26) and Moses died at 120 (Deut. 34:7).

Other scholars say that the 120 years represents a period of grace that existed prior to God unleashing His wrath on His sinning creation. Of this 120 years of grace, Peter says that "God waited patiently while Noah was building His boat. . . . He is being patient for your sake. He does not want anyone to be destroyed, but wants everyone to repent" (1 Peter 3:20; 2 Peter 3:9). Yet, our 120-year mortality cap is a grim warning that it's possible for people to reach the point of no return and then to face God's judgment. Instead of presuming on His grace, let's repent of our sinfulness today. —K.T. Sim

bound

read>
Lamentations 3:1-26
The Lord is good to those who depend on Him, to those who search for Him (v.25).

When you get into a tight place and everything goes against you, till it seems as though you could not hang on a minute longer, never give up then, for that is just the place where the tide will turn. —Harriet Beecher Stowe

When I was a kid, physical education was *not* my favorite subject. When my teacher would perch me on the chin-up bar, my arms would straighten and I would drop to the ground. Holding on for the one-minute goal was simply not possible.

Because he had set his life in faithful ministry to the Word of the Lord, Jeremiah obeyed when God spoke—even when the goal seemed to be impossible. Ministering to an apostate nation (Lamentations 3:14), this man of great faith knew what it meant to have an intimate relationship with Almighty God. What better position in life than to be God's spokesperson to a nation? As a type or reflection of Christ, however, the very people into which he poured his life ended up rejecting him. Though God was his all, all of life felt bitter (vv.17-20).

In good times, most of us have little difficulty recognizing God's faithfulness. Jeremiah, however, chose to declare the greatness of God from a position of pain. Seeing himself in the light of God's expansive mercy, he made a decision to hold fast, even when he felt like giving up.

The familiar words in Isaiah 40:31 remind us that our struggle becomes strength when we let God take control. The Hebrew word for *wait* literally means "to bind together." When we wait on the Lord, we are not passively sitting by. Rather, we are bound with Him, moving as He moves, resting as He rests (Matthew 11:29-30). Refusing to let go, we hold fast to Jesus (Revelation 2:25-26, 3:11). —Regina Franklin

more>
- Psalm 130:5-6
- Hebrews 6:18
- Hebrews 10:23

next>
When have you mistaken waiting on the Lord for passivity? Why is our attitude during waiting times as significant as our actions? In what specific area is God challenging you not to let go as you hold on to Him?

be on guard

read>
Luke 12:13-21
Then He said, "Beware! Guard against every kind of greed. Life is not measured by how much you own" (v.15).

more>
- Proverbs 1:19
- Ephesians 5:5
- Colossians 3:5

next>
How does greed affect one's relationship with God? With others? What lessons can we learn and apply from the rich fool's tragic story?

One year on Christmas Eve, a New York cab driver found more than $21,000 in cash and jewelry left in his cab by an Italian tourist. He drove more than 50 miles to return the possessions to an address he found in the purse. The woman wasn't home, so he left a note that contained his phone number. The tourist called and the driver drove back and returned her lost items, refusing to accept any kind of reward. The driver said to her, "I'm needy, but I'm not greedy."

Jesus understood the dangers of greed, and He warned His followers to be on guard against it as well. Approached by a man who demanded that his brother divide his inheritance with him, Jesus responded to his selfish request with a dramatic story about guarding against greed (Luke 12:13).

A certain rich man's land had produced an abundant crop. He was dissatisfied with his present storehouses and wanted to build bigger barns to store his crops. As he looked to the future, He anticipated many years of ease. But in the middle of his soliloquy of greed, God shook the foundations of his soul with one word: "Fool!" (v.20). He was foolish because, instead of fulfilling his moral duty of meeting the needs of others, he was storing up possessions for himself and wasn't being rich toward God (v.21). The result was eternity apart from God.

This narrative is a clear warning against one of the seductive dangers of greed—self-sufficiency. Every follower of Jesus can guard against greed by repenting of it (Luke 3:14), being on guard against it, separating ourselves from it (1 Corinthians 5:11), being content with the things God has blessed us with (Hebrews 13:5), seeking God not gain, and serving others with our wealth (1 Timothy 6:17-18). —Marvin Williams

when God arrives

read>
Isaiah 62:1-5
Never again will you be called "The Forsaken City" or "The Desolate Land" (v.4).

more>
[God] has not yet shown us what we will be like when Christ appears. But we do know that we will be like Him (1 John 3:2).

next>
How have you been tempted to believe that you can make life work on your own? Where in your life are you most in need for God to arrive?

As Haiti was reeling from a crushing earthquake, one tragic account told of a mother who had three daughters between the ages of 4 and 9. She had been cooking for her girls when the earthquake hit. Severely injured, the mom could not move or care for her children. When help arrived, the young girls had gone 2 days without food or water. The mom was convinced that her daughters would not survive. A reporter accompanying the relief workers asked, "When do you think this will end?"

"When God arrives," the mother answered.

Eventually, we humans find ourselves facing trouble beyond our expertise to fix. Inevitably, high hopes of what we can accomplish and what we can make of our world always come crashing down.

Judah repeatedly came to this point. During one calamitous cycle, under Babylon's rule and on the brink of national ruin, the prophet Isaiah prayed for his people. His heart, he said, "[could] not keep still" (Isaiah 62:1). Just as the Haitian images moved us to both sorrow and action, the devastation around Isaiah compelled him to pray for God's mercy. His prayer continued, "I will not stop praying for [Judah], until her righteousness shines like the dawn" (v.1).

Isaiah's hope for a new dawn was more than a naïve whim. He believed in God's promise of redemption for His people (and ultimately for all of God's people). Isaiah proclaimed God's intentions that the people of Judah—currently wallowing in ruin—would discover that calamity was not their end. "The Lord will hold you in His hand for all to see—a splendid crown in the hand of God" (v.3).

Isaiah pointed to a day when God would appear and make the world right again. Our sorrows will not completely end until He arrives. —Winn Collier

the weak and the afflicted

read>
1 Thessalonians 5:9-15
Take tender care of those who are weak (v.14).

more>
He feels pity for the weak and the needy, and He will rescue them. He will redeem them from oppression and violence, for their lives are precious to Him (Psalm 72:13-14).

next>
How does it reflect God's heart to care for those who are weak? What keeps you from reaching out to those who are physically impaired?

During a visit to an East Africa hospital, I met a 10-year-old boy, Joseph, who is severely disfigured. A nurse explained that when Joseph was an infant his mother set him on fire. Though he miraculously survived, his left leg was burned to a mere stub. His right is permanently bent backwards, with webbed toes that were heavily damaged by the flames. Joseph's left hand is missing two fingers, and, despite multiple operations, his wrist bone protrudes from the skin.

I held Joseph as the nurse changed his bandages, and was amazed when he confidently said to me, "The Lord's going to make me well!"

I believe Joseph is right. Though I don't know when or how God will bring healing to the child, I trust Isaiah who prophesied that one day the Lord will come, "and when He comes, He will open the eyes of the blind and unplug the ears of the deaf. The lame will leap like a deer, and those who cannot speak will sing for joy!" (Isaiah 35:5-6).

But for now, we live in an age where homes and communities around the world contain broken, hurting people. These individuals, like Joseph, are in dire need of our love and care. The apostle Paul told God's people to "take tender care of those who are weak" (1 Thessalonians 5:14). His words echo the words of King Solomon in Psalm 72 as he implored God's people to:

- Judge others in a right and righteous way (v.2).
- Let the poor always be treated fairly (v.2).
- Defend the poor and afflicted (v.4).
- Rescue the children of the needy (v.4).

What can you do today to be a blessing to a physically impaired person in your community? —Roxanne Robbins

an apology

read>
Luke 6:37-42
Hypocrite! First get rid of the log in your own eye; then you will see well enough to deal with the speck in your friend's eye (v.42).

more>
Imitate God, therefore, in everything you do. . . . Live a life filled with love, following the example of Christ (Ephesians 5:1-2).

next>
How have you acted self-righteously toward those in the homosexual community? How do you need to change the way you share God's truth in love with people who are involved in homosexuality?

A pastor friend of mine recently said that the Christian church ought to apologize and repent of the hurt it has caused to the homosexual community. That's a pretty radical statement, but I happen to agree.

Now, before you label me as someone going soft on sin, please understand that I believe the Bible teaches that homosexuality is wrong. Romans 1:26-27 plainly states that homosexual behavior is unnatural and against God's created design for sexual expression. But to reach out and show God's love to those involved in homosexuality requires much more than simply telling them it's wrong.

Unfortunately, some Christians have stigmatized and self-righteously singled out homosexuality as the worst of all sins. Many of us have acted as if this sin is greater than our own sin and condemned those who indulge in the lifestyle. It's as if we've tried to get them completely changed before we get them into God's family—let alone welcome them to sit in our pews on Sundays.

Sadly, we've responded out of an "us versus them" mentality. We have failed to understand that when the Bible tells us that Jesus was known as a friend of sinners, it didn't say, except for certain kinds of sinners (Mt. 11:18-19).

As believers in Jesus, we need to acknowledge that the homosexual community feels alienated by the church partly because of the words and behavior of some people who claim to be Christians. Yes, we are to uphold God's original design for sexual identity and expression, but we've been wrong to use the truth as a club.

Jesus, help us to see and own the mistakes we've made so we can offer a safe haven for men and women to receive the grace of Jesus—grace that can repair any life that is broken by sin. —Jeff Olson

if tomorrow never comes

read>
James 4:13-17
What you ought to say is, "If the Lord wants us to, we will live and do this or that" (v.15).

more>
Trust in the Lord with all your heart; do not depend on your own understanding. Seek His will in all you do, and He will show you which path to take (Proverbs 3:5-6).

next>
What does your planning say about you? Are you self-confident or God-reliant? How do your plans acknowledge God's plan?

A heartbreaking story on the cover of the newspaper had everyone talking. A groom was found dead hours after his wedding dinner. One of his friends said: "He was a very cheerful person and had just gotten married. Nobody could believe he was dead just hours after celebrating his wedding."

Life is truly uncertain. Everyone is just a heartbeat away from eternity. First Chronicles 29:15 states: "Our days on earth are like a passing shadow, gone so soon without a trace." It usually takes sad news, however, to drive home the reality of our frailty.

James 4:13 warns against speaking arrogantly about our future. We're too limited to even understand what lies ahead, let alone take charge of it. We're not the master of our own destiny, for we don't even know what tomorrow will bring (v.14). We're like a mist. Our lives are so short—here today, gone tomorrow.

How should we live in light of these truths? We should learn to embrace God's plan for us (v.15) and do all the good we can (v.17).

We embrace God's plan by acknowledging His sovereign rule over us. We say, "If the Lord wants us to, we will live and do this or that" (v.15). We don't make plans and then simply ask God to bless them. Instead, we should include God in every decision because He is over all of life.

Elisabeth Elliot observed, "God is God. Because He is God, He is worthy of my trust and obedience. I will find rest nowhere but in His holy will, a will that is unspeakably beyond my largest notions of what He is up to."

Next, we should do the good we can. As God's Word has instructed us in good works, we must be faithful in doing them. *That* makes for a God-honoring today and tomorrow. —Poh Fang Chia

wanting justice

read>
Jonah 3:6–4:3
Nineveh has more than 120,000 people living in spiritual darkness. . . . Shouldn't I feel sorry for such a great city? (4:11).

more>
He is the Lord our God. His justice is seen throughout the land (1 Chronicles 16:14).

next>
Why is it appropriate to want evil people to face judgment? Why is it dangerous? What happens when you take God's judgment into your own hands?

Evil is everywhere. Not far from where I was living a few years ago, 57 civilians were massacred by political rivals. Many of these people weren't simply killed. It was *brutal*. Deep in my heart, I must confess that there was a personal cry for justice—I wanted God to severely punish the perpetrators.

The whole point of the book of Jonah is not about a big fish. It's actually about a God who extends His love—even to the worst of us. Jonah was sent to announce God's judgment to the citizens of Nineveh, a city of especially brutal people. They committed horrifying acts against conquered foes.

Jonah quite naturally didn't want to take God's message to them. So he headed by ship in the opposite direction (1:1-3). That's where the big fish comes in (vv.15-17). Through divine intervention, Jonah eventually arrived in Nineveh with the Lord's message for the people. But instead of ignoring it, the people actually repented (3:7-9). Ergo, no judgment (v.10). Jonah was furious (4:1-3).

We do have a God of justice who declares: "I will take revenge. I will pay them back" (Romans 12:19). In an obscure prophecy found in the book of Nahum, God declares what He would eventually do to Nineveh (chapters 2–3). *Justice*.

But we also have a Savior who, as He was being crucified, called for His executioners to receive mercy: "Father, forgive them, for they don't know what they are doing" (Luke 23:34). Mercy.

Mercy and justice: two sides of the same coin. It's a message God wants us to convey to everyone—even to the worst among us. —Tim Gustafson

as goes the king

read>
2 Samuel 23:1-7
The one who rules righteously, who rules in the fear of God, is like the light of morning at sunrise, like a morning without clouds, like the gleaming of the sun on new grass after rain (vv.3-4).

more>
- 2 Chronicles 7:17-22
- 2 Chronicles 33:1-18

next>
Write down the names of five people who look to you for leadership. Are they happy to follow you? Why or why not? What can you do to bring them shalom?

King David's last words remind us that our lives rise and fall on leadership.

A righteous king brightens the lives of his people like a quiet sunrise, while one who "oppresses the poor is like a pounding rain that destroys the crops" (Proverbs 28:3). Leaders who bring peace and prosperity are revered and celebrated, but the names of wicked rulers are treated with contempt.

David's son Solomon was one of the good ones. His name means *shalom*, the Hebrew term for peace and prosperity, which is what his wise reign brought to Israel. The Queen of Sheba was overwhelmed by the splendor of his court and exclaimed, "How happy your people must be! . . . Because God loves Israel . . . He has made you king over them" (2 Chronicles 9:7-8).

It goes without saying that Hitler was a bad leader. As terrible as his reign was for the countries he invaded, it was even worse for his own people. During World War II, Karl Barth wrote: "We must certainly feel sorriest for the poor Germans." Many of them knew that their side was wrong, but fear led them to follow their leader.

The importance of good leadership is why Paul commands us to "pray this way for kings and all who are in authority so that we can live peaceful and quiet lives marked by godliness and dignity" (1 Timothy 2:2). As goes the king, so goes the kingdom.

Besides praying for our leaders, we must understand that we are kings too. God made us in His image to govern creation on His behalf (Genesis 1:26-28). We all sit on various sub-thrones beneath the universal reign of God. Consider your realms of responsibility—in your home, church, work, and neighborhood. Do you lead others like a warm sunrise or a driving rain? —Mike Wittmer

family feud

read>
Genesis 31:17-55
I call on the God of our ancestors . . . to serve as a judge between us (v.53).

A Sicilian man wasn't a criminal, but he asked police to arrest and jail him. When local authorities refused, he entered a nearby store and swiped a pack of gum. Then he threatened the store clerk and waited for the cops to show up! His motive? He was trying to avoid spending time with his relatives on New Year's Eve.

Some of us can relate to this guy—we're willing to do almost *anything* to evade certain family members. But avoidance rarely offers lasting peace.

Fed up with his father-in-law, Jacob packed up his family and vanished without leaving a forwarding address. When Laban finally caught up with them, he scolded Jacob for leaving so suddenly. Then, "Jacob became very angry, and he challenged Laban" (Genesis 31:36). Since his attempt to tiptoe away had failed, Jacob realized there was no way around an honest discussion of past (and present) offenses with the father of his wives.

Rehashing wrongs only intensifies our urge to escape, unless forgiveness is involved. Jacob had to forgive Laban for manipulating him relationally (29:25) and in business matters (31:7). And Laban had to forget about his missing idols (v.30) and the farewell party he never got to host (v.27). With their issues in the open, the two men promised not to harm each other (v.52). Instead of distancing himself, Jacob had taken a step closer to Laban, agreeing to leave his grievances in God's hands. Laban reciprocated and asked God to be their judge (v.53).

In the end, Laban kissed his kin and blessed them (v.55). While not every family feud has a tidy resolution, there is a better chance for harmony when we stop avoiding our family issues, face the hard work of forgiveness, and call a truce with the relatives we'd rather renounce. —Jennifer Benson Schuldt

more>
Be kind to each other, tenderhearted, forgiving one another, just as God through Christ has forgiven you (Ephesians 4:32).

next>
How might you handle a family disagreement with someone who isn't willing to discuss it openly? Why is running away counterproductive? How does God view our disputes?

ultimate healing

read›
2 Corinthians 4:7-18
We fix our gaze on things that cannot be seen. For the things we see now will soon be gone, but the things we cannot see will last forever (v.18).

more›
My health may fail, and my spirit may grow weak, but God remains the strength of my heart; He is mine forever (Psalm 73:26).

next›
What fills your heart and mind as you fix your eyes on what can't be seen? What does ultimate healing mean to you?

What Cancer Cannot Do

Cancer is so limited . . .
It cannot cripple love.
It cannot shatter hope.
It cannot corrode faith.
It cannot destroy peace.
It cannot kill friendship.
It cannot suppress memories.
It cannot invade the soul.
It cannot steal eternal life.
It cannot conquer the spirit.
—Author Unknown

I love those words. They beautifully reflect the truth found in God's Word. Paul, facing physical challenges, could say with confidence, "We ourselves are like fragile clay jars containing this great treasure" (2 Corinthians 4:7). The apostle, like you or someone you know, experienced suffering as an ever-present companion (v.10). Yet he chose to "fix [his] gaze on things that cannot be seen" (v.18).

Paul's faith and confidence flowed from the treasure within him—*God's transforming power*—and the future that awaited him—*eternity with Jesus* (v.17). He knew that when this life was over he would be forever in God's presence, where there will be "no more death or sorrow or crying or pain" (Revelation 21:4).

When suffering comes, we can pour out our hearts to God (Psalm 55:22). He is *with us* in our pain (Hebrews 13:5). We can worship Him when He chooses to heal and when He chooses not to heal. But no limited thing like disease or suffering can ever separate us from His love (Romans 8:38). An ultimate healing, as Christian composer Wayne Watson puts it, lies just ahead. Today, fix your eyes on what can't be seen—what an awesome, breathtaking view! —Tom Felten

the model church

read>
1 Thessalonians 1:1-10
You have become an example to all the believers in Greece—throughout both Macedonia and Achaia (v.7).

more>
- 1 Timothy 4:12-16
- Titus 2:7-8
- 1 Peter 2:12,21

next>
How do you measure up to the three virtues—*faithful work, loving deeds,* and the *enduring hope?* What is one good deed you can do for an unbeliever this week?

What church in the New Testament stands out as the model for the rest? This question was asked during a church growth seminar. It was no surprise that no one attempted to give the church in Corinth that honor. Understandably, everyone said it was the infant church in Jerusalem, described in Acts 2:42-47. But to the apostle Paul, the church in Thessalonica was the model church. He told them, "You have become an example [*model*, NIV] to all the believers in Greece—throughout both Macedonia and Achaia" (1 Thessalonians 1:7).

The church in Thessalonica was characterized by "faithful work, loving deeds," and the "enduring hope" (v.3). The believers boldly proclaimed the good news to people everywhere, even beyond their own country (v.8). They were a model church because they served the Lord faithfully, loved each other deeply, and expectantly longed to see the Lord at His second coming (vv.9-10). They lived changed lives—so radically altered that people felt the impact. Their godly behavior and Christlike conduct (v.6) were doing the talking. Their 100-percent commitment to God is noticed and talked about (vv.8-9). Indeed, they had "turned the world upside down" (Acts 17:6 NKJV).

Paul celebrated the fact that they exhibited a lifestyle produced by *faith*, a labor motivated by *love*, and a steadfastness anchored in *hope* (1 Thessalonians 1:3). These virtues are indispensable and unmistakable trail markers of Christian growth and maturity. They are like a compass for the maturing Christian—providing direction for the way to go. Believers in Jesus should often evaluate their own faith, love, and hope.

Why? Because Paul said these virtues are eternal. "Three things will last forever—faith, hope, and love—and the greatest of these is love" (1 Corinthians 13:13). What are you modeling to others? —K.T. Sim

face down

read>
1 Kings 18:36-46
"Go and look out toward the sea." The servant went and looked, then returned to Elijah and said, "I didn't see anything." Seven times Elijah told him to go and look (v.43).

more>
He went on a little farther and bowed with His face to the ground, praying, "My Father! If it is possible, let this cup of suffering be taken away from Me. Yet I want Your will to be done, not Mine" (Matthew 26:39).

next>
What significant experiences have shaped the way you view prayer? How does your prayer life reflect persistence?

When my father died of cancer, the inevitable question in my heart was whether he would have lived if I had shown greater faith. I lived with significant guilt that his death was somehow my fault. Rather than bringing hope, every sermon I heard on healing was like salt on an open wound. I felt spiritually attacked and harassed whenever I read verses about Jesus healing the multitudes or verses like Isaiah 53:4 and James 5:15. And I was convinced my prayers were powerless.

Our spiritual enemies want nothing less than to convince us that God is far-off, distant, and unwilling to respond to our prayers. From our human perspective, God's response or lack thereof can make the lies of our spiritual enemies feel real. But God wants us to persist in prayer (Luke 11:9-10). Not because we want to get our way. Not because He's hard to please. Not because He delights in our pain.

Persistence has a way of purifying our lives of any idolatry. Ultimately, prayer means acknowledging that only God is God. He wants us to give Him our everything, and He wants to be our everything.

A man of great faith and obedience, Elijah showed on Mount Carmel that God alone would be magnified (1 Kings 18:36-37). His faith kept him focused on what he knew was true—God was in control, worthy of deep reverence, and sovereign above all. Elijah heard with his spirit what he could not see with his eyes (v.41).

Prayer isn't supposed to be simply a crisis response or a passing thought. It's a position of consecration before the Lord, a place of continued dwelling, or—as Colossians 4:2 reminds us—an act of devotion. Prayer means staying facedown until we see God's answer—not the answer *we* want (1 Kings 18:44).

—Regina Franklin

when tragedy strikes

read>
Luke 13:1-9
You will perish, too, unless you repent of your sins and turn to God (v.3).

more>
- Luke 16:19-31
- 1 John 1:9

next>
How should we respond to the tragic death of others? If you died today, would you be ready to meet God? For what sin do you need to repent? Why is it vital that we repent of our sin?

In January 2010, people from around the world were deployed to provide relief to the citizens and land of Haiti. The tragic effects of a powerful earthquake in that country caused our family to wrestle with unsettling and troubling questions: *Why did a mind-staggering tragedy like this happen? If God is strong and powerful and loving, couldn't He have prevented the devastation in Haiti? Is God punishing the people of Haiti in some way? Are the people in Haiti more unrighteous than people in other countries?* These questions are legitimate, but they inch us away from an appropriate personal response to world tragedy.

Jesus addressed the manner in which His audience should personally respond to world crises (Luke 13). To do this, He chronicled two historical events—revealing that *death is indiscriminate* and *repentance is vital.*

In the first event, Pilate had some Galileans killed while they worshiped. The innocents died at the hands of an evil man (vv.1-2). The second event concerned a tower in Siloam that fell and killed 18 people. Those people died in a natural disaster (v.4). In light of these two tragic events, Jesus wanted His audience to ask a question of mortality: *How close am I to the end of my life?* And a question of eternity: *What's my status before God—am I ready to meet Him?* Jesus' instruction was sobering—mortality and eternity are certain, so the people needed to repent or perish spiritually.

In light of tragedies taking place around the world, we should take His teaching to heart. World tragedies should cause us to consider our own mortality and eternity, asking: *What is my status before God right now? Am I ready to meet God? How am I glorifying Him today?* To neglect these questions could prove tragic for me and you. —Marvin Williams

déjà vu

read>
1 Samuel 26
Surely the Lord will strike Saul down someday, or he will die of old age or in battle (v.10).

more>
If you are suffering in a manner that pleases God, keep on doing what is right, and trust your lives to the God who created you, for He will never fail you (1 Peter 4:19).

next>
Is there a particular experience that God is bringing you through over and over again? What lesson is he teaching you?

David was caught in a living nightmare. Once again, Saul was hot on his heels. The king had taken 3,000 of Israel's elite troops and was hunting David down in the wilderness of Ziph. The events in 1 Samuel 26 have a sense of déjà vu about them—they're remarkably similar to what took place in chapter 24.

In the first encounter, David was retreating as Saul was advancing. But in chapter 26, Saul's soldiers are camped out and David is on the offensive. His scouts located Saul's camp and David, accompanied by at least two men, goes to check it out. *What's he up to?* we wonder. *Surely, he won't attempt to assassinate Saul, for he was conscience-stricken when he previously cut off a portion of Saul's robe* (24:5).

David had come for Saul's spear and water container, and that was all. He commanded Abishai not to kill Saul for basically the same reason (v.9) he verbalized in 24:6,11. But David went beyond what he had said before, assuring Abishai, "Surely the Lord will strike Saul down someday, or he will die of old age or in battle" (26:10). After his experience with Nabal and Abigail (ch.25), David knew that God could accomplish His will in any number of ways.

It's important to note that David didn't simply know that God defends His own. He believed it. His whole plan hung on it. He staked his life on it. We see from his example that faith and action go hand-in-hand. His plan was totally dependent on God for success.

In 1 Samuel 26, David dealt with a similar situation with greater confidence and wisdom than in chapter 24. Can that be said of us? How are we living out the wisdom He has taught us through previous life experiences? —Poh Fang Chia

wisdom of a president

read>
Proverbs 1:1-7
Do not depend on your own understanding (3:5).

more>
Tune your ears to wisdom, and concentrate on understanding (Proverbs 2:2).

next>
What has God revealed to you about true wisdom? Which proverbs have you taken to heart recently?

With the death of former US President Gerald Ford in December 2006, many Americans found renewed appreciation for the man who steadfastly served following the resignation of President Richard Nixon. Many people knew that he had spent years of his life in public service before becoming President. But few knew the integral role his Christian faith had played in shaping his leadership skills.

During his years in the White House, Ford prayed Proverbs 3:5-6 every night, just as he had since he was a young boy. "Trust in the Lord with all your heart; do not depend on your own understanding. Seek His will in all you do, and He will show you which path to take." According to King Solomon, the purpose of Proverbs—as revealed in Proverbs 1—is to:

- Teach people wisdom and discipline (v.2).
- Help people understand the insights of the wise (v.2).
- Teach people to live disciplined and successful lives (v.3).
- Help people do what is right, just, and fair (v.3).
- Give insight to the simple (v.4).
- Give knowledge and discernment to the young (v.4).
- Enable the wise to become even wiser (v.5).
- Let those with understanding receive guidance (v.5).
- Develop proper fear of the Lord, the foundation of true knowledge (v.7).

President Ford understood the merit of a regular dose of Proverbs. He also embraced fellowship and accountability and surrounded himself with wise people who encouraged him to stay true to God, Christian disciplines, family, and friends.

Today, take time to meditate on the wisdom found in God's Word. It's something we all desperately need. —Roxanne Robbins

Jesus heals

read>
Luke 3:15-22
I baptize you with water, but someone is coming soon who is greater than I am (v.16).

more>
- 2 Corinthians 5:1-10
- 2 Corinthians 5:17-21
- Isaiah 54

next>
How have you experienced God's presence even in your troubles? What does it mean for you to grasp that God wants not only to be with you, but also to heal you?

By 2:00 a.m., as reports streamed in from the earthquake in Haiti, Craig Miller knew he had to go. Miller, director of the relief organization Thirst No More, had been able to have two Facebook chats with a medical contact working amid the rubble. The team's news was dire: They had seen five children die, and they couldn't provide adequate care for the survivors because they had no medical supplies.

Immediately, Miller went into action—leaving for Haiti within hours. He didn't know if he would be able to get to them in time; but "If I didn't try," he said, "I knew *for sure* they wouldn't have the supplies they needed."

Often, the best we can do for others who are in distress is to simply *be* with them in their trouble. Jesus came to be present with us, to walk amidst our pain, and to experience the fear and sorrows we face. He "faced all the same testings we do, yet He did not sin" (Hebrews 4:15).

This truth jumps to the fore in Jesus' baptism, a pivotal time in His public ministry. The other Gospels add details to the story, but Luke narrates with sparse prose. "When all the people were being baptized," Luke writes, "Jesus was baptized too" (3:21 NIV).

Jesus, who had no sin and needed no forgiveness, showed His identity with all people as He went into the water.

Yet Jesus did more than simply appear beside us. He came to heal us. At Jesus' baptism, John the Baptist proclaimed that He was the one who would baptize us "with the Holy Spirit and with fire," symbols that promised total transformation (v.16).

When Jesus has finished His work among us, we will be more than comforted. We will be changed. —Winn Collier

spiritual pursuit

read>
John 4:4-24
God is Spirit, so those who worship Him must worship in spirit and in truth (v.24).

more>
I plead with you to give your bodies to God because of all He has done for you. Let them be a living and holy sacrifice—the kind He will find acceptable. This is truly the way to worship Him (Romans 12:1).

next>
How have you tried to explore spirituality outside of God and His Word? Why can only He satisfy us?

On this day in 1963, the world was shocked by the news that John F. Kennedy, the 35th President of the United States, had been killed by an assassin's bullet. Though it's not as well known or remembered, Christian author C. S. Lewis passed away the very same day. Even fewer will remember that Aldous Huxley, author of the book *Brave New World,* died from cancer during those same 24 hours.

In 1954, Huxley published a lesser-known book titled *The Doors of Perception,* which described his experimental use of the mind-altering drug mescaline. Huxley was one of the first to write about using hallucinogens to pursue spirituality. His book inspired the popular rock band The Doors, known for their use of LSD, to name their group after Huxley's book.

Granted, Huxley and his admirers were looking in all the wrong places, but they were on an important pursuit. God made us in such a way that we're naturally drawn to spirituality (Job 32:8). And there is no greater spiritual pursuit than worshiping God.

A Samaritan woman once asked Jesus to settle an ancient dispute about the best place to worship God (John 4:19-20). Samaritans contended it was on the top of Mount Gerizim, while the Jews said it was on the temple mount in Jerusalem. Jesus told her that a day was coming where people could worship God anywhere they wanted to as long as they worshiped "in spirit and in truth" (vv.21-24).

There's no denying that people can get high on LSD or some other mind-altering drug, but they will never enter the heights of true spirituality by taking that path—not to mention the devastating effects it can have on the mind and body. It's only by worshiping God wholeheartedly—on the basis of who Jesus is—that we experience His life-altering power and presence. —Jeff Olson

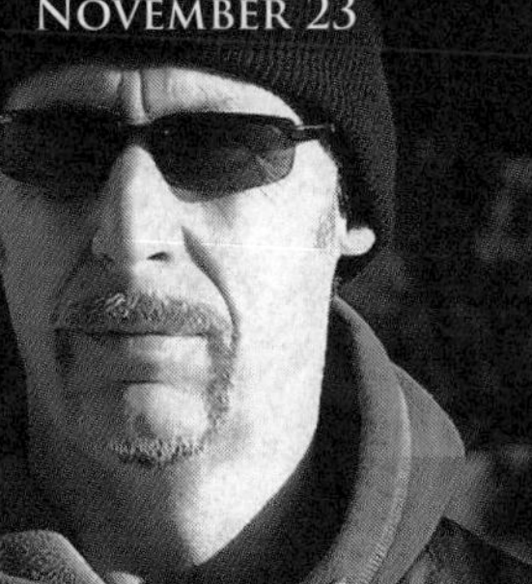

picture of pride

read>
2 Chronicles 26:3-21
When he had become powerful, he also became proud, which led to his downfall (v.16).

more>
Those who exalt themselves will be humbled, and those who humble themselves will be exalted (Matthew 23:12).

next>
When people confront sin in your life, do you respond in anger? Might this response be linked to pride? How have you experienced a loss of status or power as the result of God's humbling hand in your life?

Hoping to catch a prowler, the South Wales police published his image in a local newspaper. But the burglar was unsatisfied with the photo, so he submitted a better one—featuring him standing in front of a police vehicle! Police later captured and detained the criminal, thanks to his arrogant stunt. You might say his glamour shot led to a mug shot.

Like this bigheaded bandit, King Uzziah's oversized ego did him in. It's a shame too, because Uzziah was somewhat of a renaissance man. He defeated the Philistines, cultivated vineyards, fortified Jerusalem, and outfitted his elite military forces with some mighty fine weapons. Aided by God, his fame spread far and wide.

When Uzziah became powerful, "he also became proud, which led to his downfall" (2 Chronicles 26:16). He barged into the temple and personally ignited incense on the altar. Only the priests were allowed to do this, and when they tried to kick him out, Uzziah "became furious" (v.19) and raged at them.

Uzziah wasn't the only one who was angry—God stepped in to defend the temple workers, zapping Israel's ruler with a case of leprosy. Instantly, Uzziah's status changed from famous king to lowly outcast. He lived "in isolation in a separate house" for the rest of his life (v.21), and lost his political power.

Uzziah's life was a picture of this truth: "[God] will punish the proud" (Isaiah 2:12). Still, like the conceited king, we're all prone to adopting an inflated view of ourselves and getting angry with people who try to set us straight. Fortunately, when we "humble [ourselves] under the mighty power of God" (1 Peter 5:6), we don't have to suffer the destruction that ultimately accompanies self-importance (Proverbs 16:18). Picture this—God loves a humble heart! —Jennifer Benson Schuldt

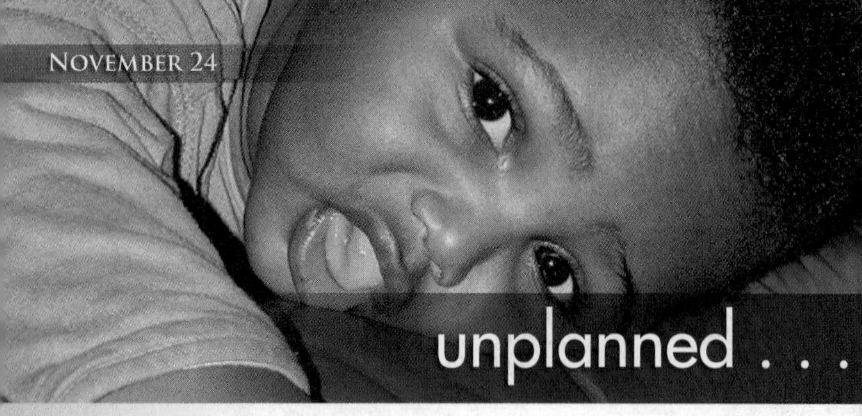

unplanned . . .

read>
Isaiah 46:3-4, 8-11
I have cared for you since you were born. Yes, I carried you before you were born (v.3).

more>
- Jeremiah 1:5
- Jeremiah 29:11

next>
Although sin can lead to a pregnancy, how does God view the new life? How can we compassionately help those who experience unwanted pregnancies?

At 17, she was in the midst of a brief season of rebellion. One night, instead of staying at a friend's house, as she had told her parents, she went to a party thrown by a guy in his twenties. Although drinking and drug use took place, she abstained and eventually fell asleep. Later, she awoke to find herself being sexually assaulted by the young man. For many weeks she kept the rape quiet. But then she found out she was *pregnant*.

Fortunately, the young woman followed some godly counsel and proceeded with the pregnancy. And a loving Christian family adopted her beautiful baby.

In Isaiah 46, God reveals some truths that help us gain a correct view of unplanned pregnancy. We learn:

- *God knows each baby.* In love, He carries the unborn and cares for them when they're born (v.3). Regardless of whether a baby is planned or unplanned, God deeply cares for him or her.
- *God forms each baby.* He says, "I made you, and I will care for you" (v.4). Each new life is made in His image and must be protected because of that great value (Genesis 1:27).
- *God knew this new life would come to be.* He declares, "I can tell you the future before it even happens" (Isaiah 46:10). An unplanned pregnancy is not a surprise to Him (Psalm 139:16).

All these truths became clear to the young woman mentioned earlier. In time, she repented and returned to living for Jesus. As she drew close to God and admitted her guilt (Isaiah 46:8), she received forgiveness from Him for her sin and rebellion. Today, she loves God just as He has always loved her.

Pregnancies can be unplanned, but for God a new life is never unknown.

—Tom Felten

faith of our fathers

read>
Ephesians 6:1-4
Fathers, do not provoke your children to anger by the way you treat them. Rather, bring them up with the discipline and instruction that comes from the Lord (v.4).

more>
- Genesis 18:19
- Proverbs 23:22-25
- Hebrews 12:5-13

next>
The one thing that most prisoners have in common is absent or abusive fathers. Why? If you are a single mother, what can you do to help your children understand the love of their heavenly Father?

I was reading upstairs when my neighbor came to pick up his son. The child must not have wanted to go yet, for I heard his small voice declare, "Someone's going to die!" My neighbor did not correct his little boy, but smiled sheepishly as he steered him toward the door. This father is failing his son. As the God-appointed authority in his child's life, he is teaching his son that it's okay to disrespect all authority figures—including God.

Our experience with our earthly father inevitably forms of our view of God. In his book *Faith of the Fatherless,* Paul Vitz observes that many of the world's leading atheists—such as Nietzsche, Hume, Russell, Sartre, and Camus—grew up without fathers. Could the absence of their earthly fathers explain why it was so hard for them to believe in the existence of a heavenly Father?

If you grew up with an absent or abusive father, you will tend to project this bad experience upon God. But if you realize this natural bent, you may be able to lay it aside. Recognize that you're the victim of bad parenting and seek out a father figure who can restore your faith in God. Above all, start with God, allowing His revelation (rather than your difficult childhood) to define what it means to be a father. Believe Jesus when He says that "your heavenly Father already knows all your needs" and is eager to "give good gifts to those who ask Him" (Matthew 6:32, 7:11).

If you're a father, know that how you love your children will determine their perception of God. Being a good dad does not guarantee that your children will love God, but a bad dad can certainly cause them to struggle in their relationship with Him. Ninety percent of parenting is just showing up, but the other 10 percent matters too. —Mike Wittmer

possible

read>
Romans 12:9-21
Do all that you can to live in peace with everyone (v.18).

more>
Turn away from evil and do good. Search for peace, and work to maintain it (Psalm 34:14).

next>
Is there a relational conflict you've been trying to control through your own actions or words? What can you do "as much as possible" to improve the situation? What aspects of this conflict need to be surrendered to Jesus?

A benefit of being a teacher, I know that Thanksgiving vacation is always an anticipated respite from the routine of waking early, grading papers, and planning lessons. What I hadn't planned for was the impending disagreements that would arise from our two children being home in close quarters with extra time. No matter how much I tried to reason with them, they couldn't seem to agree on anything. They were focused on each other's faults, while denying their own. A glutton for punishment, I grounded them from media for several days. Much to my delight, the arguments waned and they suddenly remembered that they actually liked each other.

As living sacrifices—set apart, transformed—believers in Jesus are to become living, breathing reflections of God's will (Romans 12:1-2). In the quietness of our devotional time with the Lord, this goal stirs our hearts. In the day-to-day of relationships, however, it can seem to be downright impossible.

As I deal with my children, I often hear the Lord speaking to me about my relationships with others. *It takes two to fight* (Proverbs 20:3). *You can't choose how others act, but you can choose how you respond* (Matthew 5:38-39). *Be kind, whether it's deserved or not* (Proverbs 31:26). Like my children, I can either trust the wisdom of the One who knows far more than I do or I can rely on my own perspectives (Proverbs 3:5-6).

Godly love doesn't come by finding perfect relationships; it comes when I first choose to deal with my own faults (Romans 12:9). Relational peace is not avoidance. It's a decision to act on the things for which I am responsible, while placing the things I cannot change in the hands of Jesus. I must trust a God for whom nothing is impossible (Luke 1:37; Mark 9:23). —Regina Franklin

not an option

read>
Mark 9:14-29
Jesus replied, "This kind can be cast out only by prayer" (v.29).

One Sunday, we gave our congregation a spiritual challenge—to join together in an on-site, 24-hour prayer chain. Each person was asked to consider signing up to pray for 30 minutes. Nearly 100 people signed up to participate through prayer! We gave our congregation this challenge because, unlike the disciples in Mark 9, we did not want our ministry effort to be an embarrassing failure because it lacked the power of God that comes through prayer.

The scene in Mark 9 opens with Jesus, Peter, James, and John descending from the mountain where Jesus had been transfigured. They came to the foot of the mountain, only to find the scribes arguing with the disciples who had remained behind. What were they arguing about? The argument was probably motivated by the disciples' failure to cast out a demon from a boy.

No doubt their public failure and subsequent humiliation seemed curious and strange to the disciples, for they had been given authority to cast out demons (3:14-15) and had been successful in doing so (6:7, 12-13). Jesus sighed in frustration at the faithlessness of the disciples, the scribes, the crowd, and the troubled father, and ultimately healed the boy. In the debriefing session, the disciples asked Jesus why they could not cast out the demon (9:28-29). Jesus zeroed in on the cause of their failure—they were fruitless in this ministry endeavor because they had failed to pray.

Like the disciples, as believers in Jesus we're sometimes guilty of self-sufficiency due to our abilities, knowledge, skill, and past successes. But it's extremely dangerous to do God's work without His power. To experience the power of God in our lives and spiritual efforts, we must not see prayer as optional, but as an absolute necessity. Let's depend on God—not on our technique and skill.

more>
Remain in Me, and I will remain in you. For a branch cannot produce fruit if it is severed from the vine, and you cannot be fruitful unless you remain in Me (John 15:4-5).

next>
On a scale of 1 to 10, how would you rate your prayer life? What are some actions you need to take today to improve it?

Wedding Wishes

get the party started

read>
John 2:1-11
There was a wedding celebration in the village of Cana. . . . Jesus and His disciples were also invited to the celebration (vv.1-2).

more>
When You open Your hand, You satisfy the hunger and thirst of every living thing (Psalm 145:16).

next>
What images do you have of God? Do they show God as stingy or as generous? How have you experienced God's generosity?

Pastor Robert Brearley says, "Weddings are accidents waiting to happen." I tend to agree. At one wedding where I officiated, some of the decorations in the sanctuary (which had just finished being renovated the night before—making this the first public event) caught fire, ultimately sending one of the wedding cakes up in flames. More than a few times, we've seen grooms faint and brides trip over their dresses. At my wedding, I was so nervous that for some reason I laughed uncontrollably.

John's gospel offers us a wedding scenario where, rather than an accident unfolding, the Messiah goes public. Jesus, His disciples, and His family had gathered in the village of Cana for a wedding (2:1). John's placement of the story is intentional, presenting the launch of Jesus' ministry. John lays out seven astounding miracles (or signs) that coalesce to provide the striking conclusion: *Jesus is the Son of God.*

Jewish wedding festivals were far more extensive than our affairs. Typically, the groom's family would host seven days of feasting and dancing. A severe social faux pas occurred, however, at the Cana wedding. "The wine supply ran out during the festivities" (v.3). After a conversation with His mother, Jesus told the servants to fill the six stone jars, each holding "twenty to thirty gallons," with water. Then, miraculously, the water became wine.

The writer adds details highlighting the abundant, generous nature of this act—how the jars were "filled" to the brim (v.7 NIV) and how the volume yielded at least 150 gallons of the "best" wine of the party (v.10).

Here God demonstrated His generous nature by choosing a party for His stage and by providing wine (a symbol for joy) as "the first time" to reveal Jesus' glory (v.11). —Winn Collier

honey dripping

read>
Psalm 19
They are more desirable than gold, even the finest gold. They are sweeter than honey, even honey dripping from the comb (v.10).

more>
- Psalm 119:11
- 1 Peter 2:2
- James 1:22-25

next>
What words describe how you read your Bible? What does it mean to actually live out the wisdom we find in its words?

In Eugene Peterson's *Eat This Book*, he tells the story of his 7-year-old grandson Hans who appeared to be devoutly reading his New Testament as he sat on a park bench. The boy's eyes moved back and forth across the pages of the Bible, denying the fact that *he had not yet learned how to read.*

Similarly, we can consistently "read" God's Word without comprehending its message for our lives. In Psalm 19:7-11, David lifts up the matchless wisdom of God's Word. He makes six statements about it, in which each contains the phrase "of the Lord." The title "Lord" is from the Hebrew word *Yahweh*—the covenant name of God. God is relational and He speaks to us in His Word. David reveals this important truth about Scripture: It proceeds from God Himself.

So the *way* we read the Bible is vital. Do we read it merely for information, principles, or truths that we can use to live better? Or do we read it in order to listen to God and respond in prayer and obedience?

In Psalm 19, David also lists four qualities of the Bible (perfect, trustworthy, right, clear), and the four results of following its truth (reviving the soul, making wise the simple, bringing joy to the heart, giving insight for living). Notice that the whole person is affected—the soul, the mind, and the heart.

No wonder David proclaims that God's Word is "more desirable than gold, even the finest gold" (v.10). Yes, Scripture is infinitely more precious than anything this world has to offer. And it's "sweeter than honey, even honey dripping from the comb." This imagery encourages us to savor God's Word, to eat the book and truly take in its life changing, life-sustaining wisdom.

—Poh Fang Chia

personal weaknesses

read>
John 8:1-11
They kept demanding an answer, so He stood up again and said, "All right, but let the one who has never sinned throw the first stone!" (v.7).

more>
Who can say, "I have cleansed my heart; I am pure and free from sin"? (Proverbs 20:9).

next>
When was the last time you confided in a Christian friend about one of your own personal weaknesses? What happens when we go into isolation with our sin?

When the news about a golf celebrity's numerous extramarital affairs began to leak out a few years ago, it became evident that the golfer with the squeaky-clean image wasn't so perfect after all.

At that time, there was a debate over whether or not the media was being too hard on Tiger Woods. Some said he deserved the public shame he experienced. Some pointed out that other famous people have been serial womanizers. They questioned why the media seems to look the other way when it comes to some other celebrities' sexual indiscretions, while Tiger got trashed.

John records the account of the morning when a group of Jewish religious leaders tried to draw Jesus into a moral debate (John 8:1-11). While Jesus was teaching in the temple, they brought in a woman who had committed adultery—publicly accusing her before the people (v.3).

After reminding Jesus that the Law of Moses called for her to be stoned, they asked Him what He thought they should do with her (vv.4-5). John tells us that the religious leaders were looking for Jesus to say something that would discredit Himself (v.6). If He didn't condemn her, He would be disagreeing with Moses. If He was too harsh, He might take a hit in the eyes of the masses that were attracted to His teaching.

Jesus brilliantly avoided the trap they had set by pointing out the sinfulness of the woman's accusers. He said, "Let the one who has never sinned throw the first stone!" (v.7).

Instead of discussing the moral failures of those who make headline news, let's remember that we all have weaknesses—places where sin can more easily infiltrate and ruin our lives. By humbly acknowledging our weaknesses to God and others, we can better avoid sins that will destroy us and our witness for Jesus. —Jeff Olson

acceptable apology

read>
Genesis 50:1-21
We, the servants of the God of your father, beg you to forgive our sin (v.17).

more>
- Psalm 38:18
- Romans 12:18
- 1 John 1:9

next>
What should you do if someone refuses to forgive you? How has forgiveness changed your life?

After a fight with his wife, a man decided to apologize. But his wife had already moved out. So he printed a banner with a plea for forgiveness on it, hung it near the house where his wife was living and commented, "I hope she will accept my apology and come back home."

There are lots of ways to say *I'm sorry*—banners, greeting cards, Web sites, public speeches, or just a simple hand-on-the-shoulder discussion next to the refrigerator. No matter how we express the idea, an acceptable apology should cover some basic points.

First, it's important to name the offense. Years after Joseph's brothers sold him as a slave, they sent him this message: "Please forgive your brothers for . . . their sin in treating you so cruelly" (Genesis 50:17). Although they didn't go into the details of the sale, they did address the heart of the matter, which was their cruelty.

Second, once they established the issue, the brothers focused exclusively on their own wrongdoing. They didn't remind Joseph of his bratty behavior and superiority complex back when they were growing up. Like the brothers, we should not try to justify our offense by pinning blame on the other person.

Third, sometimes an apology includes taking action to make things right. Joseph's brothers bowed before him, proclaiming, "Look! We are your slaves!" (v.18). This fulfilled a prophetic dream of Joseph's in which he would reign over his family members (37:5-8). The whole situation had come full circle and his siblings' repentant action was a final act of restitution.

The Bible urges us to "work at living in peace with everyone" (Hebrews 12:14). Sometimes this means giving an acceptable apology—identifying and owning up to our fault and then doing what it takes to made amends for our offense.

—Jennifer Benson Schuldt

never in a hurry

read>
John 5:16-19
So Jesus explained, "I tell you the truth, the Son can do nothing by Himself. He does only what He sees the Father doing" (v.19).

more>
Take My yoke upon you. Let Me teach you, because I am humble and gentle at heart, and you will find rest for your souls (Matthew 11:29).

next>
Why do you think our society struggles with "hurry sickness"? How will you seek to do only what the Father is doing today?

"Though I am always in haste, I am never in a hurry." I wish I could make these words of John Wesley my own. Most days for me are full, with numerous duties, deadlines, phone calls, e-mails, plans, and diary items to act on. Many times that peace that passes understanding (Philippians 4:7) is pushed aside by busy thoughts and knots in the stomach.

Sometimes I wonder if my problem is theological. Generally speaking, the god you worship will determine the person you become. Yes, the true God is active. He governs every single moment of creation (Psalm 104). His eyes scan the earth, looking to strengthen faith (2 Chronicles 16:9). Each day, He motivates His people to carry out His work (Philippians 2:13).

But our God is also the God who rested after creation (Genesis 2:1-3) and has a season for everything (Ecclesiastes 3:1-8). If the growth of grass and the progress of history hint at His ways, God may also be busy but He's never rushed.

When God walked the earth in the person of Jesus, He once again pushed aside all notions of being rushed. He refused to let the crowds dictate His pace (Mark 1:35-39). He assured us that the Father was active (John 5:17), and that He did only what He saw the Father doing (v.19). His pace was in step with His power. As J. B. Phillips has said: "[Christ's] task and responsibility might well have driven a man out of his mind. But He was never in a hurry, never impressed by numbers, never a slave of the clock. He was acting, as He said, as He observed God to act—never in a hurry."

The Almighty God may be busy, but He is never in a hurry. Given that we are to be imitators of God (Ephesians 5:1), how does your pace compare?

—Sheridan Voysey

late?

read>
Matthew 7:1-5
Do not judge others, and you will not be judged (v.1).

more>
- Luke 18:9-14
- Romans 14:3,10

next>
When are you most tempted to judge others? What "planks" do you need to get out of your own eyes first? Is there someone you need to humbly love, accept, and forgive today?

I normally take my kids to school 30 minutes before class begins. One morning we left the house later than normal. When we picked them up from school, my middle son insisted that they had not made it to class on time, and he had proof. He proudly presented "exhibit A": He had seen our daughter with a detention slip in her hand. The only problem with his evidence was that it was not *her* detention for being late to school—it was her classmate's. She was holding it for him until he finished tying his shoe. My son apologized for misjudging his sister. He learned an important lesson about not judging others.

When Jesus began teaching His followers, He made sure they learned the same lesson (Matthew 7:1). When He gave the "don't judge" command, however, He wasn't saying for them to put their minds in neutral and refuse to examine people's actions in order to hold them accountable to God's standards. He simply wanted them to refrain from judging others just to build themselves up. Those who judged others would find themselves being judged in the same manner by God and by others.

There are several reasons why Jesus told His followers not to judge others. First, they may have only known part of the story and didn't fully understand all the motives and issues involved (1 Corinthians 4:5). Second, when they judged others, they brought God's judgment on themselves (Romans 2:1-3). Third, God is the only One who is qualified to judge anyone (James 4:11-12). Finally, when they judged others, they were not walking in Jesus' steps (John 8:1-11).

Before we judge others, let's seek to understand all the issues and motives of the situation, examine our own lives first, leave all judging to God, and humbly love, forgive, accept, and help others in a spirit of grace and understanding.

—Marvin Williams

a tree and its fruit

read>
Genesis 3:1-21
The Lord God made clothing from animal skins for Adam and his wife (v.21).

more>
- John 3:16-18
- Romans 5:6-17
- Galatians 3:13-16

next>
God gave us the gift of salvation through Jesus' ultimate sacrifice on a tree at Calvary. Have you received that gift? How will you celebrate Christmas this year in the shadow of the cross?

Many of us place a tree in our homes this month, decorating it with colorful ornaments and lights. And, of course, gifts will be set beneath the tree, waiting to be opened on Christmas morning. What would Christmas be without the iconic Christmas tree!

In the Garden of Eden, there was a tree of knowledge of good and evil (Genesis 2:17). Eve willfully took something from that tree and changed the course of human destiny and history. Satan misled Eve to challenge the truth of God's Word—"You won't die!" (3:4), created discontent in her heart that God was withholding something better from her (v.5), and convinced her to eat the fruit so that she would "be like God" (vv.5-7). Die? Adam and Eve had no idea what dying meant. Death for human beings was ushered in by their sin. And from that time forward, we have experienced death—both spiritual and physical.

Adam and Eve were asked by God to explain their actions (vv.8-13). Satan was not, because he had no second chance for redemption. Consider the three orders of God's creation—angels, the universe, and human beings. God had already destined all the evil angels—including Satan—to hell (Matthew 25:41; 2 Peter 2:4; Jude 1:6). God will destroy the earth and re-create a new earth (2 Peter 3:7,13; Revelation 21:1). But only people will be redeemed and saved (Hebrews 2:16; 1 Peter 1:12), because they're precious to God (Psalm 8:3-5; Job 7:17).

The clothes they made for themselves (Genesis 3:7) could not cover their guilt. So God made them clothing from animal skins (v.21). As blood flowed for the very first time, they had a taste of the horrors of death. It was the first dramatic illustration of the ultimate cost to be paid at Calvary, for without the shedding of blood, there is no forgiveness of sin (Hebrews 9:22). —K.T. Sim

God's perplexing answers

read>
Habakkuk 1:5–2:1
I am doing something in your own day, something you wouldn't believe even if someone told you about it (v.5).

more>
"My thoughts are nothing like your thoughts," says the Lord. "And My ways are far beyond anything you could imagine" (Isaiah 55:8).

next>
What perplexing answer have you recently received from God? How does your perspective change when you view it through the light of His character?

My best friend's mother had just passed away. In an attempt to cheer her up, I brought her to a scenic spot in Singapore where we could watch the sunset. But upon arriving at my chosen location, I saw that the sky was overcast. The weather, it seemed, was as gloomy as our feelings. I wondered: *God, why didn't You give us a blue sky and sunshine to remind my friend of Your love? Surely it's within Your power to provide it. Why would You deny this good thing to my friend?*

Imagine Habakkuk's anguish when he heard God's reply to his complaint concerning Judah's wickedness. God told him that He would use the Babylonians, pagans who were worse than the sinning Jews, to punish His covenant people (1:6). This was definitely not what he wanted to hear!

The Babylonians were notorious for their cruelty (v.7). They were bent on violence (v.9) and worshiped nothing but their military prowess (v.11). These enemies of God's chosen people were sinful, self-centered, and ruthless. God couldn't have chosen a worse people as the means of Judah's correction.

Sometimes God answers our prayers in ways we don't want to hear. But when His ways are confusing, we need to trust His heart. God says, "I have loved you, My people, with an everlasting love" (Jeremiah 31:3).

Habakkuk ends his prayer by stating that he would watch and wait for God's answer (2:1). His response to undesired circumstances is a good example for us. Perplexing times shouldn't drive us *from* God. Rather, like Habakkuk, we should humbly bring our concerns to Him and then wait for His answer.

Habakkuk learned to look at his circumstances through the prism of God's character—instead of the other way around. Let's do the same when we receive a perplexing answer from God. —Poh Fang Chia

glorious mess

read>
Philippians 3:12-14
I don't mean to say that I have already achieved these things or that I have already reached perfection. But I press on to possess that perfection for which Christ Jesus first possessed me (v.12).

more>
Solomon loved the Lord and followed all the decrees of his father, David, except that Solomon, too, offered sacrifices and burned incense at the local places of worship (1 Kings 3:3).

next>
How have you pretended to be farther along in your maturity in Jesus than you actually are? What will you do to stop pretending?

In 1998, Dr. Larry Crabb wrote the book *Inside Out.* The book encourages Christians to stop pretending they have it all together and to be honest about what's going on in their hearts. As they do so, Crabb reveals, God can free them up to become more of who they were meant to be.

After the book was published, Larry half-jokingly said that he wished it had been titled *I'm a Mess, You're a Mess.* He knew it wasn't the most attractive title, yet it reflected something that is true of every one of us.

Take, for example, King David. Even though God considered him a man after His own heart (Acts 13:22), he was not without his struggles and faults. Second Samuel 11 records a time in David's life when he was troubled by a lack of direction and purpose. Floundering in his kingly calling, David abused his power by summoning a married woman to his bedroom, and then arranged for her husband's death to cover up what he had done.

Perhaps one of the reasons the Bible includes this sordid part of David's life is to remind us that none of us has arrived. It's not an excuse to be a mess, but it's a reminder that we're a "glorious" mess in process. In other words, we all have room to grow.

It's important to envision who we can be, but let's not deny where we are today. Referring to the life that is ours in Christ, even the apostle Paul acknowledged, "I don't mean to say that I have already achieved these things or that I have already reached perfection" (Philippians 3:12).

Don't pretend that you're farther along in the Christian life than you are. God works in our lives where we are, not where we think we should be. —Jeff Olson

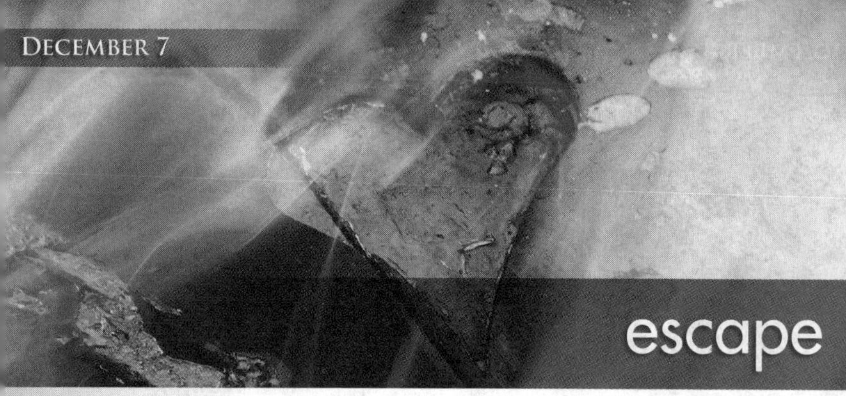

escape

read>
2 Timothy 2:23-36
Then they will come to their senses and escape from the devil's trap (v.26)

more>
I fear that somehow your pure and undivided devotion to Christ will be corrupted, just as Eve was deceived by the cunning ways of the serpent (2 Cor.11:3).

next>
Where do you feel trapped—and what lies are associated with your situation? How does Jesus' truth unveil these lies?

Seventeen-year old Shirin arrived at Afghanistan's Heart Regional Hospital with 90 percent of her body covered in third-degree burns. The official story given to hospital staff was that Shirin had suffered a cooking accident. Later in private, however, the teenager told doctors that she had set herself aflame. Sadly, such acts are not rare. Many young Afghan women feel powerless and isolated. French nurse Marie-Jose Brunel explains their predicament: "She [feels she] is here only to wash, to clean, to give baby . . . and nothing more." Trapped in a culture where they have no voice, women take drastic measures to escape.

The sensation of being trapped, confined, and bound, with no way of wresting free, is a horrible, suffocating sensation. The Scripture describes the devil as one who works to ensnare all of God's people and all of God's creation. The devil's work always results in some form of bondage: a father compulsively driven to achieve corporate prestige or to pad his reputation, a mother consumed with image—hers and her family's. Some people are addicted to heroin, but others are addicted to religious perfection. In each case, we're trapped. And eventually, we will all find ourselves desperate to be free.

The devil is the "father of lies" (John 8:44), and his traps showcase his many ways of twisting the truth. Our way to be free, then, is to "learn the truth," to see the false promises we have believed and the false hopes we have nurtured for what they are: lies that ensnare (2 Timothy 2:25-26).

And the truth we are to learn is not primarily facts or ideas, but a person—Jesus, for He is "the truth" (John 8:32). His name literally means *God saves.* This is an affirmation that He has already provided for our escape. —Winn Collier

what i need

read>
Genesis 21:8-20
Seek the kingdom of God above all else, and live righteously, and He will give you everything you need (Matthew 6:33).

Diane was devastated. Despite her husband's absence for nearly half their 8-year marriage, she had faithfully supported him in his military career. Then, abruptly, he announced that he was leaving her and their children for another woman. Now she sat in a clinic awaiting test results that would let her know if he had left her with any "parting gifts"—STDs.

An elderly woman seated across from Diane noticed her telltale red eyes. "Are you all right?" she gently inquired. With nothing to lose, the younger woman decided to share her plight. As providence would have it, this woman had also been divorced after 8 years of marriage—more than 5 decades earlier! And she, like Diane, was a follower of Jesus. She knew exactly what this young mother was going through. As her new friend quietly prayed for her in the waiting room, Diane knew that somehow God would bring her and her children through this difficult season. It was enough grace for the moment, at just the right moment.

In Genesis, we read of another woman who knew rejection and abandonment. Hagar, a servant to Sarah, had been sent into the arid wilderness by her owner (Genesis 21:8-14). Having run out of water, she put her son in the shade some distance away so she wouldn't have to watch him die (v.16). But the angel of the Lord met her there and provided for their needs.

In Jesus' Sermon on the Mount, He spoke of meeting our basic physical needs (Matthew 6:25-33). But He also provides what we need for the vast array of experiences that life throws at us. For some of our biggest needs are emotional. Life is hard. But we have Someone who knows what we're going through. He will never abandon us. He's within reach of our next heartfelt prayer.

—Tim Gustafson

more>
What does Matthew 6:25-33 tell us about how God provides for us? What does Romans 3:23-26 tell us that God did to meet our biggest need?

next>
What are your needs? How are these distinct from your wants? How are the things that you want pleasing or not pleasing to God?

little pieces

read>
Romans 6:1-13
You also should consider yourselves to be dead to the power of sin and alive to God through Christ Jesus (v.11).

more>
- Psalm 32:2
- Hebrews 12:1
- Revelation 3:19

next>
What sins have you been excusing as "not a big deal"? Why must repentance be an action as well as a posture of our hearts?

Cleaning my home is not my preferred choice of activity most days, but I do enjoy the fruit of my labor once the task is done. I don't mind the dusting or the vacuuming; it's the endless prerequisite task of straightening that bores me. The other day, when I found a small puzzle piece, I was tempted to throw it away. I had bigger tasks to tackle and didn't want to be sidetracked. I realized, though, that without that small piece the puzzle would remain forever incomplete, and the other pieces would soon follow the one into the trash.

Like throwing away an inconvenient, left-behind puzzle piece, we may find it tempting to brush aside what we define as a *small* issue of sin. We reason that its impact will be minimal because it seems inconsequential. The call for every believer, however, is to pursue character that reflects God's own (Philippians 1:6,9-11). Reminding us of God's love for us, the Song of Solomon reveals that we have a role in protecting our love relationship with Jesus: "Catch all the foxes, those little foxes, before they ruin the vineyard of love, for the grapevines are blossoming!" (2:15).

When describing the death that sin brings, Romans 6:23 doesn't differentiate between size or category. Any sin we willfully hang on to brings separation from God (Isaiah 59:2) and eventual death. In our spiritual lives, we can keep away the little foxes by:

- *Guarding our hearts.* The enemy often uses our desires and temptations to open the door to sin (Proverbs 4:23).
- *Confessing our sins.* Admitting our failings reminds us that in our own strength we miss the mark, but through God transformation is possible (Romans 6:7).

Keep dealing with the small sins in your life, before they lead to something much larger and more costly. —Regina Franklin

wrong directions

read>
Psalm 1
Oh, the joys of those who . . . delight in the law of the Lord (vv.1-2).

more>
- Psalm 144:15
- Proverbs 16:20
- Jeremiah 17:7-8

next>
How have you pursued a wrong course heading that has led to your unhappiness? What will it take for you to know true happiness?

Last summer, a couple from Sweden took a wrong turn on their way to paradise. The duo was determined to reach the beautiful island of Capri, Italy. As they headed out from Venice, however, they went the wrong way. You see, they had accidentally entered "C-A-R-P-I" into their car's GPS, not "C-A-P-R-I." So when the two found themselves in the northern town of Carpi, Italy—some 660 kilometers away from Capri—they were redirected to the place where they hoped to pursue happiness, *Capri.*

Have you and I set a course for happiness that leads to anything but that blissful state? Fortunately, the psalmist provides clear direction: "Oh, the joys of those who . . . delight in the law of the Lord" (1:1-2). When we follow hard after God and dig deep into His Word—taking it to heart—we can be blessed . . . and happy.

In verse 1, we also find that certain things don't lead to happiness:

- *Following evil advice.* Is our pursuit of happiness based in the ideals and things of this world, or in God's blessing?
- *Standing with sinners.* Who's influencing us and our path? God leads the godly to good things (v.6).
- *Joining with mockers.* How have we mocked what is sacred in our striving after what is silly and worthless?

In verse 2, the psalmist writes that we should be "meditating on [God's Word] day and night." We often "meditate" on things that can never bring happiness. We long for this and that. Objects become our focus and our passion—consuming our thoughts. But even if we get what we want, the short-lived pleasure doesn't lead to long-term happiness.

Only when we place our full focus on God and His Word will we be like "trees planted along the riverbank" (v.3), flourishing in happiness that comes only from God. —Tom Felten

patience, man

read>
Genesis 18:16-33
The Lord replied, "Then I will not destroy [Sodom] for the sake of the ten" (v.32).

more>
- Exodus 34:6-7
- Galatians 5:22
- 2 Peter 3:15

next>
How have you benefitted from God's patience? How can you exhibit Christlike patience in today's society?

After church one Sunday, our family pulled up to the drive-up window of a local fast-food restaurant. We inched up to the microphone and waited. After a lengthy pause, a voice told us it would be just another minute. I felt a surge of irritation. When my husband finally placed our order, the voice vanished again. *"Hellooooo?"* we called. The voice responded, "Patience, man." And we waited some more.

Most of us don't think of God's longsuffering ways when we picture the destruction of Sodom and Gomorrah. Images of fireballs, burning sulfur, and a fossilized woman (Genesis 19:24-26) remind us of God's judgment and His righteous anger. Still, before those events, God's patience was present.

Prior to Sodom's demise, God visited Abraham, saying, "I am going down to see if [the city's] actions are as wicked as I have heard. If not, I want to know" (18:21). The Lord took the time to personally scope out the situation before halting the city's wickedness—even though, in His divinity, He must have known all the details. God was demonstrating His patience.

Before leaving for Sodom, God endured a string of annoying questions from Abraham that began like this: "Suppose you find fifty righteous people living there in the city—will you still sweep it away and not spare it for their sakes?" (v.24). When God promised He would, Abe asked the same kind of question *five more times*!

We need to mirror God's character and "be patient with each other" (Ephesians 4:2). This might mean listening wholeheartedly to less-than-engaging dialogue, or carefully investigating when we'd rather jump to our own conclusions. In any case, it requires us to answer God's call to *have patience, man.* —Jennifer Benson Schuldt

Confirm Ignore
the "accept" button

read>
Mark 2:13-17
Healthy people don't need a doctor—sick people do. I have come to call not those who think they are righteous, but those who know they are sinners (v.17).

more>
People will come from all over the world—from east and west, north and south—to take their places in the Kingdom of God (Luke 13:29).

next>
Is there someone Jesus might be calling you to accept right now, even if that person is "unrepentant"? How did Jesus accept people without condoning their behavior?

After months of vowing not to, I finally signed up on Facebook and Twitter. My fears that these social media tools would rob me of precious writing time as I waded through endless updates have largely proven true! But the pros have outweighed the cons—particularly in keeping in touch with listeners to my radio program, *Open House*.

Open House has an audience of both believers and skeptics, each from a variety of backgrounds. So it was to be expected that I'd get a variety of folks inviting me to be their Facebook friend—including some with a lifestyle that's contrary to biblical Christianity. *How will this look to others?* I wondered for a time. *Should I press "Accept" or "Ignore" to their invitation?*

A tax collector named Levi once threw a party to celebrate his being chosen as Jesus' disciple (Mark 2:14-15). Because he made citizens pay taxes to the Romans, Levi was considered a traitor by fellow Jews and was placed in the same league as prostitutes and Gentiles. So you can imagine the friends he invited to his party! The Pharisees were disgusted to see Jesus at this celebration, sitting around in full acceptance of all this "scum" (v.16).

While Jesus attracted some colorful followers (v.15), it appears that the party was *not* filled with repentant people. And this is striking. Jesus, the Son of God, did not require repentance *before* He offered acceptance. And why was that? Because "healthy people don't need a doctor—sick people do" (v.17).

Jesus was more concerned with reaching people than with protecting His reputation. He hit "Accept" on their invitations, no matter who they were, and ended up changing them by doing so (Luke 19:5-10). Since our acceptance ends up changing us, don't you think we should offer it to others? —Sheridan Voysey

failure

read>
Matthew 26:69-75
Go and tell His disciples, including Peter, that Jesus is going ahead of you to Galilee. You will see Him there, just as He told you before He died (Mark 16:7).

more>
- 1 Kings 19:9-16
- Psalm 37:23-24
- Galatians 6:1

next>
In what ways have you failed? What truth do you need to accept as you ask Jesus to move your failure from active to inactive status?

According to columnist Perry Buffington, a licensed psychologist, failure takes on a life of its own because the brain remembers incomplete tasks or failures longer than successes or completed activities. It's called the "Zeigarnik effect." Buffington states, "When a project or a thought is completed, the brain . . . no longer gives the project priority or active working status. . . . But failures have no closure. The brain continues to spin the memory, trying to come up with ways to fix the mess and move it from active to inactive status."

Peter failed in many ways, but Jesus fixed the mounting mess of the apostle's failures and moved his blunders from active to inactive status. Peter failed in at least two ways that people most fear: *being powerless in a crisis and awkward in a social setting.*

In the most important times of his life with Jesus—the Caesarea Philippi scene (Matthew 16:20-23), the transfiguration scene (17:1-4), and the foot-washing scene (John 13:4-10)—Peter said the most inappropriate things. He failed because the deluge of his pride overpowered him, and he attempted to blanket himself in his own strength. At the arrest of Jesus, he collapsed and became a pathetic coward (Matthew 26:69-75). His heart deceived him and he denied his Teacher and Lord. But Jesus gave him a second chance and moved his failure from active to inactive (Mark 16:7; John 21:15-17).

Jesus can move our failure to inactive status when we realize that He's bigger than our failures and He's willing to give us another chance. If our failures are the result of sin, then we should confess our sins to God and genuinely repent (1 John 1:9). When we fail, we can and should get up again (Proverbs 24:16). And we should press on in Jesus' power (Acts 3). —Marvin Williams

curses and conflicts

read>
Genesis 3:1-15
I will cause hostility between you and the woman, and between your offspring and her offspring (v.15).

more>
- Romans 16:20
- Galatians 3:16
- Hebrews 2:14

next>
How have you been oblivious to the subtle temptations of the evil one? What will you do to create some healthy conflict between you and Satan?

Conflicts. I haven't found anyone who truly enjoys them. I, for one, will do anything possible to avoid conflicts. For I desire and strive to live at peace with everyone (Romans 12:18; Hebrews 12:14). Genesis 3:15 is about hostility and animosity. In this verse, God declares that He will cause enmity between Satan and Eve. Why would God deliberately create enmity between the two?

Satan had succeeded in getting Adam and Eve to disobey God (vv.1-7). But he couldn't get their *allegiance*, because God intervened. God's judgment, a curse on Satan, is tinged with hope and provides a blessing for us today. It's God's first gracious and merciful act immediately after the fall. God caused the hostility between the devil and Eve (v.15) in order to prevent Eve from giving her full allegiance to Satan.

The devil wants us to think of him as a friend (2 Corinthians 11:14). In setting up hostility between Satan and Eve, God reminds us that Satan is no friend. He's our great enemy! The apostle Peter, writing from his own painful failure (Luke 22:31-34,56-62). warns us to "stay alert! Watch out for your great enemy, the devil. He prowls around like a roaring lion, looking for someone to devour" (1 Peter 5:8).

Genesis 3:15 speaks of Eve's offspring (*seed* NKJV). Many theologians believe the seed of the woman foreshadows the virgin birth of Christ. For in nature, the seed is in the male, not the female. So it appears that the promise of the Savior was first announced in the Garden of Eden—immediately after Adam and Eve had sinned. At that early time—the grace of God was revealed that allows us to be set free from the curse and conflict that came with sin. —K.T. Sim

not a minute late

read>
Habakkuk 2:2-20
If it seems slow in coming, wait patiently, for it will surely take place. It will not be delayed (v.3).

more>
In just a little while, the Coming One will come and not delay. And My righteous ones will live by faith. But I will take no pleasure in anyone who turns away (Hebrews 10:37-38).

next>
How does the fact that God is in control change your perspective on trials? Why is it important for us to understand that God is righteous in all He does?

Jason took a trip to New York during spring break. One afternoon, he piled into a cab with some friends and headed for the Empire State Building. The ride seemed totally chaotic and dangerous to Jason. After arriving at their destination, the group headed up to the observation deck. Once there, Jason paused to take in the view—102 floors above the ground. To his amazement, he saw order and design in the city streets where—only a few minutes before—he had experienced chaos. Jason was struck by the change of perspective. Jammed in a cab amid the honking horns of turbulent traffic, he had one view of life. But his perch up on the Empire State Building gave him an entirely different take.

To Habakkuk, God seemed indifferent to the evil permeating Judah. And he was greatly disturbed when God said He would use the wicked Babylonians to judge His people (1:5-11).

God responded to Habakkuk's complaints (1:12–2:1) without explaining why He chose to use the Babylonians. Instead, He gave Habakkuk a divine perspective.

Habakkuk 2:2-20 reminds us that God is all about righteousness. He might choose to use wicked people to further His purposes, but that doesn't mean He approves of their sin. No, God will ultimately punish the wicked for the evil they've committed. It's reassuring to know that the sinful deeds of men can't thwart the purposes of God.

God is sovereign. He will work things out in our lives for His purposes. His plans will be completed and on His schedule.

As humans, our perspective is limited. We can't view the whole picture from our "cab ride" through life; only God can see it all from "His holy temple" (v.20). Things may seem chaotic in your life. But take heart, for "the Sovereign Lord is [our] strength" (3:19). —Poh Fang Chia

running from nineveh

read>
Jonah 4:1-11
Nineveh has more than 120,000 people living in spiritual darkness, not to mention all the animals. Shouldn't I feel sorry for such a great city? (v.11).

more>
God is so rich in mercy, and He loved us so much, that even though we were dead because of our sins, He gave us life when He raised Christ from the dead (Ephesians 2:4-5).

next>
How have you conveyed that some people are undeserving of God's forgiveness? How does God's grace affect your views?

Sixty-six-year-old Nita Friedman was not the sort of person you would expect to lead the police on a 15-mile car chase. But that's exactly what police chief Mike Hutter encountered on US Highway 95 in Bonners Ferry, Idaho.

After receiving a call about a reckless driver, Hutter spotted Friedman and turned on his lights and siren. Rather than pull over, however, Friedman kept on going. Apparently, she was confused and didn't think his vehicle was a real police car. Although she never exceeded the speed limit, Friedman was eventually charged with eluding a police officer.

Lately, I've been thinking a lot about a biblical character who also made a run for it. Unlike Nita Friedman, this guy intentionally ran away—not from the law, but from God. He wasn't confused. He flat out didn't want to go to the place where God had called him to go.

His name was Jonah (Jonah 1:1-3).

A part of me understands Jonah. Who in their right mind would want to go to Nineveh—a city that tortured and killed its own people? But running away from God didn't turn out so well for Jonah (vv.3-17). After he had a change of heart (ch.2), God called him again to go and warn Nineveh of its impending demise. This time he went. The city repented, God showed compassion, and Jonah was furious (ch.3–4).

It's not merely that Jonah ran. What's so problematic is *why* he ran. He bolted because he refused to accept the wildly amazing truth that God's grace is for all—even people as wicked as the Ninevites.

Are there people that we've judged as unworthy of God's grace? Perhaps because of their behavior or the way they look? It's time to reach out to them in God's love. Who is *your* Nineveh? —Jeff Olson

waiting

read>
Psalm 5:1-3
Each morning I bring my requests to You and wait expectantly (v.3).

more>
Come quickly to help me, O Lord my Savior (Psalm 38:22).

next>
When have you tried to no avail to make something happen? In what specific ways do you need to wait for God instead?

We have some friends, a young married couple, living with us. Finished with one part of their university studies, they've applied to a variety of graduate schools to continue their coursework. But they have no idea where they will end up. The possibilities are all over the map—from Boston to Vancouver to Pittsburgh to Atlanta. They've filled out many applications and requested numerous grants. There have also been interviews and carefully considered options as they've given thought to their future every which way. Now, all they can do is pray—and wait for the day when the postman brings news of what their future holds.

Psalm 5 begins with a straightforward request: "O Lord, hear me as I pray; pay attention to my groaning" (v.1). The psalmist, King David, was in a gloomy place. We don't know his situation, but David was experiencing some measure of loss, sorrow, or torment. He was in pain, "groaning." And in his difficult place, David wanted God to hear his agony. He needed God to listen to his "cry for help" (v.2).

David didn't run to his advisors or his wife or the many wise sages of his court for aid. None of them could help him. He didn't roll up his sleeves and pore over documents, figuring out some solution to his predicament. David knew he couldn't help himself. He went directly to the only One who could meet him in his darkness. "I pray to no one but You," David said (v.2). David waited, watching for God.

David's only work was to *not* work. He decided to bring his heart and his hope to God and then to "wait expectantly" (v.3). *The Message* puts it this way: "Every morning I lay out the pieces of my life on your altar and watch for fire to descend." —Winn Collier

why study?

read>
Luke 2:41-50
I have hidden Your Word in my heart that I might not sin against You (Psalm 119:11).

more>
What kind of knowledge leads to wisdom (Proverbs 9:10), and what are the benefits of studying God's Word? (Psalm 119:9-16).

next>
What are your motivations for learning? What do you do with the knowledge you have gained?

"Why do I have to study?" declared the high school student. "Life is an open-book test!" He was bright, bored, and oh-so-much-more-interested in the vital things of life—like playing online games and texting his "gf." His assertion holds a certain appeal, doesn't it? After all, information is just a mouse-click away. The problem is, he's failed to draw the distinction between knowledge and wisdom—the accurate and timely application of information.

In Luke's account of the life of Jesus, we get a unique glimpse into the Savior's childhood. At just 12 years old, Jesus displayed amazing knowledge of God's Word in the temple (Luke 2:47). "That was easy for Him," you might say. "He's the Son of God!" But the context to me indicates that Jesus was still youthfully naïve; He couldn't understand His parents' concern over His absence for several days (v.48).

Years later, when Jesus was tempted by the devil in the wilderness, He quickly countered the devil's insolent proposals with an ease that displayed a thorough and accurate knowledge of the Scriptures (see Luke 4:1-13).

Later, on the day of Jesus' resurrection from the tomb, He appeared to two travelers who didn't recognize Him. Jesus observed that they were "foolish people" because of their lack of belief in the words of the prophets. But then He explained the Old Testament prophecies to them. They would say that evening: "Didn't our hearts burn within us as He talked with us?" Jesus used His knowledge to bolster the faith of two discouraged believers (see Luke 24:13-32).

The accumulation of knowledge without wisdom will make us proud and ruthless. But biblical knowledge applied with love and discernment will keep us from bad choices, and will help us serve others. —Tim Gustafson

the fight for marriage

read>
1 Peter 3:1-12
Finally, all of you should be of one mind. Sympathize with each other. Love each other as brothers and sisters. Be tenderhearted, and keep a humble attitude (v.8).

more>
Each man must love his wife as he loves himself, and the wife must respect her husband (Ephesians 5:33).

next>
If you're married, how can you strengthen the condition of your marriage? If you're single, how can you strengthen your relationship with your first love—God?

The fight for godly marriages has raged since the fall in Eden, but in the past few years, my husband and I have become increasingly aware that the battle lines begin at our doorstep. Seeing some of our friends divorce and others separate has left us wishing for the innocence of days gone by. As we prepare to celebrate our fifteenth anniversary, we are so grateful for the work God has done in our marriage—for the gift we've been given.

God established marriage as a means of procreation (1:28), companionship (2:18), and as a reflection of God's selfless love (1 Peter 3:8; Ephesians 5:25). In short, it's so much deeper than anything this world can demonstrate to us.

We can feel dismay when we see what is taking place in the political and public arena regarding the state of marriage. When we see friends and family members struggle in their marital relationships, it can grieve us. And we're left with this vital question: How are we passionately protecting our own marriages?

To keep our marital bonds strong, we should:

- *Invest* – The greatest amount of time and investment should be in our relationship with God. Then, our relationship with our spouse must receive the second most investment—more than other relationships (1 Peter 3:1-2).
- *Trust* – We must trust God with changes we desire to take place in our spouse (vv.5,7-8). It's vital that we place our life on the altar and focus on how He wants us to change.
- *Guard* – Our interactions with members of the opposite sex must be pure and holy (vv.11-12). Unity in marriage means no hidden places.

Let's honor God by protecting our marriages. They're worth the fight.

—Regina Franklin

small sins

read>
1 Samuel 13:1-14
"How foolish!" Samuel exclaimed. "You have not kept the command the Lord your God gave you. . . . Now your kingdom must end, for the Lord has sought out a man after His own heart" (vv.13-14).

more>
- 1 Samuel 15:1-23
- Luke 16:10-13
- Acts 5:27-32

next>
Do you feel pressured by circumstances or other people to do something that you know is wrong? How might you use this opportunity to demonstrate your trust in God?

Fish farmers in the southern U.S. had a small problem. Algae was filling their ponds, so they took the seemingly innocent step of importing Asian carp—which can grow to 100 pounds and eat 40 percent of their body weight each day—to clean the bottom of their ponds. But flooding swept the carp into the Mississippi River, which they navigated until they entered the Chicago Sanitary and Ship Canal, a mere 40 miles from Lake Michigan.

Now the entire region has a large problem, for if the Asian carp reach Lake Michigan, their insatiable appetite for plankton may upset the food chain and disrupt the Great Lakes' $7 billion-per-year fishing industry.

Little acts *can* have large consequences. King Saul lost his kingdom for two *small* sins. His first mistake was not waiting for Samuel to arrive to offer sacrifices. But who can blame him? Samuel was late (from Saul's perspective) and Saul's army was slipping away. If Saul didn't seek the Lord's favor soon, he would go to war without God's blessing (1 Samuel 13:5-9).

Saul's second failure came on the heels of a signature victory. His armies defeated the Amalekites; but rather than destroy everything as God had commanded, Saul and his men "kept the best of the sheep and goats, the cattle, the fat calves, and the lambs—everything, in fact, that appealed to them" (1 Samuel 15:9).

The root of these seemingly insignificant sins was the sin of fear. Saul feared losing his army, either by not offering the sacrifice fast enough or by sacrificing something his men wanted. But he feared his men more than he feared God, and God responded by revoking his kingship.

Learn the lesson of Saul: some sins are understandable, but none are excusable—and all are devastating. —Mike Wittmer

sellout

read>
1 Kings 21:1-29
You have sold yourself to what is evil in the Lord's sight (v.20).

more>
- Colossians 3:5
- Luke 12:15
- 1 John 2:15

next>
How do you respond when someone you know has what you want? How would you complete this sentence: You can never have enough ________. Why?

Anthony Marshall conned his mother out of millions before she died at age 105 in 2007. Her money, advancing age, and struggle with Alzheimer's disease made her an attractive target. Marshall's mother was Brooke Astor—famous New York City socialite and keeper of the vast Astor family fortune. Ironically, her senior-citizen son was already wildly wealthy, and yet he conspired with his lawyer to ratchet up his inheritance!

Marshall's actions confirm what the Bible says: "Human desire is never satisfied" (Proverbs 27:20). But greed is not always about acquiring more money. It's about wanting more of something than what we need.

King Ahab wanted more land (1 Kings 21:2). He suffered from a greedy fixation on a vineyard next to his palace. Problem was, the property-owner (Naboth) wasn't selling. So Ahab went home and pouted until his wife appealed to his sense of entitlement, his status, and his ability to have anything he wanted (v.7). Acting like greed incarnate, Jezebel urged Ahab toward self-indulgence, rather than self-control.

Jezebel then hired two thugs to falsely accuse Naboth of cursing God and the king. As a result, the villagers stoned Naboth to death, and Ahab "immediately went down . . . to claim [the property]" (v.16). He never questioned Jezebel's means for procuring the vineyard. Greed says it's OK to trample people to get what we want.

Although we may not see it, God does. He does not want us to follow Ahab's example and become sellouts to greed (v.20). To avoid this, the Bible advises us to "be satisfied with what [we] have" (Hebrews 13:5). Contented living guards us against self-indulgence and a willingness to hurt others to acquire our heart's desire. It allows us to want only what we need, instead of needing what we want. —Jennifer Benson Schuldt

compassionate anger

read >
Mark 3:1-6
He looked around at them angrily and was deeply saddened by their hard hearts (v.5).

more >
- Proverbs 14:29
- Ephesians 4:26,31
- James 1:19-20

next >
Think of someone who made you angry recently. How can you show compassion to that person? If Jesus is the embodiment of God, how might Mark 3:1-6 help us understand God's wrath?

Some things make me angry. Newspaper columnists who belittle life-long marriage; radio hosts who rile against refugees; the big glossy advertisements for brothels in my local newspaper; climate-change proponents who label their critics "deniers" to silence them; climate-change critics who label their opponents "alarmists" for the same reason. *Yes, some things make me angry.*

Jesus became angry (John 2:13-17, 11:33). One Sabbath He was preaching in a synagogue when a number of His critics were present. In a provocative move, Jesus called to a man with a crippled hand and had him stand in front of the group. "Does the law permit good deeds on the Sabbath," Jesus asked, eyeing His critics, "or is it a day for doing evil?" (Mark 3:4). *Silence.* "Is this a day" (we can imagine Him speaking louder now), "to save life or to destroy it?" Still silence.

God made the Sabbath as a time for rest and renewal (Exodus 20:8), but by Jesus' day the religious leaders had made its strict observance a sign of one's righteousness. No work was to be done on the Sabbath, including, in the Pharisees' eyes, the healing of crippled men. And Jesus was *angry* about that—angry at the Pharisees' hard hearts.

But, astonishingly, we find Jesus being "deeply saddened" by them too (Mark 3:5). His anger at evil wasn't accompanied by hatred for its perpetrators, but by sadness, grief, *compassion*.

I ask myself, to what degree do I feel compassion for that columnist, radio host, or brothel owner? Do I feel sad about that angry driver or climate-change critic? I'm not sure how much of my anger is the least bit righteous, let alone combined with compassion.

To feel anger is human. To feel compassionate anger is divine. I want to be more like Jesus. —Sheridan Voysey

forgetting faces

read>
Deuteronomy 8:11-18
Remember the Lord your God. He is the One who gives you power to be successful, in order to fulfill the covenant He confirmed to your ancestors with an oath (v.18).

more>
- Psalm 106:19-22
- Isaiah 17:9-11
- Hosea 13:6

next>
In what ways have you forgotten God? What will you do today to celebrate who God is and what He has done for you?

In 2004, a woman named Claire contracted viral encephalitis. After treatment for her illness at a local hospital, she returned home. But her memory had been dramatically affected. Claire developed a condition known as prosopagnosia—the inability to recognize faces. After several years of effort, she can finally pick out her husband's countenance in a crowd, but she still can't point out her children if they're with a group of friends.

Claire's condition reminds me of something Moses warned the Israelites about—forgetting the face of God. Just prior to God's people concluding their 40 years of wandering in the wilderness, at the doorstep to the Promised Land, the prophet gave them a loving warning: "Beware that in your plenty you do not forget the Lord your God and disobey His commands" (Deuteronomy 8:11). Moses knew that in Canaan the people would trade tents for "fine homes" and manna for bountiful buffets of food that would leave them "full" (v.12).

When prosperous days come calling (v.12), you and I are often tempted to forget what God has done for us (v.15). We become proud and convinced that our goods and great success came about by our "own strength and energy" (vv.14,17). It's a subtle change that happens as we leave humility (caused by humble circumstances) and embrace arrogance and self-reliance (prompted by prosperity).

If things are going well for you today, drop to your knees and humbly thank God. "He is the One who gives you power to be successful" (v.18). Don't forget His face.

If you're being humbled by life's challenges, thank God for this "wilderness" that can cause you to seek and depend on Him. Although we sometimes forget His face, He never forgets ours. —Tom Felten

watching

read>
Psalm 59:6-10
You, O God, are my fortress (v.9).

more>
I look to the Lord for help. I wait confidently for God to save me, and my God will certainly hear me (Micah 7:7).

next>
Who or what do you watch for when you need help? What happens when we're slow to watch for God?

My young son, Wyatt, loves chess. I first taught him to play on the chessboard in our local coffee shop, and eventually he asked for his own set to enjoy at home. One time, we were playing after dinner, and Wyatt became infatuated with the knight—the piece that moves two squares, then one more square (like an "L"). His strategy was fixated on his desire to get the knight to move all over the board. So, with his focus fixed on the knight, I methodically moved one pawn (the piece that can move only one square at a time) across the entire board, taking out his pieces along the way.

We're tempted to fixate on all kinds of things: our image, another person's opinion of us, our success or our failures. When things go poorly for us (bad health news or relational disappointments or financial woes), we search everywhere and look to anyone in a flailing attempt to figure out how to change our situation. We try very hard to save ourselves.

The psalmist knew serious trouble. He spoke of violent men who were hunting him down, "snarling like vicious dogs" (Psalm 59:6). Their assaults were not merely physical: "Their words cut like swords," he wrote (v.7). Do you feel as if someone is after you or as if some circumstance has consumed you? Are you experiencing a relationship that's painful, that cuts to your soul?

Rather than working frantically to find your own remedy (which never ultimately works), Scripture invites you to turn to God, knowing that He's the only One who can rescue you. The psalmist encourages us to quiet our heart, turn fully to God, and proclaim, "I watch for *You*" (v.9 NIV). We don't watch for ourselves or our friend or our spouse. Our true help doesn't come from these sources. We watch for God. —Winn Collier

a different Christmas

read>
Revelation 21:1-7
He will wipe every tear from their eyes, and there will be no more death or sorrow or crying or pain. All these things are gone forever (v.4).

more>
It was our weaknesses He carried; it was our sorrows that weighed Him down. And we thought His troubles were a punishment from God, a punishment for His own sins! (Isaiah 53:4).

next>
Are there aspects of this Christmas season that have been difficult for you? Why must hope be something we choose and not a feeling we wait to experience?

With gifts wrapped and under the tree, Christmas Eve came to a close. God's goodness had been evident, but it had been a challenging year. Unfolding blankets and sheets, my husband and I created beds of the two couches in our family room. My husband's parents, who live in town, were using our bedroom upstairs. Three months earlier, their oldest son—and only other child—had ended his life. Keeping them close, we wanted to remind them of what they still had as they continued to grieve what had been lost.

Christmas can be complicated. While parties, gifts, and family reunions are certainly blessings, they can't take away the pain of broken relationships, absent loved ones, or unmet expectations. Without question, God is the Unchanging One who is the giver of all good gifts (James 1:17). But He is also a God who is well-acquainted with our suffering (Isaiah 53:3). Even the humble beauty of the nativity remains incomplete without the cross.

Not your typical Advent passage, Revelation 21 reminds us that we will one day experience a new heaven and new earth. The purpose in Christ putting on flesh was to restore what had been lost. *God with us* (Matthew 1:23). He not only comforts us in our sorrows, but He has promised that "He will live with [us], and [we] will be His people. God Himself will be with [us]" (v.3). The turmoil present in the world reminds us, "All creation has been groaning . . . And we believers also groan, even though we have the Holy Spirit within us . . for we long for our bodies to be released from sin and suffering" (Romans 8:22-23).

Anxiously awaiting Jesus' return, we are to celebrate His hope as He holds us in both our joy and our pain. —Regina Franklin

presence and protection

read>
Psalm 121
The Lord Himself watches over you! (Psalm 121:5).

more>
- Psalm 18:2
- Psalm 37:23-24
- Psalm 91:14-16

next>
How have you taken God's protection for granted? As you commute from your home to workplace, spend some time acknowledging His presence and protection.

A pastor gathered his wife and children together for a time of prayer, just prior to his departure for an overseas missions trip. He prayed, "Dear Lord, please protect my wife and the children while I'm gone." When he finished, his wife asked him: "Who do you think protects us while you're here?" Good question! Sometimes we take God's protection for granted and think of it only when we're faced with an emergency or events like traveling overseas. During our daily commute from home to the office, we hardly think of God's protection over us.

Known also as the "Traveler's Psalm," Psalm 121 is the second of 15 "songs of ascents" (Psalms 120–134), sung by pilgrims as they made their way up to Jerusalem to celebrate the annual feasts (Deuteronomy 16:16). Just as in ancient times, when we or our loved ones leave home for a journey, safety is on our mind. Although the travel hazards are different today, we have a similar need for protection. Psalm 121 reminds us that God is our Helper (vv.1-3) and Protector (vv.4-8).

As our Helper, the Creator of the universe (v.2) helps us as we journey through life, giving us the security and stability that we need (v.3). As our Protector, God is the vigilant watchman, fully aware of the events of our lives because He never sleeps (v.4). That reality allows us to rest in safety and serenity (Ps. 3:5, 4:8; Proverbs 3:24).

The Hebrew word for "protective shade" (121:5) can also be rendered as "protective shadow." If God is our shadow (Psalm 17:8, 57:1, 63:7), then He is present with us. Five times in Psalm 121 (vv.3,4,5,7,8) we're reminded that He "watches over" us. Because of His protective presence, we can say: "He alone is my . . . place of safety; He is my God, and I trust Him" (91:2). —K.T. Sim

winning over worry

read>
Matthew 6:25-33
Seek the kingdom of God above all else, and live righteously, and He will give you everything you need (v.33).

A few years ago, my family had much to worry about. My wife wasn't called back to her full-time teaching position (we counted on her income to help cover household expenses), my son was having recurring chest pain that we thought was due to an enlarged heart, our insurance was running out and an alternative plan was going to be more than we could afford, and—if that wasn't enough—I changed jobs. At some point these concerns turned into worry and we let them consume us. We desperately needed the wisdom Jesus spoke of in Matthew 6.

That section begins with Him commanding His followers to stop worrying and scurrying in different directions (v.25). He went on to give His followers four reasons why they shouldn't worry:

Life is more than food, drink, and clothing (v.25). Jesus understood that these are necessities in life, but they aren't the most important things in life.

God cares for His children (v.26). If He feeds the birds and clothes the flowers with beautiful color, how much more does God care for those created in His image?

Worrying doesn't accomplish anything (v.27). Jesus said that worrying doesn't add anything useful to the worrier's day; it's actually a life-draining endeavor.

Worrying is godless (v.32). Those who don't know God depend on material possessions, and they allow things to rule their lives. Jesus wants His disciples to live with the assurance that His heavenly Father is in complete control.

Let's focus on what God cares about, and then He will take care of what we worry about (v.33). This means pursuing His rule and supremacy in our lives with all we have. When we do that, He will take care of our needs.

—Marvin Williams

more>
- Philippians 4:6-8
- 1 Peter 5:7

next>
What worries or anxieties do you need to cast on God? How can you turn your worry into a prayer request today?

when God ignores

read>
Habakkuk 1:1-4
How long, O Lord, must I call for help? But You do not listen! (v.2).

more>
As for me, I will sing about Your power. Each morning I will sing with joy about Your unfailing love. For You have been my refuge, a place of safety when I am in distress (Psalm 59:16).

next>
What are some doubts you need to take to God? What happens when we deny the struggles we're facing and don't bring them to Him?

Michael felt as if his prayers were simply bouncing off the ceiling. He couldn't understand God's silence. Day after day he pleaded with Him to deal with the injustice in his workplace. But evil persisted, and God seemed absent. Can you identify with Michael? Habakkuk could. He lived during the final dark days of Judah—just before the captivity of her people. There was unrestrained wickedness and violence throughout the land—and he couldn't harmonize the prevalence of evil with the concept of God being good, just, and sovereign. The prophet cried out, "How long, O Lord, must I call for help? But You do not listen!" (1:2).

Habakkuk was disturbed with God's seeming indifference. "How long?" suggests to us that Habakkuk had brought his petitions to God over a long period of time. But God seemed to be ignoring him.

When violence and corruption abound and evil appears to rule, we may also wonder whether God really cares or if He is really in control. Habakkuk's honest dialogue with God helps us understand that we can come to God in prayer with our difficult questions.

Habakkuk had been doubting. But he turned to God in the midst of his confusion and sought God's wisdom and counsel. This is what God calls each of us to do when we're confused or when we're wrestling with tough questions. In fact, honest questions reflect a better relationship with God than superficial, outward, religious behavior.

The result of Habakkuk's search is astounding. The prophet we meet at the end of the book is not the same one we find at the beginning. He starts with questions, and he ends with praise (3:17-19). His struggle produced spiritual growth. So will your struggles when you seek God's face in complete honesty and truth. —Poh Fang Chia

too much

read>
Ecclesiastes 7:15-18
Pay attention to these instructions, for anyone who fears God will avoid both extremes (v.18).

more>
Do you like honey? Don't eat too much, or it will make you sick! Don't visit your neighbors too often, or you will wear out your welcome (Proverbs 25:16-17).

next>
Is a desire for something good (coffee, blogs, music, a person) consuming you? What would happen if you were consumed with God instead?

The other day I was putting air in my car's tires. The small wording on the side of the tires warned me, "Maximum pressure: 35 psi."

I'm no mechanic, but this is good information to know. I've been told that too much air in a tire will negatively affect braking, cornering, and overall stability. Less of the tire touches the ground when tire pressure is too high. As a result, a car will tend to bounce around on the road and its tires will lose traction. We all need air in our tires, and we won't get very far on a tire that is low or flat. But as with many things in life, too much of a good thing can be detrimental.

Take, for example, something as basic as food. We all need to eat. But the Bible clearly warns against the dangers of overeating (Proverbs 23:20-21).

Needing too much of a good thing can also show up in our relationships. For instance, the Old Testament character Leah (Rachel's older sister and Jacob's first wife) was a woman who seemed to need her husband's love too much. From the start of a marriage that was born out of deception, Jacob made no bones about the fact that he loved Rachel much more than Leah (Genesis 29:30).

Coming in second place left Leah heartbroken. Sadly, she thought she could win more of Jacob's affection and attention by giving him children (29:32,34). But her plan never worked. It only drew her deeper into a jealous rivalry with Rachel that she would never win (30:1-24).

Leah's desire for her husband's love was legitimate, but it began to consume her when it became the primary focus of her life. Is there something good in your life you need too much? —Jeff Olson

upside down

read>
1 Corinthians 1:18-25
This foolish plan of God is wiser than the wisest of human plans, and God's weakness is stronger than the greatest of human strength (v.25).

more>
"O death, where is your victory? O death, where is your sting?" . . . But thank God! He gives us victory over sin and death through our Lord Jesus Christ (1 Corinthians 15:55,57).

next>
Why was Hope the perfect name for this baby girl? Can you think of other counterintuitive truths of the Christian faith, where reality is not as it appears?

My friend's sister is due to give birth, and no one is happy about it. Her baby has Trisomy 18, a fatal disease that will likely claim the infant just minutes after she is born. It seems fiendishly upside down that the baby is alive as long as she remains within her mother, but the moment she is born she will begin to die. Cutting the umbilical cord is not her liberating path to life, but a death sentence. What should be a day of joy will commence a season of mourning.

This situation would be entirely hopeless if not for Jesus. He has reversed this tragically twisted scenario with an equally ironic moment that leads in the opposite direction. Just as this baby's birth is really a death, so Jesus' death conceals the power of life.

God may have never appeared weaker than when Jesus hung on the cross, naked and broken and bearing the guilt of the world. But this moment of weakness was actually God's greatest triumph, for Jesus took death with Him into the depths, and when He arose He left death in the dust. *Death died in the death of Christ.*

Martin Luther observed that it takes faith to believe this "theology of the cross." Most people take a commonsense view of the world, believing that what they see is what they get. But we who interpret life through the lens of the cross learn to raise a fist of defiance at death.

It may seem that death has won, for it has taken our loved ones from us. But Jesus' death and resurrection assure us that death does not have the last word, for the grave where we say goodbye is resurrection ground.

(My friend's niece was born—and died—days after I wrote this devo. Her parents named her *Hope*.) —Mike Wittmer

the right thing

read>
Philemon
It is the right thing for you to do (v.8).

Gjyste Vjerdha was busy working her nightly, graveyard-shift cleaning job at a restaurant with her 22-year-old son, Gentjan. As she tidied up a restroom, Gjyste found some women's rings worth thousands of dollars. The thought of keeping the treasures might have crossed her mind, but she chose to do the right thing and take the jewelry to her manager. Later that day, the rings were returned to a woman who had accidentally left them in the restroom. Gentjan said, "You get so many things by hard work; you don't need to steal or take from someone else."

The apostle Paul once made an appeal to his friend Philemon who had likely experienced some theft by a man named Onesimus (Philemon 1:18). During a stay in prison, Onesimus had become a believer in Jesus through Paul's ministry (v.10).

Paul wanted Philemon to welcome back this young man who had once been Philemon's slave—a pilfering one at that! The apostle wrote that to warmly receive the changed man would be "the right thing for you to do" (v.8). It was right, for Philemon's forgiveness would reflect what Jesus Himself had taught and modeled.

As believers in Christ, when we do the right thing, the word gets around and others can see the beauty of real faith (v.5). When we're forgiving, generous (v.6), loving, and kind (v.10), our actions reveal a right way of living for Jesus' sake (v.20).

more>
Keep putting into practice all you learned and received from me—everything you heard from me and saw me doing. Then the God of peace will be with you (Philippians 4:9).

next>
What issue are you wrestling with that's calling for you to do the right thing for Jesus' sake? Why is it essential that we strive to do what is right in this life?

Today you might come across something that doesn't belong to you. You might be confronted with the opportunity to forgive someone who has offended you. Each moment of your life presents a simple question: *Will you do the right thing?*

Doing what's right is a reflection of real faith in Jesus. Choose, for His sake, to do what you know is right today. —Tom Felten

how can I be sure of the Bible?

There are many factors that give the Bible unparalleled moral and spiritual authority. The Old and New Testaments are deeply rooted in a historical and geographical record that is linked to laws, poetry, and predictions that express timeless life-changing wisdom. Even the parts of the Old Testament with parallels in Mesopotamian literature (the creation story, the story of the flood, etc.) are incomparably superior to the pagan versions.[1]

Although it is an ancient document, its realism is stunning and contemporary. The records of the Bible portray people in all of their complexity and inconsistency, with not only their achievements but also their sins—and the consequences of their sins—clearly displayed.[2] J. B. Phillips expressed in a few words what countless others have noticed about the New Testament: It has the "ring of truth." There are few people of any religious tradition who are familiar with it that don't hold it in high esteem. Further, the historical accuracy of Scripture has been demonstrated time and again—often to the surprise of skeptical scholars.

The authority of the Bible is by far the most well-attested document to come out of ancient times. The reliability of the Old Testament was confirmed by the discovery of the Dead Sea Scrolls, a remarkable collection of ancient documents found preserved in caves in the Judean desert in the mid-20th century. The age of these documents, which included large portions of the Old Testament, was determined by several independent evidences, including:

- Carbon-14 tests made on the linen wrappings of the scrolls.
- Coins associated with the scrolls, which date from 325 BC to AD 68.
- The type of pottery found with the scrolls.
- Comparative paleography (science of handwriting), a science which has already been well-established for many generations.

moral and spiritual reliability?

• Linguistic analysis of Aramaic documents found in the caves.

What made the Dead Sea Scrolls such a remarkable find in confirmation of the reliability of the Old Testament was the fact that prior to their discovery the earliest text in Hebrew, the Masoretic text, dated only to the 10th century AD. Biblical scholar Gleason Archer noted that in spite of 1,000 years separating the Scrolls and the Masoretic Text, "the texts from Qumran proved to be word-for-word identical to our standard Hebrew Bible in more than 95 percent of the text. The 5 percent of variation consisted primarily of obvious slips of the pen and spelling alterations" (Gleason Archer, *A Survey of Old Testament Introduction* [Chicago, IL: Moody, 1974], p. 25).

Similarly, no serious scholar, Christian or non-Christian, has historical grounds to doubt that the modern New Testament—regardless of translation—corresponds closely to the original form in which it was written. In his book *Evidence that Demands a Verdict*, Josh McDowell quotes a number of authorities on the reliability of our Bible. Here he quotes scholar A. T. Robertson: "There are some 8,000 manuscripts of the Latin Vulgate and at least 1,000 for the other early versions. Add over 4,000 Greek manuscripts and we have 13,000 manuscript copies of portions of the New Testament. Besides all this, much of the New Testament can be reproduced from the quotations of the early Christian writers."

Historical evidence for the reliability of the text is overwhelming. But its spiritual authority can only be seen by someone who is seeking truth. It would require thousands of pages just to list the names of the outstanding people in every area of human endeavor who have looked to Scripture for their ultimate values. A random list of just a few might include:

• Philosophy: Augustine, Thomas Aquinas, Soren Kierkegaard
• Science: Francis Bacon, Galileo Galilei, Blaise Pascal
• Music: J. S. Bach
• Literature: Dante Alighieri, John Donne, John Milton, Leo Tolstoy, Fyodor Dostoyevsky, T. S. Eliot, J. R. R Tolkien, C. S. Lewis
• Politics: William Wilberforce, William Gladstone, Abraham Kuyper

The fact that the Bible provided the foundation for the personal values of some of the greatest figures of Western history doesn't constitute a "proof" of its authority. But, along with the Bible's age, textual reliability, and character as great literature, its appeal to such people certainly calls for an open-minded, respectful approach to its contents.

1 Anglican physicist/theologian/priest John Polkinghorne remarks on the value of scholarly comparison between ancient biblical and Mesopotamian texts: "Those who disdain a scholarly engagement with the same text will also miss the fact that, though the accounts are clearly influenced to a degree by neighboring Near Eastern cosmogonies, they differ in a most marked and important way from those other creation stories. It is deeply impressive that tales of conflict among the gods, with Marduk fighting Tiamath and slicing her dead body in half from which to form the earth and sky, are replaced by a sober account in which the one true God alone is the Creator, bringing creation into being by the power of the divine word. Equally significant is the insight that human beings are not destined to be the slaves of the gods (as in the Babylonian epic, Enuma Elish), but are created in the image of God and given a blessing so that they may fulfill the command: 'Be fruitful and multiply. Fill the earth and govern it' (Genesis 1:28)." (*Science and the Trinity: The Christian Encounter with Reality*, pp. 44-45).

2 To have a clear understanding of biblical authority, it is important to understand the nature of biblical inspiration. Inspiration has two aspects. One is its authority in providing truth without error in the words of Scripture. Scripture is truly the written Word of God. The other aspect of inspiration is that it was written by human beings who wrote with their own vocabulary, cultural background, and personal style. This fact does not controvert inspiration. Just as Christ was both truly man and truly God, the divine element in inspiration doesn't exclude the human limitations of the Bible's writers. For a clear discussion of the topic of inerrancy from a theological perspective, we recommend that you buy or borrow a copy of Millard Erickson's *Christian Theology*. This theology originally came out in a 3-volume set, but currently is being offered in one volume. His discussion of inerrancy can be found in chapter 10, "The Dependability of God's Word: Inerrancy."

Adapted from *Answers To Tough Questions* © 2011 RBC Ministries. Read more helpful articles like this one on the Web at questions.org